CONTACTS, BOUNDARIES & INNOVATION
IN THE FIFTH MILLENNIUM

Sidestone Press

CONTACTS, BOUNDARIES & INNOVATION
IN THE FIFTH MILLENNIUM

Exploring developed Neolithic societies
in central Europe and beyond

edited by
Ralf Gleser & Daniela Hofmann

A publication of the Institute for Pre- and Protohistoric Archaeology (Institut für Vor- und Frühgeschichtliche Archäologie) of the University of Hamburg and the Abteilung für Ur- und Frühgeschichtliche Archäologie, Westfälische Wilhelms-Universität Münster.

© 2019 Individual authors

The authors are solely responsible for the contents of their contributions

Published by Sidestone Press, Leiden
www.sidestone.com

Lay-out & cover design: Sidestone Press
Graphics cover:
- Photo: figurine from Těšetice-Kyjovice, Ralf Gleser;
- background drawing: pottery from Worms-Rheingewann, K. Riedhammer, after W. Meier-Arendt and M. Zápotocká.

Printed and bound in Great Britain by
Marston Book Services Ltd, Oxfordshire

ISBN 978-90-8890-714-2 (softcover)
ISBN 978-90-8890-715-9 (hardcover)
ISBN 978-90-8890-716-6 (PDF e-book)

In memory of István Zalai-Gáal

Contents

List of contributors	9
The fifth millennium: the emergence of cultural diversity in central European prehistory Daniela Hofmann and Ralf Gleser	13
PART ONE – DIVERSE POPULATIONS	**43**
On the periphery and at a crossroads: a Neolithic creole society on the Lower Vistula in the fifth millennium BC Peter Bogucki	45
The Brześć Kujawski culture. The north-easternmost Early Chalcolithic communities in Europe Lech Czerniak and Joanna Pyzel	59
Taboo? The process of Neolitisation in the Dutch wetlands re-examined (5000–3400 cal BC) Daan Raemaekers	91
PART TWO – INTERACTION AND CHANGE	**103**
The fifth millennium BC in central Europe. Minor changes, structural continuity: a period of cultural stability Christian Jeunesse	105
Early Middle Neolithic pottery decoration: different cultural groups or just one supraregional style of its time? Karin Riedhammer	129
The oldest box-shaped wooden well from Saxony-Anhalt and the Stichbandkeramik culture in central Germany René Wollenweber	159
A vessel with zoomorphic depiction from the Epi-Rössen horizon at Oberbergen am Kaiserstuhl: an evolutionary perspective on an unusual artefact Ralf Gleser	181
PART THREE – COMMUNITY, INTERACTION AND BOUNDARIES	**201**
Strategies of boundary making between northern and southern Italy in the late sixth and early fifth millennium BC Valeska Becker	203
The transition from the sixth to the fifth millennium BC in the southern Wetterau: pottery as expression of contacts, boundaries and innovation Johanna Ritter-Burkert	225

On the relationship of the Michelsberg culture and Epirössen groups   233
in south-west Germany in the light of absolute chronology, aspects of
culture definition, and spatial data
   Ute Seidel

Schiepzig enclosures: gaps in the archaeological record at the end of   267
the fifth millennium BC in northern central Germany?
   Johannes Müller, Kay Schmütz and Christoph Rinne

The jadeitite-omphacitite and nephrite axeheads in Europe: the case   289
of the Czech Republic
   Antonín Přichystal, Josef Jan Kovář,
   Martin Kuča and Kateřina Fridrichová

Disc-rings of Alpine rock in western Europe: typology, chronology,   305
distribution and social significance
   Pierre Pétrequin, Serge Cassen, Michel Errera, Yvan Pailler,
   Frédéric Prodéo, Anne-Marie Pétrequin and Alison Sheridan

List of contributors

Valeska Becker
Historisches Seminar
Abteilung für Ur- und Frühgeschichtliche
Archäologie
Westfälische Wilhelms-Universität Münster
Domplatz 20-22
48143 Münster
Germany
valeska.becker@uni-muenster.de

Peter Bogucki
School of Engineering and Applied Science
C-207 Engineering Quad
Princeton University
Princeton, New Jersey 08544
USA
bogucki@princeton.edu

Serge Cassen
Laboratoire de recherches archéologiques
(LARA)
Université de Nantes, BP 81227
44312 Nantes cedex 3
France
Serge.Cassen@univ-nantes.fr

Lech Czerniak
Institute of Archaeology and Ethnology
University of Gdańsk
ul. Bielańska 5
80-851 Gdańsk
Poland
lech.czerniak@ug.edu.pl

Michel Errera
Royal Museum for Central Africa
Geology and Mineralogy Department
Leuvensesteenweg 13
3080 Tervuren
Belgium

Kateřina Fridrichová
International Institute of Political Science
Faculty of Social Studies
Masaryk University
Joštova 218/10
60200 Brno
Czech Republic
219609@mail.muni.cz

Ralf Gleser
Historisches Seminar
Abteilung für Ur- und Frühgeschichtliche
Archäologie
Westfälische Wilhelms-Universität Münster
Domplatz 20-22
48143 Münster
Germany
rgles_01@uni-muenster.de

Daniela Hofmann
Department of Archaeology, History,
Cultural Studies and Religion
University of Bergen
Øysteinsgate 3
Postboks 7805
5020 Bergen
Norway
Daniela.Hofmann@uib.no

Christian Jeunesse
University of Strasburg/ Institut
Universitaire de France
CNRS, UMR 7044
5 allée du Général Rouvillois
67083 Strasbourg
France
jeunessechr@free.fr

Josef Jan Kovář
Independent researcher
josef.kovar@seznam.cz

Martin Kuča
Městské muzeum
Náměstí T. G. Masaryka 40
672 01 Moravský Krumlov
Czech Republic
muzeum@meksmk.cz

Johannes Müller
Institut für Ur- und Frühgeschichte
Johanna-Mestorf-Straße 2-6
24105 Kiel
Germany
johannes.mueller@ufg.uni-kiel.de

Yvan Pailler
Maison René Ginouvès
UMR 6554 LETG - Brest Géomer
Institut Universitaire Européen de la Mer
Rue Dumont d'Urville
Technopôle Brest Iroise
29280 Plouzané
France

Anne-Marie Pétrequin
MSHE C.N. Ledoux
CNRS et Université de Bourgogne
Franche-Comté
30, rue Mégevand
25030 Besançon Cedex
France
annemarie.petrequin@gmail.com

Pierre Pétrequin
MSHE C.N. Ledoux
CNRS et Université de Bourgogne
Franche-Comté
30, rue Mégevand
25030 Besançon Cedex
France
archeo.petrequin@gmail.com

Antonín Přichystal
Department of Geological Sciences
Faculty of Science
Masaryk University
Kotlářská 2
60200 Brno
Czech Republic

Frédéric Prodéo
INRAP Grand Sud-Ouest
156 Avenue Jean Jaures
33600 Pessac
France

Joanna Pyzel
Institute of Archaeology and Ethnology
University of Gdańsk
ul. Bielańska 5
80-851 Gdańsk
Poland
joanna.pyzel@univ.gda.pl

Daan C.M. Raemaekers
University of Groningen
Groningen Institute of Archaeology
Poststraat 6
9712 ER Groningen
The Netherlands
d.c.m.raemaekers@rug.nl

Karin Riedhammer
Independent researcher
karin.riedhammer@online.de

Christoph Rinne
Institut für Ur- und Frühgeschichte
Johanna-Mestorf-Straße 2-6
24105 Kiel
Germany
crinne@ufg.uni-kiel.de

Johanna Ritter-Burkert
Johannes Gutenberg-Universität Mainz
Institut für Altertumswissenschaften
Arbeitsbereich vor- und frühgeschichtliche
Archäologie
Schillerstraße 11
55116 Mainz
Germany
joharitter@web.de

Kay Schmütz
Institut für Ur- und Frühgeschichte
Johanna-Mestorf-Straße 2-6
24105 Kiel
Germany
kschmuetz@ufg.uni-kiel.de

Ute Seidel
Landesamt für Denkmalpflege im
Regierungspräsidium Stuttgart
Ref. 84.2, Dienstsitz Freiburg
Günterstalstraße 67
79100 Freiburg / Breisgau
Germany
ute.seidel@rps.bwl.de

Alison Sheridan
Department of Scottish History and
Archaeology
National Museums Scotland
Chambers Street
Edinburgh EH1 1JF
UK
a.sheridan@nms.ac.uk

René Wollenweber
Landesamt für Denkmalpflege und
Archäologie Sachsen-Anhalt
Richard-Wagner-Str. 9
06114 Halle/Saale
Germany
rwollenweber@archlsa.de

The fifth millennium: the emergence of cultural diversity in central European prehistory

Daniela Hofmann and Ralf Gleser

Abstract

This brief introductory contribution situates the papers collected in this volume in terms of the wider scholarly debates and challenges connected to fifth millennium archaeology in central Europe. One of the key problems we still need to address is how to deal with the co-presence of societies with very different economic strategies and ways of life, as well as different genetic heritage; in particular, we are still far from finding a satisfactory terminology. In addition, there is great variation in the degree to which societies relied on so-called "prestige goods" for their reproduction, and we need to become more explicit regarding patterns of interaction and mutual influences between such differently structured groups. Finally, as enhanced chronologies make prehistory appear more episodic across many parts of Europe, narratives concerning the rise and dissolution of specific communities provide the opportunity of linking micro-historical processes and strategies to large-scale patterns of change. All this requires not just a battery of new data and sophisticated modelling, but also a concomitant development of theoretical concepts.

Zusammenfassung: Das 5. Jahrtausend: Die Entwicklung kultureller Vielfalt in der Vorgeschichte Mitteleuropas

In dieser kurzen Einleitung werden die im vorliegenden Band zusammengefassten Beiträge in den Kontext der Debatten und Herausforderungen einer Archäologie des fünften Jahrtausends eingeordnet. Eines der wichtigsten Probleme, die es in den nächsten Jahren anzugehen gilt, ist der Umgang mit der parallelen Existenz von Gemeinschaften mit sehr unterschiedlichen wirtschaftlichen Strategien und Lebensweisen, teilweise auch genetischen Signaturen; vor allen Dingen muss hier zunächst eine zufriedenstellende Terminologie entwickelt werden. Zudem variieren Gesellschaften sehr stark darin, wie sehr sie sich in ihrer Reproduktion auf sogenannte „Prestigegüter" verlassen. Wie solche unterschiedlich strukturierten Gesellschaften interagieren und sich gegenseitig beeinflussen konnten muss noch viel expliziter diskutiert werden. Schließlich mehren sich Dank verfeinerter Chronologien die Hinweise, dass die Vorgeschichte in vielen Teilen Europas stark episodische Züge aufweist. Dies bietet die Gelegenheit, mikrohistorische Prozesse und örtlich entwickelte Strategien mit langlebigeren und extensiveren Veränderungsmustern zu korrelieren. Um all dies zu erreichen sind nicht nur neue Daten und komplexe Modelle nötig, sondern damit einhergehend auch neue theoretische Konzepte.

The fifth millennium and its relevance

In a recent contribution, John Robb[1] half-jokingly suggests that most researchers treat the Neolithic "like a hit-and-run romance: they mostly lose interest once the beginning is over". While this applies more to some regions than others, in central Europe the Mesolithic–Neolithic transition during the sixth millennium indeed dominates our accounts, for instance in terms of the space we accord it in introductory texts, in how we sell our research to funding bodies and when considering the sheer volume of output. A comparable level of interest only reappears when the next "stage" of social development is at stake, mostly some kind of hierarchisation narrative in connection to the megalithic phenomenon of the fourth millennium and/or early metallurgy. The millennium in between seems to fade into a rather unexciting blur of ceramic groups or "cultures" (Figure 1).

Yet, following Robb's statements[2], this — the fifth — millennium has a lot to offer once we change our perspective away from unilinear evolution and towards appreciating the complexity of social processes and transformations in tribal societies. From daily routines at specific sites, we can move up to longer-lasting traditions of practice and centuries-long trends punctuated by rapid tipping points of change, and from regionally shared ways of life to diversity and commonalities at an inter-regional or even continental level[3]. All this provides rich material for comparison, contrast and analysis. We would be rewarded with a much more dynamic and colourful view of what we normally lump together under a label of more or less "established" Neolithic societies.

With so much to do, this volume provides another opportunity to shift debate in these directions. It is the product of a conference jointly organised by the Universities of Hamburg and Münster and held in Münster in September 2015. The thematic focus on the fifth millennium follows on from an earlier conference, also held at Münster and published in 2012[4]. The initial call for papers of the 2012 conference[5] had identified six core themes ("tradition and regionality", "transitions, transformations, ruptures", "acculturation and interaction", "spaces and landscapes", "ritual and social action" and "achievements and innovation") and participants succeeded in discussing and publishing new research for virtually all areas of central Europe settled by Neolithic societies at this time. This already established the fifth millennium as a time of profound changes and of increasing diversity between contemporary societies, a trajectory observable at a continental scale. Its beginning sees the demise of the Linearbandkeramik (LBK) culture, which had first introduced an agricultural and largely settled way of life to vast parts of central and western Europe, while it is only towards the millennium's very end that the Neolithic expands into areas such as the North European Plain, the Alps or Great Britain, which until then were the domain of hunters and gatherers. Both processes are intensely debated, but there is much more going on. Thus, across the Balkans and the eastern Middle Danube basin around 4300 cal BC[6] we see a major shift from larger and more nucleated flat and tell settlements to

---

1 Robb 2014, 27.
2 Robb 2014, 27–28.
3 Robb 2014, 28.
4 Gleser and Becker 2012.
5 See Gleser 2012a, 7.
6 Throughout the volume, unless otherwise stated, radiocarbon dates are not further statistically modelled.

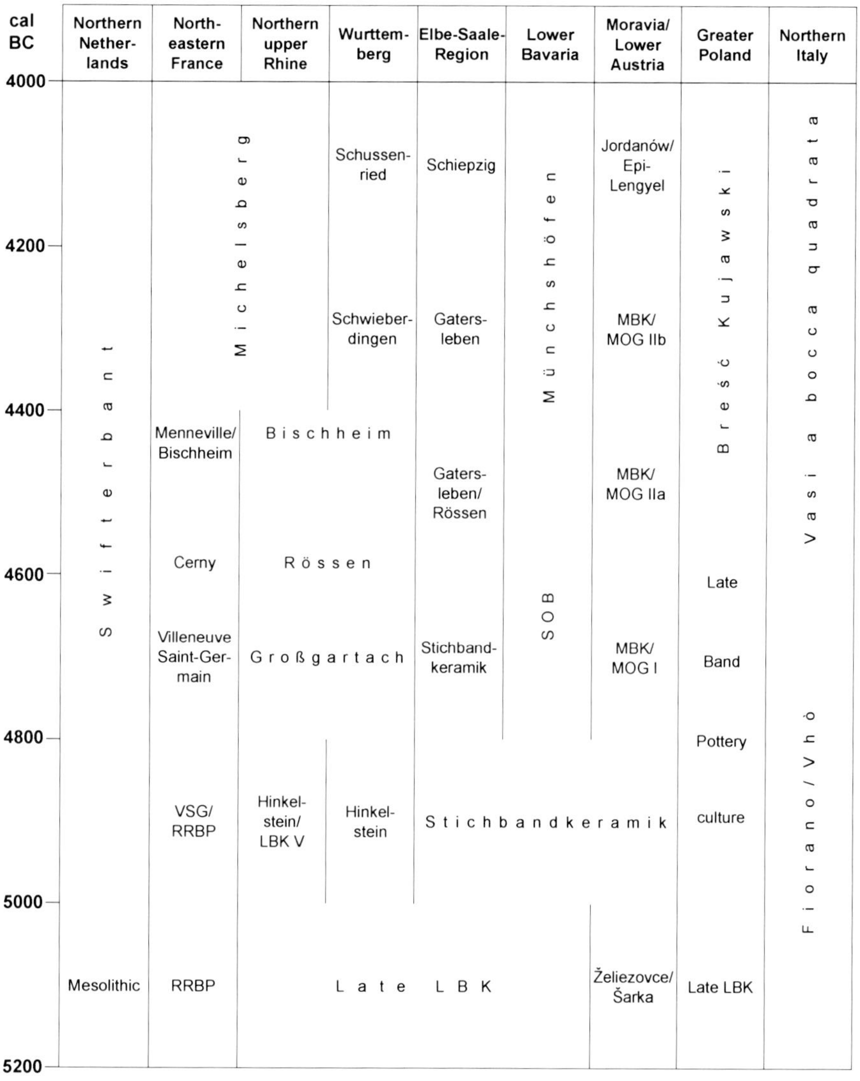

Figure 1. Simplified chronological table for the areas discussed in this book. Abbreviations:
LBK – *Linearbandkeramik;*
MBK – *Mährische Bemalte Keramik;* **MOG** – *Mährisch-Ostösterreichische Gruppe der bemalten Keramik;*
RRBP – *Rubané Récent du Bassin Parisien;*
SOB – *Südostbayerisches Mittelneolithikum;*
VSG – *Villeneuve-Saint-Germain.*

cal BC	Northern Netherlands	North-eastern France	Northern upper Rhine	Wurttemberg	Elbe-Saale-Region	Lower Bavaria	Moravia/ Lower Austria	Greater Poland	Northern Italy
4000									
	Swifterbant	Michelsberg	Michelsberg	Schussen-ried	Schiepzig	Münchshöfen	Jordanów/ Epi-Lengyel	Brześć Kujawski	Vasi-a bocca quadrata
4200									
				Schwieber-dingen	Gaters-leben		MBK/ MOG IIb		
4400		Menneville/ Bischheim	Bischheim		Gaters-leben/ Rössen		MBK/ MOG IIa		
4600		Cerny	Rössen			SOB		Late	
		Villeneuve Saint-Germain	Großgartach		Stichband-keramik		MBK/ MOG I	Band	
4800			Hinkel-stein/ LBK V	Hinkel-stein	Stichbandkeramik			Pottery culture	Fiorano/Vhò
5000		VSG/ RRBP							
	Mesolithic	RRBP	Late LBK				Želiezovce/ Šárka	Late LBK	
5200									

short-lived and dispersed sites, which is as yet hardly explored on an inter-regional scale[7]. Quite in contrast, the Andalusian Neolithic for example appears at this time to be embarking on a trajectory towards increased sedentism and settlement agglomeration[8]. Slightly earlier, the Michelsberg culture begins a fundamental transformation of the central European Neolithic, with the material record increasingly dominated by enclosure sites rather than domestic architecture, a change in the social role of pottery and a potentially more mobile lifestyle in some areas[9]. This is related to the emergence of new cultural entities across the area between the Upper Rhine and the Mediterranean, where the interaction between Danubian and maritime streams of Neolithisation resulted in a series of complex and shifting networks[10].

7   Bánffy *et al.* 2016, 292; Fischl and Krauß 2016, 323–325; Gleser 2016a, 372–373 tab.1; Gleser and Thomas 2012, 307–319 fig. VIII.20; Parkinson 2006, 185–188.
8   Molina Gonzáles *et al.* 2012, 426–427.
9   E.g. Geschwinde and Raetzel Fabian 2009; Jeunesse 2010; Kreuz *et al.* 2014.
10 E.g. Denaire *et al.* 2011.

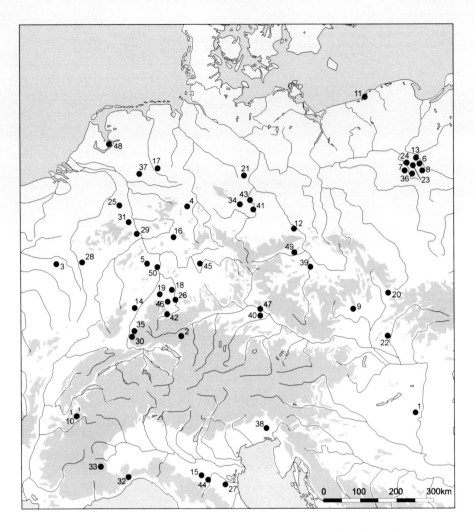

Figure 2. Localisation of selected sites discussed in this volume. 1 Alsónyék; 2 Bad Schussenried (Aichbühl and Riedschachen); 3 Bazoches-sur-Vesle; 4 Bergheim; 5 Bischheim; 6 Bodzia; 7 Bozejewice; 8 Brześć Kujawski; 9 Brno; 10 Chambéry; 11 Dąbki; 12 Dresden; 13 Dubielewo; 14 Entzheim; 15 Fiorano Modenese; 16 Friedberg; 17 Greven-Bockholt; 18 Großgartach; 19 Großvillars; 20 Hlinsko u Lipnika; 21 Hundisburg-Olbetal; 22 Jelšovce; 23 Konary; 24 Krusza Zamkowa; 25 Koslar; 26 Ludwigsburg; 27 Lugo di Romagna; 28 Mairy; 29 Mayen; 30 Merdingen; 31 Miel; 32 Monte Beigua; 33 Monte Viso; 34 Niederröblingen; 35 Oberbergen; 36 Osłonki; 37 Osterwick; 38 Pozzuolo del Friuli; 39 Praha-Bubenec; 40 Riedling; 41 Rössen; 42 Rottenburg am Neckar; 43 Salzmünde-Schiepzig; 44 Savignano sul Panaro; 45 Schernau; 46 Schwieberdingen; 47 Straubing (Lerchenhaid); 48 Swifterbant; 49 Vikletice; 50 Worms (Rheingewann).

Full geographical coverage and a detailed comparison of trajectories at a continental scale, as rewarding as they will prove to be in the future, were not the immediate aim of the second Münster conference, the papers of which are collected here[11]. Instead, using mainly case studies from central Europe (Figure 2), we asked contributors to address theoretical and methodological themes

---

11   And indeed not all the papers presented at the conference could be included. In addition to the authors represented here, we thank the following colleagues for their input and discussion in Münster: Eszter Bánffy, Andrea Dolfini, Florian Eibl, Birgit Gehlen, Detlef Gronenborn, Albert Hafner, Caroline Heitz, Thomas Link, Wolfram Schier, Zsuzsanna Siklósi and Harald Stäuble.

which could form the foundations of such more comparative exercises. In this introduction, we outline the main approaches and challenges for understanding the fifth millennium which have emerged from the presentations, discussions and the written contributions and situate the papers included here within wider debates.

Diverse populations — hunter-gatherers and farmers

Given the diversity of contemporary lifeways attested in the fifth millennium, one recurrent concern are the mechanisms of interaction between populations with different economic strategies and most likely different ancestry, both across large-scale regional boundaries and at much smaller scales, in immediately adjacent landscape zones. Recent genetic work in central Europe, for instance, has shown that admixture rates between LBK farmers and resident hunter-gatherers remained low throughout much of the fifth millennium[12]. However, archaeologically, evidence is increasing that forager populations may have survived alongside farmers in some areas, not just beyond a putative "agricultural frontier", porous and permeable though that may have been, but also right alongside or within early settled communities — a phenomenon sometimes labelled "parallel societies"[13]. In the sixth millennium, this is illustrated for instance by the continued production of La Hoguette and Limburg pottery, widely considered to be created by forager populations in contact with south-west and western Europe, but which is often found on LBK sites[14]. To this can be added the more recently collated evidence of Mesolithic-style material culture, such as stone tools, aurochs shoulder blades used for the production of bone disc rings (Figure 3) or burials with Mesolithic-style grave goods, all associated with radiocarbon dates falling into the Neolithic and in some cases the fifth millennium. These have largely been recovered from western Germany[15] and Saxony[16], but indications are mounting for other areas as well[17]. How long this coexistence lasted, and which mechanisms were in place to prevent genetic admixture between populations, is one of the great questions that will need to be addressed in coming years[18].

Genetic signatures associated with European hunter-gatherers (mitochondrial U-haplotypes) do make a re-appearance in central Europe during the fourth millennium[19], and this process potentially also begins late in the fifth millennium, with early signs at some Michelsberg culture sites[20]. The possible origins of this resurgence are currently not yet clear. In addition to any hunter-gatherers perhaps

---

12 Lipson *et al.* 2017.
13 See e.g. Heinen *et al.* 2015.
14 See e.g. Manen and Mazurié de Keroualin 2003.
15 E.g. Bokel Fenn, Banghard and Gehlen 2014; Greven-Bockholt, Heinen *et al.* 2015; Stapel and Schlösser 2014, figs 3–5; or the Blätterhöhle, Bollongino *et al.* 2013.
16 E.g. grave Schöpsdorf 1; Stäuble and Wolfram 2013; for north-east Germany: Beran 2012; for the Polish plain: Kobusiewicz 2006.
17 E.g. at Lake Schwarzenberg in Bohemia; Pokorný *et al.* 2010.
18 See also Hofmann 2015; 2016. Indeed, this kind of segregation is not limited to interactions between farmers and foragers. In their work at Alsónyék, Hungary, Bánffy and colleagues (2016, 290) could show that Sopot and LBK occupations coexisted in parallel for several generations before genetically traceable admixture took place. Although separated by only 1.5 km, a social boundary appears to have been in place.
19 Notably at the Blätterhöhle; Bollongino *et al.* 2013; Orschiedt *et al.* 2014.
20 Beau *et al.* 2017.

still surviving in central Europe itself, there are indications that foragers took a much more active role in Neolithisation across the North European Plain[21], and that this could have been preceded or accompanied by increased genetic exchange with more southerly areas[22]. From such a mixed population, hunter-gatherer-associated haplotypes could eventually have made their way back into central Europe as suggested for the Tiefstich and Bernburg communities in central Germany[23]. Western Europe, too, shows a comparatively large input of hunter-gatherer lineages to local Early Neolithic populations, so that the recently revealed Michelsberg culture "hunter-gatherer" genes could derive from such admixed Neolithic populations in France[24], especially given that the Paris Basin is mostly thought to be a likely origin point for the Michelsberg phenomenon[25].

Even this brief discussion shows the possible diversity and complexity of the social trajectories behind the genetic patterns we are confronted with at an increasing rate. At the same time, genetic data has not helped to clarify our existing terminological confusion regarding phenomena of admixture and change (see below). For instance, it has become a shorthand to speak of "hunter-gatherer" or "Near Eastern farmer" DNA, as we have done above, but this reflects the location or context of a specific genetic signature at a more or less arbitrarily defined point in time. Fifth millennium individuals living a Neolithic lifestyle in the Elbe-Saale area would most likely not have thought of themselves as "Near Eastern farmer". More troubling still, we associate the reappearance of "hunter-gatherer DNA" with a "resurgence" of the Mesolithic population and connect this to changes like the deposition of wild animal ornaments in graves[26], as if centuries of living in and alongside Neolithic societies had done nothing to alter the worldview of individuals with a U-haplotype. In fact, this "return" to wild animal symbolism occurs across a very wide area with potentially diverse hunter–farmer histories of interaction, often before the re-appearance of "hunter-gatherer" DNA, and could therefore just as well be connected to a different valorisation of hunting and the wild in the symbolic system of farmers[27]. As archaeologists, we must work harder to resist the allure of these genetic shorthands, and ideally develop a workable vocabulary. Similarly, how the "populations" of archaeogenetic texts are actually defined and where

Figure 3. Aurochs shoulder blade used for the production of bone disc rings from Greven-Bockholt, North Rhine-Westphalia, c. 4350 cal BC. Courtesy of LWL Archäologie für Westfalen; photo: St. Brentführer and U. Brieke.

---

21 Malmström *et al.* 2014; Mittnik *et al.* 2018.
22 Indeed, long-lasting contacts between Ertebølle foragers and farmers further south are evident in the material record, although they fluctuate considerably over time, see Klassen 2004, 100–108.
23 Brandt *et al.* 2013.
24 Beau *et al.* 2017, 8–9.
25 See e.g. Jeunesse 2010; Seidel this volume.
26 Jeunesse 2002.
27 E.g. Hachem 2011, 263–267; Kent 1989.

their boundaries are must be subjected to greater scrutiny. There is a danger of *a priori* categorising individuals from pre-defined archaeological "cultures" and then (inevitably) finding statistical differences between them, rather than letting the data cluster independently, although the effect of this will hopefully diminish as more information becomes available.

In the contributions collected here, the issue of hunter–farmer interaction is discussed in both papers dealing with the Brześć Kujawski culture. For Peter Bogucki, this phenomenon is the outcome of a creative fusion between strong "Danubian" elements and the hunter-gatherer cultures of the North European Plain, a process he characterises as "creolisation". Lech Czerniak and Joanna Pyzel emphasise a different facet. They show that there is actually discontinuity between the LBK and the Brześć Kujawski culture, so that any "Danubian" elements — namely longhouses and settlement burials — are most likely a deliberate re-invention or referencing of a past long ago, which could have been manipulated in inter-settlement relations. Following on from their work, it is interesting to reflect whether these acts of memory creation are part of the creativity one could expect from a "creole" society and how occasions such as burial rites could have built a new sense of identity.

Further to the west, Daan Raemaekers argues that the narrative of a long Neolithisation process that currently dominates discourse in the Netherlands is not an inevitable outcome of hunter-gatherer involvement. Indeed, it can be challenged. In his view, the social and ideological role of domesticated plants and animals is far more important to explain their adoption than economic necessity; using the notion of "taboo", he argues for a long period of interaction followed by a swift, punctuated step-change, similar to the situation in Scandinavia and the UK.

Interaction and change

The increasing role of group migration and personal mobility that is being revealed across the Neolithic sequence[28] returns us to the question of how we conceive of cultures and cultural change. Currently, with genetic data still rather patchy, there is a real temptation to connect specific material culture patterns and social structures with specific genetic signatures. Yet it is imperative to keep these two aspects apart analytically, in particular if we are interested in tracing dynamic changes over various timescales, rather than contrasting static blocks of "societies" or "cultures" with an implied essentialised identity, in the vein of Gustaf Kossinna, Gordon Childe and their successors. After the radiocarbon revolution had substantially increased the amount of time available for prehistoric social change, archaeologists had become used to thinking in terms of slow, gradual change as the default mode[29]. This is for instance both the base line for some Darwinian or evolutionary theories of change, based as they are on the notion of drift, and of various symmetrical or object-centred approaches, which de-emphasise the role of human intentionality and focus on the much slower physical or chemical transformations of objects and the persistence of things in themselves[30].

---

28 E.g. Brandt *et al.* 2015; Krause and Haak 2017.
29 As criticised e.g. in Knopf 2002, 11–31; Whittle *et al.* 2011, 3–4.
30 E.g. Ingold 2007; Olsen 2012; Shennan 2002, 217.

These narratives must now be squared with the increasingly precise date estimates provided by the statistical modelling of large numbers of radiocarbon dates[31] and by the re-establishment of factors such as climate change, demographic developments and migrations as legitimately debatable causes of social transformation[32], all of which focus our attention on rapid and potentially catastrophic change. For the fifth millennium, one of the main controversies in this respect has been the transition from the LBK to its various successor cultures at the beginning of the Middle Neolithic, probably around 4900 cal BC. The models proposed have oscillated widely between crisis and catastrophe on the one hand[33] and continuity on the other[34]. It is now clear that a single explanation will not be able to cover the whole spectrum of variability. Yet little consensus has been reached beyond a distinction between a potentially more radical break in the Rhine region, with episodes of violence and depopulation, and a seemingly more gradual process further east, in the areas of the Stichbandkeramik culture (Stroke Ornamented Pottery culture or SBK) communities[35].

A second issue to consider in this context are the interaction and communication patterns connected to the emergence of the Michelsberg phenomenon (Figure 4). At the transition from the Middle to the Late Neolithic (following west German terminology) around 4400 cal BC, this "New Neolithic" first appears in northern France, Belgium and western Germany[36]. Within a short time span, Michelsberg covers a wide distribution area from the Paris Basin to the Harz mountains[37] and beyond, reaching Saxony-Anhalt, Saxony, Brandenburg and Bohemia[38]. Even if there is discussion concerning the internal coherence of the phenomenon we label "Michelsberg": compared to other archaeological entities in the vicinity we have to admit that the degree of cultural similarity is strong, or in any case stronger within than with other contemporary and neighbouring phenomena. Is this the result of the far-reaching mobility of Michelsberg-bearing people connected to a new, more mobile cattle-oriented economy[39]? At the same time, spatially much more restricted entities, with decorated pottery that continues preceding Neolithic traditions, appear in southern Germany and the Czech Republic; amongst others, one could mention groups auch as Schwieberdingen, Aichbühl, Münchshöfen or Jordanów, all of long-standing importance in research history. Is this a reaction against the expanding Michelsberg phenomenon? Maybe these are more settled (ethnic?) groups (cf. below) in fertile regions with restricted communication systems[40], some of them also trying to expand their economic activities to the lakes of the north Alpine foreland (*e.g.* Aichbühl)? In any case, it is interesting to note that the longevity of these different entities over time varies widely, although

---

31 E.g. Bayliss *et al.* 2011; Hamilton and Krus 2018.
32 E.g. Bevan *et al.* 2017; Biehl and Nieuwenhuyse 2016; Bocquet-Appel *et al.* 2012; Shennan 2018; Weninger *et al.* 2014; for a critical appreciation see e.g. Flohr *et al.* 2016.
33 E.g. Gronenborn 2007; 2012; Zeeb-Lanz 2009.
34 E.g. Stäuble 2014.
35 E.g. Denaire *et al.* 2017; Link 2014.
36 E.g. Gleser 1998; 2012b, 68–72 fig. 12; Jeunesse 1998; Schier 1993, 34–37, fig.6.
37 Geschwinde and Raetzel-Fabian 2009, 185–188, fig. 142; Gleser 1998, 243 fig. 4.
38 Beran and Wetzel 2014; Gojda *et al.* 2002; Pavlů and Zapotocká 1979, 302; Schlenker *et al.* 2016; Strobel *et al.* 2018.
39 See the so-called „Braunschweiger Modell" by Geschwinde and Raetzel-Fabian 2009, 242–249, fig. 168.
40 Zeeb-Lanz 2006.

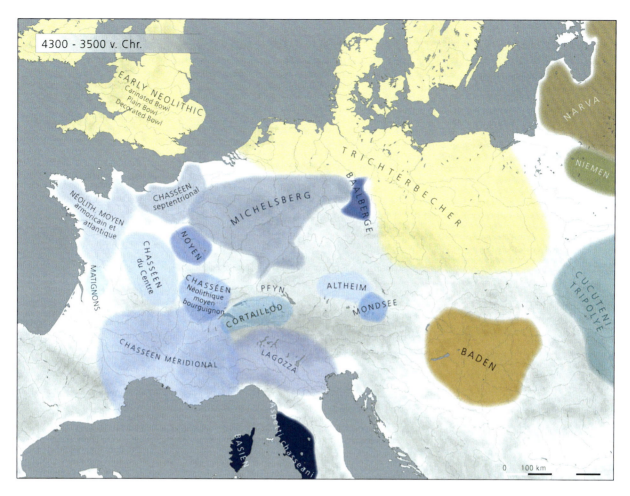

Figure 4. Map showing the extent of the Michelsberg culture and its relation with surrounding groups (from Gronenborn 2014, 45; © Creative Commons Attribution 4.0 International License, reproduced with kind permission of Detlef Gronenborn).

some aspects (for instance a certain style of lake village architecture, see below) are rather more persistent.

It may be worth considering new kinds of models for these transformative processes. For example, Timothy Pauketat[41] uses the idea of "bundling" to trace the genealogies of people, places, objects or practices and how they are entwined. The way different entities are bundled together can be more or less stable depending on how large-scale, dense and extensive their relations are. This in turn facilitates different rates and kinds of change[42], sometimes creating rapid tipping points or cascades when processes working at different speeds intersect[43], as may be the case for something like the appearance of the Michelsberg. Applying this model will need very careful consideration not just of object styles or types, but of the way in which they are embedded in the wider social context and therefore under what circumstances and at what speeds they can transform.

Alternatively, cyclical models offer a compromise solution, as they are aimed at incorporating a variety of factors working at different timescales. Indeed, these have been proposed for the end of the LBK and over the years have grown in sophistication. Where initially a fairly direct link between climate change and

---

41   Pauketat 2013, 35–39.
42   Pauketat 2013, 53.
43   See also e.g. Bentley *et al.* 2011.

social upheaval was assumed[44], more recent versions stress that these two aspects are interdependent in more complex ways[45]. However, we still need better chronological control to correlate events. In her work on personal ornamentation in the Upper Rhine area, for instance, Sandrine Bonnardin[46] identifies the most radical break in the mid-LBK, rather than between the Early and Middle Neolithic. Similarly, the fragmentation into new archaeological cultures at the beginning of the Middle Neolithic in no way means that communication between these units ceased, as several important innovations subsequently spread across multiple culture groups, ranging from increasingly trapezoidal longhouses[47] to the adoption of rondel enclosures[48]. In the same way, later in the millennium, at the onset of the Late Neolithic, causewayed enclosures or burials in grain storage pits become widespread phenomena which transcend individual culture boundaries and herald the beginning of a new kind of Neolithic with a new worldview[49], parts of which form a distinct departure from previous "Danubian" values[50]. Where exactly we draw a boundary in these continuous patterns of mutual influence and interaction is open to scrutiny, and different research questions most likely will necessitate different answers.

This is yet another recasting of the seemingly eternal controversy about culture concepts[51], which does not need to be repeated at length here. In the past few years, an ever-increasing array of terms has been proposed to help us shift from the static view of "culture history" towards characterising diversity, fusion and admixture, with creolisation, hybridity, bricolage and many others having entered the debate[52]. For instance, following Matthew Liebmann[53], *hybridity* is particularly apt in situations in which there is a clear power differential between the groups involved and stresses the subalterns' capacity for resistance, mockery and ambivalence in the adoption of "dominant" culture traits, whereas *mestizaje* focuses on the generative and creative aspects of such encounters.

While efforts at greater terminological clarity have much to commend them, the proliferation of concepts has often tended to confuse matters where definitions have been vague or inconsistently applied. In addition, terms like "hybridity" can be read to imply that at some unspecified origin point, separate and definable cultural entities existed which are then interacting. A particularly problematic aspect is to define the point when such "interaction" ends and is replaced by a new "norm", which can no longer be said to be "hybrid"; indeed this point is rarely explicitly defined[54]. Nevertheless, in spite of the always unfinished nature of social life, defining units of analysis is a fundamental step of each research endeavour; it is not only unavoidable but also fruitful as long as these units do not become reified. With this in mind, recent reworkings and extensions of the

---

44 E.g. Gronenborn 2007; 2012.
45 E.g. Gronenborn *et al.* 2014; 2017.
46 Bonnardin 2009, 292–293.
47 E.g. Coudart 1998; Mattheußer 1991.
48 E.g. Bertemes and Meller 2012.
49 E.g. Lefranc *et al.* 2010; papers in Lichter 2010.
50 Jeunesse 2017, 184.
51 In German-language literature, see e.g. Eggert 1978; Siegmund 2014; Veit 1989; Wahle 1950; Wotzka 2000.
52 E.g. Burke 2009; Greenblatt 2010; Hegmon *et al.* 2016; Liebmann 2013; 2015; Silliman 2015; Stockhammer 2012.
53 Liebmann 2013, 41.
54 Silliman 2015.

culture concept[55] show that even this discredited terminology, whose demise has long been proclaimed, can be adapted to answer a range of questions regarding the modalities of innovation and change.

Most papers in this volume address this set of issues to a greater or lesser extent, and many different scales of analysis are represented. In his contribution on theriomorphic depictions on pottery, Ralf Gleser tries to bridge the gap between, on the one hand, the sensory and cognitive effects of this kind of artefact and, on the other hand, the long-term and long-distance links revealed by the iconography, potentially back to Near Eastern roots. This illustrates how abstract, enduring cultural symbols need to be actively experienced and represented at an individual level to unfold their full potency.

At the medium scale of the archaeological culture, the volume offers three papers on the emergence of various post-LBK groupings. In her short contribution, and one scale up from Gleser's focus on individual sensory experience, Johanna Ritter tries to show how the acceptance of new pottery styles could have worked in the Wetterau region of central Germany, where LBK styles are in use for longer than in adjacent areas. Using Rogers and Shoemaker's model[56] of early innovators, majority adopters and latecomers, she suggests that the social ties in which new styles of pottery were implicated were a key factor in their adoption or rejection. This seems a far cry from models of a dramatic crisis at this point. In her case study of the emergence of the SBK, Karin Riedhammer equally emphasises social reasons for the speed of change in pottery decoration, in this case broadly concluding that SBK groups were deliberately differentiating themselves from their contemporaries and predecessors. Yet her main contribution is methodological, in that she clearly shows how tangled the picture of inter-regional interaction becomes, depending on which trait is the focus of analysis: motifs themselves or the techniques of creating them, motif structure or vessel shapes, for instance. It is difficult if not impossible to identify specific "origin points" for all these features, as ultimately this new pottery style emerges as a result of new patterns of interaction between many areas. This reading is contradicted by René Wollenweber, who uses the well at Nieder-Röblingen to argue for a more radical break between LBK and SBK and for the emergence of the SBK in western Germany, in the Hinkelstein culture. Thus, the two authors provide very different approaches for dealing with rapid and wholesale change which cannot yet be finally resolved. One can only agree with both Riedhammer and Wollenweber that the next stage of research in all these areas is to collect more data on individual mobility patterns and "boundary transgressors", to look for connections not just to former LBK regions, but also to areas beyond, to include more items than just pottery in our analyses and most particularly to build tighter absolute dating frameworks.

In contrast to all these authors, Christian Jeunesse is not concerned with rapid tipping points, but rather with the deep structural continuities which in his opinion link the entire fifth millennium. He traces a *longue durée* of practices as diverse as enclosure building, the expression of status in funerary rites, domestic architecture and the layout of settlement sites. This again is an attempt to reduce the interpretative weight of the notion of "archaeological culture", not by breaking it into smaller entities with shorter lifetimes, but by tracing the broad cultural

---

55 See e.g. Ebersbach *et al.* 2017; Furholt 2014; Heitz and Stapfer 2017; Roberts and Vander Linden 2011.
56 Rogers and Shoemaker 1971; the use of this model for Middle Neolithic western Germany was already pioneered by Eisenhauer (2002).

similarities in space and time. This approach had already gained traction over many decades, for instance through the establishment of the term *Danubian*, which includes all archaeological cultures directly deriving from the LBK. Jeunesse wants to expand the coverage of this term still further, as he sees the related cultural similarities lasting well into the fourth millennium, or indeed beyond[57]. He can identify no major break within this developmental sequence, but only externally, with the appearance of the Funnel Beaker culture. The concept is reminiscent of ideas developed by Jan Lichardus and colleagues[58] and is sure to be controversial. Many of the continuities advocated here are challenged by other papers in the volume. Nevertheless, the notion of a series of large-scale, overlapping worldviews is intriguing and will hopefully inspire, as Jeunesse himself suggests, a new kind of polyfocal mapping exercise which traces not only objects, but also the practices and contexts in which they are entwined.

Communities and boundaries: internal and external differentiation

Turning more squarely to the question of space, we must ask not just how or why cultures change, but also in how far the material culture boundaries we routinely define have real social relevance. This is ultimately the question of deliberate boundary creation with regard to others, and as a flipside the forging of a communal identity from diverse entities within, and whether this is traceable archaeologically[59].

Indeed, as Stephen Greenblatt[60] deplores, in spite of our orthodoxy of the never pure and always admixed, emerging state of culture, considerable material, social and political effort in the modern world goes into boundary creation and maintenance, and this does not just include national and territorial boundaries. Similar situations will most likely also have existed in the remote past, and we must be able to identify, understand and analyse them in their dynamic dialectic with more fluid aspects of culture. While on the one hand the emergence of post-LBK cultures may have been a process of deliberate group definition[61], on the other, as mentioned above, the internal coherence of an entity like the Michelsberg culture is increasingly being scrutinised[62]. If the notion of collectively acting groups or even ethnic groups as a label for such willed diversity is back on the agenda[63], we also need to bear in mind the divergent temporal and spatial scales of such phenomena[64].

In this context, it is vital to include the results of cultural anthropology and evolutionary biology. In principle, we can assert that although humans lived in very small groups during the Palaeolithic, they have the ability to form large communities, and indeed did so in the following periods[65]. In small-scale traditional societies, local groups consist of nuclear and extended families, also referred to as bands and

---

57 Jeunesse 2017.
58 Lichardus 1991, 785–786; Lichardus *et al.* 1985, 469–481.
59 E.g. Burmeister and Müller-Scheeßel 2006.
60 Greenblatt 2010.
61 E.g. Hofmann 2013a, 45–48; Link 2012, 281; Sommer 2011.
62 See e.g. Seidel, this volume.
63 E.g. Pechtl 2016 for the LBK.
64 Clarke 1968, 31; Wotzka 1997.
65 Wuketits 1997, 142.

clans in ethnology[66]. Merely for special occasions, for example important feasts, do local groupings aggregate, thereby also finding marriage partners, trading and forging military alliances[67]. Such endogamous units, sometimes called "mega- or macro-bands" in the archaeological literature[68] or "endogamous bands" by social anthropologists[69], can furthermore come together to form even larger groupings, which often share a dialect or language. Such entities, which consist of several regional collectives, are mostly called tribes or ethno-linguistic communities[70]. According to Christoph Antweiler, ethnic groups are defined as collectives of persons "whose norms, values, and behavioural patterns partly overlap, who have a partly common, historically developed collective identity and who marry among each other more often than with other groups"[71]. Members of ethnic groups are characterised by cultural relationships which can lead to cultural homogeneity, at least in some areas of social life. Cultural relationships encompass shared features based on common traditions in immaterial and material culture[72], independently of whether people are consciously aware of this or not.

Taking into consideration the size of settlement areas as a crucial factor, prehistoric archaeology has the possibility to search for materialisations of cultural homogeneity and indirectly for group consciousness in our source material. In this respect, for example, the Hinkelstein culture or the Schwieberdingen group, which are found over settlement areas of only around 3000 km², may well be ethnic groups[73], but they are surely different sorts of things than the long-term and large-scale boundary between northern and southern Italy explored in Valeska Becker's contribution, where many different spheres of life are affected over much larger areas. Becker suggests that the origin of the first Neolithic settlers may have had a part to play in orienting networks over the longer term, creating lasting patterns of difference, but these are certainly not simply an "ethnic" boundary across which communication nevertheless flows. To find possible "ethnic" groups within larger areas of material culture similarity, we would rather have to look for strategies of self-definition between local and regional societies which interact regularly and may even use similar material culture at a regional scale, making them very challenging to spot archaeologically[74].

The flipside to boundary creation is the building up of communities, a process that involves detailed attention to individual sites and the routines of daily life. Here, too the fifth millennium offers a variety of models. The site of Alsónyék-Bátaszék in south-west Hungary, for example, eventually turns into an impressive, large-scale aggregation of people, if only for a limited time. It is one of several substantial Lengyel culture[75] sites in the vicinity, which include both cemeteries and settlements, but its 122 houses and around 2300 graves exceed them all[76]. Recent Bayesian modelling of dates from the different occupation areas

---

66 Gamble *et al.* 2014, 53–55.
67 Wotzka 1997, 173.
68 Newell *et al.* 1990, 17, fig. 1.
69 Gamble *et al.* 2014, 41; Newell *et al.* 1990, 16–17, fig. 1.
70 Gamble *et al.* 2014, 41.
71 Antweiler 1988, 10, translation by authors.
72 Newell *et al.* 1990, 25.
73 Cf. the extent of settlement areas of ethnic groups presented in Wotzka 1997, 173 fig. 7.
74 Barth 1969.
75 In Hungary, the Lengyel culture runs from the early fifth millennium to just before 4300 cal BC (Osztás *et al.* 2016, 197), but further work on refining this is in progress.
76 Osztás *et al.* 2016, 180.

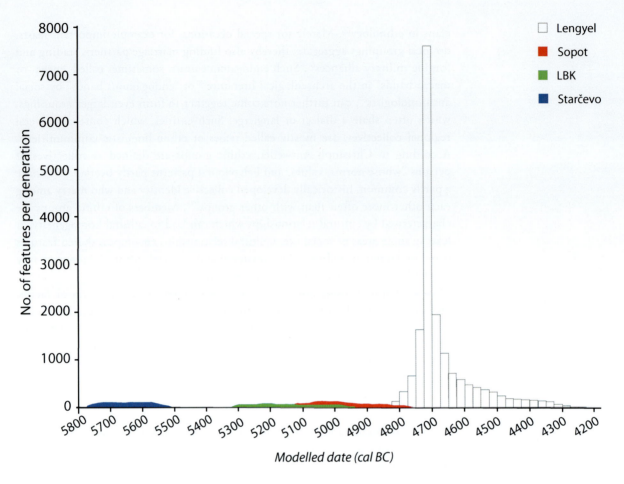

Figure 5. Number of features per generation at Alsónyék, Transdanubia, calculated from the normalised probability distributions for the use of each settlement phase (redrawn after Bánffy et al. 2016, 299 fig. 7). This shows both the overall long duration of the site and the sudden spike of activity in the Lengyel period. For more detail on the radiocarbon models and feature number estimates, see Bánffy et al. 2016. Reproduced with kind permission of Eszter Bánffy; original drawing A. Bayliss.

of Alsónyék has revealed that Lengyel activity began around 4800 cal BC, but that population then suddenly increased 50-fold, creating an exceptionally large aggregation of people (Figure 5). This high density remained in place for only one generation, followed by an equally fast dispersal[77].

The reasons both for the influx of so many people and for their eventual dispersal remain hard to grasp. The site had been settled before; indeed, the fusion of Sopot and LBK elements after a period of coexistence could be connected to the locally rapid appearance of the Lengyel culture[78]. Houses and graves form discontinuous clusters rather than planned and rigid layouts with shared, communal spaces or buildings. It is therefore possible that Alsónyék's impressive increase could be down to an agglomeration of previously separate hamlets, perhaps in response to an external threat[79], but which never managed to coalesce into a more homogenous entity. The disappearance of this threat, or some misfortune befalling the community — the authors suggest a possible outbreak of

---

77 Bánffy *et al.* 2016, 300.
78 Bánffy *et al.* 2016, 291.
79 Bánffy *et al.* 2016, 305–307; Osztás *et al.* 2016, 223–228.

tuberculosis — or quite simply the internal tensions with which large aggregations are riddled could then have been reasons for the eventual dispersal[80].

Post-excavation data for the site will continue to be published in the coming years and will no doubt allow further reflection on the social strategies that may have been attempted to attract and maintain a population of such unexpectedly large size. The display of personal wealth could have played a role, as many of the particularly richly furnished individuals date to the time of Alsónyék's boom[81]. Yet this kind of behaviour could also cause envy and encourage dispersal if it was not balanced by efforts at group cohesion.

What makes this case study particularly interesting is that tight dating has identified these explosive population movements in the first place. Yet in this, Alsónyék may not be unique. We may have to get used to a prehistory in which quite exceptional sites or behaviours appear and fade quickly, blips on our timeline, rather than being the eventual outcome of a long-term and steady process which will inexorably lead to the next logical stage. The famous cemetery at Varna may be another case in point. The available radiocarbon dates for this site have recently been remodelled in the light of possible reservoir effects[82]. Far from being the apex of development in the Late Copper Age, Varna seems to fall earlier in the sequence, in the mid fifth millennium, and with around 200 years has a relatively short use life[83]. It consists of several grave clusters which all began at approximately the same time and may represent different communities[84]. Although overall this is still a span of use of several generations, the impressive display of wealth in some graves and the pattern of a relatively short-lived peak in "complexity" followed at least locally by decline or abandonment does allow parallels to Alsónyék's boom and bust.

There are many more examples in which quick flourishes are followed by episodes of fading. For instance, at the later megasite of Valencina de la Concepción in Andalucía, the 900 years of overall use are punctuated by episodes of a "finite surge in effort"[85] in the display of wealth in the grave, as in tomb 10.049 with its ivory goods and later, in the 29th/28th century cal BC, in the Montelirio tholos. Indeed, Bayesian analysis has revealed that the overall intensity of activity at the site fluctuated, with at least two main periods of particularly intense burial activity and megalith-building between the 32nd and 24th centuries cal BC[86]. Studies of such peaks and troughs at a regional level are as yet hard to come by as they require the integration of much already published data[87] to establish tempo and duration of phases and sites, but the evidence available so far indicates that settlement density fluctuated considerably throughout, for instance in

---

80 Bánffy *et al.* 2016, 309.
81 Bánffy *et al.* 2016, 308; Osztás *et al.* 2016, 232.
82 Higham *et al.* 2018.
83 In how far the transformations evidenced at Varna then had longer-lasting effects on neighbouring societies (Chapman 2013) is another matter.
84 Higham *et al.* 2018.
85 García Sanjuán *et al.* 2018, 294.
86 See García Sanjuán *et al.* 2018, 275–301, and earlier sections of the paper for detailed statistical modelling. Nor are such punctuated biographies limited to European prehistory, see e.g. Pluckhahn *et al.* 2018.
87 See e.g. for the Middle and early Late Neolithic in western Germany Eibl 2016; Eisenhauer 2002; Friederich 2011; Knoche 2008; Lönne 2003; Spatz 1996. This is also suggested by the use of radiocarbon dates as proxies for population numbers, for instance by Bevan *et al.* 2017; Shennan *et al.* 2013, although this approach has seen its fair share of criticism, e.g. by Contreras and Meadows 2014.

fifth millennium Alsace[88]. The pulse of prehistory is quickening, and models of predictable "cycling" may not tell all of the story.

That this is not just a feature of exceptionally rich or large sites is evidenced by the waterlogged settlements of the Alpine Foreland with their wealth of dendrochronological data. Neolithic activity here begins in the last two centuries of the fifth millennium. From the start, most sites are extremely short-lived, often being in use for 20 years or less. Even these short-term agglomerations are in a state of flux, as sites are typically established by the inhabitants of two or three houses, then experience a sudden aggregation boom and begin to slowly shrink long before final abandonment[89]. Here, persistence and stability are, if present at all, to be found at other scales, for instance in the ways in which the landscape was inhabited[90]. In general, this is interpreted as reflecting a very high degree of personal and household autonomy, paired with relatively flat and unstable social hierarchies[91]. Where longer or larger aggregations did emerge, this was sometimes accompanied by special buildings, which perhaps functioned as sanctuaries or meeting places[92] and may have helped to bind larger collectivities of people together for longer.

There is a growing literature on whether and how various strategies, such as daily routines, rituals or long-range contacts, may have helped to sustain a sense of community in Alpine lake villages[93], but much of this evidence falls into the fourth millennium. Yet these debates are worth keeping in mind for earlier time horizons as well, for instance when discussing the role of enclosure sites. At Riedling in Lower Bavaria, an enclosure dating to the Münchshöfen culture is currently being studied from this point of view[94]. The Münchshöfen culture is situated between the large-scale networks of prestige goods which begin to emerge in Europe in the second half of the fifth millennium and which circulate materials such as jadeitite and copper over vast distances. In spite of far-flung connections evidenced in pottery shapes and modes of burial, the community at Riedling did seemingly not invest in such prestige items, but instead chose to destroy impressive assemblages of pottery and to deposit them in conspicuous artefact spreads in the enclosure ditches, sometimes associated with human and animal bone (Figure 6)[95]. No doubt these were intense, theatrical moments in which a sense of community belonging could have been fostered.

How long-lived this practice was, whether it could have helped to maintain a longer-lasting presence at Riedling or whether we are witnessing another boom and bust cycle of activity is still being investigated. What is important in this context is that the survival of communities over any length of time needs effort, for instance in "intense episodes of sociality"[96] in holding communities together,

---

88 See e.g. Denaire *et al.* 2017 for a diachronic study of Alsace based on Bayesian modelling of radiocarbon dates.
89 E.g. Bleicher 2009, 145–148; Ebersbach 2010a; Hofmann 2013b, 208–211.
90 Gross and Huber 2018; Hofmann *et al.* 2016.
91 E.g. Ebersbach 2010b 150–154; Ebersbach *et al.* 2017, 9.
92 E.g. Hofmann 2013b, 206–208.
93 For a summary of the main debates, see e.g. Ebersbach 2010b; Ebersbach *et al.* 2017; Hofmann 2013b; Hofmann *et al.* 2016.
94 Many thanks to the Deutsche Forschungsgemeinschaft for the generous funding of the project "Chronologie, Vernetzungen, Sozialstrukturen — Studien zur Münchshöfener Kultur am Erdwerk von Riedling, Niederbayern" (PI: D. Hofmann, Co-I: L. Husty) between 2016 and 2019.
95 E.g. Hofmann and Husty in press; Husty and Meixner 2009.
96 See Bogucki, this volume.

Figure 6. One of several sherd pavings, in this case with human remains, from the Münchshöfen enclosure at Riedling, Bavaria; photo: G. Meixner, Firma ArcTeam.

and that this took varied forms over the course of the millennium. If no coherent narrative is so far emerging, then this provides an opportunity to compare different trajectories between areas across the millennium, not only to once again give a sense of diversity, but also to help construct new models and expectations regarding these smaller-scale processes and their relation to wider patterns of transformation.

Enclosures as sites of encounter are also the topic of the contribution by Johannes Müller and colleagues. Hundisburg-Olbetal is yet another site with a short use-life, reinforcing the idea that the large-scale aggregations needed to build and maintain enclosures were not necessarily of long duration; the authors here suggest a defensive function. Yet it is also clear from the excavated material that the site's users had connections in many directions, as visible in the pottery spectrum, the enclosure's architecture and the kinds of activities carried out there. This shows that in the second half of the fifth millennium, boundaries between our cultural entities are increasingly hard to draw if not illusory; it is becoming clear that the period after 4500 BC is just as much a time of experimentation and creative recombination as the early fifth millennium was. With respect to Michelsberg and Epi-Rössen, for example, Ute Seidel, through a combination of extensive mapping and an effort at more precise dating, can show that the role of our main indicator for "cultural" attribution, pottery, may have changed over time, with more creative admixture in the early Epi-Rössen horizon and more restricted circulation of stylistic grammars, techniques and motifs in later phases (Schussenried). Following on from Andrea Zeeb-Lanz' ideas[97], this begs the question of how pottery could have functioned in emblematic and/or assertive ways and provides a welcome starting point for questioning the coherence of the "Michelsberg culture" in relation to various Epi-Rössen groups.

The fifth millennium also sees the beginnings of the circulation of so-called prestige goods, namely jadeitite and copper[98]. These items are often interpreted as the prerogative of an elite[99], creating a kind of distributed community of high status individuals with — at least implicitly — similar social strategies and goals. In the case of copper, the appearance of such artefacts and the techniques of their production, alongside the circumstances of their use, are sometimes thought to mark an elusive "new epoch" associated with a package of social, economic and

---

97 Zeeb-Lanz 2006.
98 E.g. Klassen 2004; Pétrequin et al. 2012; Rosenstock et al. 2016; Turck 2010.
99 As summarised and critically discussed e.g. in Kienlin 2012; Turck 2010.

religious innovations, even in central Europe[100]. However, at least in terms of technological innovation, it now appears the fourth millennium is more crucial than the fifth[101]. In addition, one can also question the extent to which such novel items would have had the same effect when introduced into different social contexts. In our volume, the papers by Antonín Přichystal and colleagues and by Pierre Pétrequin and colleagues focus on this aspect. In their short contribution Přichystal *et al.* present axeheads made from nephrite found in the Czech Republic and trace how these objects may have formed an alternative network to jadeitites of Alpine origin. Alongside the large-scale networks which have dominated scholarly discussion in recent years there may hence have been alternative, regional patterns of circulation, and we must now study how these interdigitate. This depends on the correct identification of the raw material, towards which this chapter forms a welcome first step. Similarly, Pétrequin and colleagues discuss the changing use of stone disc-rings, from their emergence in a Blicquy–Villeneuve-Saint Germain context, where they perhaps functioned akin to currency, to the manufacture of disc-rings from Alpine rocks. As they succeed to show, it is not just the objects which travelled. A core aspect of their success may have been the ideas and symbolic systems in which they were embedded, in this case largely concerned with gender relations.

A messier millennium? "Developed" Neolithic societies as an object of open-ended interpretations

The brief discussion above has drawn out some of the main themes discussed in the various contributions, but there are of course many more chronological and thematic connections between them which we hope our readers will extensively explore themselves. What is abundantly clear already is that the fifth millennium has far more to offer than a messy patchwork of increasingly colourful culture maps. It is this diversity, and the resulting archaeological specialisms, which make a synthetic overview of this central European Middle Neolithic difficult, let alone integrating it into the developments going on elsewhere in an increasingly connected Europe. Indeed, even a comparison of social processes in adjacent areas is rarely attempted, and in some cases the characterisation of material culture similarity and difference within and between neighbouring "cultures", as well as their precise synchronisation[102], are highly controversial. Overall, this has meant that the Middle Neolithic remains for many a rather confusing stretch of time between the well-studied LBK culture and the emergence of a fundamentally distinct Later Neolithic, an extensive period of "transition" without any importance of its own.

It is time to challenge this perspective. While the fifth millennium in central Europe quite clearly had its roots in a Linearbandkeramik world, in itself of more diverse inspiration than we generally give it credit for, fifth millennium societies were not consciously "transitioning" towards an inevitable new stage and they are therefore worthy of study in their own right. What kinds of social formations were

---

100 Cf. Lichardus 1991, 787–788 and the adaptation of this concept in Klassen 2004, 330–334; for a critical re-evaluation of the Copper Age concept see e.g. Schier 2014.
101 Hansen 2014.
102 E.g. Gleser 2016b.

created, how were they maintained, and what were the main factors of change? Such investigations must take place at multiple scales, from understanding how the routines of daily life, personal mobility and social interaction created smaller and larger communities of varying duration right up to characterising and explaining the pulses of relative material culture homogeneity and diversity which play out in central Europe and beyond over the *longue durée*. An endeavour of this kind first and foremost requires the targeted acquisition of new data obtained through careful excavation, especially seeing as the different cultural phenomena are very unevenly studied. Genetic and isotopic investigations are among the main desirables on the list, as is a robust absolute chronological framework, but even basic requirements such as reliable maps of settlement distribution and density are hard to come by for some areas. Yet we would not like to end simply with a plea for more descriptive detail. What is particularly needed are new theoretical ideas and their application as a first firm basis for comparative study at the European scale (and beyond). It is only then that the at first sight chaotic panorama of the Middle Neolithic can play its deserved part in understanding the factors behind the persistence and change of mid-level or tribal societies much more generally.

Hopefully, this volume is a further step in this direction. It is dedicated to our esteemed friend and colleague, the late István Zalai-Gáal, to whom we owe a wealth of information on the Lengyel culture in Hungary.

Acknowledgements

The Münster conference in 2015 was made possible by a generous grant of the LWL Archäologie für Westfalen. We would like to thank its director, Michael M. Rind, for his enthusiasm and support. This book is the product of a joint project of the Abteilung für Ur- und Frühgeschichtliche Archäologie at the Historisches Seminar der Universität Münster and the Institut für Vor- und Frühgeschichtliche Archäologie at the Universität Hamburg. The editors would like to express their heartfelt thanks to Renate Roling (WWU Münster) for the graphic reworking of the illustrations and to Florian Helmecke (UHH) for his editorial assistance. Corné van Woerdekom, Eric van den Bandt and Karsten Wentink at Sidestone Press have been immensely helpful in bringing this book onto the shelves — thanks are due to them also. Finally, Frank Nikulka and Alexandra Borstelmann (both UHH) kindly commented on an earlier draft of this introduction.

References

Antweiler, C. 1988. *Kulturevolution als transgenerationaler Wandel. Kölner Ethnologische Studien 13*. Berlin.

Bánffy, E., Osztás, A., Oross, K., Zalai-Gáal, I., Marton, T., Nyerges, E.A., Köhler, K., Bayliss, A., Hamilton, D. and Whittle, A. 2016. The Alsónyék story: towards the history of a persistent place. *Bericht der Römisch-Germanischen Kommission* 94, 283–318.

Banghard, K. and Gehlen, B. 2014. Das Mesolithikum in Ostwestfalen-Lippe. In M. Baales, H.-O. Pollmann and B. Stapel (eds), *Westfalen in der Alt- und Mittelsteinzeit*, 207–214. Münster.

Barth, F. 1969. *Ethnic groups and boundaries. The social organization of culture difference*. London.

Bayliss, A., Van der Plicht, J., Bronk Ramsey, C., McCormac, G., Healy, F. and Whittle, A. 2011. Towards generational time scales: the quantitative interpretation of archaeological chronologies. In A. Whittle, F. Healy and A. Bayliss (eds), *Gathering time. Dating the Early Neolithic enclosures of southern Britain and Ireland*, 17–59. Oxford.

Beau, A., Rivollat, M., Réveillas, H., Pemonge, M.-H., Mendisco, F., Thomas, Y., Lefranc, P. and Deguilloux, M.-F. 2017. Multi-scale ancient DNA analyses confirm the western origin of Michelsberg farmers and document probable practices of human sacrifice. *PLOS one* 12(7): e0179742. https://doi.org/10.1371/journal.pone.0179742.

Bentley, R.A., Earls, M. and O'Brien, M. 2011. *I'll have what she's having. Mapping social behaviour*. London.

Beran, J. 2012. Spitzhauen, Schöningen und Swifterbant — Überlegungen zu Endmesolithikum und beginnendem Jungneolithikum im nordostdeutschen Binnenland. In R. Gleser and V. Becker (eds), *Mitteleuropa im 5. Jahrtausend vor Christus. Beiträge zur Internationalen Konferenz in Münster 2010. Neolithikum und ältere Metallzeiten. Studien und Materialien 1*, 509–527. Münster.

Beran, J. and Wetzel, G. 2014. Die neolithische Siedlung der Michelsberger Kultur Wustermark 21, Lkr. Havelland. *Veröffentlichungen zur Brandenburgischen Landesarchäologie* 46, 37–141.

Bertemes, F. and Meller, H. (eds) 2012. *Neolithische Kreisgrabenanlagen in Europa. Internationale Arbeitstagung 7.–9. Mai 2004 in Goseck (Sachsen-Anhalt). Tagungen des Landesmuseums für Vorgeschichte Halle (Saale)*. Halle.

Bevan, A., Colledge, S., Fuller, D., Fyve, R., Shennan, S. and Stevens, C. 2017. Holocene fluctuations in human population demonstrate repeated links to food production and climate. *Proceedings of the National Academy of Sciences* 114, E10524–E10531.

Biehl, P. and Nieuwenhuyse, O. (eds) 2016. *Climate and cultural change in prehistoric Europe and the Near East*. Albany.

Bleicher, N. 2009. *Altes Holz in neuem Licht: archäologische und dendrochronologische Untersuchungen an spätneolithischen Feuchtbodensiedlungen Oberschwabens. Berichte zu Ufer- und Moorsiedlungen Südwestdeutschlands 5*. Stuttgart.

Bocquet-Appel, J.-P., Naji, S., Vander Linden, M. and Kozłowski, J.K. 2012. Understanding the rates of expansion of the farming system in Europe. *Journal of Archaeological Science* 36, 531–546.

Bollongino, R., Nehlich, O., Richards, M.P., Orschiedt, J., Thomas, M.G., Sell, C., Fajkošová, Z., Powell, A. and Burger, J. 2013. 2000 years of parallel societies in Stone Age central Europe. *Science* 342, 479–481.

Bonnardin, S. 2009. *La parure funéraire du Néolithique ancien dans les Bassins parisien et rhénan. Rubané, Hinkelstein et Villeneuve-Saint-Germain*. Paris.

Brandt, G., Haak, W., Adler, C.J., Roth, C., Szécsényi-Nagy, A., Karimnia, S., Möller-Rieker, S., Meller, H., Ganslmeier, R., Friederich, S., Dreseley, V., Nicklisch, N., Pickrell, J.K., Sirocko, F., Reich, D., Cooper, A., Alt, K.W. and the Genographic Consortium. 2013. Ancient DNA reveals key stages in the formation of central European mitochondrial genetic diversity. *Science* 342, 257–261.

Brandt, G., Szécsényi-Nagy, A., Roth, C., Alt, K.W. and Haak, W. 2015. Human paleogenetics of Europe — the known knowns and the known unknowns. *Journal of Human Evolution* 79, 73–92.

Burke, P. 2009. *Cultural hybridity*. Cambridge.

Burmeister, S. and Müller-Scheeßel, N. (eds) 2006. *Soziale Gruppen, kulturelle Grenzen: Die Interpretation sozialer Identitäten in der prähistorischen Archäologie. Tübinger Archäologische Taschenbücher 5*. Münster.

Chapman, J. 2013. From Varna to Brittany via Csőszhalom — was there a "Varna effect"? In A. Anders and G. Kulcsár (eds), *Moments in time. Papers presented to Pál Raczky on his 60th birthday*, 323–335. Budapest.

Clarke, D. 1968. *Analytical archaeology*. London.

Contreras, D.A. and Meadows, J. 2014. Summed radiocarbon calibrations as a population proxy: a critical evaluation using a realistic simulation approach. *Journal of Archaeological Science* 52, 591–608.

Coudart, A. 1998. *Architecture et société néolithique. L'unité et la variance de la maison danubienne*. Paris.

Denaire, A., Doppler, T., Nicod, P.-Y. and van Willigen, S. 2011. Espaces culturels, frontières et interactions au 5ème millénnaire entre la Plaine du Rhin Supérieur et les rivages de la Méditerranée. *Jahrbuch Archäologie Schweiz* 94, 21–59.

Denaire, A., Lefranc, P., Wahl, J., Bronk Ramsey, C., Dunbar, E., Goslar, T., Bayliss, A., Beavan, N., Bickle, P. and Whittle, A. 2017. The cultural project: formal chronological modelling of the Early and Middle Neolithic sequence in Lower Alsace. *Journal of Archaeological Method and Theory* 24, 1072–1149.

Ebersbach, R. 2010a. Vom Entstehen und Vergehen — Überlegungen zur Dynamik von Feuchtbodenhäusern und -siedlungen. In I. Matuschik and C. Strahm (eds), *Vernetzungen. Aspekte siedlungsarchäologischer Forschung. Festschrift für Helmut Schlichtherle zum 60. Geburtstag*, 41–50. Freiburg i. Br.

Ebersbach, R. 2010b. Soziale Einheiten zwischen "Haus" und "Dorf" — neue Erkenntnisse aus den Seeufersiedlungen. In E. Claßen, T. Doppler and B. Ramminger (eds), *Familie —Verwandtschaft — Sozialstrukturen: Sozialarchäologische Forschungen zu neolithischen Befunden*, 141–156. Kerpen-Loogh.

Ebersbach, R., Doppler, T., Hofmann, D. and Whittle, A. 2017. No time out. Scaling material diversity and change in the Alpine foreland Neolithic. *Journal of Anthropological Archaeology* 45, 1–14.

Eggert, M. 1978. Zum Kulturkonzept in der prähistorischen Archäologie. *Bonner Jahrbücher* 178, 1–20.

Eibl, F. 2016. *Die bayerische Gruppe der Stichbandkeramik und die Gruppe Oberlauterbach: Definition, Verbreitung und Untersuchungen zu Entwicklung sowie kultureller Stellung. Dissertation Universität des Saarlandes*. Saarbrücken.

Eisenhauer, U. 2002. *Untersuchungen zur Siedlungs- und Kulturgeschichte des Mittelneolithikums in der Wetterau. Universitätsforschungen zur Prähistorischen Archäologie 89*. Bonn.

Fischl, K.P. and Krauß, R. 2016. Entstehung und Ende der Tellsiedlungen im Karpatenbecken und im Ostbalkanraum — ökologische und gesellschaftliche Dynamiken im Vergleich. In V. Nikolov and W. Schier (eds), *Der Schwarzmeerraum vom Neolithikum bis in die Früheisenzeit (6000–600 v.Chr.): Kulturelle Interferenzen in der zirkumpontischen Zone und Kontakte mit ihren Nachbargebieten. Prähistorische Archäologie in Südosteuropa 30*, 321–338. Rahden.

Flohr, P., Fleitmann, D., Matthews, R., Matthews, W. and Black, S. 2016. Evidence of resilience to past climate change in Southwest Asia: early farming communities and the 9.2 and 8.2 ka events. *Quaternary Science Reviews* 136, 23–39.

Friederich, S. 2011. *Bad Friedrichshall-Kochendorf und Heilbronn-Neckargartach. Studie zum mittelneolithischen Siedlungswesen im Mittleren Neckarland. Forschungen und Berichte zur Vor- und Frühgeschichte in Baden-Württemberg 123*. Stuttgart.

Furholt, M. 2014. What is the Funnel Beaker complex? Persistent troubles with an inconsistent concept. In M. Furholt, M. Hinz, D. Mischka, G. Noble and D. Olausson (eds), *Landscapes, histories and societies in the northern European Neolithic*, 17–26. Bonn.

Gamble, C., Gowlett, J. and Dunbar, R. 2014. *Thinking big — how the evolution of social life shaped the human mind*. London.

García Sanjuán, L., Vargas Jiménez, J.M., Cáceres Puro, L.M., Costa Caramé, M.E., Díaz-Guardamino Uribe, M., Díaz-Zorita Bonilla, M., Fernández Flores, A., Hurtado Pérez, V., López Aldana, P.M., Méndez Izquierdo, E., Pajuelo Pando, A., Rodríguez Vidal, J., Wheatley, D., Bronk Ramsey, C., Delgado-Huertas, A., Dunbar, E., Mora González, A., Bayliss, A., Beavan, N., Hamilton, D. and Whittle, A. 2018. Assembling the dead, gathering the living: radiocarbon dating and Bayesian modelling for Copper Age Valencina de la Concepción (Seville, Spain). *Journal of World Prehistory* 31, 179–313.

Geschwinde, M. and Raetzel-Fabian, D. 2009. *EWBSL. Eine Fallstudie zu den jungneolithischen Erdwerken am Nordrand der Mittelgebirge. Beiträge zur Archäologie in Niedersachsen 14*. Rahden.

Gleser, R. 1998. Periodisierung, Verbreitung und Entstehung der älteren Michelsberger Kultur. In J. Biel, H. Schlichtherle, M. Strobel and A. Zeeb (eds), *Die Michelsberger Kultur und ihre Randgebiete — Probleme der Entstehung, Chronologie und des Siedlungswesens. Kolloquium Hemmenhofen 1997. Materialhefte zur Archäologie in Baden-Württemberg 43*, 237–247. Stuttgart.

Gleser, R. 2012a. Vorwort. In R. Gleser and V. Becker (eds), *Mitteleuropa im 5. Jahrtausend vor Christus. Beiträge zur Internationalen Konferenz in Münster 2010. Neolithikum und ältere Metallzeiten. Studien und Materialien 1*, 5–11. Münster.

Gleser, R. 2012b. Zeitskalen, stilistische Tendenzen und Regionalität des 5. Jahrtausends in den Altsiedellandschaften zwischen Mosel und Morava. In R. Gleser and V. Becker (eds), *Mitteleuropa im 5. Jahrtausend vor Christus. Beiträge zur Internationalen Konferenz in Münster 2010. Neolithikum und ältere Metallzeiten. Studien und Materialien 1*, 35–103. Münster.

Gleser, R. 2016a. Neue siedlungsarchäologische Daten zur frühesten Bronzezeit an der unteren Tundža. In V. Nikolov and W. Schier (eds), *Der Schwarzmeerraum vom Neolithikum bis in die Früheisenzeit (6000–600 v.Chr.): Kulturelle Interferenzen in der zirkumpontischen Zone und Kontakte mit ihren Nachbargebieten. Prähistorische Archäologie in Südosteuropa 30*, 371–389. Rahden.

Gleser, R. 2016b. Neue Überlegungen zur Chronologie der postbandkeramischen Kulturphänomene in Mitteleuropa. In J. Kovárník (ed.), *Centenary of Jaroslav Palliardi's Neolithic and Aeneolithic relative chronology. Internationale Konferenz Moravské Budejovice 2014*, 107–116. Moravské Budejovice.

Gleser, R. and Becker, V. (eds) 2012. *Mitteleuropa im 5. Jahrtausend vor Christus. Beiträge zur Internationalen Konferenz in Münster 2010. Neolithikum und ältere Metallzeiten. Studien und Materialien 1*. Münster.

Gleser, R. and Thomas, M. 2012. *"Merdžumekja"-Südosthang. Späte Kupferzeit und früheste Bronzezeit: Ergebnisse siedlungsarchäologischer Forschungen. Drama — Forschungen in einer Mikroregion 1*. Bonn.

Gojda, M., Dreslerova, D., Forster, P., Křivánek, R., Kuna, M., Vencl, S. and Zápotocký, M. 2002. Velké pravěké ohrazení v Klech (okr. Mělník). Využití nedestruktivních metod výzkumu k *poznání* nového typu areálu. Das Erdwerk Kly in Mittelböhmen. Auswertung der nichtdestruktiven Methoden zur Erkenntnis eines Siedlungsareal Typus. *Archeologické rozhledy* 54, 371–430.

Greenblatt, S. 2010. Cultural mobility: an introduction. In S. Greenblatt (ed.), *Cultural mobility. A manifesto*, 1–23. Cambridge.

Gronenborn, D. 2007. Climate change and sociopolitical crises: some cases from Neolithic central Europe. In T. Pollard and I. Banks (eds), *War and sacrifice: studies in the archaeology of conflict*, 13–32. Leiden.

Gronenborn, D. 2012. Das Ende von IRD 5b: Abrupte Klimafluktuationen um 5100 den BC und der Übergang vom Alt- zum Mittelneolithikum im westlichen Mitteleuropa. In R. Smolnik (ed.), *Siedlungsstruktur und Kulturwandel in der Bandkeramik. Beiträge der internationalen Tagung "Neue Fragen zur Bandkeramik oder alles beim Alten?!", Leipzig 23. bis 24. September 2010*, 241–250. Dresden.

Gronenborn, D. 2014. Häuptlinge und Sklaven? Anfänge gesellschaftlicher Differenzierung. In T. Terberger and Detlef Gronenborn (eds), *Vom Jäger und Sammler zum Bauern: Die Neolithische Revolution*, 39–47. Darmstadt.

Gronenborn, D., Strien, H.-C., Dietrich, S. and Sirocko, S. 2014. "Adaptive cycles" and climate fluctuations: a case study from Linear Pottery culture in western central Europe. *Journal of Archaeological Science* 51, 73–83.

Gronenborn, D., Strien, H.-C. and Lemmen, C. 2017. Population dynamics, social resilience strategies, and adaptive cycles in early farming societies of SW central Europe. *Quaternary International* 446, 54–65.

Gross, E. and Huber, R. 2018. Thinking outside the box: life beyond "house — farmstead — village" in Neolithic wetland sites. *Archäologische Informationen* 41, 255–274.

Hachem, L. 2011. *Le site néolithique de Cuiry-lès-Chaudardes — I. De l'analyse de la faune à la structuration sociale*. Rahden.

Hamilton, D. and Krus, A. 2018. The myths and realities of Bayesian chronological modeling revealed. *American Antiquity* 83, 187–203.

Hansen, S. 2014. The 4th millennium. A watershed in European prehistory. In B. Horejs and M. Mehofer (eds), *Proto-urbanisation in the 4th millenium BC? Proceedings of the International Symposium held at the Kunsthistorisches Museum Wien, Vienna 21–24 November 2012. Oriental and European Archaeology 1*, 243–259. Vienna.

Hegmon, M., Freeman, J., Kintigh, K.W., Nelson, M.C., Oas, S., Peeples, M.A. and Torvinen, A. 2016. Marking and making differences: representational diversity in the U.S. Southwest. *American Antiquity* 81, 253–272.

Heinen, M., Orschiedt, J. and Stapel, B. 2015. Parallelgesellschaften. Bauern, Hirten und letzte Wildbeuter im Neolithikum Nordrhein-Westfalens. In T. Otten, J. Kunow, M.M. Rind and M. Trier (eds), *Revolution Jungsteinzeit. Archäologische Landesausstellung Nordrhein-Westfalen*, 243–249. Münster.

Heitz, C. and Stapfer, R. 2017. Mobility and pottery production, what for? Introductory remarks. In C. Heitz and R. Stapfer (eds), *Mobility and pottery production. Archaeological and anthropological perspectives,* 11–38. Leiden.

Higham, T., Slavchev, V., Gaydarska, B. and Chapman, J. 2018. AMS dating of the Late Copper Age Varna cemetery, Bulgaria. *Radiocarbon* 60, 493–516.

Hofmann, D. 2013a. Narrating the house. The transformation of longhouses in early Neolithic Europe. In A. Chadwick and C. Gibson (eds), *Memory, myth and long-term landscape inhabitation,* 32–54. Oxford.

Hofmann, D. 2013b. Living by the lake. Domestic architecture in the Alpine foreland. In D. Hofmann and J. Smyth (eds), *Tracking the Neolithic house in Europe — sedentism, architecture and practice,* 197–227. New York.

Hofmann, D. 2015. What have genetics ever done for us? The implications of aDNA data for interpreting identity in Early Neolithic central Europe. *European Journal of Archaeology* 18, 454–476.

Hofmann, D. 2016. Keep on walking: the role of migration in Linearbandkeramik life. *Documenta Praehistorica* 43, 235–251.

Hofmann, D. and Husty, L. in press. Enclosures, structured deposits and selective innovations: Riedling and the role of the south Bavarian Münchshöfen culture in the new networks of the late Neolithic. In J. Müller and M. Hinz (eds), *Megaliths, societies, landscapes: early monumentality and social differentiation in Neolithic Europe. Proceedings of the international conference.* Bonn.

Hofmann, D., Ebersbach, R., Doppler, T. and Whittle, A. 2016. The life and times of the house: multi-scalar perspectives on settlement from the Neolithic of the north Alpine foreland. *European Journal of Archaeology* 19, 596–630.

Husty, L. and Meixner, G. 2009. Ein neues Münchshöfener Grabenwerk in Riedling, Gde. Oberschneiding, Lkr. Straubing-Bogen — Erster Vorbericht zu den archäologischen Grabungen des Jahres 2007. In K. Schmotz (ed.), *Vorträge des 27. Niederbayerischen Archäologentages,* 29–63. Rahden.

Ingold, T. 2007. Materials against materiality. *Archaeological Dialogues* 14, 1–16.

Jeunesse, C. 1998. Pour une origine occidentale de la culture de Michelsberg? In J. Biel, H. Schlichtherle, M. Strobel and A. Zeeb (eds), *Die Michelsberger Kultur und ihre Randgebiete — Probleme der Entstehung, Chronologie und des Siedlungswesens. Kolloquium Hemmenhofen 1997. Materialhefte zur Archäologie in Baden-Württemberg 43,* 29–45. Stuttgart.

Jeunesse, C. 2002. La coquille et la dent. Parure de coquillage et évolution des systèmes symboliques dans le Néolithique danubien (-5600/-4500). In J. Guilaine (ed.), *Matériaux, productions, circulations du Néolithique à l'Âge du Bronze,* 49–64. Paris.

Jeunesse, C. 2010. Die Michelsberger Kultur. In Lichter, C. (ed.), *Jungsteinzeit im Umbruch. Die "Michelsberger Kultur" und Mitteleuropa vor 6000 Jahren. Katalog zur Ausstellung im Badischen Landesmuseum Schloss Karlsruhe 20.11.2010–15.5.2011,* 46–55. Darmstadt.

Jeunesse, C. 2017. From Neolithic kings to the Staffordshire hoard. Hoards and aristocratic graves in the European Neolithic: the birth of a "Barbarian" Europe? In P. Bickle, V. Cummings, D. Hofmann and J. Pollard (eds), *The Neolithic of Europe. Papers in honour of Alasdair Whittle,* 175–187. Oxford.

Kent, S.1989. Cross-cultural perceptions of farmers as hunters and the value of meat. In S. Kent (ed.), *Farmers as hunters: the implications of sedentism*, 1–17. Cambridge.

Kienlin, T. 2012. Beyond elites: an introduction. In T. Kienlin and A. Zimmermann (eds), *Beyond elites. Alternatives to hierarchical systems in modelling social formations. Universitätsforschungen zur Prähistorischen Archäologie 215*, 15–32. Bonn.

Klassen, L. 2004. *Jade und Kupfer. Untersuchungen zum Neolithisierungsprozess im westlichen Ostseeraum unter besonderer Berücksichtigung der Kulturentwicklung Europas 5500–3500 BC. Jutland Archaeological Society Volume 47*. Aarhus.

Knoche, B. 2008. *Die Erdwerke von Soest (Kr. Soest) und Nottuln-Uphoven (Kr. Coesfeld). Studien zum Jungneolithikum in Westfalen. Münstersche Beiträge zur Ur- und Frühgeschichtlichen Archäologie 3*. Rahden.

Knopf, T. 2002. *Kontinuität und Diskontinuität in der Archäologie: quellenkritisch-vergleichende Studien. Tübinger Schriften zur Ur- und Frühgeschichtlichen Archäologie 6.* Münster.

Kobusiewicz, M. 2006. Paraneolithic — obstinate hunter-gatherers of the Polish plain. In C.-J. Kind (ed.), *After the Ice Age. Settlements, subsistence and social development in the Mesolithic of central Europe. Proceedings of the International Conference 9th to 12th of September 2003 Rottenburg/Neckar, Baden-Württemberg, Germany. Materialhefte zur Archäologie in Baden-Württemberg 78*, 181–188. Stuttgart.

Krause, J. and Haak, W. 2017. Neue Erkenntnisse zur genetischen Geschichte Europas. In H. Meller, F. Daim, J. Krause and R. Risch (eds), *Migration und Integration von der Urgeschichte bis zum Mittelalter. Tagungen des Landesmuseums für Vorgeschichte Halle (Saale)*, 21–38. Halle.

Kreuz A., Märkle, T., Marinova, E., Rösch, M., Schäfer, E., Schamuhn, S. and Zerl, T. 2014. The Late Neolithic Michelsberg culture — just ramparts and ditches? A supraregional comparison of agricultural and environmental data. *Praehistorische Zeitschrift* 89, 72–115.

Lefranc, P., Denaire, A., Chenal, F. and Arbogast, R.-M. 2010. Les inhumations et les dépôts d'animaux en fosses circulaires du Néolithique récent du sud de la Plaine du Rhin supérieur. *Gallia Préhistoire* 52, 61–116.

Lichardus, J. 1991. Die Kupferzeit als historische Epoche. Versuch einer Deutung. In J. Lichardus (ed.), *Die Kupferzeit als historische Epoche. Symposium Saarbrücken und Otzenhausen 6.–13.11.1988. Saarbrücker Beiträge zur Altertumskunde 55*, 763–800. Bonn.

Lichardus, J., Lichardus-Itten, M., Bailloud, G. and Cauvin, J. 1985. *La Protohistoire de l'Europe. Le Néolithique et le Chalcolithique entre la Méditerranée et la mer Baltique. Nouvelle Clio 1bis*. Paris.

Lichter, C. (ed.) 2010. *Jungsteinzeit im Umbruch. Die "Michelsberger Kultur" und Mitteleuropa vor 6000 Jahren. Katalog zur Ausstellung im Badischen Landesmuseum Schloss Karlsruhe 20.11.2010–15.5.2011*. Darmstadt.

Liebmann, M. 2013. *Parsing hybridity*: archaeologies of amalgamation in seventeenth-century New Mexico. In J. Card (ed.), *The archaeology of hybrid material culture*, 25–48. Carbondale.

Liebmann, M. 2015. The Mickey Mouse kachina and other "double objects": hybridity in the material culture of colonial encounters. *Journal of Social Archaeology* 15, 319–341.

Link, T. 2012. Neue Kultur oder jüngerlinienbandkeramische Regionalgruppe? Dresden-Prohlis und die Entstehung der Stichbandkeramik. In R. Smolnik (ed.), *Siedlungsstruktur und Kulturwandel in der Bandkeramik. Beiträge der internationalen Tagung "Neue Fragen zur Bandkeramik oder alles beim Alten?!", Leipzig 23. bis 24. September 2010*, 274–283. Dresden.

Link, T. 2014. Welche Krise? Das Ende der Linienbandkeramik aus östlicher Perspektive. In T. Link and D. Schimmelpfennig (eds), *No future? Brüche und Ende kultureller Erscheinungen. Beispiele aus dem 6.–2. Jahrtausend v. Chr. Fokus Jungsteinzeit. Berichte der AG Neolithikum 4*, 95–111. Kerpen-Loogh.

Lipson, M., Szécsényi-Nagy, A., Mallick, S., Pósa, A., Stégmár, B., Keerl, V., Rohland, N., Stewardson, K., Ferry, M., Michel, M., Oppenheimer, J., Broomandkhoshbacht, N., Harney, E., Nordenfelt, S., Llamas, B., Mende, B.G., Köhler, K., Oross, K., Bondár, M., Marton, T., Osztás, A., Jakucs, J., Paluch, T., Horváth, F., Csengeri, P., Koós, J., Sebők, K., Anders, A., Raczky, P., Regenye, J., Barna, J.P., Fábián, Sz., Serlegi, G., Toldi, Z., Gyöngyvér Nagy, E., Dani, J., Molnár, E., Pálfi, G., Márk, L., Melegh, B., Bánfai, Zs., Domboróczki, L., Fernández-Eraso, J., Mujika-Alustiza, J.A., Alonso Fernández, C., Jiménez Echevarría, J., Bollongino, R., Orschiedt, J., Schierhold, K., Meller, H., Cooper, A., Burger, J., Bánffy, E., Alt, K.W., Lalueza-Fox, C., Haak, W. and Reich, D. 2017. Parallel genomic transects reveal complex genetic history of early European farmers. *Nature* 551, 368–372.

Lönne, P. 2003. *Das Mittelneolithikum im südlichen Niedersachsen. Untersuchungen zum Kulturenkomplex Großgartach — Planig-Friedberg — Rössen und zur Stichbandkeramik. Materialhefte zur Ur- und Frühgeschichte in Niedersachsen 31*. Rahden.

Malmström, H., Linderholm, A., Skoglund, P., Storå, J., Sjödin, P., Gilbert, M.T.P., Holmlund, G., Willerslev, E., Jakobsson, M., Lidén, K. and Götherström, A. 2014. Ancient mitochondrial DNA from the northern fringe of the Neolithic farming expansion in Europe sheds light on the dispersion process. *Philosophical Transactions of the Royal Society B* 320, 20130373. doi: 10.1098/rstb.2013.0373.

Manen, C. and Mazurié de Keroualin, K. 2003. Les concepts "La Hoguette" et "Limbourg": un bilan des données. *Cahiers d'Archéologie Romande* 95, 115–145.

Mattheußer, E. 1991. Die geographische Ausrichtung bandkeramischer Häuser. In Seminar für Vor- und Frühgeschichte der Universität Frankfurt/M. (eds), *Studien zur Siedlungsarchäologie I. Universitätsforschungen zur Prähistorischen Archäologie 6*, 1–49. Bonn.

Mittnik, A., Wang, C.-C., Pfrengle, S., Daubaras, M., Zariņa, G., Hallgren, F., Allmäe, R., Khartanovich, V., Moiseyev, V., Tõrv, M., Furtwängler, A., Andrades Valtueña, A., Feldman, M., Economou, C., Oinonen, M., Vasks, A., Balanovska, E., Reich, D., Jankauskas, R., Haak, W., Schiffels, S. and Krause, J. 2018. The genetic prehistory of the Baltic Sea region. *Nature Communications* 442, doi: 10.1038/s41467-018-02825-9.

Molina Gonzales, F., Cámara Serrano, J.A. and López Sáez, J.A. 2012. Andalucía. In M.A. Rojo Guerra, R. Garrido Pena and I. Gárcia Martínez de Lagrán (eds), *El Neolítico en la Península Ibérica y su contexto Europeo*, 405–461. Madrid.

Newell, R.R., Kielman, D., Constandse-Westermann, T.S., van der Sanden, W.A.B. and Van Gijn, A. 1990. *An inquiry into the ethnic resolution of Mesolithic regional groups. The study of their decorative ornaments in time and space*. Leiden.

Olsen, B. 2012. After interpretation: remembering archaeology. *Current Swedish Archaeology* 20, 11–34.

Orschiedt, J., Bollongino, R., Nehlich, O. and Burger, J. 2014. Parallelgesellschaften? Die letzten Jäger und Sammler Mitteleuropas aus der Blätterhöhle, Kreis Hagen, Regierungsbezirk Arnsberg. *Archäologie in Westfalen-Lippe 2013*, 43–45.

Osztás, A., Zalai-Gáal, I., Bánffy, E., Marton, T., Nyerges, E.A., Köhler, K., Somogyi, K., Gallina, Zs., Bronk Ramsey, C., Dunbar, E., Kromer, B., Bayliss, A., Hamilton, D. and Whittle, A. 2016. Coalescent community at Alsónyék: the timings and duration of Lengyel burials and settlement. *Bericht der Römisch-Germanischen Kommission* 94, 179–282.

Parkinson, W.A. 2006. *The social organization of Early Copper Age tribes on the Great Hungarian Plain. BAR International Series 1573*. Oxford.

Pauketat, T. 2013. Bundels of/in/as time. In J. Robb and T. Pauketat (eds), *Big histories, human lives. Tackling problems of scale in archaeology*, 35–56. Santa Fe.

Pavlů, I. and Zápotocká, M. 1979. Současný stav a úkoly studia neolitu v Čechách. *Památky Archeologické* 70, 281–318.

Pechtl, J. 2016. From distribution maps to "ethnic" diversity within the southern Bavarian LBK. In L. Amkreutz, F. Haack, D. Hofmann and I. van Wijk (eds), *Something out of the ordinary? Interpreting diversity in the Early Neolithic Linearbandkeramik and beyond*, 283–311. Newcastle.

Pétrequin, P., Cassen, S., Gauthier, E., Klassen, L., Pailler, Y. and Sheridan, A. 2012. Typologie, chronologie et répartition des grandes haches alpines en Europe occidentale. In P. Pétrequin, S. Cassen, M. Errera, L. Klassen, A. Sheridan and A.-M. Pétrequin (eds), *JADE — Grandes haches alpines du Néolithique européen. Ve et IVe millénnaires av. J.-C.*, 574–727. Besançon.

Pluckhahn, T., Menz, M., West, S.E. and Wallis, N.J. 2018. A new history of community formation and change at Kolomoki (9ER1). *American Antiquity* 83, 320–344.

Pokorný, P., Šida, P., Chvojka, O., Žáčková, P., Kuneš, P., Světlík, I. and Veselý, J. 2010. Palaeoenvironmental research of the Schwarzenberg Lake, southern Bohemia, and exploratory excavations of this key Mesolithic archaeological area. *Památky Archeologické* 101, 5–38.

Robb, J. 2014. The future Neolithic: a new research agenda. In A. Whittle and P. Bickle (eds), *Early farmers. The view from archaeology and science*, 21–38. Oxford.

Roberts, B. and Vander Linden, M. (eds) 2011. *Investigating archaeological cultures. Material culture, variability and transmission*. New York.

Rogers, E.M. and Shoemaker, F.F. 1971. *Communication of innovations: a cross-cultural approach*. New York.

Rosenstock, E., Scharl, S. and Schier, W. 2016. Ex oriente lux? — Ein Diskussionsbeitrag zur Stellung der frühen Kupfermetallurgie Südosteuropas. In M. Bartelheim, B. Horejs and R. Krauss (eds), *Von Baden bis Troia. Ressourcennutzung, Metallurgie und Wissenstransfer. Eine Jubiläumsschrift für Ernst Pernicka. Oriental and European Archaeology 3*, 59–122. Rahden.

Schier, W. 1993. Das westliche Mitteleuropa an der Wende vom 5. zum 4. Jahrtausend: Kulturwandel durch Kulturkontakt? In A. Lang, H. Parzinger and H. Küster (eds), *Kulturen zwischen Ost und West. Das Ost-West-Verhältnis in vor- und frühgeschichtlicher Zeit und sein Einfluß auf Werden und Wandel des Kulturraums Mitteleuropa*, 19–59. Berlin.

Schier, W. 2014. The Copper Age in southeast Europe – historical epoch or typo-chronological construct? In W. Schier and F. Draşovean (eds), *The Neolithic and Eneolithic in southeast Europe. New approaches to dating and cultural dynamics in the 6th to 4th millennium BC. Prähistorische Archäologie in Südosteuropa 28*, 419–435. Rahden.

Schlenker, B., Wollenweber, R., Schroeter-Behrens, J. and Friederich, S. 2016. Die Michelsberger Kultur — Westeinflüsse in der Älteren Trichterbecherkultur Mitteldeutschlands. *Archäologie in Sachsen-Anhalt* 8, 11–18.

Shennan, S. 2002. *Genes, memes and human history. Darwinian archaeology and cultural evolution*. London.

Shennan, S. 2018. *The first farmers of Europe. An evolutionary perspective*. Cambridge.

Shennan, S., Downey, S.S., Timpson, A., Edinborough, K., Colledge, S., Kerig, T., Manning, K. and Thomas, M.G. 2013. Regional population collapse followed initial agriculture booms in mid-Holocene Europe. *Nature Communications* 4, 2486.

Siegmund, F. 2014. Kulturen, Technokomplexe, Völker und Identitätsgruppen: eine Skizze der archäologischen Diskussion. *Archäologische Informationen* 37, 53–65.

Silliman, S. 2015. A requiem for hybridity? The problem with Frankensteins, purées, and mules. *Journal of Social Archaeology* 15, 277–298.

Sommer, U. 2011. Tribes, peoples, ethnicity: archaeology and changing "we-groups". In E. Cochrane and A. Gardner (eds), *Evolutionary and interpretive archaeologies: a dialogue*, 169–198. Walnut Creek.

Spatz, H. 1996. *Beiträge zum Kulturenkomplex Hinkelstein — Großgartach — Rössen. Der keramische Fundstoff des Mittelneolithikums aus dem mittleren Neckarland und seine zeitliche Gliederung. Materialhefte zur Archäologie in Baden-Württemberg 37*. Stuttgart.

Stapel, B. and Schlösser, M. 2014. Zwei datierte mesolithische Knochenartefakte aus Greven, Kreis Steinfurt, Regierungsbezirk Münster. *Archäologie in Westfalen-Lippe 2013*, 46–49.

Stäuble, H. 2014. Die Krise am Ende der Linienbandkeramik? Oder ist es am Ende eine Krise der Bandkeramik-Forschung?! Ein archäologisches Feuilleton. In T. Link and D. Schimmelpfennig (eds), *No future? Brüche und Ende kultureller Erscheinungen. Fallbeispiele aus dem 6.–2. Jahrtausend v. Chr.*, 10–49. Kerpen-Loogh.

Stäuble, H. and Wolfram, S. 2013. Bandkeramik und Mesolithikum: Abfolge oder Koexistenz. In S. Hansen and M. Meyer (eds), *Parallele Raumkonzepte*, 105–134. Berlin.

Stockhammer, P.W. 2012. Conceptualizing cultural hybridization in archaeology. In P.W. Stockhammer (ed.), *Conceptualizing cultural hybridization. A transdisciplinary approach*, 43–58. Berlin.

Strobel, M., Herbig, C., Hirsekorn, V., Kaltofen, A. and Seifert, G. 2018. Trassen und Fenster in das frühe Mittelneolithikum (4500–3900 v. Chr.). Die Ausgrabungen in Wollsdorf (ZAV-03), Zävertitz (ZAV-04) und Scheerau (SCR-18). In R. Smolnik (ed.), *Ausgrabungen in Sachsen 6. Arbeits- und Forschungsberichte zur Sächsischen Bodendenkmalpflege Beiheft 33*, 59–68. Dresden.

Turck, R. 2010. *Die Metalle zur Zeit des Jungneolithikums in Mitteleuropa. Eine sozialarchäologische Untersuchung. Universitätsforschungen zur Prähistorischen Archäologie 185*. Bonn.

Veit, U. 1989. Ethnic concepts in German prehistory: a case study on the relationship between cultural identity and archaeological objectivity. In S. Shennan (ed.), *Archaeological approaches to cultural identity*, 35–56. London.

Wahle, E. 1950. *Zur ethnischen Deutung frühgeschichtlicher Kulturprovinzen*. Heidelberg.

Weninger, B., Clare, L., Gerritsen, F., Horejs, B., Krauß, R., Linstädter, J., Özbal, R. and Rohling, E.J. 2014. Neolithisation of the Aegean and southeast Europe during the 6600–6000 calBC period of rapid climate change. *Documenta Praehistorica* 41, 1–31.

Whittle, A., Healy, F. and Bayliss, A. 2011. Gathering time: causewayed enclosures in the Early Neolithic of southern Britain and Ireland. In A. Whittle, F. Healy and A. Bayliss (eds), *Gathering time. Dating the Early Neolithic enclosures of southern Britain and Ireland*, 1–16. Oxford.

Wotzka, H.-P. 1997. Maßstabsprobleme bei der ethnischen Deutung neolithischer "Kulturen". *Das Altertum* 43, 163–176.

Wotzka, H.-P. 2000. "Kultur" in der deutschsprachigen Urgeschichtsforschung. In S. Fröhlich (ed.), *Kultur—ein interdisziplinäres Kolloquium zur Begrifflichkeit*, 55–80. Halle.

Wuketits, F.M. 1997. *Soziobiologie. Die Macht der Gene und die Evolution sozialen Verhaltens*. Heidelberg.

Zeeb-Lanz, A. 2006. Überlegungen zu Sozialaspekten keramischer Gruppen. Beispiele aus dem Neolithikum Südwestdeutschlands. In S. Burmeister and N. Müller-Scheeßel (eds), *Soziale Gruppen — kulturelle Grenzen. Die Interpretation sozialer Identitäten in der prähistorischen Archäologie. Tübinger Archäologische Taschenbücher* 5, 81–102. Münster.

Zeeb-Lanz, A. 2009. Gewaltszenarien oder Sinnkrise? Die Grubenanlage von Herxheim und das Ende der Bandkeramik. In A. Zeeb-Lanz (ed.), *Krisen — Kulturwandel — Kontinuitäten. Zum Ende der Bandkeramik in Mitteleuropa. Beiträge der internationalen Tagung in Herxheim bei Landau (Pfalz) from 14.–17.06.2007*, 87–101. Rahden.

Part One

Diverse populations

On the periphery and at a crossroads

A Neolithic creole society on the Lower Vistula in the fifth millennium BC

Peter Bogucki

Abstract

During the mid to late fifth millennium BC, a distinctive Neolithic society flourished in the lower Vistula valley. First recognised in the 1930s at Brześć Kujawski, it is clear from its longhouse architecture, settlement patterns and contracted burials that this society lies in the Danubian tradition that emerged a millennium earlier and spread throughout riverine interior central Europe. At the same time, it has distinctive elements that reflect local re-interpretation of its Danubian legacy, resulting in cultural elaboration and even exaggeration. It is possible to consider the Brześć Kujawski group to be a particularly dynamic "creole" society in which ancestral customs and traditions are re-imagined and complicated across generations through the appropriation of external things and practices.

Zusammenfassung: Peripher und an der Wegscheide: eine neolithische kreolische Gesellschaft des 5. Jahrtausends v. Chr. an der Unteren Weichsel

Im mittleren und späten 5. Jahrtausend v. Chr. wurde das Tal der unteren Weichsel von einer neolithischen Kultur sehr eigener Ausprägung besiedelt. Erstmals in den 1930er Jahren als Brześć Kujawski Kultur identifiziert, ist auf Grund der Langhausarchitektur, der Siedlungsmuster und der Bestattungen in Hockerposition eindeutig klar, dass diese Gesellschaft die Tradition der sogenannten „donauländischen Kulturen" fortführt, die sich etwa ein Jahrtausend früher über die Flusssysteme Mitteleuropas ausgebreitet hatten. Andererseits finden sich jetzt auch charakteristische Elemente der materiellen Kultur, die auf eine lokale, kreative Umwandlung dieser donauländischen Tradition hindeuten, was schließlich in kultureller Entfaltung und sogar Übersteigerung mündete. Die Brześć Kujawski Gruppe kann als eine besonders dynamische „kreolische" Gesellschaft interpretiert werden, in welcher alt hergebrachte Bräuche und Traditionen neu gedacht und im Laufe der Generationen durch die Übernahme neuer Objekte und Praktiken immer komplizierter wurden.

Introduction

During the second half of the fifth millennium BC, a remarkable group of Neolithic communities emerged on the lowlands of northern Poland. Settlements of the Brześć Kujawski group, which include both domestic and mortuary features, have been known since the 1930s, starting with Konrad Jażdżewski's excavations at Brześć Kujawski. Over the last 40 years, knowledge of the Brześć Kujawski group has increased dramatically (Figure 1). Not only have many more settlements been discovered and excavated, but the geographical range of the Brześć Kujawski group has been expanded from its original heartland in Kuyavia north to the Chełmno Land, the Świecie Plateau and almost to the Vistula delta[1], as well as south-west into Wielkopolska[2]. Far from being an unusual regional anomaly confined to a handful of exceptional sites, as appeared to be the case as recently as 1985, the Brześć Kujawski group has emerged as a key cultural unit for understanding the establishment of early farming societies in central and northern Europe.

Before going further, let me clarify the terminology used here. Along with my Polish colleague Ryszard Grygiel, with whom I have worked for over 40 years in the study of these settlements, I use the term "Brześć Kujawski group" instead of "culture" or other terminology like "post-LBK" for several reasons. The first is tradition, in that we acknowledge the contributions of Konrad Jażdżewski who first recognised and named this distinctive cultural unit[3] and who encouraged our work. The second is to acknowledge that these lowland societies were so tightly coupled with the major Neolithic typological and chronological entity of the fifth millennium BC across much of east-central Europe, the Lengyel culture, that they should be seen as a variation on a much broader theme rather than a discrete cultural anomaly.

The settlements of the Brześć Kujawski group lie on the northern edge of what I have called the "Danubian World"[4], the area of riverine interior central Europe first settled by pioneer farming communities of the LBK during the second half of the sixth millennium BC. Until the end of the fifth millennium BC, this area constituted the maximum penetration of longhouse-dwelling farmers into northern and western Europe. Dated nearly a millennium after the initial diaspora of farmers in the Danubian World, the Brześć Kujawski group flourished right before the great transformations seen in Neolithic Europe at the end of the fifth millennium BC and the transition from foraging to farming in northern and western Europe. At first glance, the Brześć Kujawski group seems peripheral both geographically and chronologically to the rest of the Danubian experience.

At the same time, however, the Brześć Kujawski group is situated along the borderland between the Danubian World and the foraging societies of the Baltic coasts. When viewed from this perspective, it exhibits a dynamism that derives from its location along communication arteries and its strong connections with established Neolithic centres in the uplands to the south. The goal of this short paper is to characterise the Brześć Kujawski group as a "creole" society lying not only on the edge of the Danubian World but also at a crossroads between east and west and especially between north and south.

---

1   Bigos 2015; Czerniak 2007; Gackowski and Białowarczuk 2014.
2   Czerniak *et al.* 2016.
3   Jażdżewski 1938.
4   Bogucki 2008a.

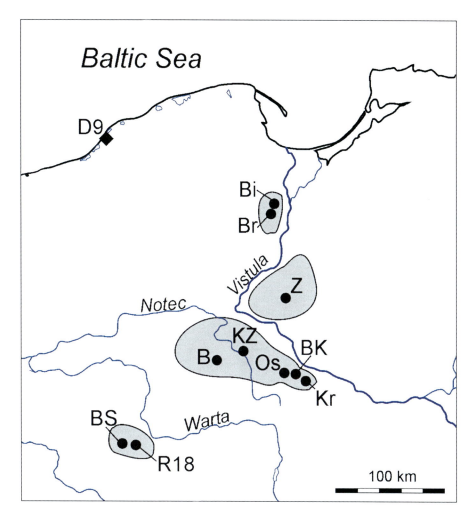

Figure 1. Map of the lower Vistula valley and adjacent areas showing the extent of settlement attributed to the Brześć Kujawski group (shaded) and locations of major sites. Key: D9 – Dąbki (Ertebølle); B – Biskupin; Bi – Bielawki; BK – Brześć Kujawski; Br – Barłożno; BS – Białcz Stary; Kr – Kruszynek, Ludwinowo; KZ – Krusza Zamkowa; Os – Osłonki, Miechowice, Konary; R18 – Racot; Z – Zelgno.

Danubian but different

The Brześć Kujawski group is clearly an heir to the great Danubian tradition of interior central Europe that began with the LBK. Its longhouses and contracted burials are the clearest markers of this heritage, in my view, since they represent deliberate choices to continue a particular general form from among a range of options. Yet the houses of the Brześć Kujawski group are very different from their LBK precursors in their shape and construction technique, as we see in Joanna Pyzel and Lech Czerniak's chapter in this volume[5], although their general dimensions remain similar. Moreover, Brześć Kujawski settlements display a preference for the same locations along glacial relict landforms like tunnel valleys and kettle ponds shown by the LBK pioneer farmers of the late sixth millennium BC. In some cases, they settled on the same sites, as at Brześć Kujawski, but they also chose new locations, like Osłonki, that lack an LBK occupation. The Brześć Kujawski

---

5   See also Pyzel 2013.

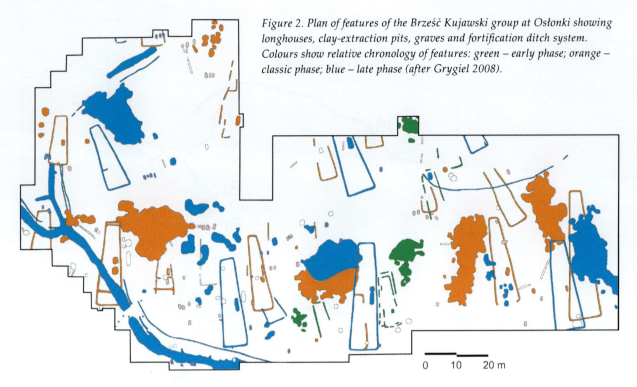

Figure 2. Plan of features of the Brześć Kujawski group at Osłonki showing longhouses, clay-extraction pits, graves and fortification ditch system. Colours show relative chronology of features: green – early phase; orange – classic phase; blue – late phase (after Grygiel 2008).

group can be said to use the general Danubian vocabulary of things and practices but with a distinctive grammar, syntax and accent.

The question is whether there was continuity between the LBK occupation of Kuyavia and the subsequent Brześć Kujawski group or if there was a hiatus in settlement. Argument from negative evidence is risky, but at the moment, traces of Neolithic occupation along the lower Vistula during the first centuries of the fifth millennium BC are exceedingly thin *compared with what is seen before and afterward*. A few widely-dispersed sites with ceramics that fit typologically into this temporal gap are known[6], but it is difficult to build a coherent pattern of settlement from them. Regional abandonments are not unheard of in other parts of the world in prehistoric times[7], but the question is whether this was the case along the lower Vistula or whether it is simply a question of archaeological visibility.

Multigenerational settlements

Brześć Kujawski-type settlements with multiple and overlapping longhouses reflect multigenerational commitments to specific locations[8]. This does not rule out the possibility of intermittent gaps and abandonments, but the sites with longhouses were occupied long enough to see one or more households through at least one generational cycle. The complexity and density of archaeological materials at these sites — particularly the co-occurrence of multiple houses and burials, greater accumulation of rubbish, and a wide range of animal species — indicates much longer occupation spans than were seen during the LBK settlement in this area during the previous millennium (Figure 2).

---

6   Bigos 2015; Czerniak 2007.
7   E.g. Nelson and Schachner 2002 on the south-western U.S.
8   E.g. Czerniak and Pyzel 2016.

 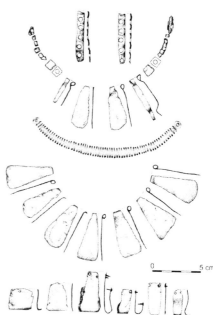

Figure 3. Burial 54 at Osłonki. On the left, skeleton of a woman aged 25–35 in the characteristic contracted position, with copper pendants visible. In the vicinity of her hands were bones of an infant between 9 and 15 months. On the right, copper ornaments found in this burial.

Larger sites like Brześć Kujawski and Osłonki had multiple household clusters in existence at any one time, giving rise to *residential landscapes*[9] across the width and length of the terrain on which they were situated. This residential landscape included houses, burials, gardens, livestock pens and other constructed elements to form highly modified openings in the lowland forests, linked by paths and trails. Within such residential landscapes and along the corridors between them, we can assume that interpersonal interactions were frequent and focused. The continued arrival in the lowlands of people from elsewhere could have added additional layers of competition for status, mates and claims to cultural authenticity.

Mortuary performance

The settlements of the Brześć Kujawski group include burials as a routine feature rather than an irregular exception. The "classic" mortuary rite of the Brześć Kujawski group is of contracted burial, men on their right side and women on their left, with heads oriented to the south or south-east. Some burials do not conform to this pattern, with occasional male skeletons on their left side, female on their right, and heads oriented in other directions. In general, however, it is very striking how the overwhelming majority of burials follow this pattern consistently.

Daniela Hofmann has discussed the performative aspects of LBK burials[10], and her observations are equally relevant to those of the Brześć Kujawski group several centuries later. Many burials are accompanied by lavish displays of copper, shell and bone ornaments, along with gender-specific grave goods such as antler T-axes. Others are barren. At Osłonki, about 24 % of the burials are accompanied by copper objects, including cylindrical beads, plaques used as pendants, and bracelets, in varying quantities. The young woman in burial 13, for example, wore a "diadem" made of copper strips (many with repoussé decoration) that

---

9   E.g. Kahn and Kirch 2013.
10 Hofmann 2009.

must have been attached to a strip of cloth or leather around her head, five trapezoidal pendants and over 200 beads. A woman and an infant in burial 54 were accompanied by multiple necklaces of copper pendants and beads, as well as calcite and shell beads (Figure 3).

The mortuary performances of the Brześć Kujawski group almost certainly played a role in the affirmation of social relationships among the living. We see this though the clustering of burials in what could be called "microcemeteries" and in the co-location of some of the richest burials. The word "microcemeteries" was first used by Chris Scarre in a review of a volume on the Villeneuve-St.-Germain group in France, where clusters of burials occur among longhouses[11]. With the Brześć Kujawski group, however, they not just cluster but rather are lined up in rows, from pairs to groups of four, five or six. Clearly burials must have been marked so that future interments could be situated next to them. While it might be assumed that the individuals so clustered might be related to each other, a recent study of a woman, a child and an infant buried close together at Krusza Zamkowa revealed that they did not share any first-degree kinship[12].

Mature agropastoral economy

The subsistence system of the Brześć Kujawski group is characterised by what I would regard as a mature, diverse agropastoral economy[13]. During the fifth millennium BC we find a mix of cattle, sheep, goat and pig, along with a small number of wild herbivores like red deer and roe deer. Here we see a strong contrast with the LBK, whose animal economy was heavily weighted toward cattle. In faunal samples of the Brześć Kujawski group, cattle comprise between 30 and 60 %, sheep and goat between 20 and 40 % and pig between 10 and 30 % of any given mammal bone assemblage. Ratios of sheep to goat reflect a herd-security strategy[14] and mortality curves show a generalised meat-production strategy rather than specialisation for secondary products.

Abundant finds of cereal grains and chaff[15], specifically from emmer and einkorn wheat, indicate that grain parching and chaff burning were widespread activities across the residential landscapes at sites of the Brześć Kujawski group. Plant assemblages also contain abundant weed taxa. The agropastoral economy was supplemented with fish, birds (aquatic, terrestrial and woodland) and tortoises. An unusual and unexplained feature of botanical assemblages from Osłonki and other sites is the large quantity of awns of feathergrass (*Stipa pennata*) which were apparently deliberately collected[16].

Landscape impact and memory

The impact of this agropastoral system and associated settlement activity was intense but localised. Palaeoenvironmental research at Osłonki indicated erosion of adjacent surfaces and eutrophication of the adjacent lakes caused by human and animal activities and wastes[17]. Such localised environmental degradation probably

---

11 Scarre 2004.
12 Juras *et al.* 2017, 37.
13 Bogucki 2008b; Bogucki and Grygiel 2015.
14 Redding 1984.
15 Bieniek 2007; Mueller-Bieniek *et al.* 2016.
16 Mueller-Bieniek and Nalepka 2010.
17 Bogucki *et al.* 2012.

provided the motivation to occupy fresh locations over time, particularly as new households formed.

Derelict residential landscapes and abandoned houses within active settlements would have held potent memories for subsequent generations. The "microcemeteries" discussed above would have been one example of what might be called "memory work" within the life-cycles of individual settlements[18]. Caches, such as a collection of flint tools and nodules in the fill above burial 56 at Osłonki, continued a widespread Danubian practice of deposits[19]. Archaeologists have only begun to consider the matter of "memory work" by which people not only memorialised their ancestors but also created a past for future generations. The Brześć Kujawski group has exceptional potential for such studies.

Borderlands: zones of intercultural penetration

The Brześć Kujawski group settlements lie along one of the great borderlands of European prehistory, the narrow zone that was not incorporated into the world of the Danubian farmers to the south or the Ertebølle foragers to the north during the fifth millennium BC. This does not mean that it was empty or deserted. Rather, as a borderland, it was a zone of intercultural penetration from both sides, through which things, practices and people moved. Borderlands are not barriers or boundaries; they are meant to be crossed. The flat north European plain could be easily crossed from all directions by foot or by watercraft. Even major rivers like the Oder and Vistula posed little obstacle, for they could be forded during times of low water and crossed on winter ice.

Connections between the Brześć Kujawski group and Neolithic communities to the south can be readily documented. The people of the Brześć Kujawski group were highly acquisitive and participated in trans-regional exchange networks. Although they used considerably less imported flint than their LBK precursors, they still obtained small quantities of chocolate and Jurassic flint from several hundred kilometres away in southern Poland. Calcite beads also came from some distance. Copper artefacts trace a trail south by south-west to Silesia and beyond. These items define the southern arc of what could be called the "interaction network" of the Brześć Kujawski group[20]. It is interesting, however, that the inhabitants of these settlements do not appear to have joined in the desire for jadeite axes that arose in western Europe during the late fifth millennium BC[21].

We can also point to markers of contact across the permeable borderland to the north[22]. These include antler T-axes, which I maintain are a more pervasive Mesolithic form than a Danubian one, along with bone decoration and bone tool types. In the meantime, finds of Neolithic pottery at the Mesolithic site of Dąbki on the Baltic coast[23] have added to the sense of permeability of this borderland. Why the Baltic foragers did not adopt agriculture sooner is a subject for another paper, but the location of the settlements of the Brześć Kujawski group make it

---

18 Bogucki 2014.
19 Kaflińska 2011.
20 See also Czerniak and Pyzel 2016, 111.
21 Pétrequin *et al.* 2012; Pétrequin and Sheridan in this volume.
22 Bogucki 2008a.
23 Czekaj-Zastawny *et al.* 2013.

Grave number (after Grygiel 2008, with clarifications)	Sex (M, F, child, indet.)	Age (after Lorkiewicz 2012)	Grave goods	Haplogroup (after Lorkiewicz et al. 2015)
K1.10	F	35–45		H
K1a.5	indet.	15–20		T2b
OS.10	M	35–45		H
OS.11	Right: child; Left: child	R: 8–10; L: ~6–7	flat bone point with perforation and punctate ornament; flake of Baltic flint	R: H5
OS.26	M	35–45	antler T-axe; antler dagger; 2 boar tusks; antler punch/retoucher; 2 bone chisels; 2 bone drills; 26 retouched blades of Baltic, Jurassic and chocolate flint	HV0
OS.38	M	25–35		U5a
OS.40	(1) F; (2) child	(1) 20–30; (2) ~1–2	2 hip belts with ~300 shell beads	(1): H5
OS.60	M	30–40		T2b
OS.63	M	~25–30	antler T-axe	H
OS.70	juvenile	14–16	copper bracelet with three loops; 5 large copper pendants (4 with repoussé ornament) with turned ends; ~30 copper beads; 21 perforated animal teeth (dog)	H5
OS.75	juvenile	~14–15	stone battleaxe with shaft hole; bone point	H1

Table 1. Burials from Konary 1 (K1), Konary 1a (K1a) and Osłonki (OS) that have been sampled for mtDNA, along with associated grave goods (compiled from Lorkiewicz et al. 2015 and Grygiel 2008).

likely that it played a role in the availability of domestic plants and animals, if only through the passage of feral livestock[24].

The initial results of archaeogenetic analyses of human skeletons of the Brześć Kujawski group undertaken by Dr Wiesław Lorkiewicz of the University of Łódź have yielded further evidence of transregional interaction and population heterogeneity[25]. An initial sample of 11 skeletons from Osłonki and Konary yielded four mtDNA haplogroups: H, U5, T and HV0 (Table 1). Of interest in this context is burial 38 at Osłonki, a male between 25 and 35 years of age, bearing haplogroup U5a, generally associated with indigenous hunter-gatherers. He was buried in the typical contracted position on his right side oriented toward the south-east. How this individual with at least some Mesolithic ancestors came to live and die at Osłonki is not known, but his presence indicates that the Brześć Kujawski group was not so bounded as to be comprised exclusively of Danubian genetic stock.

Further indications of genomic heterogeneity in the Brześć Kujawski group come from recent studies of small skeletal samples from Krusza Zamkowa and Racot. Here, the mitochondrial genome of a female between 20 and 25 years old in a contracted position on her left side has been assigned to haplogroup U5b[26], while children buried nearby belong to haplogroups K1 and H3. Interestingly, an infant lying directly on her arms shows no first-order kinship with her. Another female burial from Krusza Zamkowa is affiliated with haplogroup N1, while a female from Racot, one of the most south-western sites of the Brześć Kujawski group, belongs to haplogroup K2a[27]. Even in these small samples, the number of different haplogroups is striking.

---

24 Bogucki 1995.
25 Lorkiewicz *et al.* 2015.
26 Juras *et al.* 2017, 35.
27 Chyleński *et al.* 2017.

A Neolithic creole society

Borderland margins are where creole societies emerge[28]. I use the term "creole" in its cultural sense rather than its linguistic usage, although being at the edge between what must have been two prehistoric language families probably had linguistic consequences that we cannot now fathom. Cultural creoles are composed of the descendants of communities established through a diaspora as well as the incorporation of indigenous people, things and practices. Individuals and households make choices about how to imitate and reproduce their parent culture and how much to promote distinctiveness and even flamboyance in cultural expression. These choices often manifest themselves in household-level craft production and mortuary practices through a high level of cultural creativity while retaining ancestral forms derived from source cultures. Their diversity is the source of cultural vitality. As such, creole societies confound analytical categories.

My choice of the term "creole" to characterise the Brześć Kujawski group is intentional and stands in clear distinction to alternative but related terms such as "hybridity", "syncretism", "*bricolage*" and "*mestizaje*"[29]. A creole society is not one in which two disparate cultures meet and form a hybrid, nor is it simply a cobbling together of random cultural elements, as the term *bricolage* implies. It does not necessarily involve racial mixing, as the term *mestizaje* indicates, although some degree of inter-ethnic mixing is one dimension of a creole. Rather, a creole society is clearly rooted in a primary long-standing cultural tradition, as the Brześć Kujawski group is in the Danubian tradition that began over a millennium earlier, but by virtue of a degree of separation in space and time, it reproduces and re-interprets the traditional forms in its own way, while adding extraneous elements. A creole is not simply an amalgamation or a fusion but rather a continuing *process* of "creating something new while embodying references to its historical sources"[30].

The fluidity and ambiguity of creoles pose problems for archaeologists who seek order and harmony and clear sequences. Post-LBK continental Europe has a number of such creoles. One can make the case that Villeneuve-St.-Germain and eventually Cerny in France could fit this characterisation, while even early Tripolye in western Ukraine and Moldova is worth considering from this perspective given what we now know about the penetration of the LBK in that direction late in the sixth millennium BC. Along with the Brześć Kujawski group, they are on the margins of their ancestral societies, similar yet different, and along borderlands, positioned to engage with societies that lay beyond.

Creole societies self-consciously re-imagine ancestral things and practices in novel but familiar forms. With the Brześć Kujawski group, this characteristic is most evident in the longhouses, whose sharply-angular trapezoidal form with continuous bedding trenches is a re-interpretation of traditional Danubian posthole structures. While this may have had a functional dimension, it is also a stylistic statement. What had been atypical settlement burials became the norm, with the addition of quantities of personal ornamentation not previously seen. Thus mortuary performance is taken to a new and elaborate level, for an audience of the living within the residential landscape. Creole societies that are known from

---

28   Cusick 2000.
29   For a thorough exegesis of the tangled terminology of cultural encounters, see Stewart 2011 and papers in Baron and Cara 2011; Card 2013; Liebmann and Rizvi 2008; van Pelt 2013.
30   Baron and Cara 2003, 8.

ethnohistory often have diverse foodways that mix domestic and wild resources. For example, creole households in eighteenth-century New Orleans were more open to including wild species in their diet than colonists[31].

Creole societies have complicated social relations. A challenge for research on the Brześć Kujawski group is to untangle the relationships among the households within any one residential landscape and among settlements themselves. We see evidence for social differentiation among the burials at Osłonki and Brześć Kujawski. Some have lavish displays of grave goods, especially copper and shell ornaments and antler axes, while others are bare. Stable isotope analysis of burials from Osłonki also points to variation in dietary quality that correlates positively with copper ornaments[32]. At the same time, we see differentiation between settlements, especially those with many longhouses. For example, at Osłonki, copper was used for highly visible head ornaments and necklaces with multiple pendants of copper sheet, whereas at Brześć Kujawski, the preference was for smaller binocular pendants and bracelets. Smaller outlying settlements yielded very little in the way of copper grave goods, although their burials may be elaborate in other ways. For example, a burial of a woman aged 20–30 at Konary 1a contained a hip belt of six strands of over 8,000 shell beads[33].

Yet it does not appear that asymmetries in status and resource access translated into long-term transgenerational social differences. For that reason, I characterise the Brześć Kujawski group as "transegalitarian", a term that described societies in which social differentiation is transitory and personal rather than institutionalised and inherited[34]. Although the differentiation may have been short-lived, such an organisational structure would have required considerable negotiation and "social work" to maintain.

Such intense sociality also produced tensions and conflicts as well as everyday stresses. The skeletons of the Brześć Kujawski group reflect nutritional and occupational stress as a product of everyday life. More significantly, interpersonal violence appears to have been endemic. Eleven percent of the skeletons from Osłonki, mostly male but with at least one female, show evidence of cranial trauma, both non-lethal impacts and lethal skull penetrations. When reconstructed, the penetrations are circular and approximate the diameter of antler T-axes. One male skeleton had perimortem fractures of the shins[35], like those reported recently from an LBK mass grave at Schöneck-Kilianstädten[36], and cut marks on his skull.

This brief characterisation of the Brześć Kujawski group as a creole society is still speculative, although its settlements along the Danubian–Baltic borderland are geographically positioned to play such a role and exhibit archaeological complexity and genetic variability that point in this direction. Under such an interpretation, however, it is possible to begin to appreciate its potential role in the transmission of Neolithic things and practices from the Danubian World to the Baltic World, which culminated soon afterward with the uptake in agriculture in southern Scandinavia c. 4000 BC. Other societies that potentially qualify for creole status on the margin of the Danubian World, such as Villeneuve-St.-Germain in France, can be seen in a similar light.

---

31   Scott and Dawdy 2011.
32   Chelsea Budd, personal communication.
33   Grygiel 2008, 1179, fig. 1006.
34   E.g. Blake and Clark 1999.
35   Lorkiewicz 2011.
36   Meyer *et al.* 2015.

Conclusion

On one hand, the Brześć Kujawski group appears to occupy a peripheral spot in the Danubian world, on its northern edge geographically and in the late fifth millennium BC chronologically. At the same time, however, it lies on the edge of the borderland between the Danubian world and the Baltic foragers. Its interaction network reached south to the upper Vistula and especially to Silesia and beyond, and across the borderland to the north as well. As a result, it displays a developmental trajectory that defines it as a post-LBK creole society, as illustrated by its re-interpretation of traditional Danubian forms and its incorporation of external elements. Despite internal tensions, the Brześć Kujawski group was resilient, enabling its persistence over several centuries, until its eventual decline and disappearance at the end of the fifth millennium BC.

References

Baron, R.A. and Cara, A.C. 2003. Introduction: creolization and folklore — cultural creativity in process. *Journal of American Folklore* 116, 4–8.

Baron, R.A. and Cara, A.C. (eds) 2011. *Creolization as cultural creativity*. Jackson.

Bieniek, A. 2007. Neolithic plant husbandry in the Kujawy region of central Poland. In S. Colledge and J. Conolly (eds), *Early Neolithic agriculture in SW Asia and Europe: archaeobotanical investigations of Neolithic plant economies*, 327–342. London.

Bigos, M. 2015. Północna granica zasięgu osadnictwa kultury późnej ceramiki wstęgowej. *Folia Praehistorica Posnaniensia* 19, 7–40.

Blake, M. and Clark, J.E. 1999. The emergence of hereditary inequality: the case of Pacific coastal Chiapas, Mexico. In M. Blake (ed.), *Pacific Latin America in prehistory: the evolution of Archaic and Formative cultures*, 55–73. Pullman.

Bogucki, P. 1995. Prelude to agriculture in north-central Europe. In D.V. Campana (ed.), *Before farming: the role of plants and animals in early societies. MASCA, Research Papers in Science and Archaeology, Volume 12 Supplement*, 105–116. Philadelphia.

Bogucki, P. 2008a. The Danubian–Baltic borderland: northern Poland in the fifth millennium BC. In H. Fokkens, B.J. Coles, A. van Gijn, J.P. Kleine, H.H. Ponjee and C.G. Slappendel (eds), *Between foraging and farming. An extended broad spectrum of papers presented to Leendert Louwe Kooijmans. Analecta Praehistorica Leidensia 40*, 51–65. Leiden.

Bogucki, P. 2008b. Animal exploitation by the Brześć Kujawski group of the Lengyel culture. In R. Grygiel, *Neolit i Początki Epoki Brązu w Rejonie Brześcia Kujawskiego i Osłonek (The Neolithic and Early Bronze Age in the Brześć Kujawski and Osłonki region)*, 1581–1690. Łódź.

Bogucki, P. 2014. Planning for the past in Neolithic central Europe. In J. Osborne (ed.), *Approaching monumentality in archaeology*, 217–232. Albany.

Bogucki, P. and Grygiel, R. 2015. Pioneer farmers at Brześć Kujawski, Poland. In G. Barker and C. Goucher (eds), *The Cambridge world history volume 2: a world with agriculture, 12,000 BCE–500 CE*, 589–611. Cambridge.

Bogucki, P., Nalepka, D., Grygiel, R. and Nowaczyk, B. 2012. Multiproxy environmental archaeology of Neolithic settlements at Osłonki, Poland, 5500–4000 BC. *Environmental Archaeology* 17, 45–65.

Card, J.J. (ed.) 2013. *The archaeology of hybrid material culture*. Carbondale.

Chyleński, M., Juras, A., Ehler, E., Malmström, H., Piontek, J., Jakobsson, M., Marciniak, A. and Dabert, M. 2017. Late Danubian mitochondrial genomes shed light into the Neolithisation of central Europe in the 5th millennium BC. *BMC Evolutionary Biology* 17, 80 [doi: 10.1186/s12862-017-0924-0].

Cusick, J.G. 2000. Creolization and the borderlands. *Historical Archaeology* 34, 46–55.

Czekaj-Zastawny, A., Kabaciński, J., Terberger, T. and Ilkiewicz, J. 2013. Relations of Mesolithic hunter-gatherers of Pomerania (Poland) with Neolithic cultures of central Europe. *Journal of Field Archaeology* 38, 195–209.

Czerniak, L. 2007. The north-east frontier of the post-LBK cultures. In J.K. Kozłowski and P. Raczky (eds), *The Lengyel, Polgár and related cultures in the Middle/Late Neolithic in central Europe*, 233–248. Kraków.

Czerniak, L. and Pyzel, J. 2016. Being at home in the Early Chalcolithic. The longhouse phenomenon in the Brześć Kujawski culture in the Polish lowlands. *Open Archaeology* 2, 97–114.

Czerniak, L., Marciniak, A., Bronk Ramsey, C., Dunbar, E., Goslar, T., Barclay, A., Bayliss, A. and Whittle, A. 2016. House time: Neolithic settlement development at Racot during the 5th millennium cal BC in the Polish lowlands. *Journal of Field Archaeology* 41, 618–640.

Gackowski, A. and Białowarczuk, M. 2014. Settlement of Danubian cultures in the area of Świecie Plateau. *Analecta Archaeologica Ressoviensia* 9, 155–208.

Grygiel, R. 2008. *Neolit i Początki Epoki Brązu w Rejonie Brześcia Kujawskiego i Osłonek (The Neolithic and Early Bronze Age in the Brześć Kujawski and Osłonki region), Volume II*. Łódź.

Hofmann, D. 2009. Cemetery and settlement burial in the Lower Bavarian LBK. In D. Hofmann and P. Bickle (eds), *Creating communities: new advances in central European Neolithic research*, 220–234. Oxford.

Jażdżewski, K. 1938. Cmentarzyska kultury ceramiki wstęgowej i związane z nimi ślady osadnictwa w Brześciu Kujawskim. *Wiadomości Archeologiczne* 15, 1–105.

Juras, A., Chyleński, M., Krenz-Niedbała, M., Malmström, H., Ehler, E., Pospieszny, Ł., Łukasik, S., Bednarczyk, J., Piontek, J. and Jakobsson, M. 2017. Investigating kinship of Neolithic post-LBK human remains from Krusza Zamkowa, Poland using ancient DNA. *Forensic Science International: Genetics* 26, 30–39.

Kaflińska, M. 2011. *Społeczno-Rytualny i Gospodarczy Kontekst Depozytów Neolitycznych w Europie Środkowej*. Unpublished Ph.D. dissertation, Jagiellonian University.

Kahn, J.G. and Kirch, P.V. 2013. Residential landscapes and house societies of the late prehistoric Society Islands. *Journal of Pacific Archaeology* 4, 50–72.

Liebmann, M. and Rizvi, U.Z. (eds) 2008. *Archaeology and the postcolonial critique*. Lanham.

Lorkiewicz, W. 2011. Unusual burial from an Early Neolithic site of the Lengyel culture in central Poland: punishment, violence or mortuary behaviour? *International Journal of Osteoarchaeology* 21, 428–434.

Lorkiewicz, W. 2012. *Biologia wczesnorolniczych populacji ludzkich grupy brzesko-kujawskiej kultury lendzielskiej (4600–4000 BC)*. Łódź.

Lorkiewicz, W., Płoszaj, T., Jędrychowska-Dańska, K., Żądzińska, E., Strapagiel, D., Haduch, E., Szczepanek, A., Grygiel, R. and Witas, H.W. 2015. Between the Baltic and Danubian worlds: the genetic affinities of a Middle Neolithic population from central Poland. *PloS one* 10(2): e0118316.

Meyer, C., Lohr, C., Gronenborn, D. and Alt, K.W. 2015. The massacre mass grave of Schöneck-Kilianstädten reveals new insights into collective violence in Early Neolithic central Europe. *Proceedings of the National Academy of Sciences* 112, 11217–11222.

Mueller-Bieniek, A. and Nalepka, D. 2010. Czy znaleziska ostnicy (*Stipa* sp.) z neolitu południowych Kujaw świadczą o istnieniu muraw kserotermicznych w optimum klimatycznym? In W.H. Ratyńska and B. Waldon (eds), *Ciepłolubne murawy w Polsce — stan zachowania i perspektywy ochrony*, 235–248. Bydgoszcz.

Mueller-Bieniek, A., Kittel, P., Muzolf, B., Cywa, K. and Muzolf, P. 2016. Plant macroremains from an Early Neolithic site in eastern Kuyavia, central Poland. *Acta Palaeobotanica* 56, 79–89.

Nelson, M.C. and Schachner, G. 2002. Understanding abandonments in the North American Southwest. *Journal of Archaeological Research* 10, 167–206.

Pétrequin, P., Cassen, S., Klassen, L. and Fábregas Valcarce, R. 2012. La circulation des haches carnacéennes en Europe occidentale. In P. Pétrequin, S. Cassen, M. Errera, L. Klassen, J.A. Sheridan and A.M. Pétrequin (eds), *Jade. Grandes haches alpines du Néolithique européen. Ve et IVe millénaires av. J.-C. Cahiers de la MSHE CN Ledoux*, 1015–1045. Besançon.

Pyzel, J. 2013. Change and continuity in the Danubian longhouses of lowland Poland. In D. Hofmann and J. Smyth (eds), *Tracking the Neolithic house in Europe. Sedentism, architecture and practice*, 183–196. New York.

Redding, R.W. 1984. Theoretical determinants of a herder's decisions: modeling variation in the sheep/goat ratio. In I. Clutton-Brock and C. Grigson (eds), *Animals and archaeology 3. Early herders and their flocks. BAR International Series 202*, 223–241. Oxford.

Scarre, C. 2004. Review of "Les pratiques funéraires néolithiques avant 3500 av. J.-C. en France et dans les régions limitrophes. Table ronde SPF, Saint-Germain-en-Laye 15–17 juin 2001", edited by Philippe Chambon and Jean LeClerc, Mémoire XXXIII de la Société Préhistorique Française. Société Préhistorique Française, Paris, 2003. *Book reviews, The Prehistoric Society*, http://www.ucl.ac.uk/prehistoric/reviews/04_04_scarre.htm.

Scott, E.M. and Dawdy, S.L. 2011. Colonial and creole diets in eighteenth-century New Orleans. In K.G. Kelly and M.D. Hardy (eds), *French colonial archaeology in the Southeast and Caribbean*, 97–116. Gainesville.

Stewart, C. 2011. Creolization, hybridity, syncretism, mixture. *Portuguese Studies* 27, 48–55.

Van Pelt, W.P. (ed.) 2013. *Archaeology and cultural mixture: creolization, hybridity and mestizaje*. Archaeological Review from Cambridge 28.1.

The Brześć Kujawski culture. The north-easternmost Early Chalcolithic communities in Europe

Lech Czerniak and Joanna Pyzel

Abstract

This contribution briefly summarises the state of knowledge regarding the emergence of the Brześć Kujawski culture and discusses the importance of memory practices in its self-definition. Longhouses and their various modes of succession emerge as one of the key variables by which cultural memory is expressed, the second strand being the increasingly gendered inhumation burials on settlement sites. Differences in house and burial density are related to hierarchical relations between sites, with some emerging as ritual centres. We also briefly address how the Brześć Kujawski culture relates to both contemporary hunter-gatherer groups, with whom there appears to have been admixture, and to the perhaps partly overlapping Funnel Beaker culture, with which relations appear more confrontational. Finally, we place these debates in the context of the emergence of a "Chalcolithic" kind of society.

Zusammenfassung: Die Brześć Kujawski Kultur. Die nordöstlichsten chalkolithischen Gemeinschaften Europas

Dieser Beitrag fasst zunächst den Stand der Forschung zur Entstehung der Brześć Kujawski Kultur zusammen und erörtert dann die Rolle von Erinnerungspraktiken in deren Identitätsbildung. Langhäuser und deren Abfolge sind eine der materiellen Strategien, mit denen kollektive Gedächtnisleistungen erreicht werden. Das andere sind die immer klarer geschlechtsdifferenzierten Siedlungsbestattungen. Die unterschiedliche Belegungs- und Bestattungsdichte erlaubt die Herausarbeitung von möglichen zentralen Orten, die eine herausgehobene rituelle Funktion innehatten. Wir gehen auch kurz auf die Beziehungen der Brześć Kujawski Kultur zu benachbarten Jäger-Sammler Gruppen ein, mit denen man sich offenbar vermischte, sowie auf die Beziehungen mit der wohl teilweise gleichzeitigen Trichterbecherkultur, mit der ein eher von Konfrontation geprägtes Verhältnis bestand. Schließlich kontextualisieren wir unsere Ergebnisse im Hinblick auf die Frage der Entstehung „chalkolithischer" Gesellschaftsstrukturen.

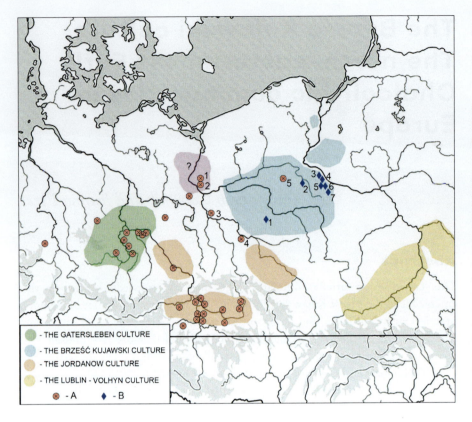

Figure 1. Extent of the Brześć Kujawski culture and surrounding "late Lengyel" cultures. A: recently discovered roundels in Poland. 1 – Nowe Objezierze; 2 – Czelin; 3 – Rąpice; 4 – Bodzów; 5 – Biskupin. B: the BKC sites mentioned in the text. 1 – Racot 18; 2 – Bożejewice 22/23; 3 – Bodzia 1; 4 – Dubielewo 8; 5 – Osłonki 1; 6 – Brześć Kujawski 4; 7 – Kruszynek 6 and Ludwinowo 3. Roundels below the black horizontal line have not been included due to their high density (modified after Literski and Nebelsick 2012, 493, Karte 1).

Introduction

Communities referred to in archaeological terms as the Brześć Kujawski culture (hereafter BKC) first appeared in the Polish Lowlands, primarily in the Kuyavia region (Figure 1), around 4350 cal BC.

We believe that the name "Brześć Kujawski culture" reflects the characteristics of this unit more accurately than the traditional "Brześć Kujawski group of the Lengyel culture", albeit the BKC undoubtedly operated within a central European contact network which can be described as *the late Lengyel interaction sphere*. This is especially visible in similar sets and decoration of pottery, but also in the presence of copper, *Spondylus* ornaments, calcite artefacts and certain lithic raw materials, as well as burial rites and social structure. However, there are also features which distinguish BKC communities from the late Lengyel background. These include elements which were greatly significant in creating a sense of identity, such as highly unified settlements with monumental, trapezoidal longhouses built on solid foundation trenches. Furthermore, a particularly distinctive aspect of these communities is the fact that they include many features adopted from hunter-gatherer communities, among them not only exotic items such as, for example, amber artefacts, but also similar dress accessories and accoutrements, such as necklaces made of wild animal teeth and T-shaped antler axes.

This article will present the particular phenomenon that was the BKC. Although an extensive study was published relatively recently by Ryszard Grygiel[1], large-scale rescue excavations carried out during the past decade have led to the discovery of a series of new, virtually complete sites that have shed fresh light on the BKC. We

---

1   Grygiel 2008.

will also examine an issue that has been inadequately addressed to date — that of a new social structure, which we define as a Chalcolithic one. In investigating this, our attention will focus in particular on the subject of memory rituals and on the role of longhouses within them, both as they reference earlier structures and as locations for burials. We also reflect on the relations between different kinds of site (central and satellite places) and on the possibility of competition between larger settlements. Another important question we will look into is that of determining absolute dates for the BKC and the general processes of cultural transformation that took place in central Europe during the fifth millennium BC. This includes the emergence of the BKC and the new kinds of relationships it established with hunter-gatherer groups, but also its striking difference to Funnel Beaker societies, which can be characterised as confrontational. Drawing on our earlier work, in which these topics are considered in more detail[2], here we aim to provide as coherent an interpretation as possible of the BKC phenomenon.

After the LBK

It is currently almost universally accepted that LBK expansion was effected by migration[3]. Its scale and extent was surprisingly large, even within the Polish Lowlands. This is indicated by the dense distribution of sites, the existence of large settlements[4], and the relatively short time span during which these migrations took place, as suggested by recent research on the radiocarbon chronology of Kuyavia[5], which shows that the LBK period in this region extended from 5400/5300 to 5100/5000 cal BC. Accepting these dates leaves us with the problem of how to interpret the fact that the end of the LBK and the emergence of the Late Band Pottery culture (hereafter LBPC = late SBK) are separated by a hiatus of around 100–200 years. This is of huge significance in interpreting the origins of the LBPC and subsequently the BKC. Were these processes also accompanied by major migrations[6]? This seems unlikely, although small-scale migration among communities as mobile as Danubian ones cannot be ruled out.

It is striking that both in Saxony and in Lower Silesia, not only is continuity evident between the LBK and the SBK, but SBK settlement also seems to have been generally stable, appearing invariable in relation to the LBK[7]. Significant changes are not apparent until the late SBK, when settlements became noticeably smaller and were occupied for shorter periods, with houses becoming much lighter in construction and smaller in size[8]. Similar patterns of continuity and stable settlement are also noted during the first half of the fifth millennium BC in the Carpathian Basin and in the Balkans[9].

Meanwhile, the situation in the Lowlands underwent drastic change, with the disappearance of settlements of the type noted during the LBK. Extensive rescue excavations carried out over the last 20 years have revealed dozens of new sites that

---

2 Czerniak 2012; Czerniak and Pyzel 2013; 2016; in prep.; Czerniak *et al.* 2016.
3 Hofmann 2016.
4 Pyzel 2010.
5 Marciniak *et al.* in prep.
6 Grygiel 2008.
7 Link 2014; a more complex situation was noted in Lesser Poland, where current findings suggest that there was also a hiatus.
8 E.g. Burgert *et al.* 2014.
9 Borič 2015; Raczky *et al.* 2014.

present a near-identical picture of settlements dated to the first half of the fifth millennium BC: a modest (occasionally moderate) number of widely dispersed pits indicative of multiple repeat visits by a small group. One or two burials are sometimes associated with these contexts. On the other hand, traces of daub and large quantities of pottery and lithics may point to prolonged occupation of these sites and to the presence of houses in the form of temporary, lightweight structures. However, there are only two recorded examples of post-built houses dating from this period in the Polish Lowlands: Konary 20 and Białcz Stary 4[10].

If LBPC communities represented a new wave of SBK colonists from the south and south-west, why did they not replicate the settlement patterns of those areas, but instead lived in small, dispersed, mobile family groups for several hundred years? How should we interpret evidence indicating that these groups settled in a significantly wider area than LBK communities, expanding into new environments (making greater use of sites on sandy soils) and entirely new regions, such as that to the east of the Middle Oder, and even to the far east of the Lower Vistula[11]?

The LBPC presence in the Polish Lowlands lasted for around 450 years (4800–4350 cal BC). So perhaps we should look at the LBPC from a slightly different angle. There appears to have been a different settlement system at the time, characterised by groups that were more mobile and scattered. Maybe then there was no hiatus between the LBK and the LBPC, but only a severe "crisis" during which LBK communities abandoned their permanent settlements, severed their network of interregional contacts and inhabited the Lowlands in dispersed, temporary settlements, leaving little evidence behind them.

The LBPC appeared in the Polish Lowlands no later than c. 4800 cal BC. The fact that these communities produced pottery that drew on the traditions of the SBK in Silesia, the SBK and the Rössen of the Middle Elbe and Saale, as well as the Malice culture in Lesser Poland[12], indicates that they must have reverted to operating within extensive, supra-regional networks at the time. The recent discovery of several roundels (Figure 1) near Biskupin on the fringes of the Kuyavia region, in Nowe Objezierze, Czelin and Rąpice on the border between Pomerania and Greater Poland, and in Bodzów between Greater Poland and Lower Silesia, as well as at several other sites[13] is key to interpreting the situation in the first half of the fifth millennium BC within the areas under discussion. These sites provide a new perspective on the picture of settlement presented above, as they probably served as centres of regional-scale social integration. Their presence points to a more mobile model of settlement, possibly linked to animal husbandry and hunting having played a more central role. This suggests that there may have been a far greater number of these sites, and that further excavations and increased use of aerial photographs and satellite images could easily lead to their discovery.

---

10 Czerniak 1994.
11 Bigos 2014; Czerniak 2007.
12 Czerniak 1994.
13 Braasch 2002; Literski and Nebelsick 2012, 456.

The Brześć Kujawski culture: dating and distribution problems

Dating the beginning of the BKC is a matter open to debate. Analysis of available radiocarbon dates using formal chronological modelling within a Bayesian framework indicates that the type of BKC sites described above can be attributed to the period from 4350 to 4000/3900 cal BC[14]. There are, however, grounds for questioning the criteria used for identifying the earliest BKC sites and interpreting the process of transformation between the LBPC and the BKC. On the one hand, there is evidence to suggest that there was a continuation in the variability of pottery characteristics between the LBPC and the BKC. A transitional phase could be represented by LBPC phase IIa (Ic), which is characterised by the limited incidence of stroke-ornamented pottery and vessel forms reminiscent of classic BKC wares[15]. Examples include the sites at Gustorzyn and Kuczyna, both of which could feasibly be attributed to the early BKC, at least in terms of their pottery assemblages[16]. This would date the beginnings of this culture to around 4600/4500 cal BC[17], or more cautiously to c. 4500/4400 cal BC[18]. However, distinctive settlements with sturdy, trapezoidal longhouses and graves signalling social change inspired by the Chalcolithic do not occur during this period. All in all, the aforementioned sites definitely indicate that the emergence of the BKC was associated with the transformation of local LBPC communities, though it is difficult to acknowledge them as the starting point of the BKC.

A different aspect of this problem is highlighted by observations on the occurrence of stroke-ornamented pottery within some BKC features. To date it has been regarded as one of the main reasons for ascribing an earlier date to the beginning of the BKC, but this can now be questioned. It seems more likely that the stroke-ornamented pottery found in these pits represents post-depositional contamination resulting from the fact that the first BKC houses were built with reference to traces of earlier settlement. Radiocarbon dating of LBPC features that may have been the source of pottery discovered in neighbouring BKC features (for example at Racot 18 and Kruszynek 6) indicate that LBPC and BKC settlement at these sites was in fact separated by a hiatus of at least 200 years[19].

In this particular context, very interesting dates were obtained for the Janowice 2 site in Kuyavia, where evidence of multiple small settlements representing LBPC phase Ic (IIa) was recorded. Notably, there was no BKC settlement at this site. LBPC feature O289B yielded a date of 4462–4338 cal BC[20], hence very close to the starting date of 4350 cal BC attributed to the BKC. This may further substantiate the claim that the beginning of the BKC coincides with LBPC phase IIb at the very earliest[21].

All things considered, it was most probably not until around 4350 cal BC that cultural changes took place, resulting in local LBPC (SBK) communities abandoning their previous more mobile way of life in small, short-term farmsteads

---

14 Czerniak *et al.* 2016.
15 Czerniak 1994.
16 Grygiel 2008.
17 Bogucki 2008; Grygiel 2008.
18 Czerniak 2012.
19 Czerniak *et al.* 2016.
20 95.4 % probability: Poz-83598: 5560 ± 40 BP; Czerniak 2016b.
21 After Czerniak 1994.

and hamlets. Thus, although it seems most likely that the emergence of the BKC was associated with cultural transformations among local LBPC communities, some factors must also have arisen to trigger such radical social and cultural change. The abandonment of a previous way of life and the transition to building monumental, standardised houses integrated into a system of long-lived villages, as well as accentuating the diverse social roles of men and women, would have required truly radical ideas to emerge and to make a meaningful impact. We will return to this subject in the final discussion.

Dating the end of the BKC is an equally contentious issue. The c. 4000/3900 cal BC date ascribed to this event[22] appears to tie in perfectly with findings concerning the earliest TRB sites in the vicinity of BKC settlements in Brześć Kujawski and Osłonki, which yielded a date of c. 3900/3800 cal BC[23]. Furthermore, DNA data from early TRB burials in this area reveals that only DNA characteristic of Danubian populations is represented, which seems to confirm that the TRB followed on from the BKC in this region[24]. Should we then completely dismiss the hypothesis that small BKC groups may have survived up until c. 3650 cal BC, undergoing transformation into the Globular Amphora culture (hereafter GAC)[25]?

It cannot be ruled out that during the 250 years or so after the demise of the robust BKC settlement system, small BKC groups may have lived on, becoming dispersed and no longer building longhouses. In other regions (*e.g.* Lesser Poland) there is clear evidence of Danubian cultures having continued to exist until the appearance of the Baden culture. Significantly, no early TRB sites, or even single features, were established in Kuyavia at multi-phase settlements encompassing the terminal BKC. In contrast, features dating from the earliest phase of the GAC are noted at such sites. This could indicate that BKC settlements remained in use for longer than suggested by radiocarbon dates, albeit on a much reduced scale. There is also evidence indicating that the TRB in Kuyavia began no later than c. 4100 cal BC, which makes the partial coexistence of communities representing both these cultures more likely. The coexistence of the TRB and GAC in Kuyavia is even more difficult to refute[26], providing grounds to regard it as an enduring phenomenon.

Another controversial issue concerning the nature of the BKC is its extent. Settlements such as the one at Brześć Kujawski, with its characteristic material culture, have been noted in Kuyavia, Greater Poland, Chełmno Land and the Lower Vistula region (Figure 1). However, the areas around the Lower Oder (including the Pyrzyce region) and between the Weser and the Lower Oder[27] — which has also recently been linked with the BKC — require closer examination. Thus far, no typical BKC houses have been recorded there, and the vast majority of pottery recovered from these areas[28] represents the late SBK rather than the BKC (including the Gurhauer group). This does not mean that the area in question could not have been inhabited by Danubian communities in the latter half of the fifth millennium cal BC. Settlement would, however, have been far less

---

22 Czerniak *et al.* 2016.
23 Grygiel 2016.
24 Borówka *et al.* 2016.
25 Czerniak 1980; 1994; Grygiel 2008; Szmyt 1999.
26 Szmyt 1999.
27 Cf. Wetzel 2014.
28 Most recently: Wetzel 2014.

concentrated than in Kuyavia and would have more likely referenced the post-Rössen sphere and Middle Elbe area rather than the BKC. The latter suggestion is substantiated by the large quantities of Rössen pottery recorded along the Lower Oder[29]. It is also probable that the earlier decline of Danubian societies in this area than in Kuyavia may have been linked to the earlier and greater presence of TRB communities in this region[30]. This problem requires further investigation.

The BKC phenomenon: longhouses

A distinctive feature of the BKC, differentiating it from other Danubian (and specifically late Lengyel) cultures, was the widespread presence at all settlements of monumental longhouses of very uniform design, set in substantial foundation trenches (Figure 2). The assertion that BKC longhouses were exceptional requires qualification, because similar houses (predominantly rectangular, but also trapezoidal) were noted in the late Lengyel, including the Jordanów culture (hereafter JC)[31] and the Tiszapolgár culture[32], as well as even further afield, for example, in the Balaton-Lasinja culture[33]. However, in all instances but the last, longhouses were a fairly unusual feature at the time and may have served a special purpose.

In terms of their principal structural and functional details, BKC houses are consistent with the wider trend of innovations which appeared during the second quarter of the fifth millennium cal BC in the Carpathian Basin. Examples include: (1) supporting the weight of the roof and — in some cases — a second storey on the posts of side walls set in foundation trenches, (2) drastically reducing the number of internal posts to several aligned in a single row, (3) reducing the size of borrow pits and locating them near the northern end wall rather than along the side walls as had been customary in the LBK, and (4) dividing the interior into two rooms and adding an annexe to some houses[34]. The distinctive trapezoidal shape of BKC houses bears certain similarities to forms noted in the western zone of late post-LBK cultures, in particular in the late phase of the SBK in Bohemia[35].

All in all, BKC longhouses are deemed exceptional because they were both widespread and numerous at central settlements (defined below) as well as at single farmsteads, and because they were built to a highly uniform design and were much larger than most, giving rise to their being referred to as monumental. In this respect, BKC houses are more readily comparable to the iconicity of LBK longhouses rather than to their contemporary late Lengyel counterparts. Their distinctiveness is especially apparent when comparing the BKC with neighbouring areas of Danubian settlement in Silesia and Lesser Poland, where houses of this type are not noted.

---

29 Dziewanowski 2016.
30 Czerniak 2018.
31 E.g. Pavúk 2012; Podborský 2011; Vokolek and Zápotocký 2009.
32 Parkinson *et al.* 2010.
33 Oross *et al.* 2010.
34 Cf. Pavúk 2012; Podborský 2011.
35 Burgert *et al.* 2014.

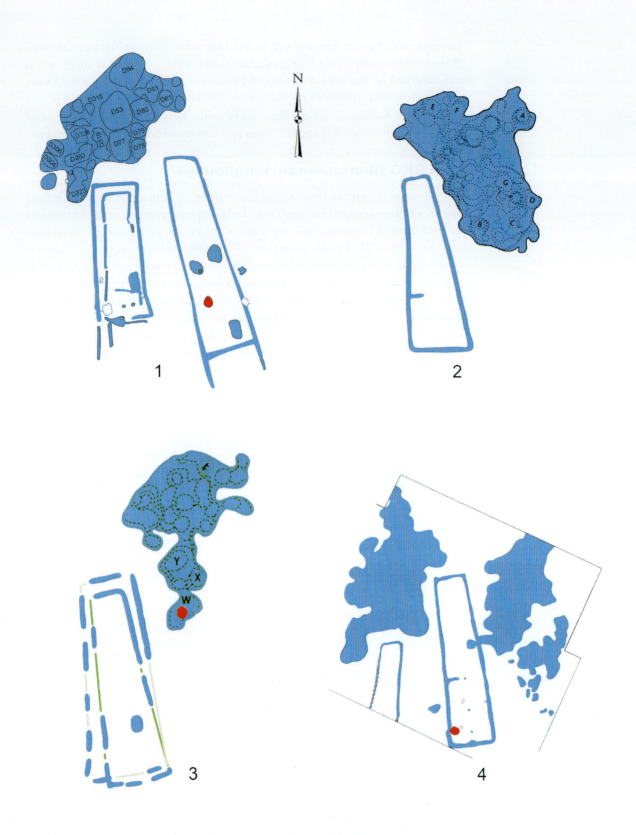

Figure 2. Examples of BKC longhouses. 1 – Dubielewo 8; 2 – Osłonki 1 (house 25); 3 – Osłonki 1 (house 7-8); 4 – Pikutkowo 6a (house 1, 5). Blue: houses and borrow pits; red: graves. Not to scale (based on Grygiel 2008, 344, fig. 298 and fig. 404; Kaczor and Żółkiewski 2015, fig. 2a).

No.	Site	No. of houses	No. of graves	Graves per house	Houses per 100m²
1.	Bodzia 1	9	3	0.333	0.048
2.	Dubielewo 8	15	12	0.800	0.224
3.	Konary 1	7	4	0.571	0.375
4.	Osłonki 1	31	96	3.097	0.230
5.	Konary 1a	4	7	1.750	0.552
6.	Miechowice 4a	14	6	0.429	0.406
7.	Miechowice 4	11	7	0.636	0.300
8.	Brześć Kujawski 4	>50	85	1.700	0.355
9.	Brześć Kujawski 3	2	6	3.000	0.115
10.	Pikutkowo 6a	5	4	0.800	0.140
11.	Kruszynek 6	12	9	0.750	0.065
12.	Ludwinowo 3	10	10	1.000	0.012
13.	Ludwinowo 2	1	0	0.000	0.024
Total		168	150		

Table 1. Characterisation of BKC settlements from the Brześć Kujawski region (after Czerniak and Pyzel 2016, 100, table 1; data for Ludwinowo 3 modified after Marchelak 2017).

Hierarchy in the BKC settlement system

Non-invasive aerial surveys[36] and large-scale open-area rescue excavations carried out prior to the construction of the A1 motorway in eastern Kuyavia revealed a high density of BKC settlements made up of longhouses, which seems to be representative of the whole of Kuyavia. These discoveries attest to the existence of a complex settlement network of considerable demographic potential. Settlements of this type were less common in the Chełmno Land and in Greater Poland, but there is no doubt that villages with identical architecture were typical across the entire area of the BKC distribution.

Despite their architectural uniformity, BKC settlements were in fact very diverse. This diversity not only pertained to the size of settlements. A more significant issue appears to have been how many houses they contained, both in terms of absolute numbers and relative to the site's surface area, which is associated with the settlement's system of internal organisation and house succession. Another important indicator of diversity is the number of graves in relation to the number of houses (Table 1). It is only once these factors have been taken into account that we can see the hierarchy of these settlements and the hierarchical system within which they operated. It was based on their relationship to central settlements as ancestral sites, which served not only as places for living and farming, but also as ritual centres.

Number of houses

Given the varied spatial distribution of houses at BKC settlements, the number of houses rather than the surface area of the site itself seems to be a better indicator of settlement size. A look at data from excavations in eastern Kuyavia illustrates this point (Table 1). Among those sites that were excavated almost in their entirety, over 50 houses were recorded at Brześć Kujawski 4, over 31 at Osłonki 1, probably little more than nine at Bodzia 1, probably little more than 12 at Kruszynek 6, around seven at Ludwinowo 3 and probably little more than 15 at Dubielewo 8. These statistics provide an important insight into the proportional size of the settlements.

---

36   Rączkowski and Ruciński 2015.

Using this criterion, we can identify at least two settlement types. The first are central settlements — a term which can only be applied to Brześć Kujawski 4 and Osłonki 1. The second category, into which all of the remaining sites listed above can be classified, consists of hamlets (or satellite settlements that were part of an interdependent network), comprising two to three contemporaneous houses in any given phase.

Density of houses

A density index of houses at settlement sites was calculated based on the number of houses per 100m² of site surface area (Table 1). This provided information that highlighted significant differences in the way that settlements were arranged, both in terms of their general layout and the approach to relocating successive houses, which will be addressed under the next subheading.

Based solely on their house density index, the excavated sites can be divided into the following three groups: (1) very low density settlements (max. index 0.1); (2) moderately built-up (0.2–0.3); and (3) densely built-up settlements (0.4+). The first group is the most easily recognisable and includes the smallest settlements, such as Bodzia 1 (Figure 6), Ludwinowo 3 and Kruszynek 6. Classifying sites to the other two groups based solely on house density can be misleading. This can be seen from a comparison of the largest two settlements: Brześć Kujawski 4 (with an index of 0.36; Figure 3) and Osłonki 1 (index 0.23; Figure 4), but is even more evident when we compare them to the small settlement at Miechowice 4A (0.41). Thus, the key to interpreting this phenomenon appears to be the system adopted for laying out houses within settlements.

Settlement layout practices

The most densely built up of the excavated settlements was Brześć Kujawski 4. The division into three phases of construction shown in Figure 3 is largely based on that used by Ryszard Grygiel[37]. Grygiel conjectured that the houses at Brześć Kujawski 4 had been built in rows[38]. Although this is a rather sweeping generalisation, it is an acceptable interpretation. By slightly modifying the original hypothesis, we can plot a radial layout of houses arranged in four rows converging at the eastern end of the settlement near house 12/12A. This building may have held a special status, as it was always the longest house, it was rebuilt to the same ground plan in phase II, and was additionally marked out by the presence of a large, rectangular enclosure (Figure 3, settlement phase I).

The same settlement layout was replicated in the next phase, with house 12A being rebuilt in exactly the same location, although it was extended both northwards and southwards. The enclosure alongside this house probably remained in use. Likewise, in the third phase the layout of buildings was largely maintained, the only difference being that the spot previously occupied by house 12/12A, where the three rows of buildings had earlier converged, was now empty, and a cluster of three houses (2–4–6) had been built in a location that interrupted the southernmost row of houses.

---

37 Grygiel 2008; for further details see Czerniak and Pyzel 2016.
38 Grygiel 2008, 310–311.

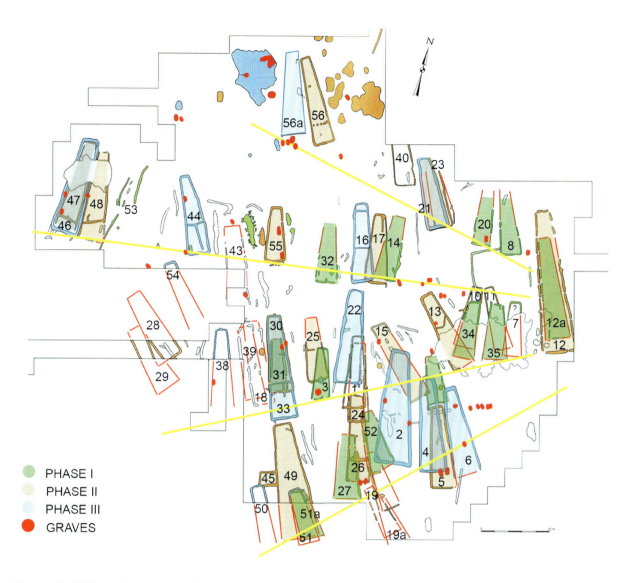

Figure 3. Brześć Kujawski 4. Schematic settlement plan with houses and graves, divided into three main phases (modified after Grygiel 2008, fig. 7).

In summary, the settlement retained the same layout of buildings from the beginning to the end of its existence, albeit in the earliest phase there was a greater concentration of houses at the site's south-east end, hence nearer the lake shore, while in subsequent phases the settlement expanded to the north-west. Another important observation is that there was a trend towards larger and more solidly built houses over time.

A different settlement layout was recorded at Osłonki 1 (Figure 4). Of all the villages noted in Kuyavia, this was the only one partly encircled by a ditch. The houses within its confines were fairly randomly arranged around a central space. Osłonki also differed in the system of house succession practised there and in featuring complexes of large clay pits between buildings, which was ultimately reflected in a much lower house density index.

In contrast, a linear arrangement of houses very similar to that at Brześć Kujawski was noted at Dubielewo 8 (Figure 5) and at Zelgno 1 in the Chełmno

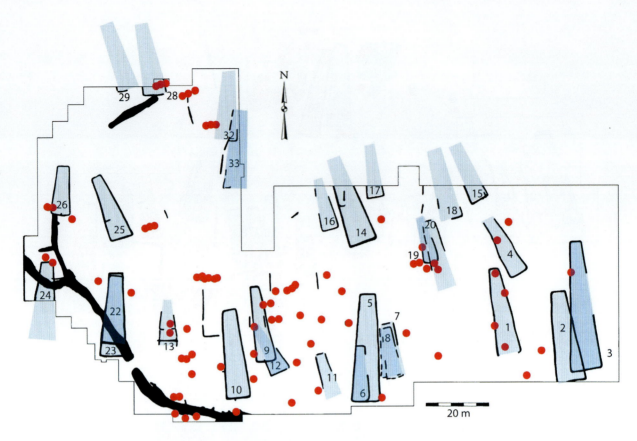

Figure 4. Osłonki 1. Schematic settlement plan with houses and graves (modified after Grygiel 2008, fig. 404).

Land[39]. However, in both instances there was only a single row of houses with solitary examples of house ground plans overlapping one another in the middle.

Irrespective of the above analysis, we believe that arranging houses in clusters was the fundamental and overriding principle governing the layout of buildings at all BKC settlements. These clusters, consisting of two to five (seldom more) houses, some synchronous and some successive, may have reflected a relatively stable division of land among individual households. This is a system which was already practised in the LBK (the yard model — modified[40]), and was also common in the SBK[41]. At Brześć Kujawski 4, houses were predominantly arranged in pairs during the first settlement phase. However, in subsequent phases, perhaps because of the increase in the average size of houses, single houses began to appear alongside pairs of houses. The third phase even sees houses configured in groups of three.

What the temporal relationships were between houses grouped in pairs and threes at both LBK and post-LBK settlements is an issue that has aroused much controversy over the years[42]. Currently, it appears that there is more than one answer to this question. The discovery of pairs of houses connected by fences in the LBK[43], as well as the SBK and Lengyel culture[44], shows that these paired houses were used synchronously as part of a compound household. There are,

---

39   Cf. Czerniak 2002.
40   See Czerniak 2016a.
41   E.g. Burgert *et al.* 2014.
42   Pleinerova 1984.
43   Czerniak 2013.
44   Burgert *et al.* 2014, 46.

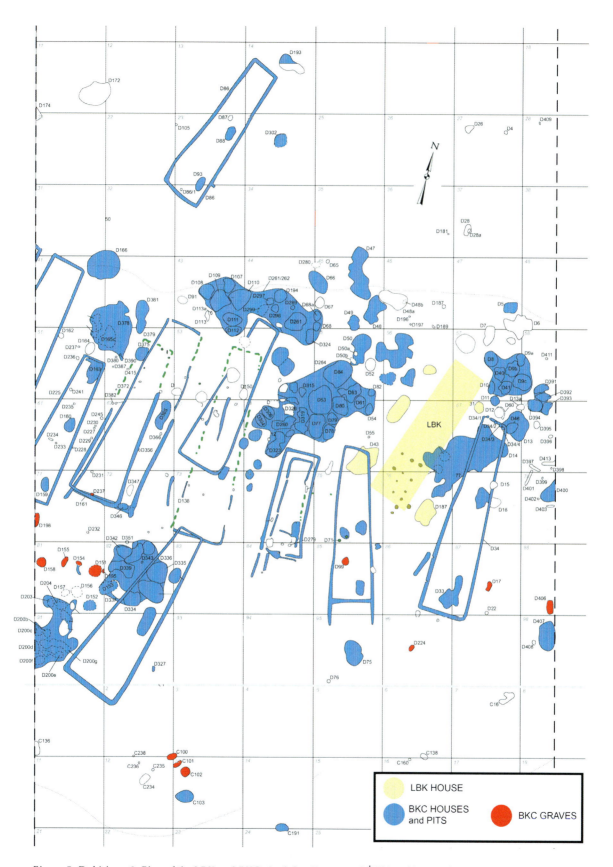

Figure 5. Dubielewo 8. Plan of the LBK and BKC site (after Kaczor and Żółkiewski 2015, fig. 2a).

however, also examples of houses attributable to different phases, and even different cultures, being connected in this fashion, as demonstrated at Straubing-Lerchenhaid[45]. A series of observations made within the BKC, for instance at Racot[46], also indicates that pairs of houses may have come into being as a result of successive building episodes. A good example of this is provided by the paired houses 56/56a at Brześć Kujawski 4, which can be relatively securely dated because they lie on the outskirts of the settlement[47].

House succession practices

Two patterns of house succession are detectable at BKC settlements where houses formed clusters. The first involved building a new house in more or less exactly the same location where an earlier one had stood. Several variations of this practice were noted, including building the new house to exactly the same ground plan as the old one, retaining the alignment of the old house, but increasing the size (usually length) of the new one, or building it so that its ground plan only partially overlapped the earlier one. In the second pattern of succession new houses were raised alongside earlier ones, though there were also numerous variations of this practice. These ranged from typical pairs of houses, recognisable because of their similar dimensions and parallel positioning (with the wider gable ends in line with one another or in Z-shaped formation), to configurations in which the alignment of each house was slightly different. In the case of the latter practice, if the buildings are not precisely dated there is no way of distinguishing between successive and synchronous pairs of houses (which could also mean that one of the houses was built slightly later than the other, but the earlier one remained in use).

At the most sparsely built-up settlements, houses were raised in isolation, either as solitary buildings or in clusters of two to four, though pairs of houses appear to have been the most common. More complex situations are witnessed at settlements with a greater density of houses. For example, at Miechowice 4[48] we can see solitary houses that became the focus of clusters which came into being as a result of houses being abandoned and then rebuilt on more or less the same spot. Therefore, in this instance, the house clusters represent the practice of raising successive buildings. Among the four clusters that can be identified at this site, reconstructions were carried out twice within two of them and three times within the other two. Each successive house tended to be bigger than the one that it replaced, which may also be indicative of why the old one was abandoned and a new one was built.

A similar layout of buildings can be seen at the neighbouring site of Miechowice 4A[49], where, in some cases, it is possible to identify as many as four successive phases of a house being built on the same spot. An example of this is provided by houses 6–7–8–6A, whose configuration suggests that the same house was rebuilt four times in the same location, each time retaining the same size.

The central settlement at Osłonki 1 had a different layout (Figure 4). Pairs of houses appear to characterise this settlement. These possibly represent a different pattern of house succession (*e.g.* houses 25–26 and 14–16), as well as

---

45 Hofmann 2013.
46 Czerniak *et al.* 2016.
47 Grygiel 1984; 2008.
48 Grygiel 2008, fig. 860.
49 Grygiel 2008, 1112, fig. 941.

the synchronous (or at least partly synchronous) use of some pairs of houses (*e.g.* houses 9–10, 15–18 and 28–29). There are also examples of solitary houses that were rebuilt in the same place, but never more than twice.

The most complicated configuration of buildings at Osłonki is that of four houses (5–6–7–8) forming an adjoining pair, each of which may have been rebuilt once in the same location. A more detailed examination of the relationships between these houses suggests that house 8 was the earliest and was succeeded by the paired houses 6–7, which were exactly the same size as house 8, with the very large house 5 being built in the third and final phase. It may have replaced not only house 6, but the pair represented by houses 6 and 7.

Brześć Kujawski 4 differs distinctly from all other settlements in eastern Kuyavia because of its high density of houses and its complicated patterns of house succession. This is probably why the boundaries of house clusters are less obvious. They are also more diverse. There are examples of multiple superimpositions and remodelling of the same house, as well as parallel houses in complex configurations of twos and threes. This situation is illustrated by houses 46–47–48 (Figure 3). House 47 may have formed a synchronous pair with house 48. During the next phase only house 46 was in use, having been superimposed on the ground plan of house 47 and made very slightly larger.

In contrast, houses 32–16–17–14 (all of similar size) formed a cluster representing three or four phases, though if we accept that houses 16 and 17 may have been remodelled (house 16 being lengthened in the process), there may even have been five phases. Houses 32 and 14 were the oldest in this group, though the fact that their alignments were slightly different could suggest that they were not built as a pair, but as independent or successive units (*e.g.* first house 14 and after its abandonment house 32). It is interesting that in the final two phases, houses 16 and 17, which overlap the outline of house 14, were similarly aligned to the neighbouring house 32. Therefore, only houses 32–16–17 could have been built successively, with the two later houses (17–16) being positioned as if to form a pair with the earliest one (32).

House 12, which was the largest at this site (246 m^2) and stood on the eastern perimeter of the village, constituted a separate unit made all the more distinctive by featuring an enclosure of approximately 20 × 18 m on its western side. It was centrally superimposed on the ground plan of the slightly smaller and earlier house 12A.

A separate problem, and the only one of its kind at this site, is presented by nine solitary houses which occupy its central portion, extending from north to south in the following sequence: 22, 1, 24, 26, 52, 27, 19B, 19 and 19A. The chronological interpretation is very difficult because not all of the stratigraphic relationships are obvious, and many potential relationships are missing due to the truncated nature of the foundation trenches. This can make it difficult to identify some of the houses. The situation is further complicated by the fact that some of the houses could have been used synchronously, such as houses 52 and 27, which appear to be the oldest in this sequence and may have functioned as a pair. Whatever the case may be, a sequence comprising at least five phases of rebuilding can be identified here (*e.g.* 52–26–24–1–22; house 22 may have been contemporary with house 2, which also overlaps house 52, but does not constitute a new phase in this sequence, as is the case with houses 19, 19A and 19B, located to the south of house 52). Overall, we can conclude that after the oldest pair of houses (52 and 27) had been abandoned, this cluster was expanded by building sequences of single houses, both to the south (houses 19B–19–19A) and — primarily — to the north (26–24–1–22).

In summary, analysis of Brześć Kujawski 4 suggests that this settlement provides a particularly significant example of house succession practices, as new houses were predominantly built at least partially within the ground plans of earlier ones. We believe that this was a conscious decision intended as an expression of symbolic continuity, rather than a move necessitated, for example, by a lack of available space. There was plenty of space at Brześć Kujawski 4 for every house to be built on a site entirely devoid of any trace of earlier occupation, as was the case at most LBK settlements. Hence, it was this practice of house succession that led to such a high density of houses and not the other way round. This appears to be a similar pattern to that observed at tell settlements, and it cannot be ruled out that this is indeed a reference to ideas that reached this region from the Carpathian Basin along with other social changes discussed below.

The second phenomenon clearly evidenced at Brześć Kujawski 4 (and at other BKC settlements) is the frequent occurrence of pairs of houses. Analysis of numerous examples has shown that these may represent either successive houses or ones that were used synchronously (as a compound household). At Brześć Kujawski 4, Osłonki 1 and other densely built-up settlements it appears that we are dealing mostly (or possibly exclusively) with synchronous pairs of houses.

Analysing only the plans of these settlement sites could lead to the conclusion that overlapping houses do not feature at sparsely built-up settlements because of the shorter lifespan of these sites. However, observations made at two almost fully excavated settlement sites (Bodzia 1 and Kruszynek 6) indicate that they were in use for just as long as Brześć Kujawski 4. Therefore, despite the large numbers of houses recorded, these were always small, but multi-generational hamlets.

The most significant observation arising from analysis of BKC settlement plans is that two systems of house succession were practised within this culture. The first entailed building a new house next to an old one; the second involved a new house being built on the site of an old one. The first of these practices can be regarded as more conservative, being rooted in LBK and SBK traditions, in which overlapping house plans are very rarely noted, whereas paired houses are a common occurrence. The second practice is reminiscent of the typical pattern of house succession seen at tell sites, and it undoubtedly first appeared in the Polish Lowlands along with the BKC. Generally speaking, these were coexisting practices; however, the latter appears to have been far less common and only occurred in exceptional circumstances. For example, at settlements where the first practice predominates, there are only isolated instances of overlapping house plans, usually at the centre of the settlement. However, the key difference appears to be the one between the two major central settlement sites in eastern Kuyavia, located barely 8 km apart: Osłonki 1 (new houses built alongside old ones) and Brześć Kujawski 4 (new houses built on top of old ones). This could point to the existence of much deeper differences and stronger rivalries between individual groups[50] than can be inferred from the unified character of material culture. Could it also reflect the different traditions drawn on by the inhabitants of these two settlements?

---

50   Lorkiewicz 2012.

Graves as indicators of settlement ranking

The number of contemporaneous houses within settlements is itself enough of an indication of settlement ranking, in which we have central settlements (Osłonki 1 and Brześć Kujawski 4) at one end of the scale and satellite settlements (hamlets) at the other. However, a more important criterion for the ranking of settlements appears to be the incidence of graves, as this tells us far more about the nature and complexity of relationships between settlements than an analysis of their size and spatial organisation.

The BKC is a culture in which burials occur exclusively within settlement sites. This is another important feature of the BKC that distinguishes it from many other contemporary Danubian cultures, where separate cemetery sites were used. We doubt, however, that in the case of the BKC we are dealing with the survival of a tradition originating in the LBK. The evident concentration of graves at central settlements appears to indicate that these sites also served as central cemeteries where the dead from smaller settlements in the region were buried.

In terms of grave numbers, two sites clearly stand out among the eastern Kuyavian settlements examined in this report: Brześć Kujawski 4 (Figure 3) and Osłonki 1 (Figure 4), where the number of graves per house amounts to 1.7 and 3.1 respectively, although given the destruction of an unknown number of graves at the first of these sites, the relevant index should really be slightly higher. At other comprehensively excavated settlements this index ranges from 0.3 (Bodzia 1) to 1.0 (Ludwinowo 3; Table 1)[51]. It is these apparently major differences which suggest that some of the dead from satellite settlements may have been buried at central settlements.

However, even at central settlements it cannot be said that the dead population is fully represented. According to some estimates, even the large numbers of burials at Brześć Kujawski 4 only represent around 20% of the dead[52]. Thus it would seem that burying the dead in the manner described herein took the form of a communal ritual in which selected individuals represented a wider section of a community's dead population. Unfortunately, we know nothing of how the remainder were buried. Presumably, the funerary practice involved was one which left no permanent trace.

It is difficult to pinpoint the criteria by which individuals were chosen for these distinctive settlement burials. Age and sex do not appear to have been guiding factors, as the age and sex composition of the dead population (as observed in the large assemblages from Brześć Kujawski 4 and Osłonki 1) does not differ significantly from that of the living population. Hence, selection may have been based on other factors, such as the date or specific circumstances of death.

In this context it should, however, be noted that single graves also occurred at smaller settlements. It is difficult to say whether they represent the survival of an earlier tradition in which some individuals were buried where they had lived, or whether we are dealing with rituals associated with the building and/or abandonment of houses.

The two aforementioned central settlements also differ from the remainder in featuring particularly lavishly furnished graves. Grygiel distinguishes between ordinary graves, graves with copper — these can be found at many different sites

---

51 For further details see Czerniak and Pyzel 2016.
52 Czerniak and Pyzel 2013.

— and exceptionally rich graves with copper, restricted only to large villages such as Brześć Kujawski and Osłonki[53]. In our opinion this does not, however, mean that central settlements played a power-related role, but rather — given that individuals from various settlements may have been buried there — they served as the founding nucleus of a larger, region-wide society, where regular meetings, exchange and rituals addressed to common ancestors took place, integrating the region's communities.

Despite the similarities evident in burial rites at the central settlements of Brześć Kujawski 4 and Osłonki, there are also certain differences. At the first of these sites there was a slight predominance of male burials (64%), while at Osłonki males account for 53% of burials. This difference may, however, be attributable to the fact that data from Brześć Kujawski 4 is incomplete.

The only form of burial rite practised at BKC sites was the deposition of bodies in pits (inhumation), 95% being buried in a contracted position, lying on their side — males on their right and females on their left. Most of the burial pits were rectangular. At Osłonki, as many as 14 individuals were buried in settlement pits; ten of them were women. In addition, two of the men buried in these settlement pits were positioned "like women" on their left side. In contrast, at Brześć Kujawski 4 there is a predominance of men among the settlement burials. All in all, it should be emphasised that the greatest deviations from standard body position and alignment are observed among settlement pit burials. Satellite settlements are notable in this respect, as 25% of burials were in settlement pits.

At Osłonki 1, 48% of graves were furnished, compared to 37% at satellite settlements. This may seem like a small difference if we disregard the number and quality of grave goods. Graves at satellite settlements were far more poorly furnished. They did not contain pottery or flint, and copper was much rarer. The presence of pottery in graves is an interesting issue. At Osłonki 1 pottery accompanies male and female burials with equal frequency, but always adult individuals. Meanwhile at Brześć Kujawski 4 pottery was only placed in women's graves. There was only ever a small number of vessels (1–2).

It is very difficult to analyse the position of graves in relation to houses within settlements, as defining the relationships between features at BKC settlements is fraught with uncertainty because of the very complicated stratigraphy of these sites. For example, at Brześć Kujawski 4 there are far more burials that can be deemed to be located within houses than there are at Osłonki 1. However, the higher density of dwellings at the former site increases the probability that houses and graves would have overlapped at some point in time. On the other hand, the pattern of house succession at Brześć Kujawski 4 involved new houses being built on top of old ones, and it cannot be precluded that the greater incidence of graves within houses noted at this site is an accurate reflection of these relationships. Even within individual settlements, such as Brześć Kujawski 4, there is considerable variation: as well as houses associated with multiple burials (*e.g.* house 6 with its seven burials), there are also those which are entirely devoid of burials (*e.g.* houses 21 and 23).

No clear pattern emerges for the location of graves situated beyond houses, although it seems that more of them were located near the southern end of nearby dwellings. At Brześć Kujawski 4 there are three instances of the same arrangement of burials within a house: one grave at the south-east end and one in the north-east

---

53   Grygiel 2008, 899.

corner. The three houses in question (55, 43 and possibly also 6) stood in close proximity to one another. There is only one example of a similar arrangement at Osłonki 1 (house 1). This site also features a variety of traditions, such as locating burials at the south-east end of a house. The large differences between houses at this site are also striking.

Comparing different sites, even those of the same category, such as the central settlements at Brześć Kujawski 4 and Osłonki 1, as well as individual houses within these sites, shows that we can see considerable differences within the ostensibly highly uniform burial rite of the BKC. These relate primarily to the number of burials, but also to the location of graves, the positioning of bodies and to grave goods. This demonstrates that the burial practices of this society were far more complex than the often assumed model of small domestic cemeteries where the residents of a given house were buried. Corroborative evidence is provided by the results of kinship analysis carried out on burials at Krusza Zamkowa in western Kuyavia, which revealed that individuals buried at a similar time and within close proximity were not closely related. Even seemingly unambiguous situations, such as a young woman buried with a baby, do not have to indicate that we are dealing with a mother and child[54]. We believe that in the BKC, people could have been buried at sites where they had never lived, for example at a central settlement. Thus, from the perspective of the inhabitants of the region, central settlements could have served a dual role of both central settlements and cemeteries, where those who traced their roots to that particular central site were buried.

Manipulating memory. Ancestors and ritual practices

Our supposition that the dead may have been buried at "ancestral settlements" is part of the wider phenomenon of memory practices (*i.e.* various references to the past) in the BKC. The key to this interpretation of the burial rite was the discovery of a BKC grave at Ludwinowo 7 in eastern Kuyavia[55]. This burial was found within a large LBK village featuring a minimum of 25 longhouses[56]. It lay in a grave that had been cut into a lateral pit next to the longest LBK house (47 m) nearly 1000 years after this house had been occupied[57]. Curiously enough, there were no houses or other settlement features of the BKC period at this site. Only evidence of various other ritual practices was recorded (see below).

A similar example of a BKC burial near an LBK house was discovered at another site in the same vicinity: Smólsk 2/10[58]. However, far more evidence exists of similar practices referencing LBK settlements. These can be interpreted as an expression of the special significance that BKC communities attributed to ritual practices aimed at highlighting references to their own past. The fact that they were addressed to very distant ancestors, who had left remains that were readily identifiable as "alien", could indicate that we are dealing with conscious manipulation based on references to "imaginary ancestors"[59].

---

54   Juras *et al.* 2017.
55   Czerniak and Pyzel 2013.
56   Pyzel 2013.
57   Czerniak and Pyzel 2013.
58   Muzolf *et al.* 2012, fig. 4.
59   For a wider discussion see Czerniak and Pyzel in prep.

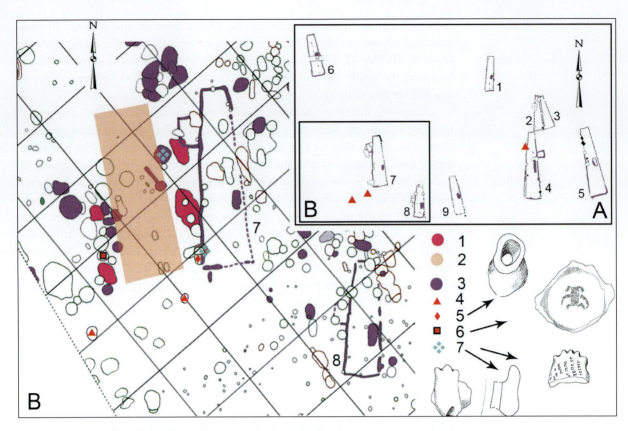

Figure 6. Bodzia 1. A: schematic plan of the site with BKC houses. B: part of the site illustrating relationships between LBK and BKC houses. 1 – LBK lateral pits; 2 – reconstructed LBK house layout; 3 – BKC house and pits; 4 – BKC graves; 5–7 – fragments of BKC ritual pots deposited in LBK pits (modified after Czerniak and Pyzel in prep.).

This issue can be looked at more broadly. Firstly, one can consider it as part of a more universal approach to "ancestors" and the past, encompassing "real" ancestors and "imaginary" ones in equal measure. Secondly, it can be perceived to some degree as a methodological problem arising from the fact that it is only at LBK settlements that we can recognise the "exceptional nature" of the presence of BKC features. It is only when viewed from both of these perspectives that we can see that many features at BKC settlements not only had a clearly ritual dimension, but were also designed to highlight connections with the past. This includes not only the settlement as a burial place, and the siting of graves in relation to a particular house, but also house succession and other practices associated with a house functioning as an ancestral dwelling (*e.g.* the burning of fires, eating of festive meals, etc.). This last category in particular is very difficult to distinguish from everyday domestic activities, and in practice this is only feasible when evidence of this kind is found within clearly earlier contexts (*e.g.* dating from the LBK). A good example is the ritual zoomorphic vessel attributable to the BKC discovered near an LBK longhouse, together with traces of digging into LBK features, at Ludwinowo 7[60].

An interesting example of references to the past is provided by Bodzia 1, a BKC settlement site consisting of nine houses. It was founded in a location that featured the remains of a single LBK longhouse. One of the BKC houses was raised in the immediate vicinity of the LBK building, in keeping with one of the patterns of house succession noted at BKC settlements (a new house alongside an old one), thus clearly demonstrating continuity. Furthermore, the borrow

---

60 Czerniak and Czebreszuk 2010; Czerniak and Pyzel in prep.

Figure 7. Plan of Bożejewice 22/23. 1 – postholes of the LBK house; 2 – LBK house and borrow pits; 3 – BKC house and cellar pit.

pits of the LBK longhouse contained a large number of so-called "special finds" attributable to the BKC, among them part of a zoomorphic vessel, sherds from a ritual vessel featuring an anthropomorphic motif and a lug in the shape of a human hand (Figure 6). These items attest to the complexity of practices associated with building new houses with reference to old ones.

A similar example was recorded at one of the largest BKC settlement sites in Kuyavia, Brześć Kujawski 4, where the remains of a small LBK hamlet, probably consisting of three houses, came to light. There were no BKC houses in the same location, which made it look as though the LBK longhouses constituted part of the BKC settlement[61]. Similar observations were made at Dubielewo 8 (Figure 5)[62].

A particularly striking example of the symbolic succession of houses comes from the site of Bożejewice 22/23 in western Kuyavia (Figure 7). It featured a BKC longhouse with a 30 m long trapezoidal foundation trench, which had been cut into an LBK longhouse 42 m long and 7.5 m wide, which was approximately 1000 years older. The BKC house fitted perfectly within the outline of the LBK one, its alignment was the same and its proportions were also comparable. All these are strong indications that the builders of the later house must have somehow made reference to the still visible remains of the older construction, and not only to the alignment of its associated borrow pits.

Other similar examples of referencing LBK longhouses can be seen at Smólsk 4 and Brześć Kujawski 3. At both of these sites a BKC house was built on exactly the same spot as an LBK house. Unfortunately, neither of them was as well preserved as the example at Bożejewice: we can only reconstruct the LBK houses at Smólsk 4[63] and Brześć Kujawski 3[64] based on characteristic pit layouts: two rows of elongated borrow pits with a house in between them.

All in all, it seems reasonable to conclude that the remains of the LBK longhouse may have been something more to BKC communities than merely a "mound" left behind by their ancestors. It is more likely that they would have recognised it as a longhouse, interpreted it and subsequently "adopted" it as "their own". This was arguably why BKC houses were positioned in the same way in relation to LBK houses as they were in relation to coexistent BKC houses. It is also understandable that a longhouse would have been chosen as the focus for rituals of memory and continuity. As a well-known and understood concept, the longhouse held a symbolic and iconic significance for these societies, creating their common identity.

An interesting observation in this context is that BKC groups avoided the remains of extensive LBK settlements when founding their own large settlements. We believe that BKC communities treated these sites as spaces that had already been built up by their ancestors and whose continuation would be assured by building new settlements either nearby or at some distance.

Farmers versus hunter-gatherers

A striking aspect of the BKC — particularly in comparison with the LBK — is the abundant evidence of contact between these communities and local hunter-gatherers. This is not only demonstrated by the large quantities of pottery, stone tools and bone ornaments found at hunter-gatherer sites[65]. There is also ample evidence that BKC groups procured products from hunter-gatherer communities, among them exotic goods made of amber (including exceptional items such as a zoomorphic figurine[66]), as well as adopting elements of dress from them (*e.g.* necklaces made of wild animal teeth). We also see syncretic objects such as armlets, which were made of *Spondylus* shell, marble and calcite among Danubian

---

61 Grygiel 2004, 184, fig. 114; 2008, fig. 7.
62 For more detail see Czerniak and Pyzel in prep.
63 Grygiel 2004, 263, fig. 181; 2008, 326, fig. 275.
64 Grygiel 2004, 142, fig. 78; 2008, 219, fig. 178.
65 Czekaj-Zastawny *et al.* 2013; Czerniak 2007; 2012; Terberger and Kabaciński 2010.
66 Grygiel 2008, 262, fig. 221.1.

communities, and out of cattle ribs in the Lowlands, where they were additionally ornately decorated in a style reminiscent of Mesolithic bone artefacts. T-shaped axes, which were very widespread in the BKC, may also have been adopted from hunter-gatherers, yet they were made by BKC communities[67] and — judging by grave goods — played the same role as stone axes in the Carpathian Basin, where they were a male status symbol. The gradual integration of hunter-gatherer and Danubian societies is also illustrated by recent DNA studies attesting the presence of women from a Mesolithic background among burials at BKC cemetery sites[68].

The presence of hunter-gatherer features is clearly perceptible in the BKC, particularly in important areas such as dress, which was linked to the expression of personal identity, ethnicity and gender. However, it is not obvious whether we are dealing exclusively with integration and cultural syncretism, or with a fashion for hunting accessories. The first scenario is suggested by BKC settlements being located close to areas inhabited by hunter-gatherers. However, the aforementioned DNA studies appear to provide more conclusive evidence. On the other hand, we are also confronted with the wider appearance of hunting symbols as part of the emergence of a distinctive "Chalcolithic cultural model" within the Danubian sphere[69]. The BKC was undoubtedly within the range of this sphere's contacts, as evidenced not only by numerous copper artefacts, but principally by gender-specific dress accessories and burial customs[70]. The absence of evidence of contact in the LBK shows that the capacity to foster relations with hunter-gatherers was not an issue of proximity but one of attitude. Thus, it also seems to have been the case with BKC communities that ideas had to first emerge that attributed new values to hunting and the tenets (ethos) associated with it.

The BKC/TRB interface and the end of Danubian cultures in the Polish Lowlands

The problem of the BKC/TRB interface is without doubt one of the most fascinating areas of research into the Neolithic of the North European Plain, primarily because of the potential links between the monumental earthen long barrows of the TRB and the longhouses of the BKC[71]. This article is too short to include a discussion of this issue[72]. We will instead focus on certain aspects of it associated with the "decline" of the BKC.

The earliest form of monumental earthen long barrows in the TRB were tombs of the "Niedźwiedź type"[73]. We believe that the use of the word "tomb" lies at the heart of the problem, as these structures were in essence imitations of longhouses, or in some cases (*e.g.* where they clearly contained no burials), they simply were longhouses. What we need to do is look at the BKC from a slightly different angle. In this culture the dead were buried in longhouses (usually abandoned ones), hence BKC burials should not be considered in isolation from BKC houses. At the same time, it is worth recalling that flat graves located next to houses were also a feature of the early TRB. The fundamental difference is that the earthen long

---

67 Kabaciński *et al.* 2014.
68 Chyleński *et al.* 2017; Lorkiewicz *et al.* 2015.
69 For a wider discussion see Kadrow 2008.
70 Derevenski 2000.
71 Bradley 1996; Childe 1949; Czerniak 1994; Hodder 1994; Rzepecki 2011; Sherratt 1990.
72 For a wider analysis see Czerniak 2018.
73 Rzepecki 2011.

barrows were not located within TRB settlements (though sometimes they were built on the site of an earlier TRB settlement). However, neither is this issue clear-cut in the BKC, given that the inhabitants of satellite settlements did not bury their dead at their own settlements, but in ancestral houses at central settlements.

Houses in the BKC can be said to have had three roles: first that of a dwelling and then — after their abandonment — of a burial place for some of the dead. The third role common to both of the aforementioned was a symbolic one. Monumental longhouses were an expression of corporate identity and of a community's "historic" land rights.

TRB societies had an almost identical approach to interpreting these structures, but used them only for symbolic and burial purposes. They also introduced changes of a nature that suggests a conscious confrontation with the BKC tradition. These changes seem to have been intended to make each burial a more universal representation of a local community, possibly of a specific extended household. We believe that this interpretation is warranted by the egalitarian nature of burial furnishings and by the almost complete departure from gender-specific grave goods and body positions. The dead of both sexes were buried in a supine position in the TRB, while gender was very discreetly indicated by the presence of a collared flask in male graves (potentially also a hunting symbol) and amphorae in female graves[74].

The confrontational nature of these differences between the TRB and the BKC makes the relatively synchronous appearance of Niedźwiedź-type tombs and BKC longhouses seem to be a rather more tempting theory[75], particularly given that this hypothesis opens up a wider view of the origins of the TRB as a phenomenon that was temporally and processually related to the emergence of the Michelsberg culture and the phenomenon of Passy-type burial structures[76]. Looked at from another angle, there may also have been a confrontational aspect to the processes of transition from the BKC to the TRB. This would leave us with an equally intriguing conundrum about the ideas that accompanied these significant social transformations.

There is no doubt that TRB communities appeared in Kuyavia (Greater Poland and the Chełmno Land) no later than c. 4100/4000 cal BC[77], hence at a time when the BKC and its hierarchical system of central and satellite settlements still existed. However, the earliest dates obtained for Niedźwiedź-type tombs are c. 3900–3800 cal BC[78], which are entirely consistent with current dating of the terminal BKC at c. 4000/3900 cal BC[79] and may indicate that the appearance of these burial monuments was connected to the BKC–TRB transition.

Fresh light is shed on this problem by discoveries made at several new early TRB sites in Kuyavia, such as Redecz Krukowy 20, Smólsk 2/10, Gustorzyn 1 and Kruszyn 10[80]. All of these sites were found in areas of dense BKC settlement, close to sites such as Brześć Kujawski 4 and Osłonki 1. Moreover, they occupied very similar habitats (though with a preference for sandy soils) to those chosen by the BKC. However, there are no examples among them of a TRB site directly overlying

---

74 Adamczyk 2013.
75 See Czerniak 1994; 2012; Rzepecki 2011.
76 Rzepecki 2011.
77 Most recently Kukawka 2015.
78 Rzepecki 2011.
79 Czerniak *et al.* 2016.
80 Papiernik 2012; Płaza 2016; for a summary analysis of these sites see Grygiel 2016.

a BKC settlement. The relatively numerous ^{14}C dates available for the sites in question range from 3900/3800 to 3600 cal BC, which Grygiel believes can be used to date the early TRB in Kuyavia[81]. He also contends that TRB communities came to Kuyavia from the lower Elbe region and brought an end to the BKC[82].

We believe that the aforementioned sites represent the later part of TRB phase I, associated with the "demise" of the BKC. Meanwhile, conclusive evidence about the relationship between the BKC and TRB comes from the results of aDNA analysis of early TRB skeletons from Kuyavia, which point to the exclusive presence of "Danubian" genes[83]. All in all, genetic continuity between the BKC and the TRB, combined with discontinuous settlement and the "confrontational" modification of burial customs indicate social and ideological causes for the decline of the BKC and transition to the TRB.

Discussion

1. The use of the term "Chalcolithic" in relation to the BKC is controversial for many reasons. In the Polish literature this period is most often referred to as the "Middle Neolithic". In light of the proposals put forward by Evžen Neustupný, the term "Eneolithic" seems appropriate for this region[84]. Conversely, the "Copper Age" appears to be a term applicable mainly to the Balkans and the Carpathian Basin[85]. Wolfram Schier has suggested that "the notion of Copper Age as a historical epoch be abandoned and the terms Eneolithic/Chalcolithic be used just as terminological conventions without culture-historical or even holistic implications [...]. The time of grand narratives may be over, but local and regional stories are equally fascinating and more adequate reflections of the dynamic cultural diversity in prehistoric Europe"[86].

The meaning and use of the term Chalcolithic is debated in the recent publication *Is there a British Chalcolithic?*[87]. The discussions therein reveal a lack of consensus about the need to use this term. However, exhaustive consideration is given to this problem, and we can draw on this as the context justifying our approach to the issue. In our opinion there are no grounds for sticking to the original definitions of the term "Chalcolithic", and in particular for restricting its use to societies involved in the production and use of copper. This is not simply a question of equivalence, as for example in the case of products made of jade[88]. The term "Neolithic" has also been redefined several times (polished stone axes and pottery — agriculture — the ideology of domestication), but it is obvious that this term means something else in relation to the Levant than it does in relation to Scandinavia. Given that the Neolithic is a useful concept, we should be consistent in using the notion of the Chalcolithic as a period characterising communities that experienced significant social and economic changes when seen in relation to the Neolithisation period.

---

81 Grygiel 2016, 942.
82 Cf. Czerniak 2018.
83 Borówka *et al.* 2016.
84 Neustupný 1981; 2008; recently also Kadrow 2015.
85 E.g. Lichardus 1991.
86 Schier 2014, 432.
87 Allen *et al.* 2012.
88 Klassen *et al.* 2012.

In the case of the BKC we can talk about the emergence of a new social structure. This was signified primarily by a complete redefinition of the social roles and identities of men and women. A distinctive gender-oriented identity can be seen, for example, in female-specific outfits and ornaments such as cattle-rib armlets, hip belts made of shells and special types of necklaces, as well as male-specific items such as axes, bone daggers and pendants. In graves, the consistent correlation between body position and biological sex — men buried lying on their right and women on their left side — can also be interpreted as an indicator of a gendered social structure. Significant changes also occurred in material culture, which is especially visible in pottery assemblages and their decoration (including the demise of stroke-ornamented pottery), and in the presence of "exotic" artefacts made of copper, *Spondylus* and calcite.

2. Around 4500/4400 cal BC we witness the collapse of the earlier settlement system within the vast territory of the "Danubian" world, resulting in the abandonment not only of tell sites, but also of large, long-lived flat settlements[89]. Not long afterwards, and entirely bucking these trends, the BKC came into being. Its distinctiveness is brought into particularly sharp focus against the backdrop of Kuyavia's nearest neighbouring cultures, the Lublin-Volhyn culture (hereafter LVC) and the Jordanów culture (JC; Figure 1).

Both the LVC and the JC practised a mobile system of settlement which lacked not only longhouses but also any other permanent dwelling structures. The solitary longhouses recorded in the JC in Bohemia have received little attention[90], and we do not know whether they served any special purpose. Instead, both of these cultures featured enclosure systems, which may have played a role in social integration. In Lower Silesia (Tyniec Mały, Dobkowice, site 12[91]) it has been suggested that they were mainly used in connection with cattle husbandry and for ritual purposes. In addition, both the LVC and the JC had separate cemetery sites with richly furnished graves (featuring fairly large numbers of copper ornaments) that were clearly differentiated according to the sex of the individual, as reflected by placing the body on its left (women) or right (men) side and by the type of grave goods with which they were buried[92].

Compared with the system represented by the BKC, two different models of settlement can be observed. The first (LVC and JC) is a model of mobile settlement in which there were no permanent houses. Instead there were enclosures and separate cemeteries. In the second model (BKC), we see a stable and hierarchical settlement network, with a built environment of monumental longhouses and cemeteries contained within central settlements. Both models featured monumental structures that were critical to local group identity: either enclosures or longhouses. The latter without doubt had a comparable iconicity to the LBK longhouse. Similarly, the blueprints for enclosures can also be sought in the LBK heritage.

---

89 Borič 2015; Parkinson *et al.* 2010.
90 Vokolek and Zápotocký 2009.
91 Furmanek *et al.* 2013.
92 Kadrow 2015.

3. What can we conclude from the above? Are we really dealing with two starkly different systems? Observations regarding monumental houses, cemetery sites and enclosures suggest that Danubian societies of the fifth millennium BC in Europe used a relatively consistent set of similar ideas and symbols inherited from the LBK, which — as with language use — were locally adapted and variously reconfigured as needed. This is why we have several local configurations that are seemingly completely different, though in essence they may be similar. Perhaps then the answer to why BKC communities turned to the symbolism of monumental longhouses lies in their choosing a sedentary form of settlement after a period of several hundred years of mobile and dispersed settlement during the LBPC. It could equally have been the other way around. It may have been the choice of the longhouse as a means of consolidating local communities[93] in the LBPC that led to sedentary settlement.

This is why the origins of the longhouse appear to hold the key to interpreting the origins of the BKC. The social role of longhouses was linked to continuity rituals addressed in equal measure to real as well as imaginary ancestors. The building of monumental houses, symbolising durability, like the diversity of rituals associated with these houses, harking back to a distant past, can be interpreted as a demonstration of ownership rights to a particular territory. Indirectly, it suggests that one of the characteristic features of the formation of the BKC was competition for access to land. The system of numerous but small satellite settlements may also attest to individual groups employing strategies of territorial expansion. Looking more widely at Danubian cultures, we can add that at the opposite ends of their territorial extent two different solutions were developed to solve the same problem of how a community's local, deep-rooted territorial rights could be marked in the landscape. In the Cerny culture this function was performed by Passy-type burial structures (some of which also, curiously enough, reference LBK longhouses[94]), in the BKC by monumental houses.

4. An interesting phenomenon within the Kuyavian BKC are the differences between two neighbouring central settlements, Osłonki 1 and Brześć Kujawski 4. These include different house succession practices, certain differences in burial rites and the existence of ditch defences exclusively at Osłonki 1. In the context of two settlements lying in such close proximity these differences are too significant to be deemed accidental. They undoubtedly signal the existence of competition between the two most important settlements in the region, which contributed to shaping the slightly different identity of their respective inhabitants. However, they could also point to the different ancestries of the founders of these villages, which would tie in with the aforementioned idea of competition for land.

5. Although BKC societies played a huge role in shaping the eastern TRB group, in particular their monumental earthen long barrows, the actual appearance of TRB communities within the BKC distribution area seems to have been a phenomenon that for at least 200 years took place in parallel with the existence of the BKC and was independent of this culture.

---

93 See Thomas 2015.
94 Midgley 2006.

References

Adamczyk, K. 2013. Communities of the Funnel Beaker culture during the era of erecting monumental tombs in the territory of Poland: rituals, vessels and social divisions. In J.A. Bakker, S.B.C. Bloo and M.K. Dütting (eds), *Current advances in Funnel Beaker culture (TRB/TBK) research: proceedings of the Borger Meetings 2009, The Netherlands. BAR International Series 2474*, 177–193. Oxford.

Allen, M.J., Gardiner, J. and Sheridan, A. (eds) 2012. *Is there a British Chalcolithic? People, place and polity in the later 3rd millennium. Prehistoric Society Research Paper 4*. Oxford.

Bigos, M. 2014. Północna granica zasięgu osadnictwa kultury późnej ceramiki wstęgowej. *Folia Praehistorica Posnaniensia* 19, 7–40.

Bogucki, P. 2008. The Danubian–Baltic borderland: northern Poland in the fifth millennium BC. *Analecta Praehistorica Leidensia* 40, 51–65.

Borič, D. 2015. The end of the Vinča world: modelling the Neolithic to Copper Age transition and the notion of archaeological culture. In S. Hansen, P. Raczky, A. Anders and A. Reingruber (eds), *Neolithic and Copper Age between the Carpathians and the Aegean Sea: chronologies and technologies from the 6th to the 4th millennium BCE*, 157–218. Bonn.

Borówka, P., Fernandes, D., Grygiel, R., Lorkiewicz, W., Marciniak, B., Pinhasi, R., Strapagiel, D. and Żądzińska, E. 2016. Przemiany populacyjne w okresie środkowego neolitu na Kujawach w świetle badań kopalnego DNA. Paper presented at the conference "Grupa wschodnia kulturz pucharów lejkowatych – w osiemdziesiątą rocznicę ogłoszenia drukiem doktoratu Profesora Konrada Jażdżewskiego", Łódź 14th–16th September 2016.

Bradley, R. 1996. Long houses, long mounds and Neolithic enclosures. *Journal of Material Culture* 1, 239–256.

Braasch, O. 2002. Aerial survey and Neolithic enclosures in central Europe. In G. Varndell and P. Topping (eds), *Enclosures in Neolithic Europe. Essays on causewayed and non-causewayed sites*, 63–68. Oxford.

Burgert, P., Končelová, M. and Květina, P. 2014. Neolitický dům, cesta k poznání sociální identity. In M. Popelka and R. Šmidtová (eds), *Neolitizace aneb setkání generací*, 29–57. Praha.

Childe, V.G. 1949. The origins of Neolithic culture in northern Europe. *Antiquity* 32, 129–135.

Chyleński, M., Juras, A., Ehler, E., Malmström, H., Piontek, J., Jakobsson, M., Marciniak, A. and Dabert, M. 2017. Late Danubian mitochondrial genomes shed light into the Neolithisation of central Europe in the 5th millennium BC. *BMC Evolutionary Biology* 17, 80. http://www.ncbi.nlm.nih.gov/pmc/articles/PMC5356262/ (accessed 25.03.2017).

Czekaj-Zastawny, A., Kabaciński, J., Terberger, T. and Ilkiewicz, J. 2013. Relations of Mesolithic hunter-gathers of Pomerania (Poland) with Neolithic cultures of central Europe. *Journal of Field Archaeology* 38, 195–209.

Czerniak, L. 1980. *Rozwój społeczeństw kultury późnej ceramiki wstęgowej na Kujawach*. Poznań.

Czerniak, L. 1994. *Wczesny i środkowy okres neolitu na Kujawach 5400–3650 p. n. e.* Poznań.

Czerniak, L. 2002. Settlements of the Brześć Kujawski type on the Polish Lowlands. *Archeologické rozhledy* 54, 9–22.

Czerniak, L. 2007. The north-east frontier of the post-LBK culture. In J.K. Kozłowski and P. Raczky (eds), *The Lengyel, Polgar and related cultures in the Middle/Late Neolithic in central Europe*, 231–248. Kraków.

Czerniak, L. 2012. After the LBK. Communities of the 5th millennium BC in north-central Europe. In R. Gleser and V. Becker (eds), *Mitteleuropa im 5. Jahrtausend vor Christus. Beiträge zur Internationalen Konferenz in Münster 2010*, 151–174. Berlin.

Czerniak, L. 2013. House, household and village in the Early Neolithic of central Europe: a case study of the LBK in Little Poland. In S. Kadrow and P. Włodarczak (eds), *Environment and subsistence — forty years after Janusz Kruk's "Settlement studies…". Studien zur Archäologie in Ostmitteleuropa/Studia nad Pradziejami Europy Środkowej 11*, 43–67. Rzeszów/Bonn.

Czerniak, L. 2016a. House and household in the LBK. In L. Amkreutz, F. Haack, D. Hofmann and I. van Wijk (eds), *Something out of the ordinary? Interpreting diversity in the Early Neolithic Linearbandkeramik and beyond*, 33–64. Newcastle.

Czerniak, L. 2016b. Osady społeczności kultur ceramiki wstęgowej. In M. Szmyt (ed.), *Osadnictwo społeczności neolitycznych na stanowisku 2 w Janowicach, woj. kujawsko-pomorskie. Studia i materiały do badań nad późnym neolitem Wysoczyzny Kujawskiej 6*, 73–124. Poznań.

Czerniak, L. 2018. The emergence of the TRB communities in Pomerania. *Prace i Materiały Muzeum Archeologicznego i Etnograficznego w Łodzi* 47, 103–129.

Czerniak, L. and Czebreszuk, J. 2010. Naczynie zoomorficzne z Ludwinowa, gm. Włocławek, stanowisko 7. *Fontes Archaeologici Posnanienses* 46, 127–136.

Czerniak L., Marciniak, A., Bronk Ramsey, C., Dunbar, E., Goslar, T., Barclay, A., Bayliss, A. and Whittle, A. 2016. House time: Neolithic settlement development at Racot during the 5th millennium cal B.C. in the Polish lowlands. *Journal of Field Archaeology* 41, 618–640.

Czerniak, L. and Pyzel, J. 2013. Unusual funerary practices in the Brześć Kujawski culture in the Polish Lowland. In N. Müller-Scheeßel (ed.), *„Irreguläre" Bestattungen in der Urgeschichte: Norm, Ritual, Strafe…?*, 139–150. Bonn.

Czerniak L. and Pyzel, J. 2016. Being at home in the Early Chalcolithic. The longhouse phenomenon in the Brześć Kujawski culture in the Polish Lowlands. *Open Archaeology* 2, 97–114.

Czerniak L. and Pyzel, J. in prep. Manipulating memory. Inventing ancestors and house foundation practices in the Early Chalcolithic in the Polish Lowlands. In C. Gibson, D. Brown and J. Pyzel (eds), *Gone… but not forgotten. Forgotten…but not gone. Mundane memories, artificial amnesia and transformed traditions*.

Derevenski, J.S. 2000. Rings of life: the role of early metalwork in mediating the gendered life course. *World Archaeology* 31, 389–406.

Dziewanowski, M. 2016. Obiekty kultur postlinearnych z wpływami kultury Rössen na Wzniesieniach Szczecińskich w świetle odkryć z lat 1995–2014. *Gdańskie Studia Archeologiczne* 5, 9–39.

Furmanek, M., Krupski, M., Ehlert, M., Grześkowiak, M., Hałuszko, A., Mackiewicz, M. and Sady, A. 2013. Dobkowice revisited. Interdisciplinary research on an enclosure of the Jordanów culture. *Anthropologie* 51, 375–396.

Grygiel, R. 1984. The household cluster as a fundamental social unit of the Lengyel culture in the Polish Lowlands. *Prace i Materiały Muzeum Archeologicznego i Etnograficznego w Łodzi* 31, 43–334.

Grygiel, R. 2004. *Neolit i początki epoki brązu w rejonie Brześcia Kujawskiego i Osłonek. Tom I. Wczesny neolit. Kultura ceramiki wstęgowej rytej.* Łódź.

Grygiel, R. 2008. *Neolit i początki epoki brązu w rejonie Brześcia Kujawskiego i Osłonek. Tom II. Część I– III. Środkowy neolit. Grupa brzesko-kujawska kultury lendzielskiej.* Łódź.

Grygiel, R. 2016. *Neolit i początki epoki brązu w rejonie Brześcia Kujawskiego i Osłonek. Tom III. Środkowy i późny neolit. Kultura pucharów lejkowatych.* Łódź.

Hodder, I. 1994. Architecture and meaning: the example of Neolithic houses and tombs. In M. Parker Pearson and C. Richards (eds), *Architecture and order. Approaches to social space*, 73–86. London.

Hofmann, D. 2013. Narrating the house. The transformation of longhouses in Early Neolithic Europe. In A.M. Chadwick and C. Gibson (eds), *Memory, myth and long-term landscape inhabitation. Celtic Studies Publications XVII*, 32–54. Oxford.

Hofmann, D. 2016. Keep on walking: the role of migration in Linearbandkeramik life. *Documenta Praehistorica* 43, 235–251.

Juras, A., Chyleński, M., Krenz-Niedbała, M., Malmström, H., Ehler, E., Pospieszny, Ł., Łukasik, S., Bednarczyk, J., Piontek, J., Jakobsson, M. and Dabert, M. 2017. Investigating kinship of Neolithic post-LBK human remains from Krusza Zamkowa, Poland using ancient DNA. *Forensic Science International: Genetics* 26, 30–39.

Kabaciński, J., Sobkowiak-Tabaka, I., David, E., Osypińska, M., Terberger, T. and Winiarska-Kabacińska, M. 2014. The chronology of T-shaped axes in the Polish Lowland. *Sprawozdania Archeologiczne* 66, 29–56.

Kaczor, W. and Żółkiewski, M. 2015. Dubielewo, stan. 8. Informacje o stanowisku. In W. Kaczor and M. Żółkiewski (eds), *Dubielewo, gm. Brześć Kujawski, stanowisko 8. Archeologiczne badania ratownicze na trasie autostrady A1 w woj. kujawsko-pomorskim*, 15–20. Poznań.

Kadrow S. 2008. Gender-differentiated burial rites in Europe of the 5th and 4th millennia BC: attempts at traditional archaeological interpretation. *Analecta Archaeologica Ressoviensia* 3, 49–95.

Kadrow S. 2015. The idea of the Eneolithic. In K. Kristiansen, L. Šmejda and J. Turek (eds), *Paradigm found. Archaeological theory, present, past and future. Essays in honour of Evžen Neustupný*, 248–262. Oxford.

Klassen, L., Cassen, S. and Pétrequin, P. 2012. Alpine axes and early metallurgy. In P. Pétrequin, S. Cassen, M. Errera, L. Klassen, A. Sheridan and A.-M. Pétrequin (eds), *Jade. Grandes haches alpines du Néolithique européen. Ve et IVe millénaires av. J.-C.* 1280–1309. Besançon.

Kukawka, S. 2015, Początki kultury pucharów lejkowatych na Niżu Polskim. *Folia Praehistorica Posnaniensia* 20, 277–299.

Lichardus, J. 1991. Die Kupferzeit als historische Epoche. Versuch einer Deutung. In J. Lichardus (ed.), *Die Kupferzeit als historische Epoche. Symposium Saarbrücken und Otzenhausen 6.–13.11.1988*, 763–800. Bonn.

Link, T. 2014. Welche Krise? Das Ende der Linienbandkeramik aus östlicher Perspektive. In T. Link and D. Schimmelpfennig (eds), *No future? Brüche und Ende kultureller Erscheinungen. Fallbeispiele aus dem 6.–2. Jahrtausend v. Chr. Fokus Jungsteinzeit. Berichte der AG Neolithikum 4*, 95–111. Kerpen-Loogh.

Literski, N. and Nebelsick, L.D. 2012. Katalog der Kreisgrabenanlagen und verwandten Tells der ersten Hälfte des 5. Jt. v. Chr. in Mittel- und Südosteuropa. In F. Bertemes and H. Meller (eds), *Neolithische Kreisgrabenanlagen in Europa. Internationale Arbeitstagung, 7.–9. Mai 2004 in Goseck (Sachsen-Anhalt). Tagungen des Landesmuseums für Vorgeschichte Halle 8*, 434–532. Halle (Saale).

Lorkiewicz, W. 2012. Skeletal trauma and violence among the early farmers of the north European plain. Evidence from Neolithic settlements of the Lengyel culture in Kuyavia, north-central Poland. In R. Schulting and L. Fibiger (eds), *Sticks, stones, and broken bones. Neolithic violence in a European perspective*, 51–76. Oxford.

Lorkiewicz, W., Płoszaj, T., Jędrychowska-Dańska, K., Żądzińska, E., Strapagiel, D., Haduch, E., Szczepanek, A., Grygiel, R. and Witas, H.W. 2015. Between the Baltic and Danubian worlds: the genetic affinities of a Middle Neolithic population from central Poland. *PLoS ONE* 10(2): https://doi.org/10.1371/journal.pone.0118316.

Marchelak, I. 2017. Osadnictwo grupy brzesko-kujawskiej kultury lendzielskiej. In I. Marchelak, A. Nierychlewska, I. Nowak and P. Papiernik (eds), *Ratownicze badania archeologiczne na stanowisku 3 w Ludwinowie pow. Włocławek, woj. kujawsko-pomorskie (trasa autostrady A-1). Via Archaeologica Lodziensis VII*, 35–83. Łódź.

Marciniak, A., Pyzel, J., Lisowski, M., Bronk Ramsey, C., Dunbar, E., Barclay, A., Bayliss, A. and Whittle, A. in prep. A history of the LBK in the central Polish lowlands.

Midgley, M. 2006. From ancestral village to monumental cemetery: the creation of monumental Neolithic cemeteries. www.jungsteinsite.de (accessed 23.03.2017).

Neustupný, E. 1981. Das Äneolithikum Mitteleuropas. In H. Behrens (ed.), Tagung über die Walternienburg-Bernburger Kultur, Halle 1977. *Jahresschrift für Mitteldeutsche Vorgeschichte* 63, 177–187.

Neustupný, E. 2008. Všeobecný přehled eneolitu. In E. Neustupný, M. Dobeš, J. Turek and M. Zápotocký (eds), *Archeologie pravěkých Čech 4*, 11–38. Praha.

Oross, K., Marton, T., Whittle, A., Hedges, R.E.M. and Cramp, L.J.E. 2010. Die Siedlung der Balaton-Lasinja-Kultur in Balatonszárszó-Kis-erdei-dűlő. In J. Šuteková, P. Pavúk, P. Kalábková and B. Kovár (eds), *Panta Rhei: studies on the chronology and cultural development of south-eastern and central Europe in earlier prehistory. Presented to Juraj Pavúk on the occasion of his 75th birthday. Studia archaeologica et medievalia 11*, 379–405. Bratislava.

Papiernik, P. 2012. Sprawozdanie z badań wykopaliskowych na stanowisku 20 w Redczu Krukowym, pow. włocławski, woj. kujawsko-pomorskie. *Prace i Materiały Muzeum Archeologicznego i Etnograficznego w Łodzi, Seria Archeologiczna* 45, 195–238.

Parkinson, W.A., Yerkes, R.W., Gyucha, A., Sarris, A., Morris, M. and Salisbury, R.B. 2010. Early Copper Age settlements in the Körös region of the Great Hungarian Plain. *Journal of Field Archaeology* 35, 163–183.

Pavúk, J. 2012. Kolové stavby lengyelskej kultúry. Pôdorysy, interiér a ich funkcia. *Slovenská Archeológia* 60, 251–284.

Pleinerova, I. 1984. Häuser des Spätlengyelhorizontes in Březno bei Louny. *Památky archeologické* 75, 7–49.

Płaza, D. 2016. Osadnictwo młodszej epoki kamienia i wczesnej epoki brązu. In W. Siciński, D. Płaza and P. Papiernik (eds), *Ratownicze badania archeologiczne na stanowisku 10 w Kruszynie, pow. Włocławek, woj. kujawsko-pomorskie (trasa autostrady A1). Via Archaeologica Lodziensis VI*, 21–136. Łódź.

Podborský, V. 2011. Fenomén neolitického domu. Sborník prací Filozofické fakulty Brněnské univerzity. *Studia Minora Facultatis Philosophicae Universitatis Brunensis* 14/15, 17–45.

Pyzel, J. 2010. *Historia osadnictwa społeczności kultury ceramiki wstęgowej rytej na Kujawach. Gdańskie Studia Archeologiczne. Seria Monografie 1*. Gdańsk.

Pyzel, J. 2013. Different models of settlement organisation in the Linear Band Pottery culture — an example from Ludwinowo 7 in eastern Kuyavia. In S. Kadrow and P. Włodarczak (eds), *Environment and subsistence — forty years after Janusz Kruk's "Settlement studies...". Studien zur Archäologie in Ostmitteleuropa/Studia nad Pradziejami Europy Środkowej 11*, 85–93. Rzeszów/Bonn.

Rączkowski, W. and Ruciński, D. 2015. Searching for hidden houses: optical satellite imagery in archaeological prospection of the Early Neolithic settlements in the Kujawy region, Poland. In D.G. Hadjimitsis, K. Themistocleous, S. Michaelides and G. Papadavid (eds), *Third International Conference on Remote Sensing and Geoinformation of the Environment (RSCy2015). Proc. of SPIE* 9535, 1–13. doi: 10.1117/12.2195618.

Raczky, P., Anders, A. and Siklósi, Zs. 2014. Trajectories of continuity and change between the Late Neolithic and the Copper Age in eastern Hungary. In W. Schier and F. Draşovean (eds), *The Neolithic and Eneolithic in southeast Europe. New approaches to dating and cultural dynamics in the 6th to 4th millennium BC. Prähistorische Archäologie in Südosteuropa 28*, 319–346. Rahden.

Rzepecki, S. 2011. *The roots of megalithism in the TRB culture*. Łódź.

Schier, W. 2014. The Copper Age in southeast Europe — historical epoch or typo-chronological construct? In W. Schier and F. Draşovean (eds), *The Neolithic and Eneolithic in southeast Europe. New approaches to dating and cultural dynamics in the 6th to 4th millennium BC. Prähistorische Archäologie in Südosteuropa 28*, 419–436. Rahden.

Sherratt, A. 1990. The genesis of megaliths: monumentality, ethnicity and social complexity in Neolithic north-west Europe. *World Archaeology* 22, 147–167.

Szmyt, M. 1999. *Between west and east. People of the Globular Amphora culture in eastern Europe: 2950–2350 BC. Baltic-Pontic Studies 8*. Poznań.

Terberger, T. and Kabaciński, J. 2010. The Neolithisation of Pomerania — a critical review. In D. Gronenborn and J. Petrasch (eds), *The spread of the Neolithic to central Europe. International Symposium, Mainz 24–26 June 2005*, 375–406. Mainz.

Thomas, J. 2015. House societies and founding ancestors in Early Neolithic Britain. In C. Renfrew, M. Boyd and I. Morely (eds) *Death rituals, social order and the archaeology of immortality in the ancient world*, 138–152. Cambridge.

Vokolek, V. and Zápotocký, M. 2009. Východní Čechy v raném eneolitu: lengyelská a jordanovská kultura. *Archeologie ve středních Čechách* 13, 567–654.

Wetzel, G. 2014. Die Brześć Kujawski-Gruppe in Brandenburg und der Lausitz. Zur Frage einer Guhrauer Gruppe. *Arbeitsberichte zur Bodendenkmalpflege in Brandenburg* 24, 89–129.

Taboo? The process of Neolitisation in the Dutch wetlands re-examined (5000-3400 cal BC)

Daan Raemaekers

Summary

This paper investigates the relevance of the notion of taboo from a diachronic perspective and focuses on the Neolithisation in the western part of the North European Plain. While taboo is a very strong cultural notion, the transition to farming by definition means a subsistence change. The notion of taboo was expanded to include three theoretical behavioural options. These are deliberate avoidance (taboo), deliberate incorporation and non-ritual adoption. In my opinion the diachronic taboo model presented here helps us to step away from the more mechanical availability model and focus on the social processes underlying the process of Neolithisation. It makes clear that the small-scale introduction of domestic animals from around 4700–4450 cal BC did not have any social relevance — at least not visible to the archaeologist. The introduction of cereals in the period 4300–4000 cal BC seems to have been of greater social relevance, resulting in new pottery types. Around 4000 cal BC the perception of domestic cattle may have changed profoundly, judging from the deposition of cattle horns. The outcome of this process around 4000 cal BC is then a society in which both cereals and domestic cattle have taken centre stage.

Zusammenfassung: Tabu? Eine Neubetrachtung des Neolithisierungsprozesses in den niederländischen Feuchtgebieten (5000-3400 cal BC)

Der vorliegende Beitrag untersucht, inwiefern das Konzept des Tabus einen fruchtbaren Ansatz für eine diachrone Perspektive zur Neolithisierung des westlichen Teils der nordwesteuropäischen Tiefebene bietet. Tabus sind sehr starke kulturelle Vorstellungen, der Übergang zu einer produzierenden Lebensweise beinhaltet aber zwangsläufig eine Veränderung in der Ernährung. Der Begriff „Tabu" wurde erweitert, um drei mögliche Verhaltensoptionen abzudecken: Bewusste Vermeidung (Tabu), bewusste Einführung und nicht-rituelle Übernahme. Das hier vorgestellte diachrone Tabumodell erlaubt es somit, sich etwas von einem rein mechanischen Verfügbarkeitsmodell zu entfernen und sich stattdessen auf die sozialen Prozesse zu konzentrieren, die der Neolithisierung zu Grunde liegen. Dadurch wird deutlich, dass die Einführung domestizierter Tiere in kleinerem Maßstab etwa 4700–4450 v. Chr. keine soziale Relevanz hatte, bzw. dass diese archäologisch nicht sichtbar ist. Dagegen scheint die Einführung von

Getreide zwischen 4300 und 4000 v. Chr. eine größere soziale Relevanz gehabt zu haben und führte zur Produktion neuer Keramiktypen. Um 4000 v. Chr. könnte sich die Wahrnehmung domestizierter Rinder dann grundlegend geändert haben, wie die Deponierungen von Rindergehörnen andeuten. Am Ende dieses Prozesses steht um 4000 v. Chr. dann eine Gesellschaft, in der sowohl Getreide als auch Rinder eine zentrale Rolle erlangt haben.

Introduction

Prehistoric archaeology finds inspiration in many other scientific disciplines. One of the continuous sources of inspiration is that of cultural anthropology. As an undergraduate student in archaeology an introduction in this discipline made clear to me that notwithstanding the immense variation of human behaviour, all human societies can be studied using descriptive frameworks such as kinship relations or gender patterns. This article focuses on one other notion from cultural anthropology, the notion of taboo. It is questioned here whether this notion can help us understand the social actions undertaken in periods of subsistence change and determine the societal relevance of these changes.

The term taboo entered the western literature thanks to the explorations by James Cook to the Pacific isles in the eighteenth century. According to Cook it referred to anything forbidden[1]. As such, the notion of taboo comprises food products, materials and actions. Some well-known present-day examples in these categories may be the taboo on eating pig by Muslims, the strict rules on the separation of milk and meat by Jews and the taboo on incest or cannibalism in many societies. This makes clear that in terms of normative behaviour, taboo regulations are very, very strong: disrespecting taboo places one outside society. When one concludes that taboo is such a strong defining aspect of any society and that it may manifest itself in both food regulations and material culture, it is surprisingly understudied within archaeology[2]. Moreover, available studies focus on topics within a specific temporal framework[3] without taking into account that notwithstanding taboos, societies change. How can we incorporate a diachronic aspect in the study of taboo?

It is proposed here to define a model in which three behavioural alternatives can be defined in response to changes in society, such as subsistence change (Neolithisation). First of all, *deliberate avoidance* may take place, in which within meaningful social arenas the new foods or materials are deliberately not integrated into existing behavioural repertoires. In other words, it is taboo. Second, the opposite may take place. The *deliberate incorporation* of new foods or materials may be seen as the second action in which a behavioural repertoire is rewritten and previous normative behaviour is replaced by new normative behaviour. The third option is that of *non-ritual adoption*, in which new foods and materials seem to play a functional role only. With this model at hand, it is now time to introduce the case study.

This model is studied using a case study from the Neolithic of north-west Europe: the Swifterbant culture (Figure 1). Remains from this archaeological

---

1 Cook and King 1821, 348.
2 E.g. Fowles 2008; Milner 2015.
3 E.g. Fowles 2008; Oestigaard 1999; Simons 1994.

Figure 1. Overview of the Swifterbant culture area with sites mentioned in the text (drawing S.E. Boersma, University of Groningen, Groningen Institute of Archaeology).

culture were found in the western part of the North European Plain, roughly between Antwerp (Belgium) and Hamburg (Germany).

Sites are concentrated in the wetlands. While this may be the consequence of preservation conditions[4], and as such provide a structural element to any interpretation concerning the "wetland adaptation" of Swifterbant communities[5], it also provides a dataset with very positive characteristics. First of all, the sites are recovered in Holocene sedimentation areas. As a result the time depth of the various sites is limited to one or a few centuries: a longer occupation of a surface is impossible thanks to the sea level rise and consequential deposition of clay or peat layers. On some sites, like the eponymous Swifterbant site, occupation surfaces were renewed with the regular deposition of reed bundles. While this activity extended the life-span of sites, it provided a site stratigraphy which can be the basis for a diachronic analysis at a site level. The case study area is therefore excellently suited to study diachronic patterns. The second reason that this area is suitable for the type of analysis presented here is strongly related. Thanks to the sedimentation history bone and plant material are well preserved. This allows a diachronic study that encompasses several find categories.

---

4 Cf. Raemaekers 1999, 106.
5 Cf. Amkreutz 2013, 308–310.

The traditional narrative

The transition to farming in the study area is studied within one dominant framework: that of the extremely long substitution phase[6] in which the subsistence base is dominated by hunting and gathering, and animal husbandry and cereal cultivation only play a minor role. Louwe Kooijmans[7] introduced the term "extended broad spectrum economy" to describe this subsistence strategy[8]. The following stepping stones can be identified in this narrative:

- the start of pottery production in Swifterbant style around 5000 cal BC at Hardinxveld-Giessendam Polderweg[9]. This marks the start of the availability phase, as the inspiration for the production of pottery is sought in the neighbouring fully Neolithic communities[10];

- the small-scale introduction of domestic animals around 4700–4450 cal BC at Hardinxveld-Giessendam De Bruin phase 3[11] and Brandwijk[12]. This marks the start of the substitution phase. It concerns small numbers of bones from domestic cattle, pig and sheep/goat. This introductory date is questioned internationally[13], probably because it interferes with a grander narrative in which the transition to farming across the British Isles and southern Scandinavia is to be dated to (or just before) 4000 cal BC;

- the introduction of small-scale cereal cultivation around 4300–4000 cal BC at various sites of the Swifterbant culture[14]. The archaeological evidence concerns cereal grains, small-scale forest clearings in pollen diagrams[15], the presence of quern stones (mostly in Swifterbant itself[16]) and horticultural fields at three levee sites in Swifterbant[17];

- the occurrence of sites in which the evidence for animal husbandry and cereal cultivation is so abundant that one might suppose a "true" Neolithic subsistence base. This consolidation phase is reached with Schipluiden, dated around 3500 cal BC[18]. This last stage in the process of Neolithisation is left out of consideration here.

The dogma of the millennium-long Neolithisation is so strong within the Dutch discourse that diverging notions raise serious objections. I concluded in 2004 that the start of the substitution phase was based on the evidence from coastal sites and that the coastal landscape before 4000 cal BC was probably absent due to erosion. This absence of evidence allows for a second model of Neolithisation in which the substitution phase was reached much earlier[19]. This

---

6 Zvelebil 1986.
7 Louwe Kooijmans 1993.
8 E.g. Amkreutz 2013, 46–47; Out 2009, 363; Raemaekers 1999, 112–115.
9 Louwe Kooijmans 2003; Raemaekers 2001.
10 E.g. Raemaekers 1999, 141; *par excellence* Ten Anscher 2012, 131–153.
11 Oversteegen *et al.* 2001.
12 Raemaekers 1999, 59–61, based on Robeerst 1995.
13 E.g. Krause-Kyora *et al.* 2013; Rowley-Conwy 2013.
14 Cappers and Raemaekers 2008; Out 2009, table 11.2.
15 Bakker 2003; Kramer *et al.* 2013.
16 Devriendt 2014, 61–126.
17 Huisman and Raemaekers 2014.
18 Kubiak-Martens 2006; Louwe Kooijmans 2006.
19 Raemaekers 2003.

hypothesis has received ample, but critical attention[20]. The find of a cereal field at Swifterbant S4[21] was important to, first of all, conclude that local cultivation took place, but it also made clear that cereal cultivation was a structural part of the subsistence strategies of the Swifterbant people[22]. While not even proposing that this find would lead to the consequence of a much earlier consolidation phase, the interpretation of the Swifterbant culture as a not fully/truly Neolithic society has remained dominant[23].

Case studies 1 and 2: the introduction of domestic animals

The first case study in which the taboo model is applied pertains to the introduction of domestic animals in the Swifterbant culture. Most Swifterbant find contexts are interpreted as settlements, and the bone material as refuse. This makes it difficult to analyse the role domestic animals played in terms of material culture to think with. We therefore focus on two specific contexts in which deliberate action forms the basis of the archaeological record. The first context is that of the selection of bones for the production of tools; the second context is that of depositions.

The production of bone tools on the basis of the raw material available has the unwanted effect that the most diagnostic parts of a bone, the proximal and distal parts, are often removed. The outcome is that while a large number of bone tools have been documented on various sites from the period under study, the number of bone tools of which the species has been identified is very limited. In this analysis the bones and bone tools from the type site of Swifterbant S3, dated to c. 4300–4000 cal BC, are presented[24]. The starting point in this analysis is the idea that when producing a bone tool, all bones from an assemblage are available as raw material. If non-ritual adoption of domestic animals explains the handling of these bones, one should expect that the proportion of domestic animals is rather similar in both the general bone assemblage and the bone tool assemblage. Table 1 indicates that tools were produced from bones of both wild and domestic species. Due to the small number of bone tools, it is difficult to interpret the observed pattern. Nevertheless it is proposed that this table provides no evidence of either deliberate avoidance or deliberate incorporation of domestic animals in this behavioural repertoire. An interpretation in terms non-ritual adoption of domestic animals seems to fit the data better.

The second context in which the social role of domestic animals can be studied is that of depositions. Again, it is a study based on a small number of finds. It is clear that deposition of animal parts predates the introduction of domestic animals in the region. Finds include red deer antlers and aurochs skulls. Of eight dated red deer antlers, four stem from the Mesolithic[25]. Antler depositions dated to the Neolithic are absent, but two finds dated to the Bronze Age indicate that it may be a continuous or reinvented practice. The aurochs finds are of greater concern here[26]. Three aurochs skulls were found at Hoge Vaart/A27 and can be dated to

---

20 Amkreutz 2013, 407–408; Louwe Kooijmans 2007.
21 Huisman *et al.* 2009.
22 Cf. Cappers and Raemaekers 2008.
23 E.g. Amkreutz 2013, 317–318; Out 2009, 409–412.
24 Bulten and Clason 2001; Zeiler 1997.
25 Ufkes 1997.
26 Peeters 2007, 201–203.

	Number of bones	Number of tools	Number of expected tools
Aurochs	2	1	0.0
Red deer	118	2	1.6
Cattle	321	2	4.3
Horse	2	1	0.0
Total	**443**	**6**	**5.9**
Wild (aurochs + red deer)	120	3	1.6
Domestic (cattle + horse)	323	3	4.4

Table 1. Bone tools from Swifterbant S3 (from Bulten and Clason 2001; Zeiler 1997).

	GrN	date BP	Cal BC (2σ)	Species
Een	20381	5530 ± 30	4460–4330	Aurochs
Drenthe	20386	5360 ± 60	4340–4000	Aurochs
Buinerveen	20373	4960 ± 40	3900–3650	Domestic cattle
Westerbork	20384	4880 ± 60	3790–3510	Domestic cattle
Odoorn	20375	4780 ± 60	3690–3370	Domestic cattle

Table 2. Cattle horns ^{14}C-dated to before 3400 cal BC (start of Drouwen TRB) (from Prummel and Van der Sanden 1995).

the ceramic Mesolithic phase of the site (4950–4460 cal BC). One of the skulls has been found at the bottom of the gully located directly next to the inhabited sand ridge; the other two derive from the bank of the same gully and were found together in spatial association with a standing oak post. The deposition of cattle horns continued after the introduction of the first domestic cattle — it concerns a dataset of five ^{14}C-dated cattle horns from the peat area in the province of Drenthe[27]. The ^{14}C dates (Table 2) make clear that there are two subsets. There is a group of two dated to the second half of the fifth millennium and a group of three dated to the first half of the fourth millennium. Notwithstanding the small numbers, the two oldest cattle horns indicate the continuation of Mesolithic deposition because they concern aurochs finds, an example of deliberate avoidance. The three younger cattle horns are from domestic animals and indicate deliberate incorporation. The data suggest that an important change in the perception of domestic cattle occurred somewhere around 4000 cal BC.

Case study 3: the introduction of cereals

The societal relevance of the introduction of cereals is studied on the basis of the ceramics from the type site, Swifterbant S3. There are several reasons to focus on this site and on its ceramics. It is the largest ceramic assemblage available, it is a stratified site, it is well-published[28] and functional analysis of its ceramics has been carried out[29]. The available ^{14}C dates indicate that the site was occupied somewhere in the period 4300–4000 cal BC. Due to a plateau in the calibration curve it is not possible to date the site more precisely. The time depth of the site is probably much less than three centuries.

In general the pottery from Swifterbant S3 is plant-tempered, thick-walled (9–10 mm) and of poor quality. Decoration may consist of rows of impressions

---

27 Prummel and Van der Sanden 1995.
28 De Roever 2004.
29 Raemaekers *et al.* 2013.

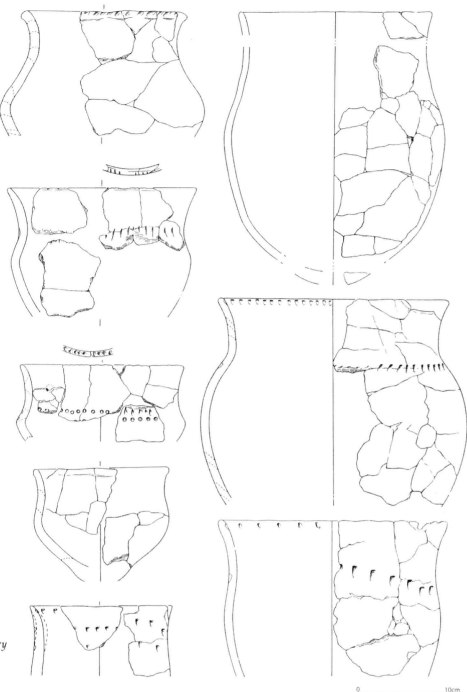

Figure 2. Subgroup A pottery from Swifterbant S3 (from Raemaekers 2015, fig. 5).

on the shoulder and the rim zone. A striking characteristic of Swifterbant pottery is that some pots are decorated with rows of impressions on the inside of the rim. While this general description holds true, some internal variation can be found. Throughout the occupation history of S3 there are also pots with stone temper, with thinner walls and of high quality[30].

A more detailed ceramic analysis focuses on the correlations between the different aspects recorded for each individual pot. There are three subgroups

---

30   De Roever 1979; 2004, 43–58; Raemaekers 1999, 31–33; 2015.

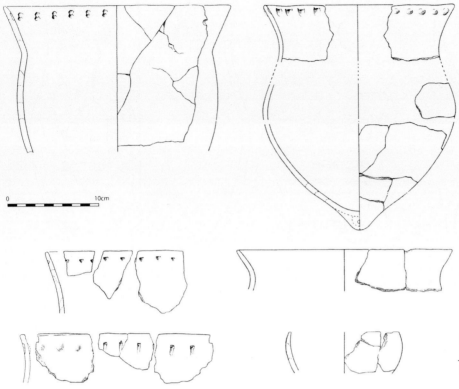

Figure 3. Subgroup B pottery from Swifterbant S3 (from Raemaekers 2015, fig. 6).

	Subgroup A	Intermediate	Subgroup B
Top part (layer F)	42%	19%	39%
Middle part (layer G)	40%	43%	17%
Lower part (layers H-I-K)	40%	53%	8%

Table 3. Chronological development of pottery subgroups at Swifterbant S3 (after Raemaekers 2015: table 4).

proposed. Subgroup A comprises pots which are plant-tempered, thick-walled and of poor quality (Figure 2). Subgroup B comprises pots which are stone-tempered, thin-walled and of high quality (Figure 3). The third subgroup comprises pots with intermediate characteristics.

When this subdivision of the pots is combined with their stratigraphic position it becomes clear that the proportion of subgroup A pots is constant throughout the occupation period (40–42 %). The proportion of subgroup B pots increases strongly from 8 % in the lower part of the find layer to 39 % in the top part. Of course this increase is at the expense of the group with intermediate characteristics (Table 3). We see that over time the production of pottery changed from a tradition in which the pottery aspects studied here were loosely connected to a tradition in which two norms of pottery production dominate the production process[31].

How is this pottery development connected to the introduction of cereals? First of all it needs to be borne in mind that under the find layer — therefore before the occupation — there is evidence of a cultivated field[32]. Moreover, even in the lowermost spits cereal grains were recovered[33]. Both observations make clear

---

31 Raemaekers 2015.
32 Huisman and Raemaekers 2014.
33 Van Zeist and Palfenier-Vegter 1981.

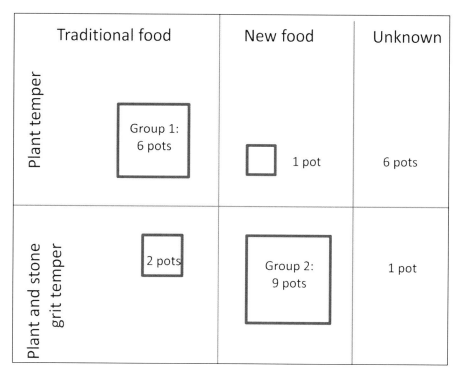

Figure 4. Correlation between temper and function of pots at Swifterbant S3. The size of the square is related to the number of pots (from Raemaekers et al. 2013, fig. 13).

that from the start of the occupation cereals were available as raw material to think with. The changes in pottery characteristics indicate that these thoughts led to the development of two opposite stereotypes. The functional analysis of 25 pots from Swifterbant S3 subsequently indicates a strong correlation between subgroup B pots with meals that comprised emmer wheat and subgroup A pots with meals without emmer wheat (Figure 4)[34].

The subgroup B pots seem to be a new development firmly rooted in older Swifterbant pottery, as one can monitor its "birth" during the Swifterbant S3 occupation. It is the correlation between temper, wall thickness, quality and function that sets these pots apart from the rest of the assemblage. It is proposed that the introduction of cereals in Swifterbant societies is an example of deliberate incorporation in which the consumption of new foods was mirrored in the development of a new type of pots, the incipient form of the Funnel Beaker culture in the western part of the North European Plain[35].

Conclusions

This paper has investigated the relevance of the notion of taboo from a diachronic perspective and focused on the Neolithisation in the western part of the North European Plain. While taboo is a very strong cultural notion, the transition to farming by definition means a subsistence change. How was this change dealt with in terms of behavioural patterns? The notion of taboo was expanded to include three theoretical behavioural options. These are deliberate avoidance (taboo), deliberate incorporation and non-ritual adoption. The three case studies indicate that all three behavioural options were practised. The selection of bones

---

34   Raemaekers *et al.* 2013.
35   Raemaekers 2015; Ten Anscher 2012, 63-129; 2015.

for the production of tools at Swifterbant S3 (4300–4000 cal BC) suggests that bones from domestic and wild animals were considered to be equally suited. The deposition of cattle horns provided evidence of at first deliberate avoidance (prior to 4000 cal BC) and subsequent deliberate incorporation (after 4000 cal BC). It is proposed that this pattern is the result of an important change in the perception of domestic cattle somewhere around 4000 cal BC. In the third case study we see that the introduction of cereals at Swifterbant S3 (4300–4000 cal BC) correlates with an important restructuring of the production of pottery. I argue that this is much more than a correlation: the new pottery type is the result of the new meals. As such it is an example of deliberate incorporation.

In my opinion the diachronic taboo model presented here helps us to step away from the more mechanical availability model and to focus on the social processes underlying the process of Neolithisation. It makes clear that the small-scale introduction of domestic animals from around 4700–4450 cal BC did not have any social relevance — at least not visible to the archaeologist. The introduction of cereals in the period 4300–4000 cal BC seems to have been of greater social relevance, resulting in new pottery types. Around 4000 cal BC the perception of domestic cattle may have changed profoundly, judging from the deposition of cattle horns. The outcome of this process around 4000 cal BC is then a society in which both cereals and domestic cattle have taken centre stage.

This paper thus indicates that the introduction of domestic animals around 4700–4450 cal BC was not only of limited scale, but also of limited social importance. The "true" transition to a New Neolithic[36] took place in the final centuries of the fifth millennium cal BC. As a result, the Dutch case study area now fits better into the general grander narrative in which the transition to farming across the British Isles and southern Scandinavia is to be dated to (or just before) 4000 cal BC[37].

References

Amkreutz, L.W.S.W. 2013. *Persistent traditions. A long-term perspective on communities in the process of Neolithisation in the Lower Rhine Area (5500–2500 cal BC).* Leiden.

Bakker, R. 2003. *The emergence of agriculture on the Drenthe Plateau. A palaeobotanical study supported by high-resolution 14C-dating. Archäologische Berichte 16.* Groningen.

Bulten, E.E. and Clason, A. 2001. The antler, bone and tooth tools of Swifterbant, the Netherlands (c. 5500–4000 cal. BC) compared with those from other Neolithic sites in the Netherlands. In A.M. Choyke and L. Bartosiewicz (eds), *Crafting bone: skeletal technologies through time and space. BAR International Series 937*, 297–320. Oxford.

Cappers, R.T.J. and Raemaekers, D.C.M. 2008. Cereal cultivation at Swifterbant? Neolithic wetland farming on the north European plain. *Current Anthropology* 49, 385–402.

Cook, J. and King, J. 1821. *A voyage to the Pacific Ocean: undertaken by command of His Majesty, for making discoveries in the Northern Hemisphere: performed under the direction of Captains Cook, Clerke, and Gore in the years 1776, 1777, 1778, 1779 and 1780 being a copious, comprehensive and satisfactory abridgement of the voyage.* London.

De Roever, J.P. 1979. The pottery from Swifterbant — Dutch Ertebølle? *Helinium* 19, 13–36.

---

36 Cf. Raemaekers 1999.
37 E.g. Rowley-Conwy 2013.

De Roever, J.P. 2004. *Swifterbant-aardewerk. Een analyse van de neolithische nederzettingen bij Swifterbant, 5e millennium voor Christus. Groningen Archaeological Studies 2.* Groningen.

Devriendt, I. 2014. *Swifterbant stones. The Neolithic stone and flint industry at Swifterbant (The Netherlands): from stone typology and flint technology to site function. Groningen Archaeological Studies 25.* Groningen.

Fowles, S.M. 2008. Steps towards an archaeology of taboo. In L. Fogelin (ed.), *Religion, archaeology, and the material world*, 15–37. Carbondale.

Huisman, D.J. and Raemaekers, D.C.M. 2014. Systematic cultivation of the Swifterbant wetlands (The Netherlands). Evidence from Neolithic tillage marks (c. 4300–4000 cal. BC). *Journal of Archaeological Science* 49, 572–584.

Huisman, D.J., Jongmans, A.G. and Raemaekers, D.C.M. 2009. Investigating Neolithic land use in Swifterbant (NL) using micromorphological techniques. *Catena* 78, 185–197.

Kramer, A., Bittmann, F. and Nösler, D. 2013. New insights into vegetation dynamics and settlement history in Hümmling, north-western Germany, with particular reference to the Neolithic. *Vegetation History and Archaeobotany* 23, 461–478.

Krause-Kyora, B., Makarewicz, C., Evin, A., Girdland Flink, L., Dobney, K., Larson, G., Hartz, S., Schreiber, S., von Carnap-Bornheim, C., von Wurmb-Schwark, N. and Nebel, A. 2013. Use of domesticated pigs by Mesolithic hunter-gatherers in northwestern Europe. *Nature communications* 4, 2348.

Kubiak-Martens, L. 2006. Botanical remains and plant food subsistence. In L.P. Louwe Kooijmans and P.F.B. Jongste (eds), *Schipluiden. A Neolithic settlement on the Dutch North Sea coast, c. 3500 cal BC. Analecta Praehistorica Leidensia 37/38*, 317–338. Leiden.

Louwe Kooijmans, L.P. 1993. Wetland exploitation and upland relations of prehistoric communities in the Netherlands. In J. Gardiner (ed.), *Flatlands & wetlands. Current themes in East Anglian archaeology. East Anglian Archaeology 50*, 71–116. Oxford.

Louwe Kooijmans, L.P. 2003. The Hardinxveld sites in the Rhine/Meuse Delta, The Netherlands, 5500–4500 cal BC. In L. Larsson, H. Kindgren, K. Knutsson, D. Loeffler and A. Åkerlund (eds), *Mesolithic on the move. Papers presented at the Sixth International Conference on the Mesolithic in Europe, Stockholm 2000*, 608–624. Oxford.

Louwe Kooijmans, L.P. 2006. Schipluiden: a synthetic view. In L.P. Louwe Kooijmans and P.F.B. Jongste (eds), *Schipluiden. A Neolithic settlement on the Dutch North Sea coast, c. 3500 cal BC. Analecta Praehistorica Leidensia 37/38*, 485–516. Leiden.

Louwe Kooijmans, L.P. 2007. The gradual transition to farming in the Lower Rhine Basin. In A. Whittle and V. Cummings (eds), *Going over. The Mesolithic–Neolithic transition in north-west Europe*, 287–309. London.

Milner, N. 2015. Taboo. In T. Insoll (ed.), *The Oxford handbook of the archaeology of ritual and religion*, 105–114. Oxford.

Oestigaard, T. 1999. Food rituals and taboos: an ethnoarchaeological study among Brahamans and Magars in the Balung district of western Nepal. In R.B. Chhetri and O. Gurung (eds), *Anthropology and sociology of Nepal: cultures, societies, ecology and developments*, 48–55. Kathmandu.

Out, W.A. 2009. *Sowing the seed? Human impact and plant subsistence in Dutch wetlands during the Late Mesolithic and Early and Middle Neolithic (5500–3400 cal BC). Archaeological Series Leiden University 18.* Leiden.

Oversteegen, J.F.S., Van Wijngaarden-Bakker, L.H., Maliepaard, C.H. and Van Kolfschoten, T. 2001. Zoogdieren, vogels en reptielen. In L.P. Louwe Kooijmans (ed.), *Hardinxveld-De Bruin: een kampplaats uit het Laat-Mesolithicum en het begin van de Swifterbant-cultuur (5500–4450 v. Chr.)*, 209–297. Amersfoort.

Peeters, J.H.M. 2007. *Hoge Vaart-A27 in context: towards a model of Mesolithic–Neolithic land use dynamics as a framework for archaeological heritage management.* Amersfoort.

Prummel, W. and Van der Sanden, W.A.B. 1995. Runderhoorns uit de Drentse venen. *Nieuwe Drentse Volksalmanak* 112, 8–55.

Raemaekers, D.C.M. 1999. *The articulation of a "New Neolithic". The meaning of the Swifterbant culture for the process of Neolithisation in the western part of the North European Plain. Archaeological Series Leiden University 3.* Leiden.

Raemaekers, D.C.M. 2001. Aardewerk en verbrande klei. In L.P. Louwe Kooijmans (ed.), *Hardinxveld-Giessendam Polderweg. Een mesolithisch jachtkamp in het rivierengebied 5500–5000 v. Chr.*, 105–117. Amersfoort.

Raemaekers, D.C.M. 2003. Cutting a long story short? The process of Neolithization in the Dutch delta re-examined. *Antiquity* 77, 780–789.

Raemaekers, D.C.M. 2015. Rethinking Swifterbant S3 ceramic variability. Searching for the transition to the Funnel Beaker culture before 4000 calBC. In J. Kabaciński, S. Hartz, D.C.M. Raemaekers and T. Terberger (eds), *The Dąbki site in Pomerania and the Neolithisation of the north European lowlands (c. 5000–3000 calBC). Archäologie und Geschichte im Ostseeraum 8*, 321–334. Rahden.

Raemaekers, D.C.M., Kubiak-Martens, L. and Oudemans, T.F.M. 2013. New food in old pots — charred organic residues in Early Neolithic ceramic vessels from Swifterbant, The Netherlands (4300–4000 cal. BC). *Archäologisches Korrespondenzblatt* 43, 315–334.

Robeerst, A. 1995. *De Neolithische fauna van de Donk het Kerkhof bij Brandwijk, Alblasserwaard.* Leiden.

Rowley-Conwy, P. 2013. North of the frontier: early domestic animals in northern Europe. In S. Colledge, J. Conolly, K. Dobney, K. Manning and S. Shennan (eds), *The origins and spread of domestic animals in southwest Asia and Europe*, 283–311. Walnut Creek.

Simons, F.J. 1994. *Eat not this flesh. Food avoidances in the Old World.* Madison.

Ten Anscher, T.J. 2012. *Leven met de Vecht. Schokland-P14 en de Noordoostpolder in het Neolithicum en de Bronstijd.* Amsterdam.

Ten Anscher, T.J. 2015. Under the radar: Swifterbant and the origins of the Funnel Beaker culture. In J. Kabaciński, S. Hartz, D.C.M. Raemaekers and T. Terberger (eds), *The Dąbki site in Pomerania and the Neolithisation of the north European lowlands (c. 5000–3000 calBC). Archäologie und Geschichte im Ostseeraum 8*, 335–357. Rahden.

Ufkes, A. 1997. Edelhertgewei uit natte context in Drenthe. *Nieuwe Drentse Volksalmanak* 114, 29–56.

Van Zeist, W. and Palfenier-Vegter, R.M. 1981. Seeds and fruits from the Swifterbant S3 site. Final reports on Swifterbant IV. *Palaeohistoria* 23, 105–168.

Zeiler, J.T. 1997. *Hunting, fowling and stock-breeding at Neolithic sites in the western and central Netherlands.* Groningen.

Zvelebil, M. 1986. Mesolithic prelude and Neolithic revolution. In M. Zvelebil (ed.), *Hunters in transition. Mesolithic societies of temperate Eurasia and their transition to farming*, 5–16. Cambridge.

Part Two

Interaction and change

The fifth millennium BC in central Europe. Minor changes, structural continuity: a period of cultural stability

Christian Jeunesse

Abstract

The fifth millennium in central Europe is often seen as a time of great historical change. The aspects most often cited are the emergence of copper metallurgy, the establishment of an extensive distribution network for jadeite axes, the first monumental funerary architecture, increasing social hierarchy and so on. It is argued that these innovations mark the origin of a new world view which fundamentally differs from that dominating in the Linearbandkeramik. In truth however, these changes, which are taking place within a region still settled by Bandkeramik successor cultures, are of a merely quantitative nature and should be seen as the concrete manifestations of a set of possibilities whose roots go back to the Early Neolithic. The only significant change is the development of the Michelsberg/Funnel Beaker cultural complex at the margins of central Europe. The stability of cultural forms of expression is particularly evident in three areas, treated in greater depth in this contribution: burial rites, the spatial organisation of settlements and the morphology of enclosures.

Zusammenfassung: Das 5. Jahrtausend in Mitteleuropa. Kleinere Veränderungen, strukturelle Kontinuität: Eine Zeit kultureller Stabilität

Das 5. Jahrtausend in Mitteleuropa wird oft als ein Zeitalter großer historischer Veränderungen aufgefasst. Besonders oft zitiert werden in diesem Zusammenhang die Herausbildung der Kupfermetallurgie, der Aufbau eines extensiven Verbreitungsnetzwerkes für Jadeitbeile, das Auftreten erster monumentaler Grabbauten, eine Verstärkung vertikaler sozialer Differenzierung, usw. Diese Neuerungen seien der Ursprung einer neuen Weltordnung, sehr anders als diejenige, die während der Linearbandkeramik vorherrschte. In Wahrheit sind diese Veränderungen innerhalb einer Region, die noch immer von bandkeramischen Folgekulturen bewohnt wird, nur quantitativer Art und sollten als die konkrete Ausformung von Möglichkeiten verstanden werden, deren Wurzeln bereits im Frühneolithikum angelegt wurden. Die einzige signifikante Veränderung ist die Herausbildung des Kulturkomplexes MK/TRB in den Randgebieten Mitteleuropas. Die Stabilität kultureller Ausdrucksformen zeigt sich vor allem in drei Bereichen, die in diesem Beitrag näher beleuchtet werden: Bestattungssitten, räumliche Organisation der Siedlungen und Morphologie der Erdwerke.

Résumé : Le 5ème millénaire en Europe centrale, une période de stabilité culturelle

Le 5ème millénaire est souvent présenté comme une période de grands changements historiques en Europe centrale. Parmi les indices les plus souvent cités figurent l'émergence de la métallurgie du cuivre, la mise en place d'un vaste réseau de diffusion des jadéites alpines, l'apparition des premières architectures funéraires monumentales, un accroissement du degré de différenciation verticale, etc. Ces mutations seraient à l'origine d'un monde nouveau, très différent de celui qui caractérisait la Culture à céramique linéaire. En réalité, dans une région qui reste occupée par le Néolithique danubien, ces changements sont uniquement quantitatifs et doivent être vus comme la réalisation concrète de virtualités déjà présentes, à l'état de germes, dans le Néolithique ancien. Le seul changement significatif est, à la périphérie du domaine centre-européen, l'apparition du complexe culturel MK/TRBK. La stabilité des usages se manifeste en particulier dans trois domaines que nous examinons successivement dans cet article : les pratiques funéraires, l'organisation spatiale des habitats et la morphologie des enceintes.

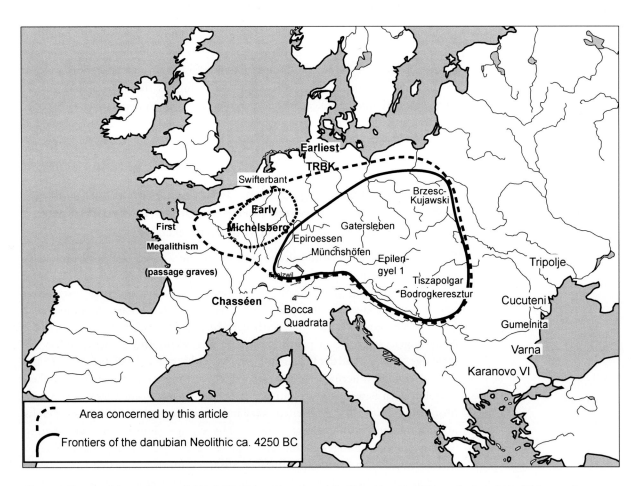

Figure 1. Extent of the study area (5600–3600 BC) and location of the Danubian Neolithic and selected Neolithic complexes or cultures of surrounding areas around 4250 cal BC.

Introduction

The fifth millennium BC is frequently presented as a time of momentous historical changes in central Europe. Among the evidence most often cited is the emergence of copper metallurgy, the development of a vast distribution network of Alpine jadeites, the first monumental funerary architecture, an increasing degree of vertical differentiation, etc. From these changes a brand new world, very different from the one which formerly characterised the Linear Pottery culture, is said to have arisen. In truth, in a region still occupied by Danubian Neolithic groups, these changes are simply quantitative and should be regarded as the practical realisation of potentialities, the roots of which were already present in the Early Neolithic. The only truly decisive change is the emergence during the last three centuries of the millennium, on the western and northern fringes of central Europe, of a new Neolithic civilisation embodied by the early phases of the Michelsberg culture and of the Funnel Beaker culture (TRB) (Figure 1).

This latter aspect will not be discussed in our paper, which deals with the cultures classically attributed to the so-called Danubian Neolithic. Even though this concept is considered outdated by some researchers, for me it remains utterly relevant and has kept all its heuristic legitimacy. In a nutshell, one could say it forms a complex which comprises all the cultures which derive from the Linear Pottery culture (LBK), from the first main cultures of the *Mittelneolithikum* (Großgartach, Stichbandkeramik, Lengyel) to the last occurrences of the Lengyel-Polgár cycle (Lublin-Wolhynie and Hunaydihalom) (Figure 2); I will later give a more precise definition. In the area occupied by this complex, between the Carpathian Basin and north-eastern France, most of the fifth millennium is characterised by a noticeable stability, visible in particular in funerary practices, spatial organisation of settlements and enclosure morphology.

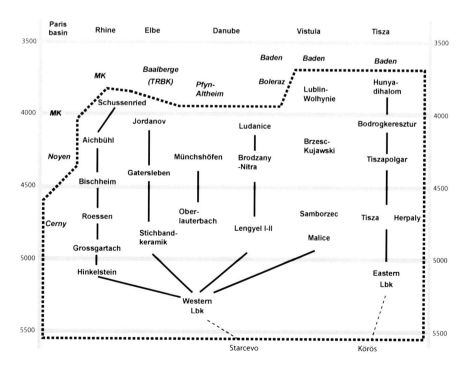

Figure 2. Genealogical tree and schematic chronology of the Danubian Neolithic. In italics: non- or only partly (Cerny) Danubian cultures.

Funerary practices: the Danubian funerary system

The Danubian Neolithic has a homogenous funerary system, enduring without noticeable modification from its implementation during the early LBK across the whole period, to its last occurrences during the first half of the fourth millennium. Single graves, cemeteries located outside settlement areas, frequent and various grave goods among which precious goods play a major part, the existence of a well-marked gender dualism, and a social status displayed mostly through the composition of the grave goods assemblage are the main distinctive traits of this system. Analysing the degree of wealth of the graves shows that there are two or three levels, depending on the cemeteries studied. As regards the LBK period, these situations are illustrated respectively by the Nitra[1] and Aiterhofen[2] cemeteries (Figure 3). Graves 185 from Aiterhofen and grave 1 from Bajč (Figure 4) illustrate the third level for male graves. These are "warrior" graves prefiguring the graves of the "battle-axe bearers" of the fifth millennium[3]. The existence at the same period of rich graves of women and very young children — the latter evoking hereditary status transmission — completes the picture of the still restricted elite which occupies the third level of the social hierarchy.

This system perpetuates itself, unchanged, in the fifth millennium cultures. Minor changes occur, for instance the development of a whole range of regional traditions[4] (Figure 5), of battle axes different in shape from working axes, the use of metal objects, or the emergence of gender display through lateralisation of body positions[5]. The basic principles however remain unchanged, as does the three-level vertical structure. The male graves from Alsónyék (Figure 6), Tiszavalk-Kenderföld and Zlota, along with the female grave from Krusza Zamkova (Figure 7), are perfect examples of level 3 graves. One can indeed note the appearance of new types and of copper artefacts, but these changes are not sufficient to postulate the existence of a fourth level and hence a significant increase in the degree of vertical social differentiation.

For the fifth millennium, level 4 should in my opinion be reserved for the great Carnac graves ("*tumulus carnacéens*") from southern Brittany and for the richest burials in the Varna cemetery, two small corpora located outside our study area. It does not seem justified to insist on the exceptional nature of Alsónyék's grave 3060, presented as marking a strong break with the previous situation[6]. To me this grave indicates an intense competition among the elites of the Lengyel culture, and nothing more than that. This is the final resting place of a local chieftain, possibly a bit richer and more influential than his peers and the "chiefs" from Bajč or Aiterhofen, but in no way comparable to the "princes" from Varna or the Carnac tombs. The difference to the graves of the LBK elite is a matter of degree, and not of kind. The presence of metal objects in the fifth millennium Danubian graves should not create an illusion to the contrary: they simply take the place of earlier precious raw materials and nothing allows us to state that their appearance triggers significant social changes.

---

1 Pavúk 1972.
2 Nieszery 1995.
3 Jeunesse 2011a.
4 Jeunesse 2006.
5 Kadrow 2011.
6 Zalai-Gaál *et al.* 2011, 79–80.

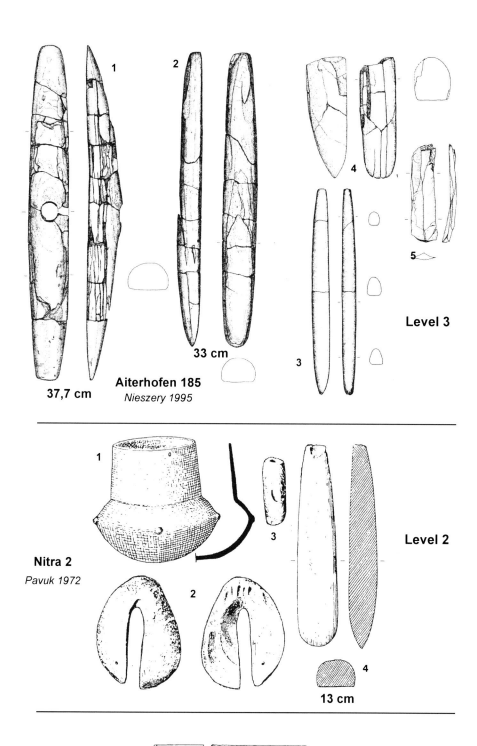
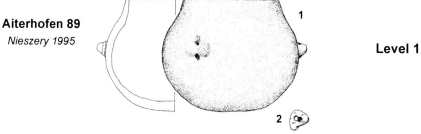

Figure 3. Grave goods of the Linearbandkeramik culture: the three levels of wealth (Aiterhofen 89 and 185: after Nieszery 1995, 355 and 379–380; Nitra 2: after Pavúk 1972, 41).

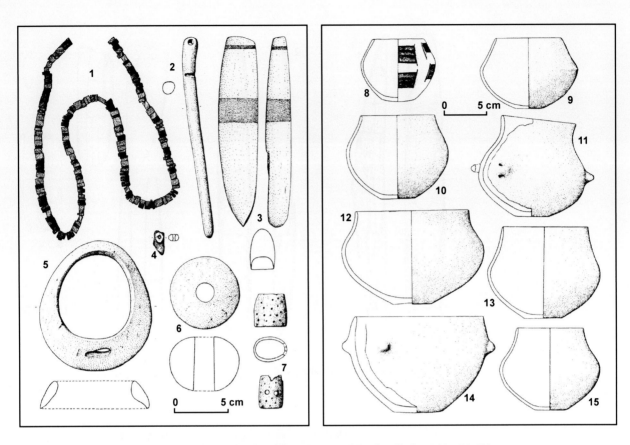

Figure 4. Grave goods from the Bajč level 3 male grave (Slovakia, late LBK; after Cheben 2000, 76–77).

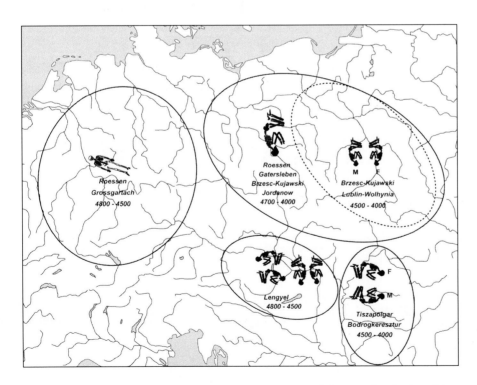

Figure 5. Internal variability of the Danubian funerary system. Schematic distribution of the main funerary traditions in the fifth millennium Danubian Neolithic.

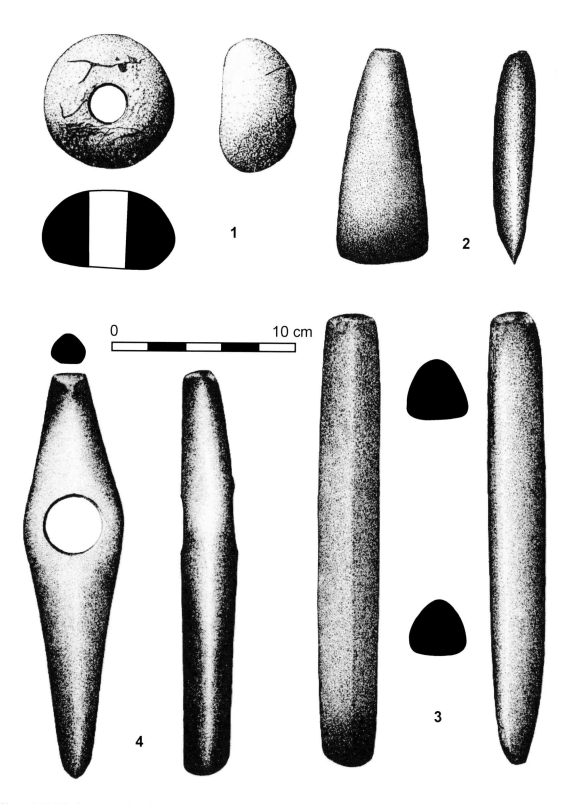

Figure 6. Polished stone artefacts from grave 3060 in the Alsónyék Lengyel cemetery (Hungary; after Zalai-Gaál et al. 2011, 73–74).

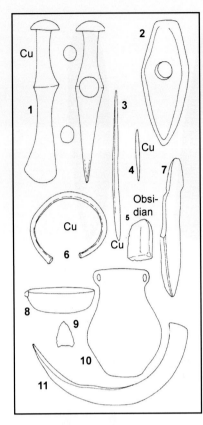  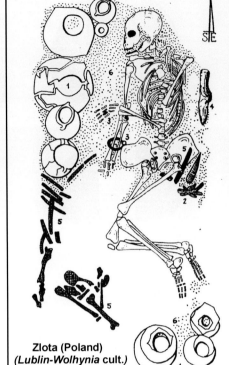

This uniqueness of the funerary system, the originality of which is even clearer when compared to other Neolithic systems, for instance those of the first (passage grave complex) and the second megalithism (gallery grave complex)[7] and of the Michelsberg/TRB complex, forms the first pillar for the definition of the "Danubian Neolithic". The second one is to be found in the principles of internal spatial layout of the settlements, which also remain unchanged over the whole period.

Figure 7. Three level 3 Danubian graves of the second half of the fifth millennium: Tiszavalk-Kenderföld (male; after Lichter 2001, 324); Złota (after Kulczycka-Leciejewiczowa 1979, 158); Krusza-Zamkova (female; after Czerniak 1980, fig. 40).

Organisation of settlements: the Danubian pattern

As regards settlements *largo sensu*, what has so far attracted attention are the continuities one can observe in the architecture. The most remarkable is illustrated by the huge longhouses which were built over 1500 years, from the beginning of the Linear Pottery culture to the end of the Brześć-Kujawski culture. Yet, a second architectural type (bipartite trapezoidal or rectangular houses with supporting walls), which appears during the early Lengyel (around 4800 cal BC) and forms a new phylum, breaks through the architectural homogeneity of the Danubian Neolithic. However, this subdivision, which has to be considered within the broader frame of Danubian architectural variability during the fifth millennium (Figure 8), does not impact the spatial organisation of settlements. They display a remarkable uniformity, the main characteristics of which we are now going to describe.

---

7   The terms first and second megalithism refer to two different funerary systems current in western and northern Europe, which are distinguished by their architectural choices (passage graves or gallery graves), by the number of deceased interred in these monuments, the duration of use of the sites and the use of space inside the funerary chambers (Chambon 2003).

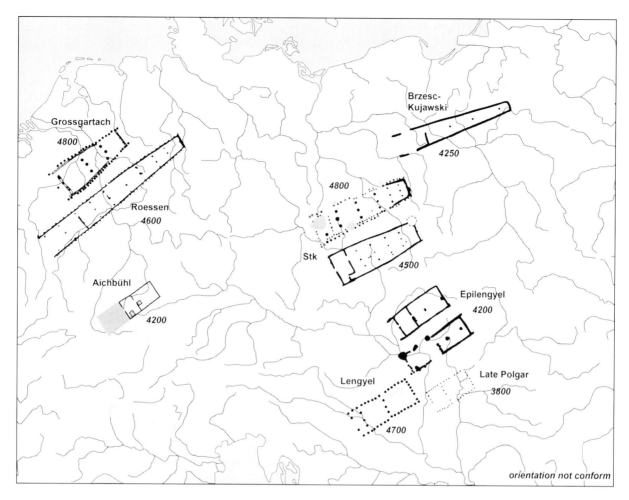

Figure 8. Schematic distribution of the regional architectural traditions in the fifth millennium Danubian Neolithic.

We will not deal here with the issue of the Linear Pottery dwellings arranged in lines of parallel houses, which has been hotly debated for a decade[8], since this layout is clearly attested only for some of the Danubian cultures and hence cannot, as it is, be used in a definition of spatial organisation relevant for all settlements in the entire Danubian complex. A Danubian settlement is made up of rectangular or trapezoidal houses usually placed well apart, all having the same orientation and opening on the same side. There are no visible privileged pathways, nor an empty space that could be considered as a village square[9]. This pattern can be applied to all the Danubian cultures for which settlements have been excavated on a large enough scale. A replication of the Linearbandkeramik culture's organisational structure has been clearly identified for the central European cultures with very large houses (Großgartach, Stichbandkeramik, Rössen, Brześć-Kujawski) and the extensive excavations carried out recently on settlements belonging to the Lengyel culture, in particular Alsónyék[10], show that it can also be applied to the area of the Lengyel type houses.

---

8 Jeunesse 2016; Link 2012; Rück 2008.
9 The role of a square as a gathering place for the community could have been fulfilled in some cultures — Linearbandkeramik, Lengyel, Rössen, Großgartach, Stichbandkeramik — by small enclosures (of the Langweiler 8 type during the Linearbandkeramik culture, and of the type *Kreisgrabenanlage* or *Kreispalisadenanlage* during the Middle Neolithic) located alongside the settlements.
10 Osztás *et al.* 2012.

If I am not mistaken, nobody has so far stressed the fact that this way of partitioning and organizing space is also shared by later cultures from the so-called "Epi-Lengyel/ Epi-Polgár" and "Epi-Rössen" complexes. The settlements at Jelšovce (Ludanice group; Figure 9) and Tiszalúc-Sarkad (Hungary, Hunyadihalom group; Figure 10) are good examples of this trait for the first complex mentioned. As regards the second one, the best examples are found in the eponymous site of the Aichbühl group and in the Schussenried settlement of Bad Buchau "Taubried" (Figure 11). It may be surprising for some of our readers, accustomed to have these two settlements automatically classed into the category of "lake or wetland site" given their architecture and location, that these two sites are taken into account here. Besides the fact that the architecture of the houses has its roots in the architectural tradition of the Lengyel culture, they clearly match the criteria which characterise Danubian settlements, including the above-mentioned layout in lines of parallel (but not necessarily contemporaneous) houses. The only difference with the traditional picture of the Danubian settlement is that the houses are closer to one another. However, a rapid survey of the Danubian corpus shows that this trait is a mere variation that can also be found in the earliest Linearbandkeramik, for instance in Brunn (Figure 12). Moreover, we must not forget that for the villages of Aichbühl and Bad Buchau, which were excavated a long time ago, all the houses have been mapped together without taking into account the possibility of internal periodisation.

In our attempt to define the nature of settlements in the Danubian Neolithic, another trait, which is not directly linked to internal organisation, has to be

Figure 9. Map of the Jelšovce settlement, Ludanice group (after Pavúk and Bátora 1995, 50).

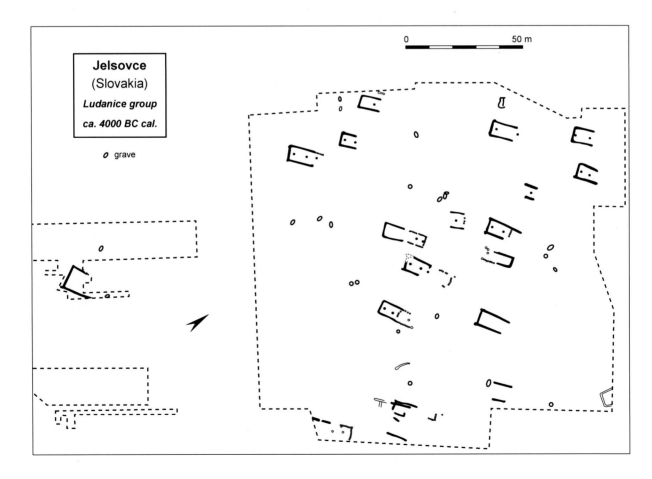

Figure 10. Map of the Tiszalúc-Sarkad settlement (Hungary, Hunyadihalom group; after Kienlin 2010, fig. 5.20).

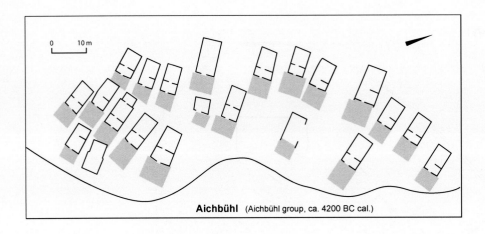

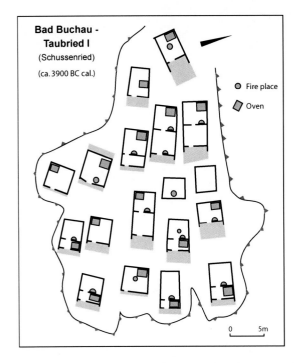

Figure 11. Simplified map of the Aichbühl (Aichbühl group) and Taubried (Schussenried culture) settlements, south-west Germany (after Strobel 2000, 63 and 259).

mentioned: the great stability of villages occupied often over several centuries. This contrasts with the quite short duration of the houses, even though these are solidly built with durable materials. This paradox explains why on many Danubian dwelling sites, house plans are often recut in very large numbers.

As with the funerary system, the originality of the Danubian settlement system stands out even better when compared with the other types of organisation known in the European Neolithic and Chalcolithic. Lines of small contemporaneous houses facing each other on both sides of a central axis in Neolithic lake dwellings of the circum-Alpine area, closely spaced buildings on the Bulgarian tells from the middle of the fifth millennium, the radial layout of the Michelsberg[11] settlement at Mairy (north-eastern France), the radiating layout of elliptical settlements from the late phase of the Tripolje culture in Ukraine (Figure 13) — all are different

---

11 Or maybe post-Michelsberg (second half of the fourth millennium), as studies in progress suggest.

Figure 12. Map of a portion of the Brunn settlement (Lower Austria), earliest LBK (after Lenneis 2008, 169).

Figure 13. Spatial organisation of settlements in some non-Danubian Neolithic or Chalcolithic cultural complexes. Poljanica (after Todorova 1982, 206); Maidanets'ke (after Videjko 1995, 49); Mairy (after Marolles 1989, 119); Zürich-Mozartstrasse (after Stöckli et al. 1995, 208); Pestenacker and Stockwiesen (after Schlichtherle 2006, 171).

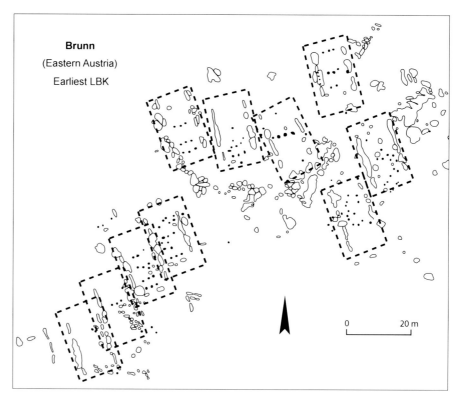

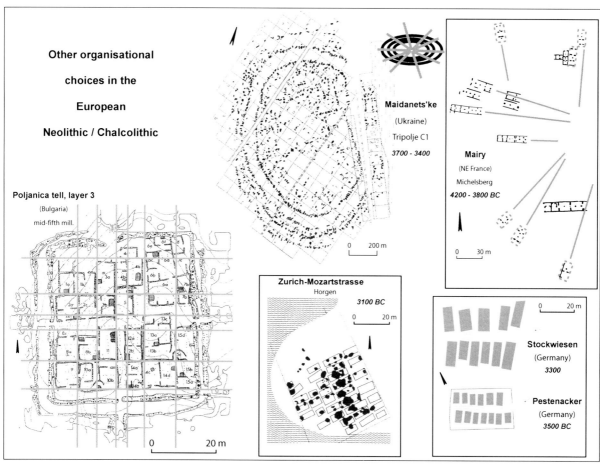

JEUNESSE | 117

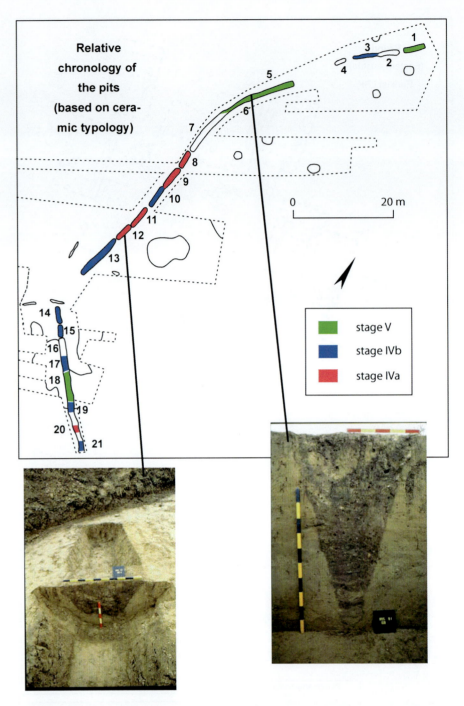

Figure 14. The LBK pseudo-ditch enclosure of Rosheim (Alsace, France; after Jeunesse and Lefranc 1999, 31).

configurations which, each in its own way and as a means of contrast, illustrate the singularity of the Danubian pattern and the model of social life that it reflects.

Causewayed enclosures

The long-lasting tradition of building causewayed enclosures is the third element of continuity inside the Danubian block. Causewayed enclosures are one of the main types of enclosures in the European Neolithic. They are composed of lines

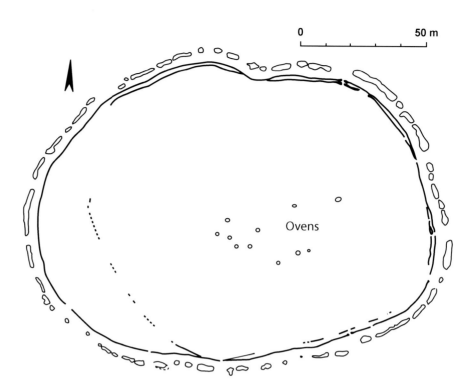

Figure 15. Balloy "les Réaudins" causewayed enclosure (Seine-et-Marne, France; Cerny culture; after Mordant 1997, 94).

of pits separated from one another by narrow interruptions. I recently suggested[12] that, at least in some cases, these pits could have been dug successively, possibly by different groups of people, over a period that could span several generations. Since the oldest pits are already at least partially backfilled when the most recent ones are dug, and since the ditch hence never forms a continuous ring, I suggest using the term "pseudo-ditch" enclosure. Each time excavations of a causewayed enclosure have been carried out according to the appropriate procedure, the existence of this type of enclosure could be proven. Concerning the Danubian Neolithic, they are known in the Early (LBK) and Middle (Rössen and Epi-Rössen) Neolithic of western central Europe (Rhine Basin), yet there is no reason to exclude a wider distribution area. The causewayed enclosure, with or without a pseudo-ditch, actually exists within the entire Danubian world, from the Paris Basin to Poland, and ranging chronologically from the Early Neolithic (LBK) to the Middle Chalcolithic (late Danubian cultures of central and southern Poland).

Like the Rosheim monument (Figure 14), the earliest causewayed enclosures can be attributed to the Linearbandkeramik culture. At Rosheim, the various shapes displayed by the pits, the numerous intercuttings between pits as well as their respective dates show unequivocally that this is indeed a pseudo-ditch. The discontinuous ditch continues in the Middle Neolithic cultures. Balloy (Seine-et-Marne, France), which belongs to the Cerny culture, is the best preserved and best studied monument of the whole Danubian world (Figure 15). Since erosion has hardly affected the surface, one can reject the suggestion that the interruptions between the pits result from the erosion of continuous ditches of irregular depth. Deposits of pottery and animal bones from the pit fills and ovens found inside are strong arguments in favour of a ceremonial function, comparable to what has

---

12   See Jeunesse 2011b for the most recent synthesis on the subject.

been suggested for the small enclosures located next to dwellings in the northwestern LBK[13]. Giving a detailed description of all the causewayed enclosures in the Danubian complex would go too far here[14]. The three examples from Poland (Figure 16) will simply help us to show that this type of feature is geographically and chronologically widely distributed, stretching both to the easternmost borders of the Danubian Neolithic and to the latest manifestations of this complex.

For the sake of completeness we must add that this type of ditch, even though it indisputably appears in the LBK culture, is not specific to the Danubian complex, since it can also be observed in the Michelsberg/TRB complex as early as the second half of the fifth millennium in northern France, Belgium and the Rhine Basin, and later in areas into which this complex expands during the fourth millennium (central and northern Europe and the British Isles)[15]. Since the causewayed enclosure (either with a pseudo-ditch or with a ditch made of synchronous pits, if this second type exists) is a creation of the Danubian complex and widely distributed both in time and in space, it can safely be considered a constitutive feature in the definition of the Danubian Neolithic.

Synthesis

The causewayed enclosure thus finds its place alongside the funerary system, the principles which guide the spatial organisation of the settlements and the stability of these settlements. To these features we can also add the social and symbolic importance of pottery (Figure 17).

Taken individually, most of these aspects are not specific to the Danubian complex:

- Similar funerary systems are known in other Neolithic cultural complexes, for instance in Spain in the Sepulcro de fosa culture (first half of the fourth millennium), in northern Italy in the Bocca Quadrata culture (fifth millennium), or else in Early Chalcolithic cultures (3500–2500 BC) of Italy, for instance Remedello and Spilamberto;
- As previously mentioned, the causewayed enclosure also exists outside the Danubian complex;
- There are other complexes in which pottery serves as identity emblem and social marker;
- Tells from south-eastern Europe exhibit the same stability as the Danubian settlements, etc.

What makes the specificity of the Danubian cultural complex in recent European prehistory is the way these different traits combine and relate to one another.

These features share the fact that they all appeared within the LBK and endured without major changes throughout the fifth millennium. The changes which take effect throughout the millennium, for instance architectural innovations, or reinforcement of gender dualism in some cultures (shown by placing the deceased on one side of the body or the other), should be regarded as epiphenomena which change nothing in the fundamentals of the Danubian civilisation. The stability

---

13 Boelicke 1988.
14 For a more detailed inventory, see Jeunesse 2011b.
15 Andersen 1997; Jeunesse 2011b.

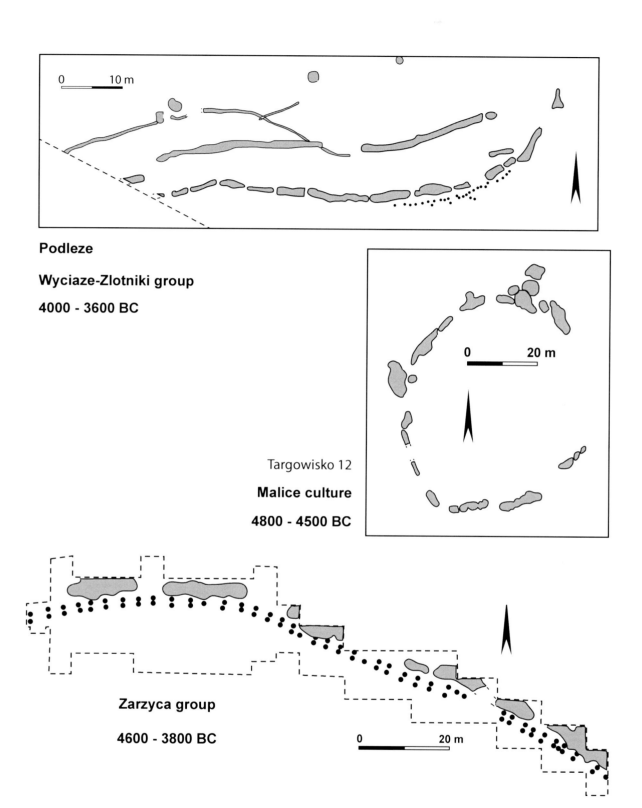

Figure 16. Three causewayed enclosures in the Polish late Danubian cultures. A: Podleze (Wyciaze-Złotniki group; after Nowak et al. 2007, 453); B: Targowisko (Malice culture; after Czerniak et al. 2007, 478); C: enclosure from the Zarzyca group (after Kulczycka-Leciejewiczowa 1993, 80).

of practices over two millennia (5600–3600 BC) testifies to a strong cultural coherence which very likely reflects the existence of common values, norms and a unique symbolic system[16].

As already mentioned for the grave goods, copper only marginally modifies the functioning of the fifth millennium Danubian societies. It simply replaces materials that were previously used (*Spondylus*, semi-precious stones such as jadeite, and so on) to make certain types of prestige goods which keep their traditional symbolic function and are found in funerary assemblages structurally identical to those predating the emergence of metalworking. As I suggested in a study on adze deposits[17], and as W. Schier brilliantly reminded us in a recent article[18], it is thus illusory to believe that copper triggered the emergence of a new "historical period"[19].

The really major historical changes are more likely to be found in the emergence, to the west and north of the Danubian complex, of two new cultural complexes, namely the first megalithism (which produced the passage graves) and the Michelsberg/TRB block. The differences between these two complexes and the Danubian Neolithic are perfectly known, so there is no need to go into more detail. Considering only the funerary practices and the expressions of these complexes before 4000 cal BC[20], one can note the existence of collectives graves, the absence of cemeteries[21], few grave goods which are used neither to indicate the gender nor the social status of the dead, and among which there are never any precious objects[22]. These differences are so large that one could almost speak of "another Neolithic", as I took the liberty of doing in a comparative study of the Danubian Neolithic and the Michelsberg culture[23].

I am thus convinced that the most realistic representation of the history of the European Neolithic and Chalcolithic is one which, far from the legacy of an evolutionist vision picturing different stages of development following on from each other like in a chest of drawers, favours a division into large, partly overlapping cultural complexes (Figure 18). During the second half of the fifth millennium, four such blocks coexist in the western half of Europe (from the Vistula river to the Atlantic Ocean): the last phase of the north European Mesolithic (Ertebølle, Swifterbant); the Danubian Neolithic, still strongly established in central Europe; the earliest phase of the Michelsberg/TRB complex; and the first megalithism. Their differences appear clearly in the specific issues raised in this paper and in others which are just as important as well, such as the subsistence system or, more broadly, the actual and symbolic relationships with the natural environment. On this point one can refer for instance to the very enlightening studies by Kalis and Meurers-Balke[24] on the forms of environmental exploitation by the Danubian

---

16 On the symbolic system of the Linearbandkeramik culture, see Jeunesse 2009.
17 Jeunesse 1998.
18 Schier 2014.
19 Lichardus 1991.
20 The emergence after 4000 cal BC of mixed forms makes the contrasts less stark. This is for instance the case for TRB funerary practices, in which the ideology of the MK/TRB complex is weakened by the adoption of practices pertaining to the Danubian system.
21 Or, in the partly acculturated TRB complex, their coexistence with other funeral forms.
22 It is important here to stress that in our opinion the Carnac graves with their sumptuous grave goods (jadeite axe heads, variscite ornaments) do not belong to the passage grave world and hence are not part of the first megalithism.
23 Jeunesse 2010.
24 Kalis and Meurers-Balke 1988.

Danubian Neolithic (5600 -3600 BC)

Funeral practices

- Graveyards with individual graves
- Grave goods reflecting status and gender
- Strong gender dualism
- Precious goods (shell, stone, metal)

Settlements

- Large settlements / big rectangular or trapezoidal houses / all opening on the same side
- stability of settlements (up to 500 years)
- Particular organizational pattern

Others :

- Social and symbolic importance of decorated ware
- Causewayed enclosures with pseudo-ditches

Figure 17. Main characteristics of the Danubian Neolithic.

Neolithic and Michelsberg/TRB complex respectively, and to the synthesis by Schier[25] on the role of extensive slash-and-burn agriculture in the expansion of a Neolithic economy.

I am perfectly aware that favouring this kind of division leads to the rehabilitation of a conception close to the one which was built around the notion of *Kulturkreis* in the anthropological research of the first half of the twentieth century. This notion was created by the German ethnologist Leo Frobenius in 1898, and later more completely defined by Fritz Graebner in his "*Methode der Ethnologie*"[26]. Far from being archaic, this notion and the methodological framework of which it is the emblem remain perfectly relevant today, once one discards the diffusionist excesses it has led to[27]. Besides, they form the implicit conceptual structure of many current discourses on the European Neolithic and indisputably reflect the historical reality of recent prehistory better than the usual classification into periods (Early, Middle, Late…) subdivided into cultures. A profitable substitute for this classification system could be a three-level tree diagram with cultural complexes (or civilisations) subdivided into traditions (funerary or architectural, such as those roughly mapped on Figures 7 and 8, or ceramic traditions), which can themselves be divided into various facies. Levels 2 and 3 would allow us to bypass the far too rigid framework of the archaeological culture and account for

---

25   Schier 2009.
26   Graebner 1911.
27   As well as, of course, the scandalous interpretations resulting from its exploitation by Nazi research.

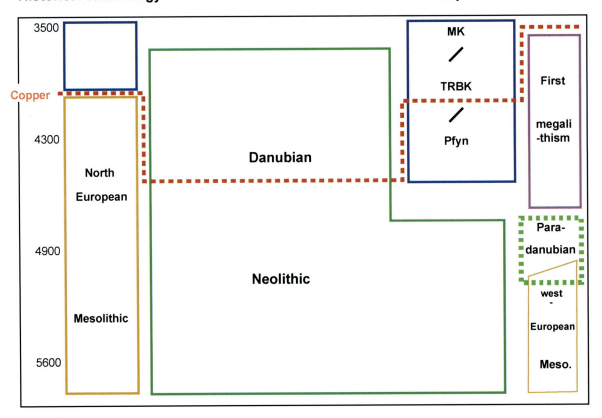

the polythetic dimension of the reality of the Neolithic period. The example of the two funerary traditions sharing the area of the ceramic culture traditionally called "Rössen" (Figure 19) shows very well the existence of distinct geographic logics which are the source of the non-correspondence of the two mapped subsystems.

This approach, freed from the horizontal "development stages" of the chronological frame commonly used today, has led to the particular view of the

Figure 18. Chronology of the Neolithic and Chalcolithic in central and western Continental Europe.

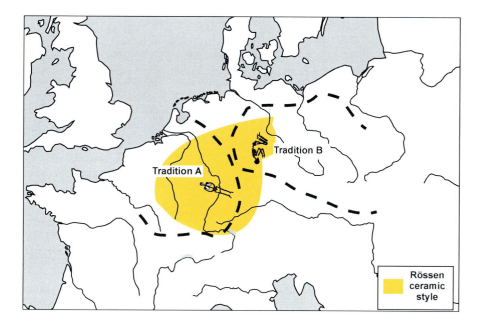

Figure 19. Distribution areas of the so-called "Rössen" ceramic style and of the two funerary traditions represented within its territory.

fifth millennium in central Europe which is summarised in this contribution. Innovations pointed out by other researchers as major changes are for me mere epiphenomena which do not modify the substance of a Danubian Neolithic staying true to its fundamentals. The profound changes actually occur on the margins, through the birth and development of new cultural complexes.

References

Andersen, N.H. 1997. *The Sarup enclosures. Jutland Archaeological Society Monographs.* Moesgaard.

Boelicke, U. 1988. Das Erdwerk. In U. Boelicke, D. von Brandt, J. Lüning, P. Stehli and A. Zimmermann (eds), *Der bandkeramische Siedlungsplatz Langweiler 8. Rheinische Ausgrabungen 28*, 395–427. Köln.

Chambon, P. 2003. *Les morts dans les sépultures collectives néolithiques en France. Du cadavre aux restes ultimes. 35ème supplément à Gallia Préhistoire.* Paris.

Cheben, I. 2000. *Bajč — eine Siedlung der Želiezovce-Gruppe. Entwicklungsende der Želiezovce-Gruppe und Anfänge der Lengyel-Kultur. Universitätsforschungen zur Prähistorischen Archäologie 68.* Bonn.

Czerniak, L. 1980. *Rozwój społeczeństw kultury późnej ceramiki wstęgowej na Kujawach.* Poznań.

Czerniak, L., Golanski, A. and Kadrow, S. 2007. New facts on the Malice culture gained from the rescue excavations at the A4 motorway section east of Krakow. In J.K. Kozłowski and P. Raczky (eds), *The Lengyel, Polgár and related cultures in the Middle/Late Neolithic in central Europe*, 471–486. Krakow.

Graebner, F. 1911. *Methode der Ethnologie.* Heidelberg.

Jeunesse, C. 1998. A propos de la signification historique des dépôts dans le Néolithique danubien ancien et moyen. In B. Fritsch, M. Maute, I. Matuschik, J. Müller and C. Wolf (eds), *Tradition und Innovation — Prähistorische Archäologie als historische Wissenschaft. Festschrift für Christian Strahm*, 31–50. Rahden.

Jeunesse, C. 2006. Les traditions funéraires du Néolithique moyen en Europe centrale dans le cadre du système funéraire danubien. In K. Alt, R.-M. Arbogast, C. Jeunesse and S. van Willigen (eds), *Archéologie funéraire du Néolithique danubien. Nouveaux enjeux, nouvelles approches. Actes de la table ronde de Fribourg-en-Brisgau, 17, 18 octobre 1998*, 3–26. Zimmersheim.

Jeunesse, C. 2009. Le front de colonisation occidental (entre Rhin et Seine) et l'identité rubanée. Réflexion sur les systèmes symboliques dans le Néolithique danubien. In J. Kozłowski (ed.), *Interactions between different models of Neolithization north of the central European agro-ecological barrier*, 151–176. Krakow.

Jeunesse, C. 2010. Die Michelsberger Kultur. In Badisches Landesmuseum Karlsruhe (eds), *Die „Michelsberger Kultur" und Mitteleuropa vor 6000 Jahren*, 46–55. Karlsruhe.

Jeunesse, C. 2011a. Masses perforées et haches de combat. La question des sépultures « armées » dans le Néolithique centre-européen. In L. Baray, M. Honegger and M.-H. Dias-Meirinho (eds), *L'armement et l'image du guerrier dans les sociétés anciennes. Actes de la table ronde internationale de Sens, juin 2009*, 43–70. Dijon.

Jeunesse, C. 2011b. Enceintes à fossé discontinu et enceintes à pseudo-fossé dans le Néolithique d' Europe centrale et occidentale. In A. Denaire, C. Jeunesse and P. Lefranc (eds), *Nécropoles et enceintes danubiennes du 5ème millénaire dans le Nord-Est de la France. Actes de la table ronde de Strasbourg, 2 juin 2010*, 31–71. Strasbourg.

Jeunesse, C. 2016. Spatial organization in European Neolithic settlements: example of the central-european Danubian Neolithic (5600–3600 BC). *Musaica Archaeologica* 1–2, 7–26.

Jeunesse, C. and Lefranc, P. 1999. Rosheim "Sainte-Odile" (Bas-Rhin), un habitat rubané avec fossé d'enceinte. Première partie: les structures et la céramique. *Cahiers de l'Association pour la Promotion de la Recherche Archéologique en Alsace* 15, 1–111.

Kadrow, S. 2011. Kupferzeitliche Sozialstrukturen. In S. Hansen and J. Müller (eds), *Sozialarchäologische Perspektiven: Gesellschaftlicher Wandel 5000–1500 v. Chr. zwischen Atlantik und Kaukasus. Internationale Tagung Kiel, Okt. 2007*, 107–121. Mainz.

Kalis, A.J. and Meurers-Balke, J. 1988. Wirkungen neolithischer Wirtschaftsweisen in Pollendiagrammen. *Archäologische Informationen* 11, 39–53.

Kienlin, T.L. 2010. *Traditions and transformations: approaches to Eneolithic (Copper Age) and Bronze Age metalworking and society in eastern central Europe and the Carpathian Basin*. Oxford.

Kulczycka-Leciejewiczowa, A. 1979. Pierwsze społeczenstwa rolnicze na ziemiach polskich. Kultury kregu naddunajskiego. In M. Godlowska, A. Kulczycka-Leciejewiczowa, J. Machnik and T. Wislanski (eds), *Prahistoria Ziem Polskich, Tom II, Neolit*, 19–164. Wroclaw.

Kulczycka-Leciejewiczowa, A. 1993. *Osadnictwo neolityczne w Polsce południowo-zachodniej: próba zarysu organizacji przestrzennej (Neolithic settlement in south-western Poland. An outline of spatial organization)*. Wrocław.

Lenneis, E. 2008. Perspectives on the beginnings of the earliest LBK in east-central Europe. In D.W. Bailey, A. Whittle and D. Hofmann (eds), *Living well together*, 164–178. Oxford.

Lichardus J. 1991. Kupferzeit als historische Epoche. Eine forschungsgeschichtliche Einleitung. In J. Lichardus (ed.), *Die Kupferzeit als historische Epoche. Saarbrücker Beiträge zur Altertumskunde 55*, 13–32. Saarbrücken.

Lichter, C. 2001. *Untersuchungen zu den Bestattungssitten des südosteuropäischen Neolithikums und Chalcolithikums*. Mainz.

Link, T. 2012. „Hofplatz" und „Zeilensiedlung": konkurrierende Modelle oder zwei Seiten derselben Medaille? In R. Smolnik (ed.), *Siedlungsstruktur und Kulturwandel in der Bandkeramik. Beiträge der internationalen Tagung „Neue Fragen zur Bandkeramik oder alles beim Alten?!", Leipzig 23. bis 24. September 2010*, 43–46. Leipzig.

Marolle, C. 1989. Le village Michelsberg des Hautes-Chanvières à Mairy (Ardennes). I. Etude préliminaire des principales structures. *Gallia Préhistoire* 31, 93–118.

Mordant, D. 1997. Le complexe des Réaudins à Balloy: enceinte et nécropole monumentale. In C. Constantin, D. Mordant and D. Simonin (eds), *La culture de Cerny. Nouvelle économie, nouvelle société au Néolithique. Actes du colloque international de Nemours, 9–11 mai 1994*, 449–479. Nemours.

Nieszery, N. 1995. *Linearbandkeramische Gräberfelder in Bayern. Internationale Archäologie 16*. Espelkamp.

Nowak, M., Dziegielewski, K. and Szczerba, R. 2007. Late Lengyel-Polgár in western Little Poland reflected by excavations in Podleze near Krakov. In J.K. Kozłowski and P. Raczky (eds), *The Lengyel, Polgár and related cultures in the Middle/Late Neolithic in central Europe*, 449–470. Krakow.

Osztás, A., Zalai-Gaál, I. and Bánffy, E. 2012. Alsónyék-Bátaszék, a new chapter in the research of Lengyel culture. *Documenta Praehistorica* 39, 377–396.

Pavúk J. 1972. Neolithisches Gräberfeld in Nitra. *Slovenská Archeológia* 20, 5–106.

Pavúk, J. and Batora, J. 1995. *Siedlung und Gräber der Ludanice Gruppe in Jelsovce*. Nitra.

Rück, O. 2008. New aspects and models for Bandkeramik settlement research. In D. Hofmann and P. Bickle (eds), *Creating communities. New advances in central European Neolithic research*, 159–185. Oxford.

Schier, W. 2009. Extensiver Brandfeldbau und die Ausbreitung der neolithischen Wirtschaftsweise in Mitteleuropa und Südskandinavien am Ende des 5. Jahrtausends v. Chr. *Prähistorische Zeitschrift* 84, 15–43.

Schier, W. 2014. The Copper Age in southeast Europe — historical epoch or typo-chronological construct? In W. Schier and F. Draşovean (eds), *The Neolithic and Eneolithic in southeast Europe. New approaches to dating and cultural dynamics in the 6th to the 4th millennium BC*, 419–435. Rahden.

Schlichtherle, H. 2006. Chemins, roues et chariots: innovations de la fin du Néolithique dans le sud-ouest de l'Allemagne. In P. Pétrequin, R.-M. Arbogast, A.-M. Pétrequin, S. van Willigen and M. Bailly (eds), *Premiers chariots, premiers araires. La diffusion de la traction animale en Europe pendant les IVe et IIIe millénaires avant notre ère*, 165–178. Paris.

Stöckli, W.E., Niffeler, U. and Gross-Klee, E. (eds) 1995. *La Suisse du Paléolithique à l'aube du Moyen-Age. II, Néolithique*. Basel.

Strobel, M. 2000. *Die Schussenrieder Siedlung Taubried I (Bad Buchau, Kr. Biberach)*. Stuttgart.

Todorova, H. 1982. *Kupferzeitliche Siedlungen in Nordostbulgarien. Materialien zur Allgemeinen und Vergleichenden Archäologie 13*. München.

Videjko, M. 1995. Großsiedlungen der Tripol'e-Kultur in der Ukraine. *Eurasia Antiqua* 1, 45–80.

Zalai-Gaál, I., Gál, E., Köhler, K. and Osztás A. 2011. Das Steingerätedepot aus dem Häuptlingsgrab 3060 der Lengyel-Kultur von Alsónyék, Südtransdanubien. In H.-J. Beier, R. Einicke and E. Biermann (eds), *Varia Neolithica VII. Dechsel, Axt, Beil & Co — Werkzeug, Waffe, Kultgegenstand? Aktuelles aus der Neolithforschung*, 65–83. Langenweissbach.

Early Middle Neolithic pottery decoration

Different cultural groups or just one supraregional style of its time?

Karin Riedhammer

Abstract

With the end of the Linear Pottery culture (LBK), a clear break in pottery development is observed everywhere in central Europe. While the Stichbandkeramik culture (SBK) emerged in the east, the new beginning in the west was characterised by the Hinkelstein group. Many different opinions have been voiced regarding the genesis of the new styles and the timing of this new beginning, as summarised in this paper. Besides the adoption of characteristics from the preceding regional stylistic groups of the LBK, the pottery of this early Middle Neolithic horizon shows a series of stylistic similarities over far distances, which in the past were interpreted as directions of influence in a diffusionist sense and partly explained by migration. In recent years, the publications on transitional settlements in northern Bohemia and the Dresden Elbe valley have given new impulses. Advances in absolute dating show that the Middle Neolithic probably began at about the same time everywhere.

The supraregional stylistic similarities of the early Middle Neolithic were examined in the course of a larger study on the development of pottery, absolute dating and certain aspects of settlement in the South-East Bavarian Middle Neolithic (*Südostbayerisches Mittelneolithikum*, SOB), recently completed by the author. A focus was placed on analysing stylistic aspects and absolute dates from the end of the LBK and the beginning of the Middle Neolithic in central Europe as a whole in order to understand the transition in general and to integrate the results developed for southern Bavaria into a larger context. Here, I present a subset of this data regarding the regional pottery characteristics of the early Middle Neolithic, which play a key role in understanding the beginning of the Middle Neolithic and the newly emerging contact networks after the breakdown of the LBK.

Zusammenfassung: Keramikverzierung im frühen Mittelneolithikum – verschiedene Kulturgruppen oder nur ein überregionaler Stil?

Nach dem Ende der Linearbandkeramik ist überall in Mitteleuropa ein deutlicher Bruch in der Keramikentwicklung zu beobachten. Während im Osten die Stichbandkeramische Kultur entstand ist der Neuanfang im Westen durch die

Gruppe Hinkelstein gekennzeichnet. Zur Genese der neuen Stile und zum zeitlichen Ablauf dieses Neuanfanges gab es in der Vergangenheit viele unterschiedliche Meinungen, die in diesem Artikel zusammenfassend dargestellt werden. Neben der Übernahme von Eigenheiten aus den vorangegangenen regionalen Stilgruppen der LBK ist die Keramik dieses frühen mittelneolithischen Horizontes durch eine Reihe von stilistischen Ähnlichkeiten über weite Entfernungen hinweg gekennzeichnet, die in der Vergangenheit als Einflussrichtungen im diffusionistischen Sinne gedeutet und zum Teil mit Migration erklärt wurden. Die Publikationen zu Übergangssiedlungen in Nordböhmen und dem Dresdner Elbtal haben in den letzten Jahren hier neue Impulse gegeben. Fortschritte in der absoluten Datierung zeigen, dass der Neubeginn wahrscheinlich überall in etwa gleichzeitig einsetzte.

Die überregionalen stilistischen Ähnlichkeiten des frühen Mittelneolithikums wurden im Rahmen einer größeren Studie zur Entwicklung der Keramik, zu Siedlungsaspekten und zur absoluten Datierung des Südostbayerischen Mittelneolithikums (SOB) genauer beleuchtet. Innerhalb dieser Studie lag ein Fokus in der stilistischen und absolutchronologischen Untersuchung des Endes des Altneolithikums und des Beginns des Mittelneolithikums in Mitteleuropa insgesamt, um den Übergang allgemein zu verstehen und die für Südbayern erarbeiteten Ergebnisse in einen größeren Kontext einbinden zu können. Die hier vorgestellte Teilanalyse der regional auftretenden Keramik-Charakteristika des frühen Mittelneolithikums spielt dabei eine besondere Rolle um den mittelneolithischen Neuanfang und die sich neu bildenden Kontaktnetzwerke nach dem Zusammenbruch der LBK besser zu verstehen.

The beginning of the Stichbandkeramik culture and Hinkelstein from the point of view of different research traditions and researchers

At the end of the Linear Pottery culture (LBK) a striking typological break in pottery style is obvious across central Europe. Only in northern Bohemia (Figure 1) one can recognise a gentler transition from the LBK to the archaic Stichbandkeramik (Stroke-Ornamented Pottery culture, or SBK). This is the reason why M. Zápotocká[1] suggested many times that the SBK originated in northern Bohemia and spread out from there. In recent years, she has explicitly spoken about the spread of a pottery style and not about the spread of people[2]. The SBK appears in the region of the preceding Šárka style, which belongs to the last phase of the LBK. The transition is — in Zápotocká's opinion — more an expression of changing social and religious aspects than an expression of changing economic aspects, because the geographical positions of sites and the economic techniques do not seem to change very much[3]. She recognises her phase SBK IIa in the Saxon Elbe region, in north-west Bohemia and in the central Bohemian Basin around Prague (Figure 1).

From her phase SBK IIb onwards, Zápotocká[4] counts south-western Bohemia, the Plzeň Basin and Lower Bavaria with the sites Aiterhofen-Ödmühle, district

---

1 Zápotocká 1970; 2007, 200–207 figs 2, 6; 2013, 38–44 pl. 1b.
2 Zápotocká 2013, 38–44.
3 Zápotocká 2007, 199–200; see also Spatz 2002; 2003.
4 Zápotocká 2007, 200–202 fig. 2B.

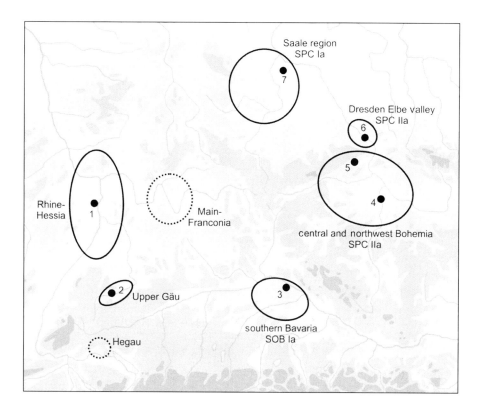

Figure 1. Regions with early Middle Neolithic pottery, schematically indicated. Dashed line: early Middle Neolithic not sufficiently known. Important sites: 1 Worms; 2 Rottenburg am Neckar; 3 Straubing; 4 Prague; 5 Vikletice; 6 Dresden; 7 Wulfen. SPC = SBK. Base map: RGK.

of Straubing-Bogen[5], and Straubing-Lerchenhaid[6] to the distribution area of the archaic SBK. But a close look at these Bavarian pottery assemblages shows that there are many similarities to the characteristic Bohemian assemblages from the graves of Praha-Bubeneč (compare Figure 2 and Figure 4)[7] and the famous grave of Vikletice (compare Figure 3 and Figure 5). So these inventories from Lower Bavaria must be contemporary to phase SBK IIa after Zápotocká[8].

In the western part of Germany, in Rhine-Hesse, a new pottery style appears at the beginning of the Middle Neolithic[9] period that we call Hinkelstein (HST). Using stylistic comparisons, Zápotocká parallels Hinkelstein (Figure 6) with her phases SBK IIb and III[10]. In the context of the emergence of Hinkelstein, she earlier suggested the possibility of an influx of SBK people into the Rhine region[11]. Later she saw this "regional process" as being caused by a more general kind of influence from the central SBK[12]. Contrary to Zápotocká, W. Meier-Arendt[13] advanced the opinion that Hinkelstein developed out of the regional LBK without any participation of the SBK. Based on her analysis of the decoration, Zápotocká[14] concludes that eastern Bohemia, Silesia, Austria and the east German

---

5   Nieszery 1995, pl. 64.6–7: cremation grave 229.
6   Riedhammer 1994a; 1994b.
7   Zápotocká 1998a, pl. 32–39.
8   Riedhammer 2015.
9   This is a term used in the west German research tradition. In Bohemian research this horizon belongs to the Late Neolithic period.
10 Zápotocká 1998b, 299.
11 Zápotocká 1970, 19; 1972, 310.
12 Zápotocká 2007, 202 fig. 2B, 204; see also Zápotocká 1998b, 299.
13 Meier-Arendt 1975, 158.
14 Zápotocká 2007, 204–207 figs 4–6a.

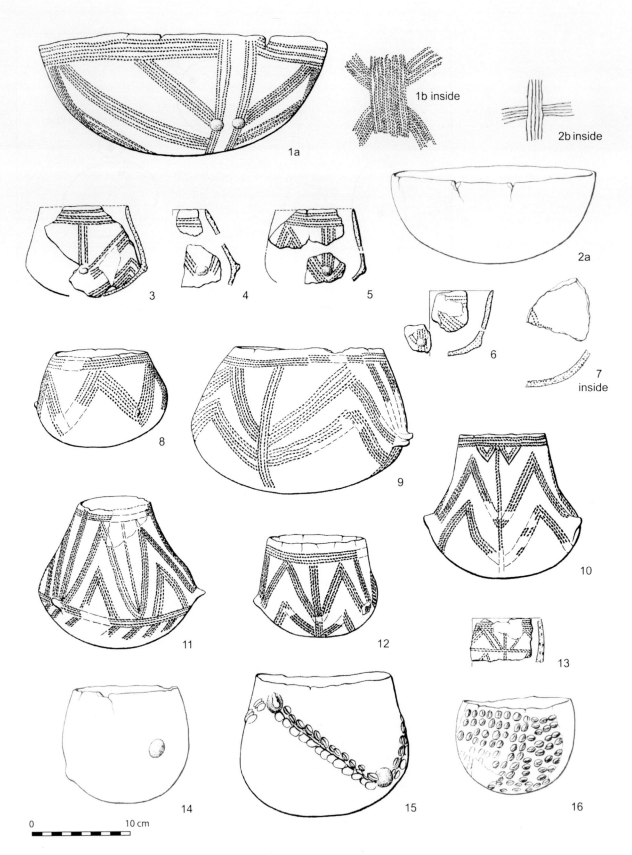

Figure 2. Prague-Bubeneč, central Bohemia, Czech Republic. Selection of pottery from SBK IIa graves (after Zápotocká 1998a, pl. 32–39) that is comparable to pottery from Straubing-Lerchenhaid (see Figure 4).

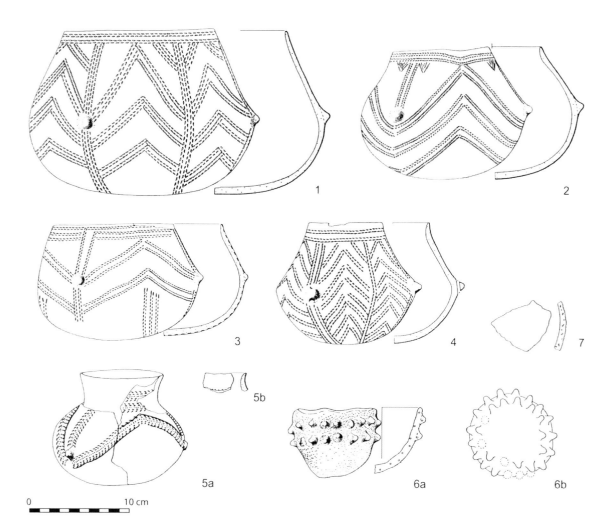

Figure 3. Vikletice, north Bohemia, Czech Republic, grave 2/64. SBK IIa pottery (Zápotocká 1986).

Saale region were not part of the SBK distribution area until her phase III[15]. Her main arguments for equating D. Kaufmann's phase Ia with the Bohemian phase III is that in east Germany, from the very beginning only one decorating chevron band is found on SBK vessels (Figure 7), and having only one chevron band is typical for Bohemian phase III[16]. However, the phase Ia chevron bands from the Saale region are very narrow in comparison to those from Bohemian phase III[17]. Narrow chevron bands are, in contrast, typical for Bohemian phase IIa, but here two or more chevron bands are arranged one above the other (see Figures 2–3). There are differences between the vessel shapes in the early SBK of both regions. But in both deep bowls (Figures 7.8–9.18)[18] and wide vessel forms (Figures 2.8–9, 3.3, 7.6–7) are common. This could suggest that the SBK in the Saale region does not begin as late as Zápotocká supposes, because in the later developmental phases round and pear-shaped vessels become relatively narrower and higher in both regions.

---

15 In earlier publications Zápotocká (e.g. 1998b, 291 fig. 75, 296 fig. 76) parallels Kaufmann's (1976) phases Ia and Ib with her own phases IIb and III.
16 Zápotocká 2013, 45 fig. 15.
17 Kaufmann 1976, pl. 1.
18 Zápotocká 1998a, pl. 32.6, 35.9, 37.13–1, 39.16.

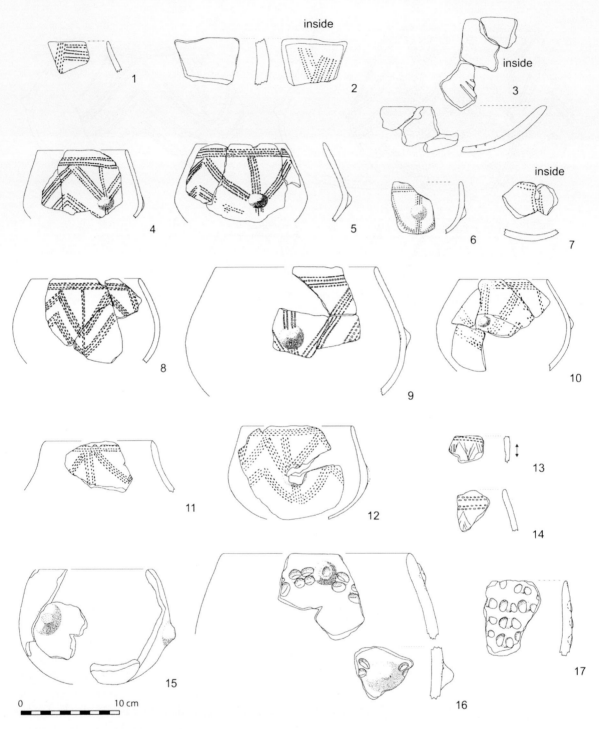

H. Spatz pointed out that Hinkelstein must more likely be connected with east Germany than with Bohemia, because many of the Hinkelstein vessels also are decorated with only one chevron band (see Figure 6). Today we know that the so-called SBK pots from the Hinkelstein cemeteries do not come from Bohemia or east Germany, they are merely imitations of that style. Spatz parallels the examples from Trebur, southern Hesse, with the east German phases Ia and Ib defined by Kaufmann[19].

Figure 4. Straubing-Lerchenhaid, Lower Bavaria, settlement finds. Selection of SBK IIa, i.e. SOB Ia, pottery (Riedhammer 2016, 132 fig. 4) that is comparable to pottery from graves at Prague-Bubeneč (see Figure 2).

---

19 Spatz 1999, 251–252; 2002, 285.

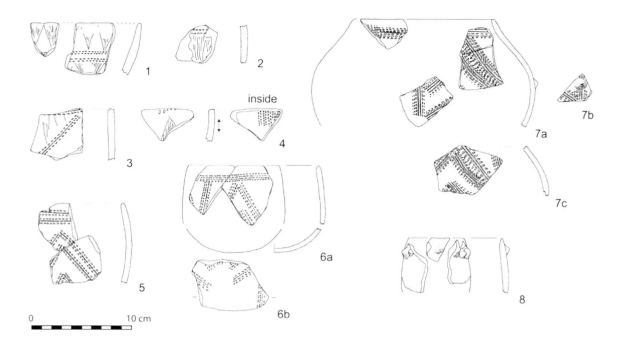

Figure 5. Straubing-Lerchenhaid, Lower Bavaria, settlement finds. Selection of SBK IIa, i.e. SOB Ia, pottery (Riedhammer 2016, 133 fig. 5) that is comparable to pottery from Vikletice, grave 2/64.

Kaufmann argues that not only the east German SBK but the SBK in all regions developed out of the LBK without any break. In his opinion the requirements for such a transition existed in all regions. Some aspects of SBK religious life, such as cremation graves or anthropomorphic depictions, already emerged during the LBK. For this reasons he reduces the seemingly clear break between LBK and SBK to nothing more than a change of vessel shapes and pottery decoration, something that for him is simply a shift of fashion[20]. The emergence of the SBK in the Saale region, in Kaufmann's opinion[21], is a transformation on a regional basis including western LBK elements. Until the year 2004 he thought it probable that the Bohemian and east German SBK could have emerged at about the same time[22]. Yet with the publication of the material from Hrbovice, northern Bohemia[23], he recognised a seamless development from LBK to SBK in northern Bohemia that is not visible to the same degree in the whole east German region. After a stylistic comparison of the different east German regional LBK stylistic groups, he concluded that some LBK groups probably continued to exist while the SBK arose in neighbouring regions. He sees a need for more research to clarify the questions concerning the genesis of the SBK in east Germany[24].

C. Jeunesse and H.-C. Strien expressed the opinion that the beginning of the Middle Neolithic period is to be found in the west and the emergence of the SBK began later than that of Hinkelstein. They argue this based on a variety of import finds. These are mainly sherds with a Šárka style decoration which have been found

---

20 Kaufmann 2009, 267–269.
21 Kaufmann 1976, 109; 2009, 269.
22 Kaufmann 1987, 288; 2009, 269 footnote 3. In his early work, Kaufmann (1976, 106 fig. 25) let the SBK begin a little earlier in the Saale region than in Bohemia.
23 Zápotocká and Muška 2007.
24 Kaufmann 2009, 268 fig. 1, 269–280.

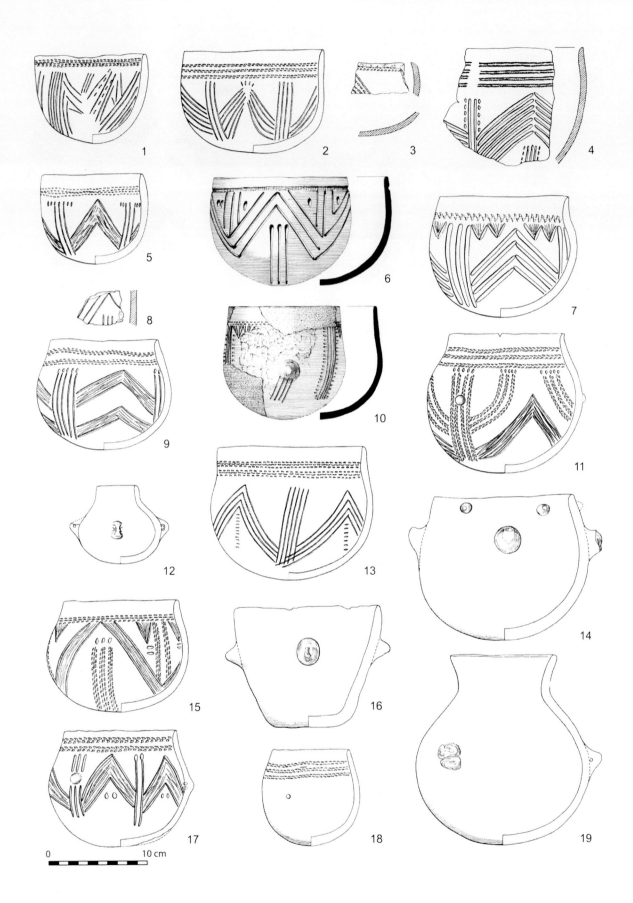

Figure 6 (opposite page). Worms, Rhine-Hesse, Rhineland-Palatinate. Selection of graves thought to be Hinkelstein I. Worms "Rheingewann": 1–4 grave XLIV; 5 grave LV; 6.10 isolated finds; 7.11 grave L; 8–9 grave XLIX; 14–19 grave LIX; Worms-Rheindürkheim: 12–13 grave VII (after Meier-Arendt 1975; Zápotocká 1972).

in material of other regional LBK stylistic groups[25]. Many of the authors' arguments are acceptable. Thus, the parallelisation of the youngest LBK in Württemberg (Strien's phase 8 A/B) with the youngest LBK in Herxheim (Palatine group), with phase IIb/c of the Rhineland chronology "or later" and with the youngest LBK Elster-Saale style and the Bohemian Šárka style is convincing. All these contact finds support my own conclusions that in west Germany, the LBK ended at about the same time everywhere[26]. For Jeunesse and Strien, the Hinkelstein style and also the SBK imitations from Hinkelstein graves derive entirely from western LBK decorations. But this is no more plausible than deriving the imitated SBK decorations from the SBK itself: the decoration is executed with instruments with two prongs that were pushed into the pot surface in an alternating rhythm. This is generally typical for the beginning of the Middle Neolithic period.

Spatz[27] already pointed out the special position of the early Middle Neolithic sites around Tübingen (Upper Gäu) and near the Bodensee (Hegau). In these regions, early Middle Neolithic pottery shows more dotted decoration (Figure 8) than the Hinkelstein style in Rhine-Hesse[28]. It is true that these finds should not be split into HST and SBK sherds and that their decoration concepts have more to do with HST than with SBK[29]. But Jeunesse and Strien claim that contacts between these regional style groups and the central SBK area did not even exist. This is not convincing, as many flint finds originating from the Franconian and southern Bavarian mining areas underscore the mediating character of the area around Tübingen and the Bodensee with its geographical position between Rhine-Hesse and southern Bavaria[30]. It is very likely that a contact route ran along the river Danube[31]. Jeunesse and Strien's assertion that chevron motifs were dominant only in the western LBK and could only have entered the general Middle Neolithic stylistic canon from there[32] must also be contradicted. Although curvilinear patterns predominate, rectilinear and chevron motifs are present in the late Šárka style[33] and the Middle Neolithic vertical separating motifs can be derived from the vertical structuring motifs of the Bavarian[34] and Bohemian LBK[35] as much as from the western LBK *Zwickel* motifs[36]. Their reasoning that the emergence of HST from the west German LBK is smoother than the development from the LBK to the SBK in Bohemia and east Germany[37] is disproved by the find complexes from northern Bohemia and the Dresden Elbe valley[38]. Similarly, the idea that early SBK incised anthropomorphic representations can be traced back to a Hinkelstein influence[39] overlooks the fact that very similar motifs already occur during the

---

25 Jeunesse and Strien 2009, 243–244.
26 Riedhammer 2017.
27 Spatz 1996, 422 footnote 1365; 1999, 258.
28 Bofinger 1996; 2005; Dieckmann 1987.
29 Jeunesse and Strien 2009, 242.
30 Bofinger 1996, 57; 2005, 184–185; Dieckmann *et al.* 2000.
31 E.g. Spatz 2002, 285–286.
32 Jeunesse and Strien 2009, 244.
33 Vencl 1961; Zápotocká 2013, 30 fig. 6, 39 fig. 11.
34 E.g. Neubauer 1955.
35 E.g. Vencl 1961, pl. 23.28, 26.10.
36 The small, generally simple motifs near the top of the vessel which fill the empty spaces between the main bands.
37 Jeunesse and Strien 2009, 245.
38 Link 2014b; Zápotocká and Muška 2007.
39 Jeunesse and Strien 2009, 245.

LBK in Bavaria and Bohemia[40]. In any case, it is clear that Hinkelstein follows the LBK in Württemberg. Jeunesse and Strien argue for an immediate transition from LBK 8A to HST I in the surroundings of Heilbronn and for the immediate transition from LBK 8B to HST II in the area of Stuttgart, without considering the possibility of a longer break between the LBK and the Middle Neolithic. It is only fair to point out that in 2009, the duration of this process was not backed up well enough by radiocarbon dating. But in the meantime, the situation concerning absolute dating has improved especially in west Germany and Alsace[41]. There, the break between LBK and HST which Stöckli already drew attention to in 2002 is still recognisable and cannot be completely filled by the available dates and finds.

Jeunesse and Strien's conclusion that the beginning of HST has to date before the genesis of the SBK and that influences causing the rise of the SBK come from HST, rather than the other way around, is ultimately based on two premises: that the LBK in Württemberg ended earlier than in the Rhineland and that the latest LBK in the Rhineland existed simultaneously with Hinkelstein in south-west Germany[42]. If one takes the step of throwing these "conventional" ideas overboard, Jeunesse's and Strien's statements still leave many arguments for the idea that the central European LBK (with the exception of its western areas of distribution in France and Belgium) ended everywhere at about the same time[43] and that the Middle Neolithic period started everywhere at around the same time. One can share the authors' opinion that there must have been relatively great mobility of at least single individuals at the end of the LBK and the beginning of the Middle Neolithic. The "convergences" in pottery decoration suggest knowledge of each other's style. Evidence of genuine contact finds is lacking at the beginning of the Middle Neolithic period or has not been identified archaeometrically. While imitations of SBK pottery in Hinkelstein graves are known, the first evidence of a vessel decorated in HST I style in SBK territory comes from the site of Hrdlovka, north-west Bohemia[44]. It was found in connection with SBK IIa pottery.[45] Such contact finds are known in higher numbers in later Middle Neolithic phases[46]. In contrast, the distribution of Bavarian chert to west Germany is evident already from early Middle Neolithic times[47].

For southern Bavaria, I have previously suggested a settlement hiatus between the LBK and the Middle Neolithic[48]. The reasons for this were the clear typological break with the preceding LBK, the fact that a seamless transition from the LBK to the Middle Neolithic had at the time not been identified anywhere[49] and the clear gap in the absolute dates between the LBK and early South-East Bavarian

---

40 Pechtl 2009, pl. 19.403-1, 79.1169-240, 100.1509-89; Spatz 2003, 575; Zápotocká 1970, 6; 1998a, pl. 10a.1–2, 11a.1.
41 Denaire 2009; 2011; Denaire *et al.* 2017.
42 Jeunesse and Strien 2009, 245.
43 Compare Pechtl 2009, 111–112; Vencl 1961, 139.
44 Vondrovský 2015, App. plate 2.25/4/vessel number 6547.
45 While the site is believed to be settled without a break from the LBK until the SBK, the authors (Vondrovský 2015; Vondrovský *et al.* 2016) have not yet published SBK phase I pottery.
46 E.g. Gleser 2012.
47 Spatz 2002, 286.
48 Engelhardt *et al.* 2006, 65; Riedhammer 2005, 70.
49 Neither in Hienheim, district of Kelheim (van de Velde 1979; 1986a; 1986b) nor in Regensburg–Harting-Nord (Herren 2003) is a continuous settlement activity convincing, as early Middle Neolithic pottery is missing at both sites (Riedhammer 2015; 2016).

Middle Neolithic (SOB)[50]. The close typological links between the pottery from Straubing-Lerchenhaid (Figure 4) and the Bohemian SBK graves from Praha-Bubeneč (Figure 2) in central Bohemia[51] led to the idea that the bearers of the early SBK had migrated from Bohemia to Bavaria.

A closer look at the excavation of Regensburg–Harting-Nord[52] and the re-analysis of Straubing-Lerchenhaid, as well as a supraregional evaluation of radiocarbon dates[53], led me to share the opinion of T. Link[54]. He warns against the idea that the SBK spread out just from northern Bohemia and the Dresden Elbe valley. In his opinion, the examples of Dresden-Prohlis and Hrbovice-Chabařovice show that even in the core area of the SBK this new style seemed to be a completely new phenomenon for a long time. Only through detailed investigations and only at individual sites is it possible to identify a smoother beginning rooted in the LBK. It cannot be ruled out, and it is indeed quite probable, that with improved research, regional transition phases from LBK to SBK will also be identified in other areas in the future. Following Link, a polyfocal beginning of the Middle Neolithic period can be suggested. The development in the different regions probably began under similar conditions. Differences in the early Middle Neolithic archaeological material — above all the ceramics — are probably due to the different traditions of the preceding regional LBK groups. However, the great similarities in the pottery decoration are striking, so one can speak of a common period style.

Selected pottery characteristics and their distribution at the start of the Middle Neolithic period

If one accepts, like Link, Zápotocká and P. Vencl[55], that the Bohemian SBK I is not a separate chronological phase in Bohemia and Saxony but an ornament style that existed simultaneously with the latest Šárka style, then the SBK proper, and thus the Middle Neolithic period according to west German terminology, starts with phase SBK II[56]. Accordingly, the Middle Neolithic period begins with HST I in Rhine Hesse and the Neckar region[57], with phase SBK Ia[58] in east Germany and with phase SOB I in southern Bavaria[59]. Some elements, shapes and decoration motifs of early Middle Neolithic pottery are supraregional, but do not occur everywhere in the same proportions. And not every single element or motif is present in each region. In Figure 10, selected pottery characteristics are compiled to reveal similarities and differences in style between the regions. All regions with sufficiently documented early Middle Neolithic sites and assemblages are compared (Figure 1).

50 Riedhammer 2012.
51 Zápotocká 1998a, pl. 32–39.
52 Herren 2003; Riedhammer 2015; 2016.
53 Riedhammer 2017.
54 Link 2014b, 219–220.
55 Link 2014b; Vencl 1961; Zápotocká 2009a.
56 Zápotocká 1970.
57 Meier-Arendt 1975; Spatz 1996.
58 Kaufmann 1976.
59 Nadler *et al.* 1994.

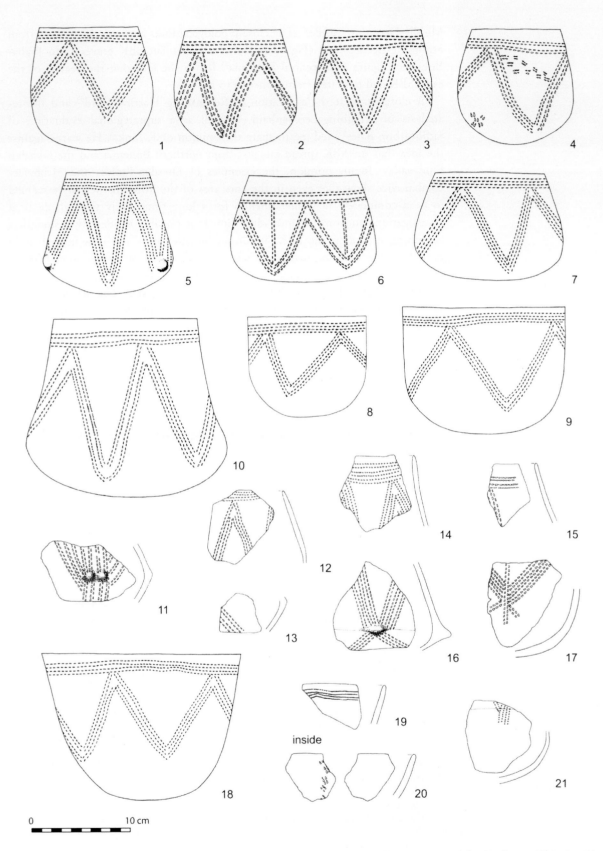

Figure 7. Osternienburger Land-Wulfen, Saxony-Anhalt. Settlement pit. Selection of SBK Ia pottery (after Kaufmann 1976, pl. 1–2).

The source for the east German Saale area is Kaufmann's 1976 monograph, in which he defined his phase SBK Ia mainly by means of the assemblage from Wulfen, Osternienburger Land, district of Anhalt-Bitterfeld, Saxony-Anhalt (Figure 7). Other sites that yielded SBK Ia pottery were also included[60].

For Rhine-Hesse the assemblages of the cemeteries Worms "Rheingewann" and Worms-Rheindürkheim were considered, which are treated here as falling early within the HST I phase due to close typological relations to LBK decorations (Figure 6)[61]. In addition, further assemblages of phase HST I from the Worms area[62] and the Hessian cemetery of Trebur, district of Groß-Gerau[63], were examined.

For the Upper Gäu region, Baden-Württemberg, it is not easy to find early Middle Neolithic pottery. A good assemblage, which however consists only of small sherds, comes from Rottenburg am Neckar Flur "Beim Lindele", district of Tübingen. In addition to the earliest Middle Neolithic finds (for a selection, see Figure 8.1–11), there are Middle Neolithic finds dating to the early Großgartach and later. No HST II finds were made[64]. It is even more difficult to recognise early Middle Neolithic finds from Ammerbuch-Reusten, Flur "Stützbrunnen", district of Tübingen. The settlement excavation revealed material from the earliest LBK right up to the Young Neolithic Schussenried group[65]. In some cases, the assemblages were thoroughly mixed. In addition to the early Middle Neolithic, there are finds that date to HST II[66], Großgartach[67] and Rössen[68]. For the characterisation of the early Middle Neolithic, sherds from pit B10[69] and pit B8[70] — except for the LBK and La Hoguette sherds also recovered — and single surface finds[71] were taken into account. A selection of the finds from pit B8 is compiled in Figure 8.12–24. For both sites it is important to note that apart from typical HST incised decoration, they have a greater number of dotted ornaments.

Similar observations have been made in the Hegau[72] (Figure 1), but too little material has so far been published, so that the region could not be taken into account here.

Hinkelstein and early SBK finds are also known from Main-Franconia (Figure 1), which indicates that here both distribution areas meet[73]. More precise statements on the relationship between the pottery styles are not yet possible, we are awaiting the results of research by S. Suhrbier[74].

In addition to the finds from Straubing-Lerchenhaid (Figures 4–5)[75] and grave 229 at Aiterhofen-Ödmühle, district of Straubing-Bogen[76], further finds

---

60   Kaufmann 1976, plates.
61   Riedhammer 2017.
62   Meier-Arendt 1975, 191–223.
63   Spatz 1999, plates.
64   Albert 1987; Bofinger 1996.
65   Bofinger 2005, pl. 44–89.
66   Bofinger 2005, pl. 75.14, l. 77.4–5.7.10. The vessels illustrated by Bofinger (2005, pl. 75.15, 76.7) belong to the transitional phase HST II/fGG.
67   Bofinger 2005, pl. 78–79.
68   Bofinger 2005, pl. 80–81.
69   Bofinger 2005, pl. 75B, 84, 85A.
70   Bofinger 2005, pl. 82B, 83.
71   Bofinger 2005, pl. 77, 85B, 86.
72   Dieckmann 1987, 25 fig. 5.4–7; compare Spatz 2002, 286.
73   Suhrbier 2012.
74   Stefan Suhrbier's dissertation on the Middle Neolithic of Lower Franconia will be published shortly. I owe him heartfelt thanks for the possibility to view unpublished material and for the stimulating scientific exchange.
75   Riedhammer 1994a; 1994b.
76   Nieszery 1995.

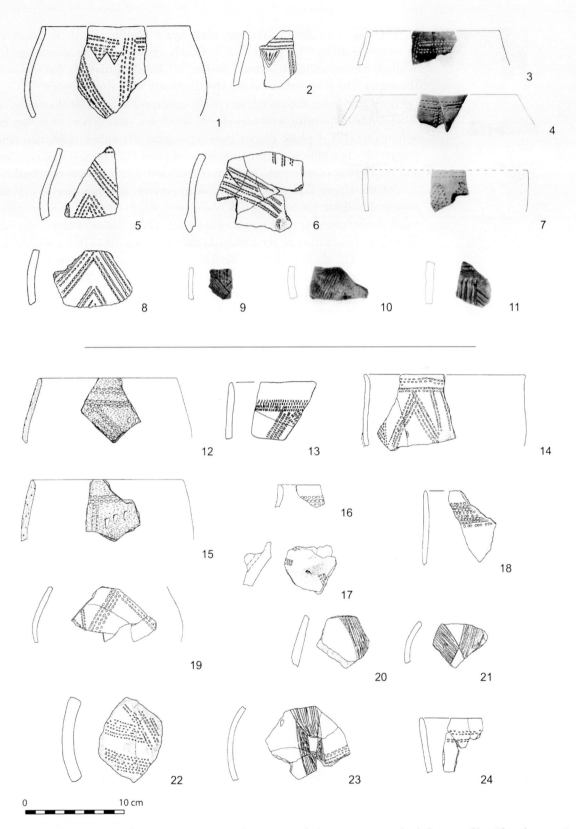

Figure 8. 1–11: Rottenburg am Neckar, Flur "Beim Lindele", survey finds; 12–24: Ammerbuch-Reusten, Flur "Stützbrunnen", pit B8. Both Baden-Württemberg, Upper Gäu. Selection of early Middle Neolithic pottery (after Albert 1987; Bofinger 1996; 2005).

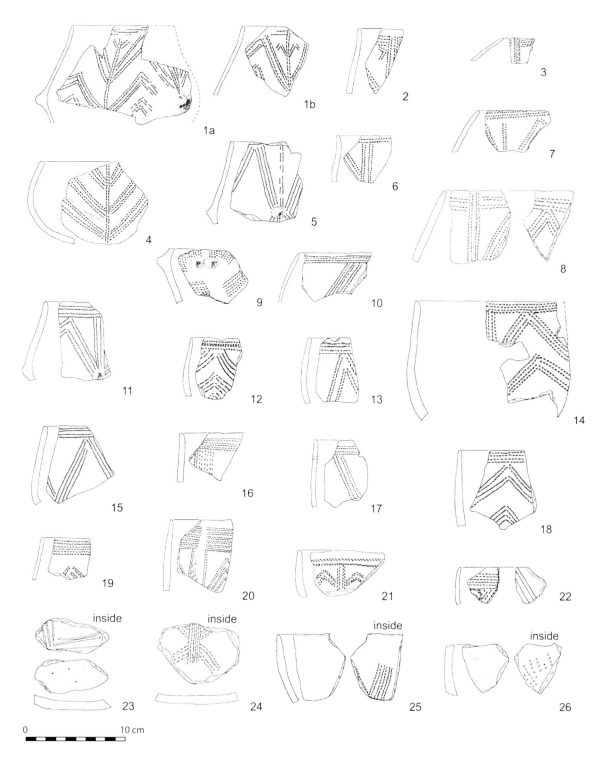

Figure 9. Dresden-Cotta, Saxony, settlement finds. Selection of SBK IIa pottery (after Pratsch 1999).

from Köfering-Kelleräcker II, district of Regensburg, and Altdorf-Aich, district of Landshut[77] were taken into account for southern Bavaria.

The assessment of the Bohemian SBK was based on the assemblages from the early graves at Praha-Bubeneč (Figure 2) and other sites[78], but phase IIa settlements were also considered[79]. For Bohemia — the region with the largest number of sites from this horizon — it seems likely that future research will reveal regional differences in pottery decoration.

I also took a more precise look at the SBK IIa pottery of the Dresden Elbe valley. Here, the published settlement at Dresden-Cotta[80] yielded LBK finds and material from phases SBK IIa to SBK IV, with a focus in phase IIa (Figure 9). The pottery from Dresden-Prohlis[81] was not taken into account, as the allocation of individual sherds to phase SBK I or SBK II is difficult.

Figure 10 shows which characteristics are present (value 1 and higher) or missing (value 0) in the pottery of the various regions. Grey coloured table cells containing a value of 1 mean that the trait exists, but is rare in the region. Higher values do not accurately reflect differences, they merely represent estimates relative to the occurrences in other regions.

One of the most important characteristics of early Middle Neolithic pottery is the decoration system of closed vessel shapes, which consists of a horizontal motif beneath the rim, a chevron motif running around the vessel and a vertical separating motif, the latter often passing over a handle. Comparing the regions, it is striking that this system is least strictly adhered to in the Saale region. Here, the separating motif is often missing, especially in the earliest assemblages (Figure 7). But also in Bohemia (Figure 2.4.8), in the Dresden Elbe valley (Figure 9.15) and in southern Bavaria[82] the separating motif is not present on all vessels. The decoration system appears to have been adhered to relatively strictly in those HST I assemblages which are thought to be early. However, a few vessels are also decorated in a deviating system, for example only with horizontal dotted bands (Figure 6). Considering all HST I assemblages from Worms "Rheingewann" and Worms-Rheindürkheim[83], less than half of the vessels are decorated in this system. In most cases the separating motif is missing, while other decorations, such as triangles, can also occur as main motifs. Where one can find the closest similarities can consequently differ: the HST I assemblages thought to be early are more similar to the SBK of Bavaria and Bohemia, while the HST I phase as a whole, according to Meier-Arendt[84], can be compared better with the SBK of the Saale region. For the Upper Gäu, if a vessel fragment is large enough, a separating motif can generally be found on it. However, the assemblages are so small that no definite conclusions can be drawn.

Looking at the shapes of early Middle Neolithic vessels, different main types can be recognised and compared across the regions, even if they differ slightly from each other. In all regions, there are broad forms, which are narrower towards the mouth (Figures 2.8–9, 3.2, 4.8–9, 6.2.4–6, 7.6–7, 8.1.12.15, 9.14.18). These

---

77 Eibl 2011, 89 fig. 7.2943; Matuschik 1992, 26 fig. 2.2; Nagel 1999.
78 Zápotocká 1998a, pl. 32–39, 78.1–2 bottom, 88, 98.1–4 top, 102, 106, 107.3–4 top.
79 Končelová and Květina 2015; Kuna 1991; Pavlů 1992; Pavlů et al. 1993; Zápotocká 1982; 2009b.
80 Pratsch 1999.
81 Link 2014b.
82 Matuschik 1992, 26 fig. 2.2.
83 Meier-Arendt 1975, plates.
84 Meier-Arendt 1975.

broad forms can be regarded as a common, supraregional characteristic of the early Middle Neolithic. While in following SBK phases the shape of the vessels becomes proportionately higher compared to vessel width[85], shapes remain relatively broad in the west during Großgartach[86].

A portion of the early broad vessel forms has a relatively narrow mouth and a rounded base and continues the three-quarter-spherical shapes (so-called *bombenförmige Kümpfe*) of the LBK. This type is known from Hinkelstein as well as from the south Bavarian and Bohemian SBK (Figures 2.8–9, 4.8–10, 6.9, 8.4, 9.7–8.). It is not present in the Saale region, where there are either broad shapes with slightly flattened bases (*e.g.* Figure 7.6–7) or spherical profiles, which are as wide as they are high (Figure 7.1–4).

In contrast, deep, U-shaped vessels are frequently found in the Saale region (*e.g.* Figure 7.8–9). In other regions U-shaped vessels are present occasionally, but they are by no means as deep as in the Saale region and can therefore be referred to as bowls (*e.g.* Figures 2.13, 4.6, 6.2, 8.13–14). In the Dresden Elbe valley, the latter form appears somewhat more frequently (Figure 9.16–18, 9.20–22).

Vessels with slightly S-shaped profiles and rounded body, which were retained from the LBK, appear to be completely absent in the early SBK of the Saale region (compare Figure 7). This vessel type occurs relatively frequently in the early HST of Worms (Figure 6.7.11.13.15.17) and in the Upper Gäu (Figure 8.2.5.16), whereas it is absent in Bohemia. It occurs only very rarely in the SBK of southern Bavaria[87] and the Dresden Elbe valley (Figure 9.6).

In Bohemia and the Elbe valley, vessels with a slightly curved profile have a slightly flattened base and a low centre of gravity. They form the low variant of the typical SBK pear-shaped vessels (Figures 2.12, 3.1–4, 9.1.5). This type is also known from the Saale region (Figure 7.10)[88] and from southern Bavaria (Figure 5.7). It is completely absent from Hinkelstein assemblages.

High pear-shaped vessels — the main type of the following phase SBK III — occur early in Bohemia (Figure 2.10–11). Rare examples are also recorded in the Dresden Elbe valley (Figure 9.5.9), in the Saale region (Figure 7.16–17) and in southern Bavaria (Figure 4.11). They rarely occur in the HST I phase. From the Alzey cemetery, district of Worms, two examples are known, but the composition of the grave assemblages, and thus the dating into a given HST phase, are uncertain[89]. From the Trebur cemetery, another three examples from graves 86 (HST I), 103 (HST I/II) and 124 (HST I) are known[90].

Vessels with a narrow mouth, a straight shoulder and a gently carinated body are present across the whole distribution area of the early SBK (Figures 2.3–5, 4.4–5, 7.12, 9.11). They are absent from Hinkelstein assemblages around Worms and in the Upper Gäu.

Another characteristic which connects all regions is the main decoration technique. Using instruments with two prongs, alternating strokes were placed on the pottery surface, forming the ornaments built up of bands. At the beginning of the Middle Neolithic period this technique was known in all regions. On the basis of

---

85 Kaufmann 1976, 16–22; Zápotocká 2013, 43 fig. 14, 45 fig. 15.
86 Spatz 1996, 55 fig. 6.
87 Riedhammer 1994b, 135 fig. 4,27.
88 Kaufmann 1976, pl. 5.1–9.
89 Meier-Arendt 1975, pl. 34.3, 38.4.
90 Spatz 1999.

this stroking technique, therefore, no source area in the sense of a diffusionist cultural interpretation, for example from Hinkelstein to SBK or vice versa, can be identified.

Other decoration techniques were also used (Figure 10). Single impressed dots are frequently found in the Hinkelstein style (Figure 6.2.4.6.10.11.13.15.17), they are also present in the Upper Gäu (Figure 8.12.15.23), whereas they occur exceptionally and rarely in the SBK regions (Figures 2.7, 4.7, 9.26). Here they are used only for the inner surface decoration of bowls. An example from the Saale region is dated to the LBK by Kaufmann[91].

Alternating strokes made with an instrument with three and more prongs are relatively frequent around Worms (*e.g.* Figure 6.1.9.13.15), in the Upper Gäu (Figure 8.16.18) and in southern Bavaria (Figure 5.3.5–7). In Bohemia this technique is known from the SBK IIa graves at Vikletice. Here it is found not only on the vessel assigned to the Rhineland LBK by Zápotocká (Figure 3.5), but also on an SBK vessel of a second burial[92]. According to Zápotocká, instruments with three and more prongs were used very rarely in phase SBK II. Indeed, the regular occurrence of this technique defines phase SBK III. Thus, while it is not completely unknown in the SBK II of Bohemia, it does not appear in the early Middle Neolithic period in the Elbe valley and in the Saale region[93].

The decoration with deeply incised broad lines is characteristic for the Hinkelstein style (see Figure 6). Although strokes are predominant in the Upper Gäu, deeply incised broad lines are regularly present (Figure 8.9–11). In southern Bavaria, this technique is known exclusively from the inner surface of bowls (Figure 4.3). In Bohemia and in the Dresden Elbe valley, incised lines are known as inside decoration of bowls, but triangles or chevrons executed in deeply incised broad lines can also occasionally be found as secondary motifs (Figures 2.2.10, 9.23). In Dresden-Cotta, both LBK and SBK pottery was found, so it is not entirely certain whether the selected example dates to the SBK (Figure 9.23). An SBK pot decorated with dotted bands and incised triangles comes from Großweitzschen-Strocken, district of Mittelsachsen. The site is located 80 km north-west of Dresden. It could still be part of the sphere of influence of the Dresden Elbe valley[94]. In the Saale region, deeply incised broad lines from the inside of bowls seem to date only to the LBK[95].

Bands of fine incised lines, bands filled with fine hatching and triangular secondary motifs filled with fine hatching are typical for the early Hinkelstein style (*e.g.* Figure 6.5.7.9.11.15). In the Upper Gäu this technique is also relatively frequent (Figure 8.20–21.23). Fine incised lines are also characteristic of the southern Bavarian early Middle Neolithic phase SOB Ia. Here they do not form bands, but smaller triangular secondary motifs (Figures 4.13–14, 5.1–4). It is not easy to decide from the publication, but in Bohemia, the filling of such small triangles on a vessel from Vikletice also seems to consist of fine incised lines (Figure 3.2). A vessel decorated with a dotted band beneath the rim, a dotted separating band and a chevron band of fine incised parallel hatching

---

91   Kaufmann 1976, 81–82 fig. 19.1.
92   Zápotocká 1998a, pl. 106.2 top.
93   However, since this technique is typical for the middle phase of the SBK, some early examples of its use may be incorrectly dated. An early example is recorded from pit 31 at Hrbovice, which is classified as an SBK I assemblage (Zápotocká 2009, 309 fig. 6). In Dresden-Prohlis, too, there are isolated examples of this technique (Link 2014b, 58).
94   Hoffmann 1963, l. 55.3.
95   Kaufmann 1976, 81–82 fig. 19.2.

was discovered at Hrdlovka, north-west Bohemia[96] in association with SBK IIa pottery. This vessel is a perfect example of the early Hinkelstein style (compare Figure 6.5.9.11.15). Whether it originally comes from the region around Worms or was made in Bohemia should be established by scientific provenance studies.

The main motif of the early Middle Neolithic is the chevron band encircling the vessel. In Hinkelstein occasionally two chevrons are arranged one above the other (Figure 6.9.11), but the great majority of closed HST I vessel forms are decorated only with one chevron band. This is also the case in the Saale area, so both regions were often compared to each other (see above). In the Upper Gäu both possibilities are present, either one chevron band (Figure 8.1.14.19) or at least two bands (Figure 8.5.8). In southern Bavaria, the ratio is opposite to that in Hinkelstein: there are almost always several chevron bands arranged around the vessel (Figures 4–5), exceptions are rare (Figure 4.6). The situation is similar in Bohemia and the Elbe valley: vessels with only one chevron band are the exception (Figures 2, 3, 9). In most cases, the vessels from these regions decorated in this manner show a slight carination on the body; this vessel type does not appear in the following phases (Figures 2.4–5.8, 9.11.15).

Small triangles or chevrons have already been mentioned as secondary motifs. Zápotocká[97] described such a motif on a vessel from grave 1/64 at Vikletice (Figure 3.2) as foreign to Bohemia and connected it with Hinkelstein. This provides a good reason to look more closely at these motifs. They occur frequently in the entire early Middle Neolithic period, either at the angle between the band beneath the rim and the separating motif, where they may also occur in duplicate (see Figures 2.10, 3.2, 6.7.10.15, 8.1–2, 10) or strung along horizontal bands (Figures 2.13, 4.13, 5.1). These secondary motifs can be incised as well as dotted, even combinations of the two techniques appear (Figures 2.10, 8.1). Only the early assemblages of the Saale region do not have a single one of the described variants. They seem to appear here no earlier than phase SBK Ib after Kaufmann[98] and then only dotted and strung along vertical bands. The strung variant is particularly frequent in Hinkelstein[99]. Strictly speaking, these are secondary motifs that accompany main motifs, but in effect they play the role of main motifs. While for Meier-Arendt this type of motif is dated to his phase HST II, according to Spatz some simple incised examples date to phase HST I[100]. Standing and hanging triangles are found in southern Bavaria on closed vessel forms under the band beneath the rim (Figure 4.14) and more frequently on horizontal bands running around bowls (Figure 5.1.4). Like the Hinkelstein style, they always consist of incisions. A bit later, in phases HST II and SOB Ib, dotted variants also occur, again accompanying horizontal bands encircling vessels[101]. While these motifs were incised in the early Middle Neolithic around Worms and in southern Bavaria, they were almost exclusively dotted in Bohemia and the Elbe valley of Dresden. Exceptions are the combination of both techniques in the Upper Gäu (Figure 8.1) and at Praha-Bubeneč (Figure 2.10), as well as an example of an incised triangle

---

96 Vondrovský 2015, pl. 2.25/4/vessel number 6547.
97 Zápotocká 1986.
98 Kaufmann 1976, pl. 15.
99 E.g. Meier-Arendt 1975, pl. 36.1–2, 37.1.3, 39.22.
100 His motif 391: Spatz 1996, 267, 281 fig. 105.
101 Koch 2005, 29–30 fig. 20; Meier-Arendt 1975, pl. 112.1; motif 802 according to Spatz 1996, 267, 281 fig. 105.

from the Saxon SBK[102]. Standing small triangles — in principle triangles rotated by 180° — are present in Bohemia[103] and in the Dresden Elbe valley, occurring in the space between the rim band and the separating band (*e.g.* Figure 9.1b.21). A variant rotated by 90° (Figure 9.2) is a specialty of the SBK of Bohemia and Saxony — possibly with a distribution focus in north-west Bohemia. Examples are known from Třebenice[104], Chcebuz-Brocno[105] and Lovosice[106]. All these sites lie in the Litoměřice district and date to phase SBK IIa. These secondary motifs are interpreted together with corresponding bowl decorations as arms and legs of anthropomorphic symbols[107]. Comparable to these secondary motifs positioned on both sides of a separating motif, the early tree motifs appear in the Hinkelstein style, and exclusively there[108].

Another common characteristic of the early Middle Neolithic is the interrupted rim band. It occurs everywhere (Figures 10, 2.1.9, 4.1, 6.4, 7.15, 9.20)[109], being very common in both Hinkelstein phases. In southern Bavaria (Figure 4.1.10), Bohemia (Figure 2.1.11) and in the Dresden Elbe valley (Figure 9.1–2), rim band interruptions are often limited by separating motifs. The latter often continue through the rim band to the edge of the rim. This variant is known with and without a gap in the rim band. It also appears in the Upper Gäu (Figure 8.1) but is unknown in Hinkelstein assemblages around Worms and the Saale region[110].

Another characteristic of Hinkelstein is that the separating bands and the chevron peaks often end before they touch the band beneath the rim (Figure 6.1–2.4–5.7.9.13.17). This is rarely the case in the Upper Gäu, in southern Bavaria (Figure 5.5), Bohemia (Figure 2.10) and in the Dresden Elbe valley (Figure 9.7). In the Saale region, on the other hand, these motifs generally reach up to the rim band.

Also, filling motifs in variable positions and secondary motifs that form band ends are not known everywhere in the same frequencies. While they occur relatively frequently in Rhine-Hesse (Figure 6.2.5.6.9.11.15.17) and in the Upper Gäu (Figure 8.12.15.23), they are rare in the Saale region (Figure 7.4). In southern Bavaria, Bohemia, and in the Dresden Elbe valley, they are unknown during the SBK, with the exception of grave 2/64 at Vikletice (Figure 3.3).

In the early Middle Neolithic, the accompanying secondary motifs are also a speciality of the Hinkelstein style around Worms (Figure 6.4) and the Upper Gäu[111]. In southern Bavaria, as already described, incised triangles can be classified as accompanying motifs (Figure 5.1).

Deeply incised broad lines on the inside of bowls have already been mentioned. They are unknown in the Hinkelstein style and relatively frequently present in the repertoire of the early SBK of southern Bavaria (Figure 4.3) and Bohemia (Figure 2.2). There are also examples from east Germany (see above) and the Dresden Elbe valley (Figure 9.23) but it is possible that they date to the LBK.

---

102 Hoffmann 1963, pl. 55.3.
103 Zápotocká 2009b, pl. 16.1.
104 Pavlů *et al.* 1993, fig. 10, Obj. 62, 11, Obj. 80.
105 Zápotocká 2009b, pl. 1.4.
106 Zápotocká 2009b, pl. 14.11.
107 Kaufmann 1976, 80–88; Spatz 1999, 245–247; 2002, 286–287; Zápotocká 2013, 88.
108 Bofinger 1996, 92 fig. 36.2; Spatz 1996, 267, 281 fig. 105 motif 704; 1999, 204–206 motifs 704 and 908.
109 Bofinger 2005, fig. 77.2, 85.7.
110 Undatable examples come from Worms "Rheingewann" (Meier-Arendt 1975, pl. 106.4). Examples from the Saale region seem to be younger (Kaufmann 1976, pl. 10.1, 31.3).
111 Bofinger 2005, l. 77.2.

	Saale SBK Ia	Rhine-Hessia HST I	Upper Gäu HST I	southern Bavaria SOB Ia	Bohemia SBK IIa	Dresden SBK IIa	Saale SBK IIa
rim + chevron + separating motif	2	5	5	8	8	8	2
three-quarter-spherical vessels	0	1	1	1	1	1	0
deep U-shaped vessels	3	1	1	1	1	2	3
S-shaped vessels	0	2	2	1	0	1	0
low pear-shaped vessels	1	0	0	1	2	2	1
high pear-shaped vessels	1	1	0	1	2	0	1
vessels with gentle carination	1	0	0	1	1	1	1
single impressed dots	0	5	2	1	1	1	0
alternating strokes using tools with three or more points	0	5	2	2	1	0	0
deeply incised, broad lines	0	5	3	1	1	1	0
fine incised lines / hatching	0	4	4	2	1	0	0
one chevron	5	5	3	1	1	1	5
two or more chevrons	0	1	3	5	5	5	0
small hanging triangles / chevrons as secondary motifs	0	1	0	1	1	1	0
small upright triangles / chevrons as secondary motifs	0	1	0	1	1	1	0
small triangles / chevrons, rotated 90°, as secondary motifs	0	0	0	0	1	1	0
incised small triangles / chevrons	0	2	2	2	1	1	0
dotted small triangles / chevrons	0	0	1	0	1	1	0
early tree motifs	0	1	1	0	0	0	0
interruption of rim band	1	2	2	0	1	0	1
separating motif continuing through rim band	0	0	1	1	1	1	0
separating motif and chevron do not touch rim band	0	5	1	1	1	1	0
filling motifs in variable positions and secondary motifs forming band ends	1	2	2	0	1	0	1
accompanying secondary motifs	0	1	1	1	0	0	0
deeply incised lines on inside of bowls	0	0	0	2	2	0	0
strokes inside of bowls	1	0	0	2	2	2	1
small bulges on rim of bowls	0	1	1	1	0	0	0
fingertip impressions cover whole surface	0	1	0	1	1	0	0
rows of small projections	0	0	0	1	1	0	0

Figure 10. Comparison of early Middle Neolithic pottery characteristics from different regions. 0: characteristic is missing; 1: characteristic is present. The numbers 2 and higher represent estimates of frequency in relation to other regions.

Also, dotted ornaments on the inner surface of bowls do not occur in Hinkelstein assemblages, but are common throughout the entire SBK distribution area (Figures 2.1.7, 4.2.7, 7.20, 9.24).

Bowls with rims that have small upright bulges are an inheritance of the LBK. They are only known from HST inventories around Worms[112] and from southern Bavaria[113] while they do not seem to appear in any of the other regions mentioned. Examples from the Upper Gäu cannot be dated with certainty to either the LBK or the Middle Neolithic period[114]. Fingertip decoration covering the whole surface of coarse ceramic vessels is known from southern Bavaria (Figure 4.17) and Bohemia (Figure 2.16). An example from Worms cannot be dated securely[115]. Rows of small

---

112 Meier-Arendt 1975, pl. 59.3, 73.3, 79.3.
113 Riedhammer 2017, pl. 4.3, 42.4.
114 Bofinger 2005, l. 53.4, 86.18.
115 Meier-Arendt 1975, l. 103.1.

projections beneath the rim of otherwise undecorated vessels occur in southern Bavaria (Figure 5.8) and Bohemia (Figure 3.6).

The selection of characteristics and motifs was made subjectively. Because of a lack of absolute dates, it cannot be guaranteed that the selected finds assemblages compared here always come from the exact same time horizon. But the current dating situation[116] supports the idea that the horizon discussed here begins at about 4950 cal BC in all regions. Furthermore, it is not possible to reliably count the frequency of single characteristics by checking selected publications. Nevertheless, attempts were made to show tendencies in the similarity or dissimilarity of the pottery assemblages from the different regions and to describe them not only in text form, but also graphically in Figure 10. Looking at the columns in the table reveals that regional similarities and differences can be clearly identified.

Thus, greater similarities between Rhine-Hesse and the Upper Gäu become obvious. There is also a greater similarity between the Bohemian SBK and the SBK of the Dresden Elbe valley. The southern Bavarian early Middle Neolithic pottery seems to be a connecting factor between Hinkelstein and the central SBK region. The Saale region shows the largest differences to all other regions studied here. Many of the characteristics I have compared are missing here. Some of these are, as stated, quite present in the preceding LBK or even the following SBK development. In order to show the similarities and differences of the early Middle Neolithic pottery of the compared regions in a different graphical form, the values in Figure 10 were converted into a correspondence analysis (Figures 11–12)[117]. Here, the correspondence analysis is thus not used for the investigation of a development, but for the representation of the similarities of approximately simultaneous assemblages from different regions.

Astonishingly, the result (Figure 11) exactly replicates the geographic position of the examined regions to each other. In the right half of the X-axis (first principal dimension, positive values) lie the SBK regions southern Bavaria, Bohemia and the Dresden Elbe valley. One could call this grouping the Bohemian-influenced SBK. In the left half of the X-axis (first principal dimension, negative values) lie Rhine-Hesse and the Upper Gäu. From the tight grouping of the two regions, it can be concluded that the pottery from the Upper Gäu can be counted to the Hinkelstein sphere in spite of some similarities with the SBK style. Between these two groupings, the Upper Gäu and southern Bavaria are closer to each other, thus illustrating their mediating position between the Hinkelstein style and the Bohemian-influenced SBK style. The Saale region lies far away from both groupings in the positive area of the Y-axis (second principal dimension), thus illustrating its greater independence from the other regions. Rather near to the Saale region lies the Dresden Elbe valley which, in spite of showing some similarities with the Saale region, shares far more characteristics with Bohemia.

Looking at the distribution of the individual characteristics (Figure 11, numbers; see Figure 12 for the number coding used and for the values on the first two principal dimensions) reveals that certain characteristics are responsible for the locations of the regions. The extreme location of the Saale region is due to the distribution of the characteristics of "deep U-shaped vessels" (Figure 11.21) and "one chevron" (Figure 11.11), which is not surprising. "Early tree motifs"

---

116 Denaire *et al.* 2017; Link 2014a; Riedhammer 2012.
117 The program PAST version 2.17c (February 2013) was used: Ø. Hammer *et al.* 2001, 1–9. Download: http://folk.uio.no/ohammer/past. The graphics have been reworked.

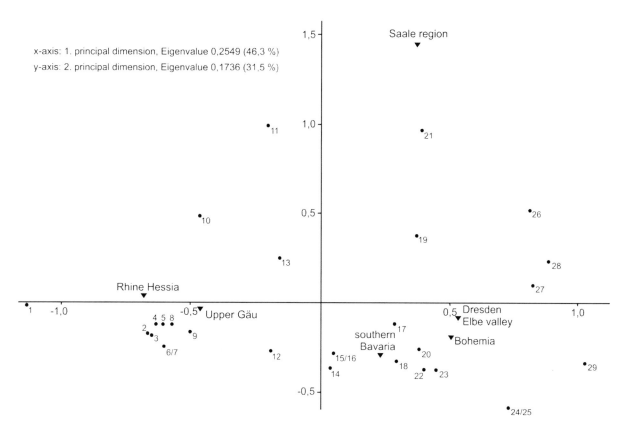

Figure 11. Correspondence analysis of the early Middle Neolithic pottery characteristics from different regions. For code list and values, see Figure 12.

(Figure 11.1) influence the location of Rhine-Hesse and the Upper Gäu. "Deeply incised lines inside bowls" (Figure 11.24), "rows of small projections" (Figure 11.25), "strokes inside bowls" (Figure 11.27) and "triangles as secondary motifs rotated by 90°" (Figure 11.29) are responsible for the position of southern Bavaria, Bohemia and the Dresden Elbe valley.

The characteristics "incised triangles as secondary motifs" (Figure 11.12), "fingertip impressions covering the whole surface" (Figure 11.14), "three-quarter-spherical vessels" (Figure 11.15) and "hanging triangles or chevrons as secondary motifs" (Figure 11.16) mediate between Hinkelstein and the Bohemian-influenced SBK.

It is obvious to interpret the location of the regions within the correspondence analysis in such a way that geographically neighbouring regions maintained stronger contacts and exchanges and thus more similarities in the design of the pottery were achieved. The great dissimilarity — or rather the autonomy — of the Saale region, even in comparison to the geographically near Dresden Elbe valley, could indicate that the transformation from the LBK to the early Middle Neolithic took place at a time when there were few contacts with other regions. Characteristics shared with other regions, which are present in the next phase of the SBK of the Saale region, suggest that more such contacts begin a little later.

Interesting is the centre of this almost triangular distribution of regions with early Middle Neolithic finds (Figure 11). If the distribution of regions in the plot is indeed due to their geographic location, the early Middle Neolithic of Main Franconia would have to lie here. In this case it would be possible to expect a mixed style of Hinkelstein and SBK, characterised by "one chevron" (Figure 11.11), "filling motifs in variable positions and secondary motifs that form band ends"

	Characteristics	1st principal dimension	2nd principal dimension
1	early tree motifs	−1.1297	−0.018767
2	alternating strokes using tools with three or more points	−0.66308	−0.1735
3	fine incised lines / hatching	−0.64701	−0.18463
4	deeply incised, broad lines	−0.63156	−0.12258
5	single impressed dots	−0.6032	−0.12372
6	accompanying secondary motifs	−0.59994	−0.24796
7	small bulges on rim of bowls	−0.59994	−0.24796
8	separating motif and chevron do not touch rim band	−0.56853	−0.12512
9	S-shaped vessels	−0.50013	−0.165
10	filling motifs in variable positions and secondary motifs forming band ends	−0.46362	−0.48317
11	one chevron	−0.20428	−0.99141
12	incised small triangles / chevrons	−0.1925	−0.27056
13	interruption of rim band	−0.15798	−0.24801
14	fingertip impressions cover whole surface	−0.03888	−0.36694
15	three-quarter-spherical vessels	−0.051959	−0.28412
16	small hanging triangles / chevrons as secondary motifs	−0.051959	−0.28412
17	rim + chevron + separating motif	−0.28689	−0.12133
18	small upright triangles / chevrons as secondary motifs	−0.29375	−0.32736
19	high pear-shaped vessels	−0.37072	−0.37465
20	dotted small triangles / chevrons	−0.38147	−0.26263
21	deep U-shaped vessels	−0.39171	−0.96638
22	separating motif continuing through rim band	−0.40099	−0.37356
23	two or more chevrons	−0.44768	−0.37764
24	deeply incised broad lines on inside of bowls	−0.73039	−0.58723
25	rows of small projections	−0.73039	−0.58723
26	vessels with gentle carination	−0.81372	−0.51478
27	strokes inside of bowls	−0.82486	−0.096583
28	low pear-shaped vessels	−0.88575	−0.2304
29	small triangles / chevrons, rotated 90°, as secondary motifs	−1.0298	−0.33836

Figure 12. Correspondence analysis of the early Middle Neolithic pottery characteristics from different regions. Code list and values.

(Figure 11.10), the "interrupted rim bands" (Figure 11.13), "high pear-shaped vessels" (Figure 11.19) and "deep U-shaped vessels" (Figure 11.21).

In fact, for the early Middle Neolithic of Main Franconia only single finds from field surveys are known so far, some of which can be attributed to the Hinkelstein style and others to the early SBK[118]. One pit assemblage from Geldersheim, district of Schweinfurt, Lower Franconia[119] may not date to the earliest Middle Neolithic horizon because of the multiple structured band decorations present (Figure 13). Fragments of two closed forms — one with an S-shaped profile and

---

118 Engelhardt *et al.* 2006, 66–67. The individual sherds, which can be attributed to the HST or SBK style, could originate from one and the same site. I want to thank Stefan Suhrbier for the opportunity to see photographs of unpublished sherds.
119 Rosenstock and Wamser 1982, 329 fig. 18.

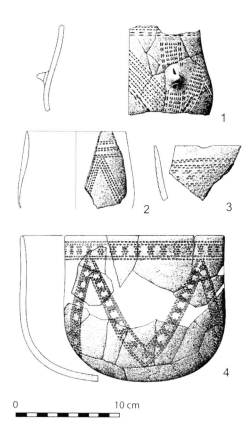

Figure 13. Geldersheim, district of Schweinfurt, Lower Franconia. Settlement pit (after Rosenstock and Wamser 1982, 329 fig. 18).

the other probably a low pear shape — and a third deep U-shaped vessel each have only got one, in two cases very narrow, chevron running around the vessel. The deep U-shaped pot definitely has no separating motif. In this assemblage, characteristics that connect the Bohemian-influenced and the east German SBK style appear together. It remains to be seen whether future finds of early Middle Neolithic Main Franconian inventories can actually be placed in the centre of this distribution of characteristics.

Conclusions

In any case, the investigations presented here lead to the conclusion that the Middle Neolithic period emerged everywhere at about the same time on the regional basis of the preceding LBK[120]. However, the regional divergences of style at the beginning of this period are not as predominant as in the preceding regional stylistic groups of the LBK, which can be interpreted more in the sense of regional cultural identity groups. At the beginning of the Middle Neolithic period, the striking similarities of style spread over the whole geographical area investigated here, in spite of the scattered nature of early settlement (Figure 1). While Neolithic pottery in general is understood as a domestic product, made by women for use in their own household, this rather uniform distribution of stylistic characteristics can be interpreted as a constant marriage network reaching across regions without known settlement sites. So it is not unlikely that after the

---

120 See also Link 2015.

end of the LBK the Middle Neolithic period started with a rather low population density[121], making it necessary to maintain contact over considerable distances. As an interim development, these stylistic similarities express a re-unification of the central European Neolithic sphere after the split of the LBK world into small regional groups and its final breakdown. Out of this rather uniform early Middle Neolithic stylistic world, new regional spheres had developed by the time of the middle Middle Neolithic period. The west German variety of the Middle Neolithic established itself with the Großgartach style, and by the time the Bohemian SBK IV and the southern Bavarian SOB II style had emerged, the emancipation from the Linear Pottery culture heritage was finally completed in all regions mentioned. These stylistic changes and spheres surely reflect cultural changes and contacts, but whether they should be interpreted as cultural units must be seen critically and will be discussed in detail in another paper[122].

References

Albert, S. 1987. Zur jungsteinzeitlichen Besiedlung von Rottenburg. Forschungen und Funde. Beiträge zur Forschungsgeschichte und Archäologie von Rottenburg und Umgebung. *Sülchgau* 29/30, 61–69.

Bofinger, J. 1996. Die mittelneolithischen Siedlungsreste von Rottenburg a. N., Lkr. Tübingen, "Lindele" – Bereich der Wüstung Sülchen. Die Grabungen 1984–1990. *Fundberichte aus Baden-Württemberg* 21, 13–105.

Bofinger, J. 2005. *Untersuchungen zur neolithischen Besiedlungsgeschichte des Oberen Gäus. Materialhefte zur Archäologie Baden-Württemberg 68*. Stuttgart.

Denaire, A. 2009. Radiocarbon dating of the western European Neolithic: comparison of the dates on bones and dates on charcoals. *Radiocarbon* 51, 657–674.

Denaire, A. 2011. Chronologie absolue de la séquence Hinkelstein-Grossgartach-Roessen-Bischheim dans le sud de la plaine du Rhin supérieur et le nord de la Franche-Comté à la lumière des dernières données. In A. Denaire, C. Jeunesse and P. Lefranc (eds), *Nécropoles et enceintes danubiennes du Ve millénaire dans le nord-est de la France et le sud-ouest de l'Allemagne. Actes de la table ronde internationale de Strasbourg organisée par l'UMR 7044, Rhin Meuse Moselle 5*, 9–30. Strasbourg.

Denaire, A., Lefranc, P., Wahl, J., Bronk Ramsey, C., Dunbar, E., Goslar, T., Bayliss, A., Beavan, N., Bickle, P. and Whittle, A. 2017. The cultural project: formal chronological modelling of the Early and Middle Neolithic sequence in Lower Alsace. *Journal of Archaeological Method and Theory* 24, 1–78.

Dieckmann, B. 1987. Ein mittelneolithischer Fundplatz bei Mühlhausen im Hegau. Stratifizierte Funde der Hinkelsteingruppe, der Stichbandkeramik und der Großgartacher Gruppe. *Archäologische Nachrichten aus Baden* 38/39, 20–28.

Dieckmann, B., Hoffstadt, J., Lohrke, B., Maier, U. and Vogt, R. 2000. Archäologie und Landesgartenschau 2000: Neue Ausgrabungen auf den "Offwiesen" in Singen, Kreis Konstanz. *Archäologische Ausgrabungen in Baden-Württemberg 2000*, 27–32.

Eibl, F. 2011. Die Bayerische Gruppe der Stichbandkeramik und die Gruppe Oberlauterbach – zum Stand der Forschung. In M. Chytráček, H. Gruber, J. Michálek, R. Sandner and K. Schmotz (eds), *Fines Transire 20*, 79–100. Rahden.

---

121 In some regions we have signs of woodland regeneration between the LBK and the Middle Neolithic (Kalis *et al.* 2003, 44–49; Meurers-Balke *et al.* 1999, 26–27).
122 Riedhammer 2017.

Engelhardt, B., Riedhammer, K. and Suhrbier, S. 2006. Mittelneolithikum – Eine neue Zeit mit alten Wurzeln. In Gesellschaft für Archäologie in Bayern (ed), *Archäologie in Bayern – Fenster zur Vergangenheit*, 65–75. Regensburg.

Gleser, R. 2012. Zeitskalen, stilistische Tendenzen und Regionalität des 5. Jahrtausends in den Altsiedellandschaften zwischen Mosel und Morava. In R. Gleser and V. Becker (eds), *Mitteleuropa im 5. Jahrtausend vor Christus. Beiträge zur Internationalen Konferenz in Münster 2010. Neolithikum und ältere Metallzeiten. Studien und Materialien 1*, 35–103. Münster.

Hammer, Ø., Harper, D.A.T. and Ryan, P.D. 2001. PAST: Paleontological Statistical software package for education and data analysis. *Paleontologica Electronica* 4, 1–9.

Herren, B. 2003. *Die alt- und mittelneolithische Siedlung von Harting-Nord, Kr. Regensburg/Oberpfalz – Befunde und Keramik aus dem Übergangshorizont zwischen Linearbandkeramik und Südostbayerischem Mittelneolithikum (SOB)*. Bonn.

Hoffmann, E. 1963. *Die Kultur der Bandkeramik in Sachsen. 1. Die Keramik. Forschungen zur Vor- und Frühgeschichte 5*. Berlin.

Jeunesse, C. and Strien, H.-C. 2009. Bemerkungen zu den stichbandkeramischen Elementen in Hinkelstein. In A. Zeeb-Lanz (ed.), *Krisen – Kulturwandel – Kontinuitäten. Zum Ende der Bandkeramik in Mitteleuropa. Beiträge der Internationalen Tagung in Herxheim bei Landau (Pfalz) vom 14.–17. 06. 2007*, 241–247. Rahden.

Kalis, A.J., Merkt, J. and Wunderlich, J. 2003. Environmental changes during the Holocene climatic optimum in central Europe — human impact and natural causes. *Quaternary Science Review* 22, 33–79.

Kaufmann, D. 1976. *Wirtschaft und Kultur der Stichbandkeramiker im Saalegebiet. Veröffentlichungen des Landesmuseums für Vorgeschichte Halle 30*. Berlin.

Kaufmann, D. 1987. Linien- und Stichbandkeramik im Elbe-Saale Gebiet. In T. Wiślański (ed.), *Neolit i początki epoki brązu na ziemi Chełmieńskij: Materiały z międzynarodowego sympozjum, Toruń, 11–13 XI 1986. The Neolithic and Early Bronze Age in the Chełmno Land. The materials from the international symposium, 11–13 XI 1986*, 275–301. Toruń.

Kaufmann, D. 2009. Anmerkungen zum Übergang von der Linien- zur Stichbandkeramik in Mitteldeutschland. In A. Zeeb-Lanz (ed.), *Krisen – Kulturwandel – Kontinuitäten. Zum Ende der Bandkeramik in Mitteleuropa. Beiträge der Internationalen Tagung in Herxheim bei Landau (Pfalz) vom 14.–17. 06. 2007*, 267–282. Rahden.

Koch, H. 2005. Neolithische Erdwerke aus Irlbach. *Das Archäologische Jahr in Bayern 2004*, 27–30.

Končelová, M. and Květina, P. 2015. Neolithic longhouse seen as a witness of change in the post-LBK. *Anthropologie* 53, 431–446.

Kuna, M. (ed.) 1991. *Neolitické sídliště v Roztokách – Die neolithische Siedlung in Roztoky I–II, Muzeum a současnost 10/I–II*. Roztoky.

Link, T. 2014a. Welche Krise? Das Ende der Linienbandkeramik aus östlicher Perspektive. In T. Link and D. Schimmelpfennig (eds), *No future? Brüche und Ende kultureller Erscheinungen. Fallbeispiele aus dem 6.–2. Jahrtausend v. Chr. Fokus Jungsteinzeit*, 95–111. Kerpen-Loogh.

Link, T. 2014b. *Die linien- und stichbandkeramische Siedlung von Dresden-Prohlis. Eine Fallstudie zum Kulturwandel in der Region der oberen Elbe um 5000 v. Chr. Veröffentlichungen des Landesamtes für Archäologie Sachsen 60*. Dresden.

Link, T. 2015. New ideas in old villages. Interpreting the genesis of the Stroked Pottery culture. *Anthropologie* 53, 351–362.

Matuschik, I. 1992. Neolithische Siedlungen in Köfering und Alteglofsheim, Landkreis Regensburg, Oberpfalz. *Das Archäologische Jahr in Bayern 1991*, 26–29.

Meier-Arendt, W. 1975. *Die Hinkelsteingruppe. Der Übergang vom Früh- zum Mittelneolithikum in Südwestdeutschland. Römisch-Germanische Forschungen 35*. Berlin.

Meurers-Balke, J., Kalis, A.J., Gerlach, R. and Jürgens, A. 1999. Landschafts- und Siedlungsgeschichte des Rheinlandes. In K.-H. Knörzer, R. Gerlach, J. Meurers-Balke, A.J. Kalis, U. Tegtmeier, W.D. Becker and A. Jürgens (eds), *Pflanzenspuren. Archäobotanik im Rheinland: Agrarlandschaft und Nutzpflanzen im Wandel der Zeiten. Materialien zur Bodendenkmalpflege im Rheinland 10*, 11–66. Köln.

Nadler, M., Zeeb, A., Böhm, K., Brink-Kloke, H., Riedhammer, K., Ganslmeier, R., Poensgen, U., Riedmeier-Fischer, E., Spatz, H., Rind, M.M. and Blaich, F. 1994. Südbayern zwischen Linearbandkeramik und Altheim: Ein neuer Gliederungsvorschlag. In H.-J. Beier (ed.), *Der Rössener Horizont in Mitteleuropa*, 127–189. Wilkau-Hasslau.

Nagel, A.E. 1999. *Keramik und Befunde der neolithischen Siedlung von Köfering-"Kelleräcker II", Lkr. Regensburg*. Unpublished Master Dissertation, University of Heidelberg.

Neubauer, H. 1955. Wallersdorf (Ldkr. Landau a.d. Isar). *Bayerische Vorgeschichtsblätter* 21, 172–173.

Nieszery, N. 1995. *Linearbandkeramische Gräberfelder in Bayern. Internationale Archäologie 16*. Espelkamp.

Pavlů, I. 1992. Nové neolitické naleziště v Nynicích (okr. Plzeň-sever). – A new Neolithic site in Nynice. *Archeologické rozhledy* 44, 356–365.

Pavlů, I., Salač, V. and Zápotocká, M. 1993. Neolitická sídliště u Třebenic. Neolithische Ansiedlungen bei Třebenice. *Archeologické rozhledy* 45, 185–211.

Pechtl, J. 2009. *Stephansposching und sein Umfeld. Studien zum Altneolithikum im bayerischen Donauraum*. Unpublished PhD dissertation, University of Heidelberg.

Pratsch, A. 1999. *Die linien- und stichbandkeramische Siedlung in Dresden-Cotta. Eine frühneolithische Siedlung im Dresdner Elbkessel. Beiträge zur Ur- und Frühgeschichte Mitteleuropas 17*. Weissbach.

Riedhammer, K. 1994a. *Die mittelneolithische Keramik des Fundplatzes Straubing-Lerchenhaid, Stadt Straubing, Niederbayern (Grabung 1980–82)*. Unpublished Magister dissertation, University of Frankfurt a. M.

Riedhammer, K. 1994b. Die Stichbandkeramik von Straubing-Lerchenhaid. In M. Nadler, A. Zeeb, K. Böhm, H. Brink-Kloke, K. Riedhammer, R. Ganslmeier, U. Poensgen, E. Riedmeier-Fischer, H. Spatz, M.M. Rind and F. Blaich, Südbayern zwischen Linearbandkeramik und Altheim: Ein neuer Gliederungsvorschlag. In H.-J. Beier (ed.), *Der Rössener Horizont in Mitteleuropa*, 132–136. Wilkau-Hasslau.

Riedhammer, K. 2005. Sternenkundler und Bergbauspezialisten. *Antike Welt* 36, 69–76.

Riedhammer, K. 2012. Möglichkeiten und Grenzen der absoluten Datierung des Südostbayerischen Mittelneolithikums. In A. Boschetti-Maradi, A. de Capitani, S. Hochuli and U. Niffeler (eds), *Form, Zeit und Raum. Grundlagen für eine Geschichte aus dem Boden. Festschrift für Werner E. Stöckli zu seinem 65. Geburtstag. Antiqua 50*, 69–78. Basel.

Riedhammer, K. 2015. 450 post LBK years in southern Bavaria. *Antropologie* 53, 387–398.

Riedhammer, K. 2016. Zwischen Großgartach, Stichbandkeramik und Mährisch Bemalter Keramik. In J. Kovárník *et al.* (eds), *Centenary of Jaroslav Palliardi's Neolithic and Aeneolithic relative chronology (1914–2014)*, 127–148. Ústí nad Orlicí.

Riedhammer, K. 2017. *Typologie und Chronologie des Südostbayerischen Mittelneolithikums unter besonderer Berücksichtigung der Fundplätze Straubing-Lerchenhaid und Geiselhöring-Süd, Lkr. Straubing-Bogen, Niederbayern.* Unpublished PhD dissertation, University of Bern.

Rosenstock, D. and Wamser, L. 1982. Ausgrabungen und Funde in Unterfranken 1980–1982. I. Steinzeit bis Urnenfelderzeit. *Frankenland Neue Folge* 34, 301–380.

Spatz, H. 1996. *Beiträge zum Kulturenkomplex Hinkelstein – Großgartach – Rössen. Der keramische Fundstoff des Mittelneolithikums aus dem mittleren Neckarraum und seine zeitliche Gliederung. Materialhefte zur Archäologie in Baden-Württemberg 37*. Stuttgart.

Spatz, H. 1999. *Das mittelneolithische Gräberfeld von Trebur, Kreis Groß-Gerau. Materialien zur Vor- und Frühgeschichte in Hessen 19*. Wiesbaden.

Spatz, H. 2002. Bäumchen und Sichel: Aspekte und Überlegungen zum Übergang vom frühen zum mittleren Neolithikum in Zentraleuropa. *Archeologické rozhledy* 54, 279–300.

Spatz, H. 2003. Hinkelstein: Eine Sekte als Initiator des Mittelneolithikums? In J. Eckert, U. Eisenhauer and A. Zimmermann (eds), *Archäologische Perspektiven. Analysen und Interpretationen im Wandel. Festschrift für Jens Lüning zum 65. Geburtstag*, 575–587. Rahden.

Stöckli, W.E. 2002. *Absolute und relative Chronologie des Früh- und Mittelneolithikums in Westdeutschland (Rheinland und Rhein-Main-Gebiet). Basler Hefte zur Archäologie 1*. Basel.

Suhrbier, S. 2012. Multikulti in Mainfranken – Der Beginn des Mittelneolithikums. In R. Gleser and V. Becker (eds), *Mitteleuropa im 5. Jahrtausend vor Christus. Beiträge zur Internationalen Konferenz in Münster 2010. Neolithikum und ältere Metallzeiten. Studien und Materialien 1*, 141–149. Münster.

Suhrbier, S. 2018. *Das Mittelneolithikum in Mainfranken. Chronologie und Siedlungsentwicklung.* Unpublished PhD dissertation, Freie Universität Berlin.

Van de Velde, P. 1979. On Bandkeramik social structure. An analysis of pot decoration and hut distributions from the central European Neolithic communities of Elsloo and Hienheim. *Analecta Praehistorica Leidensia* 12, 1–242.

Van de Velde, P. 1986a. Die Entwicklung der Keramikverzierung in der Hienheimer Bandkeramik. In P.J.R. Modderman (ed.), *Die Neolithische Besiedlung bei Hienheim, Ldkr. Kelheim. II–IV. Materialhefte zur Bayerischen Vorgeschichte 57*, 43–50. Kallmünz.

Van de Velde, P. 1986b. Die Hienheimer Keramikverzierung in einem breiteren Kontext. In P.J.R. Modderman (ed.), *Die Neolithische Besiedlung bei Hienheim, Ldkr. Kelheim. II–IV. Materialhefte zur Bayerischen Vorgeschichte 57*, 88–95. Kallmünz.

Vencl, P. 1961. Studie über den Šárka-Typus. *Sborník Národního muzea, řada A* 15, 93–140.

Vondrovský, V. 2015. *Neolitický sídelní areál Hrdlovka: Analýza keramického materiálu.* Unpublished diploma dissertation, University of České Budějovice.

Vondrovsky, V., Beneš, J., Divišova, M., Kovačikova, L. and Šida, P. 2016. From LBK to SBK: pottery, bones, lithics and houses at the Neolithic site of Hrdlovka, Czech Republic. *Open Archaeology* 2016/2, 303–327.

Zápotocká, M. 1970. Die Stichbandkeramik in Böhmen und Mitteleuropa. Unpublished manuscript for: H. Schwabedissen (ed.), *Die Anfänge des Neolithikums vom Orient bis Nordeuropa. 2. Östliches Mitteleuropa. Fundamenta A3 II*. Köln.

Zápotocká, M. 1972. Die Hinkelsteinkeramik und ihre Beziehungen zum zentralen Gebiet der Stichbandkeramik. Analyse und Auswertung der Gräberfelder Worms-Rheingewann und Rheindürkheim. *Památky Archeologické* 63, 267–374.

Zápotocká, M. 1982. Chlustina, okr. Beroun. Příspěvek k neolitickému osídlení Hořovicka. Ein Beitrag zur neolithischen Besiedlung des Hořovicer Raumes. *Archeologické rozhledy* 34, 121–159.

Zápotocká, M. 1986. Die Brandgräber von Vikletice. Ein Beitrag zum chronologischen Verhältnis von Stich- und Rhein-Bandkeramik. *Archeologické rozhledy* 38, 623–649.

Zápotocká, M. 1998a. *Bestattungsritus des böhmischen Neolithikums (5500–4200 B.C.). Gräber und Bestattungen der Kultur mit Linear-, Stichband- und Lengyelkeramik*. Praha.

Zápotocká, M. 1998b. Die chronologische und geographische Gliederung der postlinearkeramischen Kulturgruppen mit Stichverzierung. In J. Preuß (ed.), *Das Neolithikum in Mitteleuropa, Teil B: Übersichten zum Stand und zu Problemen der archäologischen Forschung*, 286–306. Weissbach.

Zápotocká, M. 2007. Die Entstehung und Ausbreitung der Kultur mit Stichbandkeramik in Mitteleuropa. In J.K. Kozłowski and P. Raczky (eds), *The Lengyel, Polgár and related cultures in the Middle/Late Neolithic in central Europe*, 199–215. Kraków.

Zápotocká, M. 2009a. Der Übergang von der Linear- zur Stichbandkeramik in Böhmen. In A. Zeeb-Lanz (ed.), *Krisen – Kulturwandel – Kontinuitäten. Zum Ende der Bandkeramik in Mitteleuropa. Beiträge der Internationalen Tagung in Herxheim bei Landau (Pfalz) vom 14.–17. 06. 2007*, 303–315. Rahden.

Zápotocká, M. 2009b. *Neolitické sídelní regiony v Čechách (ca 5300–4400 př. Kr.). Region Litoměřicko. Neolithische Siedlungsregionen in Böhmen (ca 5300–4400 v. Chr.). Die Region Litoměřice. Archeologické Studijní Materiály 18*. Praha.

Zápotocká, M. 2013. *The Neolithic. The prehistory of Bohemia 2*. Praha.

Zápotocká, M. and Muška, J. 2007. *Hrbovice, Okres Ústí nad Labem. Výzkum 1978. Sídelní areál kultury s keramikou lineární a vypíchanou. Hrbovice, Kreis Ústí nad Labem. Ausgrabung 1978. Ein Siedlungsareal mit der Linear- und Stichbandkeramik*. Praha.

The oldest box-shaped wooden well from Saxony-Anhalt and the Stichbandkeramik culture in central Germany

René Wollenweber

Abstract

Data from Niederröblingen (district of Mansfeld-Südharz in Saxony-Anhalt) show, at the level of settlement structure, a dynamic and continuous development from the Linear Pottery culture (LBK) to the Stichbandkeramik culture (Stroke-Ornamented Pottery culture, or SBK). This development manifests itself through a restructuring of the settlement and, in general, through a slight decrease in settlement activities between LBK and SBK.

This is in line with or in contradiction to — depending on whether one is following the eastern or the south-western point of view — current interpretations of settlement development itself. Thus, the Early Neolithic settlement of Niederröblingen occupies a key position in the discussion of cultural change from LBK to SBK, and between the principle of discontinuity preferred in the south-west and the principle of continuity preferred in the east.

As a first result, it becomes clear that the development of the SBK has to be differentiated at a large scale and chronologically. It seems that the original SBK evolved in the western part of the LBK distribution in the form of the early Hinkelstein culture (HSK). During its eastward spread, the SBK phenomenon then falls on more or less fertile ground.

Zusammenfassung: Der älteste hölzerne Kastenbrunnen aus Sachsen-Anhalt und die Stichbandkeramik in Mitteldeutschland

Die Daten aus Niederröblingen (Landkreis Mansfeld-Südharz, Sachsen-Anhalt) zeigen auf der Siedlungsebene eine dynamische und kontinuierliche Entwicklung von der Linienbandkeramik (LBK) zur Stichbandkeramik (SBK). Diese Entwicklung manifestiert sich durch eine Siedlungsumstrukturierung und eine zwischenzeitliche, leichte Abnahme der Siedlungstätigkeit.

Dies steht in Einklang und gleichzeitig im Widerspruch – je nach Sichtweise – zu gängigen Annahmen der Siedlungsentwicklung, entweder südwestlicher oder östlicher Prägung. Die bandkeramische Siedlung aus Niederröblingen steht damit im Spannungsfeld der Diskussion zum Kulturwandel von LBK zur SBK und zwischen dem im Südwesten präferierten Diskontinuitäts- und dem im Osten bevorzugten Kontinuitätsprinzip.

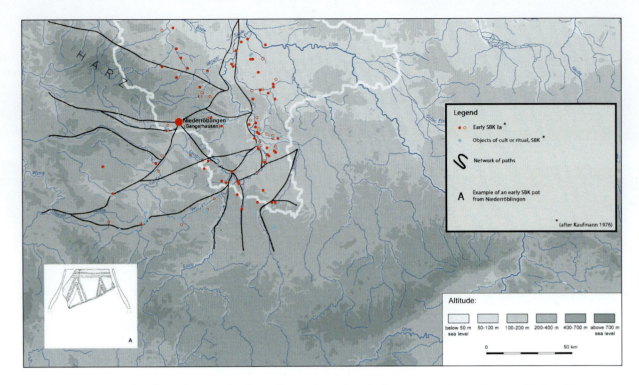

Figure 1. Niederröblingen. Location, paths and the early SBK in western central Germany. The site is also close to the early SBK site of "Sangerhausen Erfurter-Bahndamm" mentioned by Kaufmann (1976, 182 map 15).

Als ein erstes Ergebnis lässt sich feststellen, dass das Aufkommen der SBK großräumig und zeitlich differenziert zu betrachten ist. Es scheint sich herauszukristallisieren, dass die ursprüngliche SBK im westlichen Bereich der LBK in Form der frühen Hinkelsteinkultur (HSK) entsteht und im Zuge ihrer Ausbreitung oder Weitergabe nach Osten auf unterschiedlich „fruchtbaren" Boden fällt.

Introduction

The starting point for dealing with the cultural change at the transition from the sixth to the fifth millennium was the excavation of an LBK/SBK box-shaped wooden well, preserved in waterlogged conditions, and its associated Early Neolithic settlement at Niederröblingen. Niederröblingen is situated at a nodal point in an important (pre)historic path network, which has remained accessible to western and southern influences until today. It is therefore not surprising that a centrally placed site like Niederröblingen should also yield evidence for the chronologically early stage of the SBK[1] (Figure 1) and many other archaeological Neolithic cultures, up to the Bronze and Iron Ages.

The ongoing evaluation of the well and the data from the Early Neolithic settlement suggest two main possibilities for interpreting cultural change in Niederröblingen. On the one hand it seems possible to support arguments for a continuous and on the other hand for a more discontinuous sequence between LBK and SBK.

Without knowing the chronological resolution of the backfilling processes of the settlement pits (for instance pits next to houses and postholes), which alongside graves and wells are the main source of information at Niederröblingen and contain the archaeological finds assemblage, it is difficult to provide plausible

---

1   Stage SBK Ia/b after Kaufmann 1976.

estimates regarding the simultaneous or successive deposition of finds of different cultures. This of course also applies to all archaeological finds and cultures in general. The following statements are based on the premise that the use of pots and the deposition of whole vessels — or even fragments of them — into the soil of a highly frequented settlement site are mostly not chronologically equal. If material is incorporated into a pit at different points in time, even repeatedly, or if older material was rearranged and redeposited several times, then without a typology-independent method of dating it cannot be established whether the mixed material was in use at the same time or not. A pit cannot be dated by the ceramics alone. Further observations relating to the archaeological features, such as their structure or absolute dates, are essential for a more reliable interpretation. A monocausal interpretation, based on typological considerations only, is necessarily speculative and naive. So only a few pits out of thousands or only some layers from these few pits may contain material of a chronologically related sequence[2]. That soon became clear once the first absolute dating of the well was obtained.

Some aspects of the well and of the settlement at Niederröblingen

A sample of an oak plank was already analysed by M. Friedrich during the excavation[3]. The first date, obtained on sapwood, was 5108 ± 10 BC. Thus, it was clear that a section of the well dated to the late LBK. AMS samples of organic material from the backfill of the well, as well as sherds of the LBK/SBK interface, cover a duration from the 53rd to the 49th century BC[4]. In the absence of a complete dating series of all oak timbers, which is still in progress, it cannot yet be decided whether the well was in use continuously, or whether the overall use life of 400 years comprised several separate phases. At the time a preliminary report was written (late 2015), the results of the dendrochronological dating were not yet completely available and therefore it seemed unwarranted to simply assume a continuous use of the well[5].

Until the final results of the scientific analyses are available (planned for 2019), investigations had to rely mainly on the ceramic material and some first AMS dates. Only the SBK sherds show fresh fractures, have preserved original surfaces, show a lower degree of fragmentation and edge rounding and provided refits. Given that the SBK sherds reach down to the base of the well shaft, it can be concluded that the main part of the backfill was deposited no later than during the stage of the early SBK[6] (Figure 2). It was conspicuous that the earliest AMS dates within this backfill were exclusively obtained on carbonised cereals which date to the late LBK.

So it can be assumed that only carbonised cereals have survived in greater quantities within the backfill of the well shaft during dry periods, given the long duration of the well, its cleaning out and the special taphonomic conditions pertaining to organic micro- and macroremains in this environment. Thus, it became doubtful whether the well had indeed been in use continuously.

---

2 Undisturbed graves may be equated in their chronological relevance to these rare layers of settlement pits, as can the last backfilling stage of a well.
3 M. Friedrich, Universität Hohenheim, Institut für Botanik.
4 B. Kromer, CEZ Archäometrie GmbH Mannheim.
5 Cf. Wollenweber 2016, 10.
6 Stage SBK Ib after Kaufmann 1976.

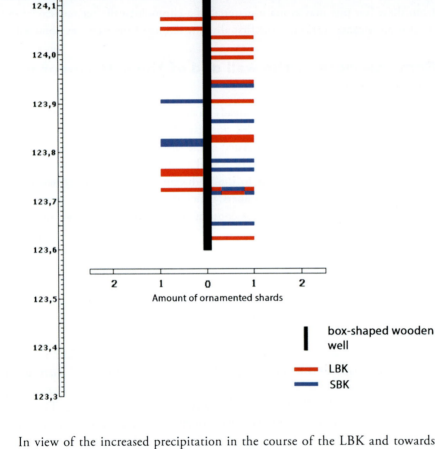

Figure 2. Niederröblingen, well feature 6565. Distribution of LBK and SBK fragments in the box-shaped wooden well. It is obvious that the SBK sherds (blue) reach down to the bottom of the well.

In view of the increased precipitation in the course of the LBK and towards its end[7], it is also possible that a higher water level in the well prevented its being backfilled with datable material. In that case, the impression of discontinuity in the use of the well and in settlement activity would be erroneous[8].

With these at first glance contradictory results for the well in mind, it became possible to critically scrutinise other settlement features with mixed assemblages

---

7   B. Schmidt *et al.* 2004.
8   First dendrochronological series from the well do manifest a chronological gap in repairing the bottom of the well shaft during the 50th century BC. According to hydrological GIS-based modelling, the bottom of the well could not be reached as a result of increasingly humid conditions after very dry phases in the late 52nd century (Wollenweber in prep.).

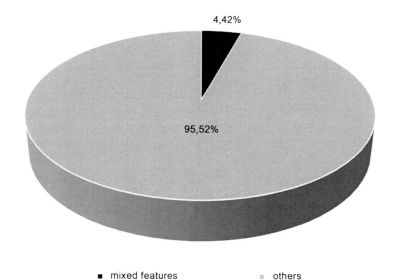

Figure 3. Niederröblingen. Pie chart showing only 4.42 % of the features in Niederröblingen contain ornamented pottery from both the LBK and the SBK.

of LBK and SBK material. It became apparent that the mixture of SBK and LBK material in features at Niederröblingen is very rare in comparison to the total amount of features containing Early Neolithic material. Only 44 features (out of 995 with finds material), including the well, contain mixed material of both LBK and SBK decorated ceramics. This corresponds to only 4.42 % of all Early Neolithic features in the excavated part of the settlement (Figure 3).

Additionally, many of the features cannot be interpreted as "closed" assemblages, but as pits with secondary or indeed multiple intrusions. These pits can be seen as "disturbed" pits in a narrow sense. Frequently, Bronze Age and Iron Age ceramics also appear within the features, which provides an additional taphonomic filter. The degree of rounding of the sherds was also recorded and divided into three levels. Regarding the features with mixed ceramic material, this showed that the LBK and SBK sherds were often not deposited, and hence also not used, at the same time. Together with the contradictory data from the well, there are serious arguments for a slight decrease of settlement activities between the LBK and SBK at Niederröblingen.

Although settlement activities seemed to decrease between LBK and SBK, transitional pottery forms, such as very rare pots decorated only with rows of single incisions, are in evidence and suggest a degree of settlement continuity. Such items are absent in the well (Figure 4). These characteristic elements, such as parallel rows of single incisions and the absence of incised lines, seem to be imitations of SBK precedents and appear to stand in an LBK tradition. This technique of ornamentation — in the case of the LBK in combination with incised lines — is well-known throughout the later LBK in the northern Harz region[9] and also in eastern Thuringia[10].

Alongside these critical considerations concerning the features, one must always bear in mind the question concerning the transition between the LBK and

---

9 Cf. Einicke 1993, plate 9.
10 Cf. Einicke 2014, 174, 816.

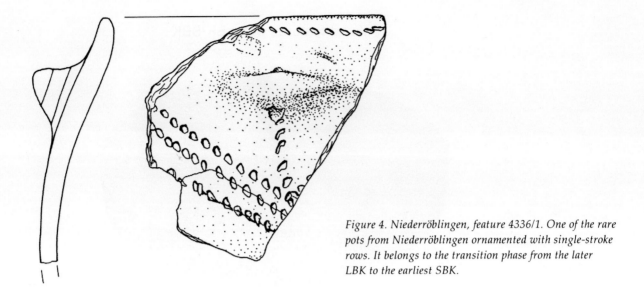

Figure 4. Niederröblingen, feature 4336/1. One of the rare pots from Niederröblingen ornamented with single-stroke rows. It belongs to the transition phase from the later LBK to the earliest SBK.

SBK cultures more generally. In this context, the spatial and temporal relation between the LBK and SBK deserves special attention.

Some aspects of research history

The turn of the fifth millennium in central and south-west Germany is characterised by the appearance of stroke-ornamented pottery, which is supposed to evolve out of an LBK context. For instance, H. Behrens explicitly stated for central Germany that the SBK "has such a clear connection to the LBK in terms of vessel shapes that one cannot doubt the existence of a genetic dependency"[11]. Given the current state of research, this scenario certainly seems applicable at least to the relationship between LBK and early Hinkelstein (HSK) in Rhenish Hesse (Rhineland-Palatinate)[12].

In detail, however, this idea may not be transferred to the whole LBK distribution. The simplifying biologism of a "genetic dependency" or continuity is often merely used as a placeholder, which obscures a much more complex problem of intra-LBK variability and of the timings and modalities of cultural change.

What we can say for now is that the early stage of the "archaic" SBK[13] is of very short duration. This provides an interesting parallel for other periods in the Neolithic, when we can recognise that times of cultural stability are followed by very sudden events, as for instance in the dissemination of the Michelsberg phenomenon or the spread of the LBK itself.

After all, one could just as well reject the idea of continuous development from LBK to SBK and instead stress that the 500-year long tradition of incised decoration on pottery was discontinued, new types of pots and houses were established, rondels were finally introduced from the Lengyel culture area and burial customs changed, with graves and cemeteries almost completely absent during the early

---

11 Behrens 1973, 43: "Sie [i.e. the SBK] besitzt eine so deutliche Formenverwandschaft mit der Linienbandkeramik, dass an einem genetischen Abhängigkeitsverhältnis nicht zu zweifeln ist". A very similar term was already used by M. Zápotocká 1970, 1.
12 Cf. Biermann 2001, 378.
13 Stage Ia after Kaufmann 1976.

SBK in central Germany. Therefore, the emergence of the SBK may not only be adequately subsumed under the heading of "fashionable innovations"[14]. It could also be a real cultural break and the beginning of something new.

This cultural new beginning, pointedly characterised by H. Spatz as a "sect"[15], starts in the south-west of Germany no later than Strien's stage LBK 7[16] (or with Dohrn-Ihmig's stage LBK 2c[17]) and is represented by the early HSK. This transition can be pinpointed in an area near the city of Worms (Rhineland-Palatinate) and in the Kraichgau just to the north[18]. Following this model, the early HSK does not develop from the SBK, as conventional models would have it. Much more plausible is an inverted model according to which the SBK develops from the HSK. However, it must be mentioned that there is currently no direct evidence of the contact between western LBK/HSK and the SBK in central Germany[19], an aspect which needs further research; efforts are already under way[20]. In any case, this pattern is not surprising given the general decrease of settlement activities at the end of the LBK.

The typological and technological similarities between the early SBK in central Germany and the early HSK are undeniable[21]. Yet it remains problematic that the available absolute dates for the early HSK are few and are only useable with reservations[22].

A further model for the development of the SBK is its polycentric formation, including a simultaneous development of stylistic elements in different regions and a fast expansion[23]. However, this model is currently not backed up by any absolute dates or spatial vector data[24]. This idea assumes a kind of shared cultural superstructure and rightly emphasises the connection between regions through exchange systems and networks. However, it seems problematic that the possible areas of origin and formation of the SBK (which, until proven otherwise, may well have existed) are treated as chronologically equivalent. This means that from the start, there is no further attempt at identifying chronological depth within the early SBK. Yet even a synchronous development should be influenced by adjacent regions. Another question is whether we can measure the probably rather short period of proliferation of the SBK with archaeological methods and with the rare early SBK sources. This is not a question of interpreting the structure of a culture, but in the first instance a methodological problem (see below).

So far, the polycentric model seems to completely reject both diffusion and colonisation or migration as potential drivers of cultural change[25]. It is therefore a rather convenient model, which neglects both the difficulties and opportunities

---

14 Kaufmann 1976, 109: "modische Neubildungen".
15 Spatz 2002; 2003.
16 Strien 1990, 63–64.
17 Dohrn-Ihmig 1979.
18 Jeunesse and Strien 2009, 244; Strien 2013.
19 Spatz 1996, 507.
20 Cf. Einicke 2016; Siller 2016; Wollenweber in prep.
21 Cf. Spatz 1999, 251ff.
22 E.g. the AMS dates from the cemetery of Trebur show a systematic error and seem to be 100 or 200 years too young (cf. Müller 2002, 151–152). Additionally, only a very small number of AMS dates are available for the HSK in general.
23 Cf. Link 2012a, 127; Wolf-Schuler 2009, 298.
24 Link 2014b, 228.
25 Cf. Link 2014b, 229.

offered by absolute and relative dating methods. A recent study[26] questioning the SBK development stated plausibly that the former opinion of the development of the SBK from the Bohemian *Šárka horizon* is far from certain at the moment. Unfortunately, this study provided no breakthrough in explaining the early SBK phenomenon[27].

The fact remains that there currently exist several serious gaps in our understanding, which prevent a plausible solution for the origin of the SBK. These are:

- lack of absolute dates concerning the end of the LBK, in particular any regional diversity in the timing of this end
- two radiocarbon plateaus corresponding to the periods of interest (the early 51st century for Hinkelstein development and the transition from the 50th to the 49th century for the SBK phenomenon in central Germany)
- lack of temporal and spatial resolution regarding the occurrence of the earliest elements of the SBK
- lack of differentiation between the concepts of continuity in settlement structure and the continuity of archaeological cultures on the site in general
- a continuous development from LBK to SBK does not automatically imply an immediate proximity to the SBK epicentre
- variable definitions of the characteristics of the earliest SBK
- the dogma of *ex oriente lux*, which claims that innovations came only from the east
- LBK-centrism, which results in the LBK being mainly seen as a contributing culture, neglecting its capacities for absorption
- the assumption of a one-sided "culture-giving" behaviour of the LBK; this neglects the possibility of an inter- and extracultural source of the SBK-phenomenon
- regionalism of research — researchers preferentially see their study region as the area of formation of the SBK and/or try to differentiate it as much as possible from neighbouring regions

On this basis, it is still difficult to satisfactorily position the SBK phenomenon spatially and temporally. Nevertheless, it seems possible to make some models of SBK development more probable than others, based on the principle of exclusion, combined with the results of recent excavations, absolute dating and computer-based typologies.

The break within the correspondence analyses

An important indication that the "genetic dependency" should be questioned is the difference of the ceramics between the SBK and LBK. This is reflected in central Germany by several correspondence analyses of ceramic material, which have repeatedly shown that LBK and SBK are not reconcilable with each other. This is in spite of some core categories of ceramic description, such as angled

---

26   Wolf-Schuler 2009, 298.
27   Cf. Kaufmann 2014, 535.

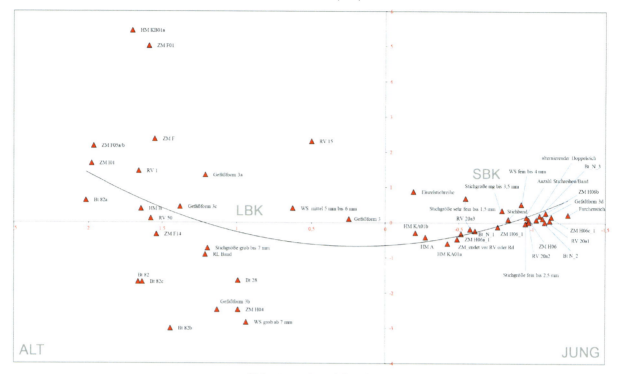
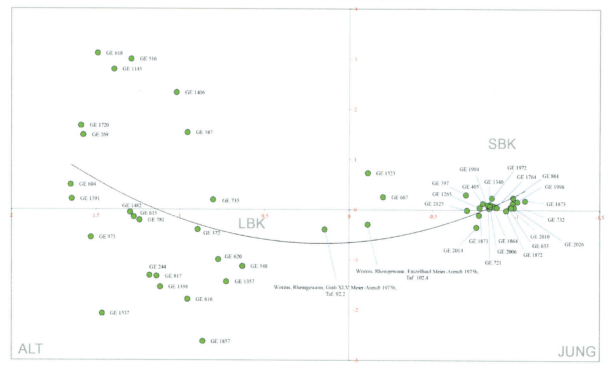

Figure 5. Niederröblingen, correspondence analysis. The clusters belonging to LBK and SBK are obvious. The weakly defined transition phase in Niederröblingen unsatisfactorily fills the gap with the technique (variables) of single-stroke rows, globular pots (Gefäßform 3) and rectilinear motifs (top graph). Pots of the exogenous HSK cemetery of Worms-Rheingewann (objects) also fall into this gap (bottom graph). For further information on the variables and objects used in the production of this figure, see Wollenweber in prep.

ribbons and the technique of the double stroke, being very well known from both cultures and especially from their mutual transition phase.

For example, in a correspondence analysis based on randomly selected LBK and SBK material from Niederröblingen and comprising 47 representative pots, LBK and SBK form two markedly different groups or clusters (Figure 5). This applies to visualisations at the level of both pots and attributes. Interestingly, in the case of Niederröblingen only two additionally included pots from the HSK burial ground of Worms-Rheingewann[28] are situated centrally in the middle of the curve (see Figure 5). This is not surprising if the curve records a chronological gradient and if we accept the early position of the HSK within SBK development. Only in a HSK context do we find examples which include the technique of the alternating double stroke as well as the tradition of incised lines on globular pots. This combination of a specific ornamentation and a typical LBK pot type are exclusively known in the early HSK and together form the typological missing link between LBK and SBK.

The same applies to a correspondence analysis of the LBK/SBK settlement of Dresden-Prohlis (district of Dresden, Saxony), which shows a marked break between SBK and LBK[29]. Despite the clear break at Dresden-Prohlis, an interpretation of continuous settlement activity between LBK and SBK can be suggested[30].

Furthermore, the Dresden Elbe valley and Bohemia have been repeatedly suggested as regions of origin for or as being close to the epicentre of the SBK[31]. It is of interest that the emergence of the SBK has been seen in connection with the formation of a new SBK group identity[32]. Recently, even Bohemain colleagues have doubted the polyfocal model proposed by Link[33].

Another break between LBK and SBK is visible in a correspondence analysis of ceramic material for the extensively excavated settlement of Zwenkau/Eythra (district of Leipzig Land, Saxony)[34]. A contiguous curve can only be recognised within the LBK or SBK developments themselves. A similar picture has been obtained at the LBK/SBK site of Hrdlovka (Czech Republic) in a correspondence analysis of the assemblages from cut features[35].

In conclusion, so far the differences between LBK and SBK have been interpreted as a problem of ornamentation technique or as a methodological problem, and not as evidence for a hiatus, transformation or decrease of settlement activities. The differences are not explicitly discussed from a chronological point of view.

At the level of ornamentation it seems indeed difficult to create the preferred motif of the LBK, the spiral, using the technique of the alternating double stroke. This could therefore be one reason why rectilinear main motifs were preferred in the SBK[36]. However, combined patterns of incised lines and (parallel) rows of double strokes in the later LBK show that when using variations of this technique, spiral main motifs could also be realised[37]. Several pots ornamented

---

28 Meier-Arendt 1975, Tab. 92.2, 102.4.
29 Link 2012b, 278, figs 4–5; 2014b, 71ff.
30 Link 2014a, 97; 2014b, 196, 216.
31 Link 2012b, 281; 2014b, 217.
32 Link 2014b, 226.
33 Vondrowsky et al. 2016, 323; contra Link 2014b.
34 Frīdrich 2016, fig. 6.2.
35 Vondrowsky et al. 2016, fig. 3B.
36 Cf. Kaufmann 1976, 43; 2009b, 47.
37 E.g. Einicke 1993, tabs 17, 19, 24, 27, 28, 34; Leinthaler and Bogen 2012, figs 25, 42.

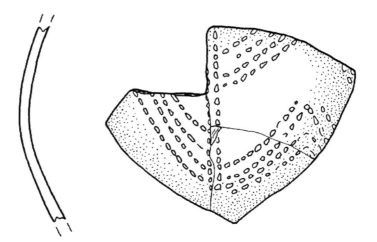

Figure 6. Niederröblingen, feature 8799. A spiral-like main motif realised in the technique of the alternating double stroke.

with the technique of the alternating double stroke, but with curvilinear motifs, are the exception which proves the rule (Figure 6). Conversely, main motifs in a rectilinear style also played a large role in the LBK.

As the technique of the parallel double stroke is generally combined with spiral main motifs, it can be argued that this technique exclusively occurs in the LBK. Similarly, the typical, low-centred pots in combination with the alternating double stroke and the rectilinear main motif are defining for the SBK.

The discrepancy between LBK and SBK in the correspondence analysis so far seems to be down to a mixture of chronological and methodological reasons.

What is typical for early SBK ware?

The first useful definition of the early SBK in central Germany was formulated by D. Kaufmann[38]. The striking nature of the selected characteristics led him to define an "archaic" SBK, as he thought he could recognise an isolated early variant in central Germany[39]. Based on this early central German stage of the SBK, the following essential criteria were defined:

- the good quality and low wall thickness of the vessels, especially in stages SBK Ia/b
- a high firing temperature
- globular pots with a straight upper part, sometimes slightly everted
- pear-shaped pots with a low centre of gravity
- beaker-like shapes ("Bechernapf")
- simple rows of double strokes, narrow angular bands and a strictly angular motif structure
- the upper and lower apices of the stroke ribbons coincide
- rows of double strokes with small (< 1.5 mm) incisions, which increase over the course of the SBK
- the alternating double stroke

---

38   Kaufmann 1976.
39   SBK stage Ia after Kaufmann 1976.

These criteria already make spatial differences and relations visible. For instance, it is striking that variants of globular pots with a straight upper part (see point 3 above) and pear-shaped pots (point 4), both ornamented with the alternating double stroke, occur together with incised lines as a retarding effect of the LBK, but do so only in the HSK[40]. These types of pots can be derived from typical later LBK shapes and may show the western origin of the SBK phenomenon. Similarly, beaker-like pots (point 5) also find their predecessors in the western LBK/HSK, while these pots are nearly absent in Saxony and Bohemia[41]. We can now add some chronologically sensitive criteria (see Figure 8).

In contrast, the criterion of increasing stroke size over the course of the SBK seems to be of limited applicability, as it does not apply to the early HSK. Instead, the relatively big strokes in the HSK could show that small strokes only emerged during the spread of the SBK and only became an important identifier upon the arrival of the SBK in central Germany. This could be interpreted as a slight chronological offset for the beginning of early HSK in contrast to the beginning of the early SBK in central Germany.

The alternating double stroke

A defining characteristic of the early SBK is the alternating double stroke[42]. It provides a technological distinction between SBK and later LBK, which at least in central Germany does not use this technique. This technique is of essential importance because it later became the tremolo technique, which dominated the further development of decoration in all SBK regions and chronological stages. It must be distinguished from the tremolo stroke, which has to be carried out with a simple chisel-shaped instrument applied in an alternating technique[43].

In particular, the transition from the parallel to the alternating double stroke deserves a closer look. Typologically, this transition can first be observed in the material of the early HSK. Only in the early HSK can the transition be seen as an autochthonous development, as this is supported by several further characteristics[44]. This sequence of stroke techniques seems indeed to have taken place multiple times in several regions, but has to be differentiated by region and time. While some authors see the parallel double stroke as a predecessor for the alternating double stroke[45], it can also be argued that the alternating double stroke is a strategy of imitation outside the HSK distribution. This does not necessarily mean a continuous development from LBK to SBK outside the HSK area. So far, the early HSK is the only case where this technological transition indicates a broader continuity, as the development can be observed on the pots as the smallest closed unit. Therefore, the alternating double stroke and the evolving SBK derive from the genesis of the early HSK out of its local LBK substrate.

Furthermore, as the alternating double stroke requires slightly greater technological know-how, it can be seen as the first reflection of the tremolo technique in the SBK. The tremolo technique itself is plausibly a result of a

---

40 Cf. Meier-Arendt 1975; Zápotocká 1972.
41 Kaufmann 1976, 18.
42 Kaufmann 1976, 29–30.
43 Cf. Zápotocká 1978, 526.
44 Meier-Arendt 1975, esp. tabs 92, 102.4; cf. Zápotocká 1972, 338ff.
45 E.g. Link 2014a, 95.

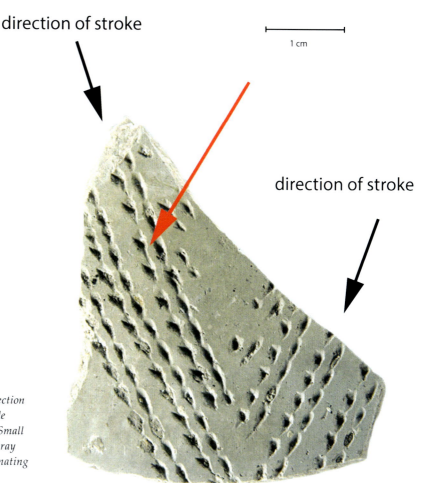

Figure 7. Niederröblingen, feature 4509. Direction (black arrows) and depth of the strokes provide insight into the technique of ornamentation. Small imperfections in the use of the instrument betray the tremolo technique (red arrow) of the alternating double stroke.

transfer of technology (and more?) from the Cardial-influenced Villeneuve-Saint-Germain culture and its predecessors into the LBK and the HSK[46].

Another possibility to produce a — so to speak — pseudo-alternating double stroke is to use an instrument with offset points. In this case, we would have to speak of a modification of the parallel double stroke and a pure LBK innovation. However, this scenario can be neglected based on observations regarding the depth and direction of the strokes on SBK pots (Figure 7). The instruments used for producing the alternating double stroke were simple, split pieces of wood or bone which were then "walked" across the surface of the pot in a manner similar to movement on two legs.

Only in the early HSK can we clearly observe the transition in the stroke ornamentation, in the vessel shapes and in the rudimentary elements, such as incised lines. The early HSK in Rhenish Hesse thus is either very near the region of origin of the SBK, or indeed is itself that region. Consequently, variations of stroke techniques, for instance the parallel single or double rows of strokes, can be seen as LBK imitations of or responses to the alternating double stroke of the SBK/HSK. They are therefore not merely predecessors of the new technique, but

---

46 Jeunesse and van Willigen 2010, 595.

rather a sign of cultural contact between the Cardial and the LBK, which then becomes independent over time.

Interestingly, most authors discussing the origin of the SBK generally look for preliminary forms and possible origin points only within the LBK itself[47]. Few broaden their search for possible regions of influence beyond the spatial and chronological limits of the LBK. Where such ideas are voiced[48], they are not pursued and soon rejected.

In this context, the Cardial cultures of France could play an important role, as the origin of the tremolo technique is to be found there[49]. Whether this transfer of technology in ceramic ornamentation is accompanied by other aspects of culture (such as economy, ritual, religion and so on) needs further investigation.

SBK in Bohemia

It is often argued that the formation of the SBK took place in Bohemia. This idea depends on the assumption of a local, autochthonous development of the SBK out of the LBK[50], which in turn relies on a suggested continuous sequence of transition between the later LBK *Šárka horizon* (Západocká's StK I) and the developed stage of the SBK (STK II after Západocká). This transitional horizon is characterised by the simultaneous use of rows of single incisions and (parallel) double strokes in Bohemia. Its definition relies on only few published assemblages, and mainly on one feature — Obj. 31 from Hrbovice-Chabařovice[51]. The assemblage from this pit originates from an older excavation and seems to be problematic in its composition, as the multi-phase use of the site could have led to redeposition of the Šárka finds. This is supported by the relatively small size of the the older LBK sherds in comparison to the SBK ware in this pit[52]. Indeed, there are other arguments against the Šárka style as a precursor for the early SBK[53]. Recently, Bohemia has once again been suggested as region of origin for the SBK[54].

The appearance of the Šárka style with several late LBK pottery styles in the pits of the ritual enclosure at Herxheim (district of Südliche Weinstraße, Rhineland-Palatinate) makes possible its relative dating. This means that the Šárka style is much too young to function as a predecessor of the SBK, because SBK elements had at this point already been established in HSK[55].

Although the Šárka argument has thus been invalidated, attempts were made to retain the superseded model of a development of the SBK in the east[56]. Of special interest in this case is Dresden-Prohlis (district of Dresden, Saxony), where parallel rows of single strokes and the parallel double stroke technique, as well as pear-shaped pots, were interpreted as transitional between LBK und SBK. However, this neglects the existence of typologically earlier steps in the west and the fact that the continuity at Dresden-Prohlis is not based on a series of absolute dates[57].

---

47 E.g. Kaufmann 2009a, 269.
48 Cf. Kaufmann 1977; Mauser-Goller 1969, 36.
49 Cf. Jeunesse and van Willigen 2010.
50 Západocká 1970, 60–61.
51 Západocká 2009, fig. 5, 308; Západocká and Muška 2007, 258ff.
52 Cf. Západocká and Muška 2007, 258ff.
53 Kaufmann 1976, 109.
54 Kaufmann 2009a, 269.
55 Jeunesse and Strien 2009, 243.
56 Link 2014b, 217.
57 Link 2014b, 184.

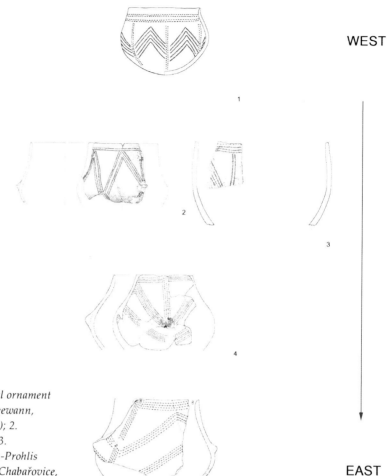

Figure 8. Suggested development of the vertical ornament separators from west to east. 1. Worms-Rheingewann, grave LVIII (after Zápotocká 1972, 355, fig. 30); 2. Niederröblingen, features 9835/2 and 9613/7; 3. Niederröblingen, feature 9970/276; 4. Dresden-Prohlis (after Link 2012b, 277, fig. 3.15); 5. Hrbovice-Chabařovice, Obj. 31/3 (after Zápotocká 2007, 260, plate 48.8).

Returning to the ceramics, one important element of comparison that has so far been neglected are the vertical anthropomorphic separating ornaments[58], which are fully developed both in the HSK in Rhenish Hesse and the early, "archaic" SBK of central Germany[59]. This archaic phase seems to be of short duration in adjacent regions also[60]. The fact that the rim ornamentation is not reached, and especially not interrupted, by these vertical ornament separators supposedly indicates an early stage of SBK development (Figure 8). It is remarkable that in Saxony and Bohemia, the rim ornamentation is very often reached and frequently interrupted (see Figure 8, 4–5). Where the vertical anthropomorphic separating ornaments do not reach the rim, in Bohemia the separators are often combined with typological elements of the later SBK, for instance bigger strokes or late vessel shapes[61]. If this observation has chronological relevance, we could assume a quite fast but delayed spread of the SBK to the east.

---

58 Ornament 706 after Spatz 1999, 79, fig. 39.
59 Stage 1a after Kaufmann 1976.
60 Riedhammer 2016, 140.
61 Cf. Burgert 2012; 2016, fig. 13.1., fig. 14.4; Burgert *et al.* 2014, fig. 3.1.

Following these suggestions, Bohemia belongs to an early, but developed stage of the SBK and not to the earliest stage. The SBK does not seem to originate in Bohemia. However, given Bohemia's LBK monopoly of amphibolite quarrying and trading, one could assume that elements of the SBK spread to Bohemia very quickly. As a typological consequence, the parallel double stroke does not indicate an epicentre of the evolving SBK, but is a sign of a retarded development and an imitation of the alternated double stroke — as already observable in later LBK groups in central Germany.

A little bit later, Bohemia is more likely a conservative region in terms of pottery, as the later SBK still exports adze blanks to the Rössen culture in central Germany[62]. Maybe this conservative attitude must also be taken into account as a factor in the local transition from LBK to SBK in this region. The Lengyel complex is not a possible region of origin for the development of the SBK[63].

SBK in central Germany

In the past, central Germany has been regarded as the region of origin of the SBK by D. Kaufmann[64]. Interestingly, Kaufmann recognised in 1976 a strong influence from the western LBK in the formation of the SBK. After discussions with M. Zápotocká, he changed his opinion in favour of SBK formation in Bohemia[65]. Recently, Kaufmann has rightly stated that vessels of the later LBK in central Germany cannot be seen as a predecessor of the SBK but as a result of contact with the SBK[66]. At the same time, he has interpreted the delayed transition from LBK to SBK in some regions of central Germany as a reluctance to accept SBK elements[67]. This seems to stand in contrast to the assumption that the SBK has developed "without clearly identifiable influences from the latest LBK"[68]. If the SBK evolved as a "fashionable innovation"[69], we would need to assume a more willing acceptance. That this could not have been the case indicates a hostile environment or a temporal gap between both cultures. This is currently based upon only a few, but weighty arguments:

- the decrease of settlement activity on some sites with continuity between LBK and SBK
- the complete cessation of settlement activities on some sites after the latest LBK (*e.g.* Schönebeck/Elbe, district of Salzlandkreis)
- the breaks in the correspondence analysis, which result from a mixture of qualitative, quantitative, cultural and chronological reasons; there is no type of pot which includes both definitely LBK and clear SBK criteria together

---

62   Kaufmann 2012, 394.
63   Kaufmann 1976, 102.
64   Kaufmann 1976, 109.
65   Kaufmann 2009a, 269. D. Kaufmann was convinced by illustrations of the material from Hrbovice-Chabařovice shown to him by M. Zápotocká at the conference "Neolithic circular enclosures in Europe", held in Halle (Saale) in May 2004 (Kaufmann 2009a, note 3). As Zápotocká did not hold a lecture at this conference, the change of opinion seems to be based on a comparatively short conversation.
66   Kaufmann 2009a, 270ff.
67   Kaufmann 2009a, 279.
68   Kaufmann 2009a, 267: "ohne deutlich erkennbare Einflüsse aus der jüngsten Linienbandkeramik".
69   Kaufmann 1976, 109.

- the fortifications of late LBK settlements (*e.g.* Eilsleben), especially those in close proximity to early SBK settlements; this substantiates the impression of a partial displacement of the LBK by the SBK
- the co-occurrence of LBK and SBK on settlement sites is not automatically evidence for a "genetic dependency"; first and foremost, it shows that the SBK chose favourable settlement areas and it reflects the high degree of landscape development by the LBK
- the absence of graves and cemeteries especially during the early SBK

This latter point may be linked with a smaller population during the transition between LBK and SBK in general. Ritual and religious developments or a change in inheritance law may have taken place in the background. During the preceding LBK a larger population, which was bound by territorial inheritance claims, may have necessitated cemeteries and more graves[70]. This territorial claim was not important in the early SBK in consequence of a lower population density.

One of the few published early SBK graves in Saxony-Anhalt, that of Großkorbetha (district of Burgenland, Saxony Anhalt), must be redated to a later stage of the SBK[71], based on the vessel decoration with relatively large strokes, the type of pot and the fact that the apices of the angular ornaments do not meet. It is also conspicuous that there is no SBK evidence from Zwenkau-Harth (district of Leipzig Land, Saxony)[72]. Furthermore, we have to acknowledge a hiatus between the later LBK (here Elster-Saale-style) and the middle SBK.

Other forms of settlement re-use could be to build a rondel on a former LBK settlement site, as observed in Quedlinburg (district of Harz, Saxony-Anhalt)[73]. Many sites which are completely abandoned after the later LBK, such as Schönebeck (district of Salzlandkreis, Saxony-Anhalt), show knowledge of SBK pottery elements by the LBK[74]. This indicates regionally different absorption capacities of SBK elements. Given the results from Niederröblingen, the crucial point to stress is that there are indications for continuity and discontinuity, at least for some places and regions in central Germany. Further investigations, especially comprising absolute dates for selected examples, in combination with continuous efforts in settlement archaeology, are essential to further our understanding of regional differences in cultural change at the transition from the sixth to the fifth millennium.

---

70 Strien 2011.
71 Stage SBK Ib after Kaufmann 1976; cf. Nitzschke 1966.
72 Kaufmann 2009a, 274.
73 Cf. H. Schmidt 2006, 67.
74 Cf. Leinthaler and Bogen 2012.

References

Behrens, H. 1973. *Die Jungsteinzeit im Mittelelbe-Saale-Gebiet. Veröffentlichungen des Landesmuseums für Vorgeschichte Halle 27*. Halle (Saale).

Biermann, E. 2001. *Alt- und Mittelneolithikum in Mitteleuropa. Untersuchungen zur Verbreitung verschiedener Artefakt- und Materialgruppen und zu Hinweisen auf regionale Tradierungen*. Köln.

Burgert, P. 2012. K vnitřní chronologii sídliště kultury s vypíchanou keramikou v Libišanech (okr. Pardubice). *Archeologie východních Čech* 4, 5–54.

Burgert, P. 2016. Součkova cihelna v Plotištích nad Labem – zapomenutý pramen poznání kultury s vypíchanou keramikou ve východních Čechách. *Praehistorica* 33, 97–115.

Burgert, P., Končelová, M. and Květina, P. 2014. Neolitický dům, cesta k poznání sociální identity. In M. Popelka and J. Bartík (eds), *Neolitizace aneb Setkání Generací*, 29–57. Prague.

Dohrn-Ihmig, M. 1979. Bandkeramik an Mittel- und Niederrhein. *Beiträge zur Urgeschichte des Rheinlandes III. Rheinische Ausgrabungen 19*, 191–362.

Einicke, R. 1993. *Die Tonware der jüngsten Linearbandkeramik aus Eilsleben, Kreis Wanzleben, aus den Grabungsjahren 1974 bis 1986. Teil II: Katalog, Tafeln, Karten, Beilagen*. Diploma dissertation, University of Halle, available at https://www.academia.edu/13836431/; last accessed July 2015.

Einicke, R. 2014. *Die Tonware der Linienbandkeramik im östlichen Thüringen. Bd. 1, Text. Alteuropäische Forschungen 6*. Langenweissbach.

Einicke, R. 2016. Linienbandkeramik ohne Linie – Auf der Spur jüngerlinienbandkeramischer Stilregionen Mitteldeutschlands. In J. Beran, R. Einicke, V. Schimpff, K. Wagner and T. Weber (eds), *Lehren – Sammeln – Publizieren. Hans-Jürgen Beier zum 60. Geburtstag gewidmet*, 81–99. Leipzig.

Fridrich, C. 2016. Typochronologie der verzierten Keramik. In H. Stäuble and U. Veit (eds), *Der bandkeramische Siedlungsplatz Eythra in Sachsen. Studien zur Chronologie und Siedlungsentwicklung. Leipziger Forschungen zur Ur- Frühgeschichtlichen Archäologie 9*, 61–112. Leipzig.

Jeunesse, C. and Strien, H.-C. 2009. Bemerkungen zu den stichbandkeramischen Elementen in Hinkelstein. In A. Zeeb-Lanz (ed.), *Krisen – Kulturwandel – Kontinuitäten. Zum Ende der Bandkeramik in Mitteleuropa. Beiträge der internationalen Tagung in Herxheim bei Landau (Pfalz) vom 14.–17. 06. 2007. Internationale Archäologie, Arbeitsgemeinschaft, Symposium, Tagung, Kongress 10*, 241–247. Rahden.

Jeunesse, C. and van Willigen, S. 2010. Westmediterranes Frühneolithikum und westliche Linearbandkeramik: Impulse, Interaktionen, Mischkulturen. In D. Gronenborn and J. Petrasch (eds), *Die Neolithisierung Mitteleuropas. Internationale Tagung Mainz, 24. bis 26. Juni 2005. Römisch-Germanisches Zentralmuseum Tagungen 4*, 569–605. Mainz.

Kaufmann, D. 1976. *Wirtschaft und Kultur der Stichbandkeramik im Saalegebiet. Veröffentlichungen des Landesmuseums für Vorgeschichte Halle (Saale) 30*. Berlin.

Kaufmann, D. 1977. Die Stichbandkeramik im Saalegebiet. In J. Češka, (ed.), *Sborník prací Filozofické fakulty brněnské univerzity: řada archeologicko-klasická, Bd.24-25, Heft E20-21 (1975-1976)*, 63–71. Brünn.

Kaufmann, D. 2009a. Anmerkungen zum Übergang von der Linien- zur Stichbandkeramik in Mitteldeutschland. In A. Zeeb-Lanz (ed.), *Krisen – Kulturwandel – Kontinuitäten. Zum Ende der Bandkeramik in Mitteleuropa. Beiträge der internationalen Tagung in Herxheim bei Landau (Pfalz) vom 14.–17. 06. 2007. Internationale Archäologie, Arbeitsgemeinschaft, Symposium, Tagung, Kongress 10*, 267–282. Rahden.

Kaufmann, D. 2009b. Einige notwendige Bemerkungen zur Stichbandkeramik. In L. Husty, M. Rind and K. Schmotz (eds), *Zwischen Münchshöfen und Windberg. Gedenkschrift für Karl Böhm. Internationale Archäologie, Studia Honoria 29*, 45–52. Rahden.

Kaufmann, D. 2012. Rössenzeitliche Amphibolithgeräte aus Mitteldeutschland. In R. Gleser and V. Becker (eds), *Mitteleuropa im 5. Jahrtausend vor Christus. Beiträge zur Internationalen Konferenz in Münster 2010. Neolithikum und ältere Metallzeiten. Studien und Materialien 1*, 389–408. Berlin.

Kaufmann, D. 2014. Rezension zu A. Wolf-Schuler, Untersuchungen zur Chronologie und strukturellen Entwicklung der Kultur mit Stichbandkeramik. *Jahresschrift für mitteldeutsche Vorgeschichte* 94, 531–544.

Leinthaler, B. and Bogen, C. 2012. Die linienbandkeramische Siedlung von Schönebeck. In H. Meller (ed.), *Von Egeln bis Schönebeck: Archäologie und Straßenbau in der Magdeburger Börde. Archäologie in Sachsen-Anhalt. Sonderband 20*, 29–44. Halle (Saale).

Link, T. 2012a. Stilwandel contra Siedlungskontinuität – Zum Übergang von der Linien- zur Stichbandkeramik in Sachsen. In R. Gleser and V. Becker (eds), *Mitteleuropa im 5. Jahrtausend vor Christus. Beiträge zur Internationalen Konferenz in Münster 2010. Neolithikum und ältere Metallzeiten. Studien und Materialien 1*, 115–132. Berlin.

Link, T. 2012b. Neue Kultur oder jüngerlinienbandkeramische Regionalgruppe? Dresden-Prohlis und die Entstehung der Stichbandkeramik. In R. Smolnik (ed.), *Siedlungsstruktur und Kulturwandel in der Bandkeramik. Beiträge der internationalen Tagung „Neue Fragen zur Bandkeramik oder alles beim Alten?!" Leipzig 23. bis 24. September 2010. Arbeits- und Forschungsberichte zur sächsischen Bodendenkmalpflege, Beiheft 25*, 274–283. Dresden.

Link, T. 2014a. Welche Krise? Das Ende der Linienbandkeramik aus östlicher Perspektive. In T. Link and D. Schimmelpfennig (eds), *No future? Brüche und Ende kultureller Erscheinungen. Beispiele aus dem 6.–2. Jahrtausend v. Chr. Fokus Jungsteinzeit. Berichte der AG Neolithikum 4*, 95–111. Kerpen-Loogh.

Link, T. 2014b. *Die Linien- und Stichbandkeramische Siedlung von Dresden-Prohlis. Eine Fallstudie zum Kulturwandel in der Region der oberen Elbe um 5000 v. Chr. Veröffentlichungen des Landesamtes für Archäologie Sachsen 60*. Dresden.

Mauser-Goller, K. 1969. *Die relative Chronologie des Neolithikums in Südwestdeutschland und der Schweiz. Schriften zur Ur- und Frühgeschichte der Schweiz 15*. Basel.

Meier-Arendt, W. 1975. *Die Hinkelstein-Gruppe. Der Übergang vom Früh- zum Mittelneolithikum in Südwestdeutschland. Römisch-Germanische Forschungen 35*. Berlin.

Müller, J. 2002. Zur Belegungsabfolge des Gräberfeldes von Trebur: Argumente der typologieunabhängigen Datierungen. *Prähistorische Zeitschrift* 77, 148–158.

Nitzschke, W. 1966. Ein stichbandkeramisches Grab von Großkorbetha, Kr. Weißenfels. *Ausgrabungen und Funde* 11, 11–12.

Riedhammer, K. 2016. Zwischen Großgartach, Stichbandkeramik und Mährisch Bemalter Keramik. In Jaromír Kovárník *et al.* (eds), *Centenary of Jaroslav Palliardi's Neolithic and Aeneolithic Relative Chronology (1914–2014)*, 127–148. Ústí nad Orlicí.

Schmidt, B., Gruhle, W. and Rück, O. 2004. Klimaextreme in bandkeramischer Zeit (5300 bis 5000 v. Chr.). Interpretation dendrochronologischer und archäologischer Befunde. *Archäologisches Korrespondenzblatt 34*, 303–307.

Schmidt, H. 2006. Das Frühneolithikum. In H. Meller (ed.), *Archäologie XXL. Archäologie an der B 6n im Landkreis Quedlinburg. Archäologie in Sachsen-Anhalt, Sonderband 4*, 65–69. Halle (Saale).

Siller, J. 2016. Grenzgebiete? Ein Projekt zur Linearbandkeramik in Unterfranken und Thüringen. In J. Pechtl, T. Link and L. Husty (eds), *Neue Materialien des Bayerischen Neolithikums. Tagung im Kloster Windberg vom 21. bis 23. November 2014. Würzburger Studien zur Vor- und Frühgeschichtlichen Archäologie 2*, 63–76. Würzburg.

Spatz, H. 1996. *Beiträge zum Kulturkomplex Hinkelstein-Großgartach-Rössen: Der keramische Fundstoff des Mittelneolithikums aus dem mittleren Neckarland und seine zeitliche Gliederung. Materialhefte zur Archäologie in Baden-Württemberg 37*. Stuttgart.

Spatz, H. 1999. *Das mittelneolithische Gräberfeld von Trebur, Kreis Groß-Gerau. Materialhefte zur Vor- und Frühgeschichte in Hessen 19*. Wiesbaden.

Spatz, H. 2002. Bäumchen und Sichel: Aspekte und Überlegungen zum Übergang vom frühen zum mittleren Neolithikum in Zentraleuropa. *Archeologickè rozhledy 54*, 279–300.

Spatz, H. 2003. Hinkelstein, eine Sekte als Initiator des Mittelneolithikums? In J. Eckert, U. Eisenhauer and A. Zimmermann (eds), *Archäologische Perspektiven. Analysen und Interpretationen im Wandel. Festschrift für Jens Lüning zum 65. Geburtstag. Internationale Archäologie, Studia honoraria 7*, 575–587. Rahden.

Strien, H.-C. 1990. *Untersuchungen zur Bandkeramik in Württemberg. Universitätsforschungen zur prähistorischen Archäologie 69*. Bonn.

Strien, H.-C. 2011. Friedhöfe und Rechtsgeschichte: Warum wurden bandkeramische Gräberfelder angelegt? Unpublished lecture given at the 7. Deutscher Archäologiekongress, Bremen 05.–06.10.2011.

Strien, H.-C. 2013. Besiedlungsgeschichte des Zabergäus. In C. Schrenk and P. Wanner (eds), *Heilbronnica 5. Beiträge zur Stadt- und Regionalgeschichte. Quellen und Forschungen zur Geschichte der Stadt Heilbronn 20. Jahrbuch für schwäbisch-fränkische Geschichte 37*, 35–50. Heilbronn.

Vondrowsky, V., Beneš, J., Divisova, M. and Kovačiková, L. 2016. From LBK to SBK: pottery, bones, lithics and houses at the Neolithic site of Hrdlovka, Czech Republic. *Open Archaeology 2*, 303–327.

Wolf-Schuler, A. 2009. *Untersuchungen zur Chronologie und strukturellen Entwicklung der Kultur mit Stichbandkeramik. Universitätsforschungen zur Prähistorischen Archäologie 171*. Bonn.

Wollenweber, R. 2016. One house like another? – Access to water wells as an indicator of social inequality in the Linear and Stroke Ornamented Pottery cultures. In H. Meller (ed.), *Arm und reich. Zur Ressourcenverteilung in prähistorischen Gesellschaften. Tagungsband des 8. Mitteldeutschen Archäologentages 22–24.10.2015 Halle (Saale). Tagungen des Landesmuseums für Vorgeschichte Halle (Saale) 14*, 165–181. Halle (Saale).

Wollenweber, R. in prep. *Niederröblingen (Helme). Studie zu frühneolithischen Siedlungsstrukturen in der Helmeaue*. PhD thesis, Universität Leipzig.

Zápotocká, M. 1970. Die Stichbandkeramik in Böhmen und in Mitteleuropa. In H. Schwabedissen (ed.), *Die Anfänge des Neolithikums vom Orient bis Nordeuropa. Teil 2: östliches Mitteleuropa. Fundamenta Reihe A, Band 3*, 1–66. Köln.

Zápotocká, M. 1972. Die Hinkelsteinkeramik und ihre Beziehungen zum zentralen Gebiet der Stichbandkeramik. *Památky Archeologické* 63, 267–374.

Zápotocká, M. 1978. Ornamentace neolitické vypíchané keramiky: Technika, Terminologie a způsob dokumentace. *Archeologické rozhledy* 30, 504–534.

Zápotocká, M. 2009. Der Übergang von der Linear- zur Stichbandkeramik in Böhmen. In A. Zeeb-Lanz (ed.), *Krisen – Kulturwandel – Kontinuitäten. Zum Ende der Bandkeramik in Mitteleuropa. Beiträge der internationalen Tagung in Herxheim bei Landau (Pfalz) vom 14.–17. 06. 2007. Internationale Archäologie, Arbeitsgemeinschaft, Symposium, Tagung, Kongress 10*, 303–315. Rahden.

Zápotocká, M. and Muška, J. 2007. *Hrbovice, okr. Ústí nad Labem. Výzkum 1978. Sídelní areál kultury s keramikou lineární a vypíchanou. (Hrbovice, Kreis Ústí nad Labem. Ausgrabung 1978. Ein Siedlungsareal mit der Linear- und Stichbandkeramik)*. Prague.

A vessel with zoomorphic depiction from the Epi-Rössen horizon at Oberbergen am Kaiserstuhl

An evolutionary perspective on an unusual artefact

Ralf Gleser

Abstract

This contribution has two main aims. First, it offers an interpretation for an artefact which is unique in the Epi-Rössen context of south-west Germany. This is achieved through an inter-regional comparison, which in the present case leads to Thrace and Anatolia. Second, it focuses attention on the special importance of pottery and stone vessels in general as spherical artefacts, as well as on their function as image-bearing objects in the process of cultural evolution. Artefacts of this kind appear from the global beginnings of sedentism in the Near East. Based on the results of evolutionary biology, pottery and stone vessels are here seen as representatives of an unusual category of artefact, as they combine two mental concepts — the circle and the container. Adding a horizontal image frieze creates an artificial horizontal orientation with an upper and lower demarcation. What is more, turning the object and passing it from hand to hand enables the illusion of movement, while repeated rotation creates an impression of "endlessness". Such artefacts, used in stationary settings, make it possible to simulate the dynamic character of the environment and lifeworld in a domestic context.

Zusammenfassung: Tongefäß mit Tierdarstellung des Epi-Rössener Horizontes von Oberbergen am Kaiserstuhl: Ein außergewöhnlich gestaltetes Artefakt aus evolutionsbiologischer Perspektive

Im vorliegenden Beitrag werden zwei Ziele verfolgt. Einerseits geht es darum, ein im Epi-Rössen Südwestdeutschlands singuläres Artefakt durch überregionalen Vergleich, der im vorliegenden Fall nach Thrakien und Anatolien führt, einer Interpretation zu unterziehen. Andererseits wird auf die besondere Bedeutung sowohl von Keramik bzw. Steingefäßen an sich als sphärisch gebildeten Artefakten als auch deren Funktion als Bildträger im Prozess der kulturellen Evolution aufmerksam gemacht. Solche Artefakte sind seit der erstmaligen Sesshaftigkeit des Menschen im vorderasiatischen Raum feststellbar. Tonware und Steingefäße werden im Beitrag in Anlehnung an die Ergebnisse evolutionsbiologischer Forschung als Vertreter einer besonderen Artefaktkategorie akzentuiert, die zwei mentale Konzepte vereinigt – Kreis und Hohlform. Durch das Anbringen eines horizontalen Bildfrieses daran wird beim Betrachten derselben nicht nur der besonderen Ordnung einer artifiziellen Horizontalen mit oberem und unterem Abschluss Rechnung getragen. Es wird beim Drehen und Herumreichen auch die figurative Illusion von Bewegung möglich und durch wiederholte Rotation jene von „Unendlichkeit" der räumlichen Ausdehnung. Durch solche stationär gehandhabten Artefakte scheint der dynamische Charakter der Um- und Mitwelt im häuslichen Umfeld zu simulieren möglich.

Introduction: the Anatolian roots of the central European Neolithic

At first glance, the Early and Middle Neolithic of central Europe[1] appear as a heterogeneous constellation of regionally diverse societies. Nevertheless, many characteristics of these two periods are based on a unified repertoire of cultural traits and practices which were introduced wholesale through the migration of agricultural communities. Both the cultural repertoire and the people themselves have their roots in the Aegean and Balkan areas, which were in turn settled over the course of the seventh millennium cal BC by populations spreading westwards from the core areas of the south-west Asian variety of the Neolithic, that is to say from south-eastern Anatolia, Upper Mesopotamia and the Levant. That these earliest Neolithic cultures in central Europe continued the traditions of their areas of origin is most clearly evident in the case of the first fully agricultural communities, the Early Neolithic Linearbandkeramik culture (LBK). On the one hand, the cultural character of these groupings can be interpreted as an adaptation to the ecological and environmental conditions prevalent in central Europe, on the other hand it is the result of specific practices and ideas. However, as a technological foundation of a given way of life, this set of traits has preserved all the hallmarks of its area of origin, in particular concerning the plant and animal species involved, the tools used and not least the presence of pottery. Other components of the cultural life of this central European phenomenon, which are less well accessible to prehistoric archaeology, also have recognisable roots in south-east Europe, and ultimately the Near East. These are aspects connected to worldview and its varied forms of expression, by which I mean the so-called sociotechnic and ideotechnic artefacts[2]. For the Linearbandkeramik culture, this would also include clay idols or figurines[3]. In this context, there have already been many attempts to trace symbolic forms of expression in general back to Anatolian forerunners and models, both stylistically and in terms of content, for example the ornaments on pottery of the LBK and the Middle Neolithic Stichbandkeramik (Stroke-Ornamented Pottery culture or SBK) which follows it[4]. Some authors have even identified the enduring influence of traditions with alleged Anatolian roots as late as the Late Neolithic of south-west Germany. Recently, Helmut

---

1   I use these period names following Lüning 1996. The Early Neolithic thus comprises the period from c. 5500 to 4900 cal BC, the Middle Neolithic lasts from about 4900 to 4400 cal BC.
2   In the sense of Binford 1962.
3   See e.g. Bánffy 2003.
4   See especially Soudský and Pavlů 1966, 118 fig. 19.

Schlichtherle has interpreted aurochs horn cores and vertebrae from Late Neolithic "cult buildings" at Sipplingen and Ludwigshafen-Bodman on the German shore of Lake Constance in the context of the well-known hunting scenes from the Early Neolithic settlement of Çatalhöyük East in Turkey, dating to the seventh millennium cal BC[5]. Currently, it remains uncertain whether these Late Neolithic cultural phenomena are based on LBK and hence indirectly on Anatolian roots, which in this case would have had a largely latent influence for over a millennium, or whether they go back to traditions and "influences" of the later Lengyel culture in Hungary and Austria, which can be recognised in numerous aspects of the south-west German material from the middle of the fifth millennium onwards and had a decisive impact on the cultural changes defining the transition from the Middle to the Late Neolithic across southern Germany.

In the context of the Late Neolithic, in this contribution I would like to draw attention to an object from Oberbergen near the Kaiserstuhl mountain, which has been known for a long time, but has remained relatively undiscussed[6]. It seems well suited to draw out certain mental concepts of Neolithic European populations, concepts which are closely connected to the processes by which anatomically modern humans became sedentary in the course of the Holocene in western Asia and which are of considerable importance for the further post-glacial cultural developments. In the course of this interpretation, I will attempt to relate insights from evolutionary biology to new sets of knowledge which emerged during the technological development of *Homo sapiens* after the last Ice Age.

Epi-Rössen around the Kaiserstuhl

At the end of the 1970s, extensive land consolidation programmes of wine-growing areas took place in the central Kaiserstuhl area in Upper Baden. This also affected plots north-west of the village of Oberbergen, near Vogtsburg im Kaiserstuhl, district of Breisgau-Hochschwarzwald (Baden-Württemberg). In the area of the well-known vineyard at "Baßgeige", the heritage management division at Freiburg identified and excavated settlement remains and graves of different Neolithic periods. This included the Linearbandkeramik culture, but also a more regional cultural phenomenon of the late Middle Neolithic and the beginning of the Late Neolithic, which on the basis of its characteristic decorated pottery was originally named the Wauwil group, after the eponymous settlement in north-west Switzerland[7]. From the 1990s onwards, these kinds of finds have then been generally referred to by the term Bruebach-Oberbergen, narrowing down the chronological range and cultural affiliation[8]. Pottery in the Bruebach-Oberbergen style is overwhelmingly found around the Kaiserstuhl and in the southern Upper Rhine plain. Alongside other neighbouring groups, this regional phenomenon is part of a larger Epi-Rössen horizon. The Bruebach-Oberbergen group first attracted the interest of archaeologists in 1972, with the discovery of a burial during earth removal activities in Sasbach, in the north-western foothills of the

---

5   Schlichtherle 2016, 184.
6   I would like to thank the Landesamt für Denkmalpflege im Regierungspräsidium Stuttgart, Archäologische Denkmalpflege Freiburg, and in particular Dr. Gabriele Keller-Nitsche, for the permission to reproduce the photograph shown here as Figure 2. I would also like to thank Dr. Ute Seidel for further information pertaining to this image.
7   Amongst others, see Dieckmann 1978, 14–17; 1990, 7–13.
8   Gleser 1995, 240–242; Jeunesse 1990.

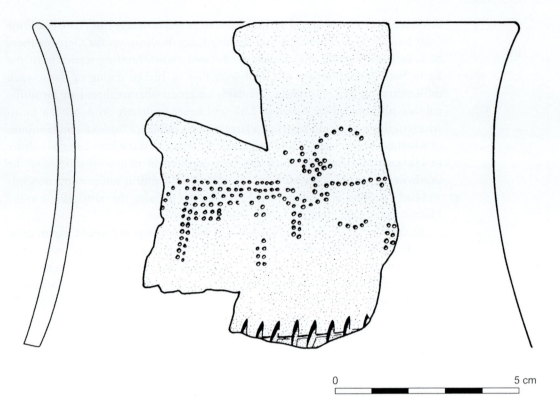

Figure 1. Vogtsburg-Oberbergen, district Breisgau-Hochschwarzwald, Germany. Drawing of vessel remains from the Epi-Rössen horizon with depiction of an animal (after Dehn and Fingerlin 1979, 15 fig. 5; courtesy of the Landesamt für Denkmalpflege im Regierungspräsidium Stuttgart, Archäologische Denkmalpflege Freiburg).

Figure 2. Vogtsburg-Oberbergen, district Breisgau-Hochschwarzwald, Germany. Photograph of the vessel remains (courtesy of the Landesamt für Denkmalpflege im Regierungspräsidium Stuttgart, Archäologische Denkmalpflege Freiburg).

Kaiserstuhl. The individual, extended on his back, was buried with a symmetrical axe blade[9], one of several examples in southern Germany — others are for instance known from the lake dwelling of Aichbühl in the Federsee area — which can be linked to a type first produced in the area of the western Hungarian Lengyel culture. Thus, during the Epi-Rössen horizon in the mid-fifth millennium BC, we can begin to identify a transfer of goods and ideas, which is also manifested in other aspects of the contemporary lifeworld. While it is unknown whether the Sasbach axe reached the Kaiserstuhl during a direct exchange transaction, the find nevertheless illustrates that specific long-lived aesthetic conventions had a certain validity over very large distances.

The decorated vessel from Oberbergen and its characteristics

Among the Bruebach-Oberbergen pottery from the settlement of Oberbergen-"Baßgeige" are the rim and neck fragments of a globular beaker, collected as surface finds. The outside of the vessel shows a highly-stylised animal in a standing posture, its head to the right, formed of small, rounded incisions (Figures 1 and 2). Near the lower edge of the sherds, towards the main body of the beaker, a horizontal line accompanied by grain-shaped incisions remains just about visible. This line originally surrounded the entire vessel. The shape of the beaker and the decorative techniques are so typical for the Epi-Rössen phenomenon that there is no doubt as to the cultural and hence also the chronological attribution of this item, even though the piece was only cursorily published in the late 1970s[10] and subsequently did not receive the attention it deserves.

The figure[11], this much is certain, is a depiction of a large horned mammal and is rendered schematically from the side. The decorative technique chosen did not allow the inclusion of much detail. Front and back legs are shown as two parallel vertical lines of incisions, with the front legs incompletely preserved nearer the body. The neck is slightly separated and, like the front part of the body, is outlined by three rows of incisions. The back half of the body is depicted by four lines of incisions. A single, only partially preserved row of incisions seems to form a long tail. The short double line in front of the back legs appears to show secondary sexual characteristics, but it cannot be stated with certainty whether this is a male or a female animal. In contrast to the neck, the head area creates a rather confused impression, especially as part of the vessel is missing here. Overall, the head consists of three quarters of a circle, but two short parallel lines running abruptly downwards from the head are a little puzzling — perhaps these are meant to show an elongated snout, or, with all due reservations, a wattle. Similarly, the incisions placed within the circle make little sense to a modern-day viewer — all the more so since several breaks in the vessel run together here. On the other hand it is tempting to interpret the arched line, beginning on the putative forehead and open towards the base, as a very large horn. However, it is unclear how this relates to a second line running from the head quite straight towards the right. If this is supposed to be the second horn, then the depiction deviates from the principle

---

9 Dehn and Dieckmann 1985, 474–476 with fig. 13.1; cf. Denaire and Lefranc 2014, 105 with fig. 38.
10 Dehn and Fingerlin 1979, 15 fig. 5; cf. Gleser 1995, plate 24.11.
11 This follows the main points of my description of this image published in Gleser 1995, 61, which was, however, written solely on the basis of the published drawing.

of a strict lateral view and the head would be shown horizontally from a slightly oblique perspective[12]. Perhaps the intention was to show the head turned towards the viewer. Near the right edge of the sherd, just before the break, a further two vertical parallel rows of incisions are visible and could depict legs. It can therefore not be excluded that originally there was a second animal. This is also supported by the inclusion of a possible tail, a short arched line open towards the top which is just about visible to the right of the completely preserved animal, at about chest height. It is hence possible, albeit speculative, that originally several examples of the same or different animal species were arranged around the neck of the vessel, forming a "frieze".

Interpretation of the depiction on the Oberbergen vessel

It hence seems that the topic of the image can be reconstructed more or less successfully, yet the question remains whether the image shows a real animal and which species could be represented. The possibilities are drastically circumscribed by the marked head with its impressive horns. In my opinion, the image does indeed reference existing animals, leaving us with the possibility of horned animals (*bovidae* or *caprinae*), or those carrying antlers (*cervidae*). Given the long tail and the fact that the horns are not branching, red deer can be excluded. The tail could be used to argue for one of the small ruminants, *i.e.* sheep or goat, but the long, forward-slanting curve of the horns contradicts this interpretation. Thus, the Oberbergen animal depiction most likely shows a species of cattle (*bovidae*)[13]. In Neolithic central Europe, the wisent (*Bos bonasus*) and the aurochs (*Bos primigenius*) are the potential wild species[14], but the everyday life of Neolithic farmers was of course strongly influenced by the presence of domesticated cattle. Indeed, the markedly straight and low line of the neck and shoulders could suggest a domestic animal (*Bos taurus*). This reading gains further plausibility if the suggested sexual characteristics are interpreted as an udder, as this organ can be visually more marked in domestic breeds due to the potentially increased rate of milk production[15]. In the Late Neolithic of central Europe, *i.e.* by the second half of the fifth and the first half of the fourth millennium, there are clear indications that dairying did play a certain role[16].

Comparable artefacts

My aim at this point is not to collate Neolithic depictions of cattle from the Near East and Europe and to use this comparison as a basis for investigating the roles and importance of these animals in the daily and ritual lives of past communities[17]. Furthermore, my focus is not cattle in prehistory more generally, nor the intentions of the potters and their motivations for adding such decorations to their vessels. Rather, I want to concentrate on the mental concepts which may

---

12 This perspective, which is more precise compared to a strict lateral view, is already used in Ice Age depictions of animals, for instance at Lascaux: Delluc and Delluc 2008, 308–309, 330, 332–333.
13 Cf. Gleser 1995, 61.
14 Benecke 1994, 260–264 with fig. 143.
15 On udder size in Neolithic cattle, see Masson and Rosenstock 2011, 88.
16 Ebersbach 2002, 203.
17 Cf. Falkenstein 2007; Krauß 2016; Masson and Rosenstock 2011; Molist 2003; Rind 2016.

underlie the making and use of the Oberbergen artefact. For this reason, my comparison is limited to pieces which fulfil three conditions. First, they must have been made in a manner similar to the Oberbergen vessel; second, it must be possible to use them in the same way; and third, they should be similarly visually concise, *i.e.* have a similar effect on their viewers. Even after more than 20 years, it is not easy to identify such *structurally congruent* and *perceptionally equivalent*[18] artefacts for the Oberbergen vessel and its pictorial programme, whether from the nearer or further surroundings[19]. Defining the main characteristics of the piece as being the depiction of large mammals, their horizontal arrangement into a frieze and their placement on a vessel of the fifth millennium BC, then the number of similar artefacts, whether roughly of the same age or older, is rather reduced. The region under consideration here comprises the entire area of distribution of Neolithic civilisations in the Near East and Europe.

The first point of note is that depictions of any kind are extremely rare in the Middle and early Late Neolithic in south-west Germany, especially in the case of the Rössen and Epi-Rössen phenomena[20]. In contrast, numerous depictions of animals are known from the preceding Linearbandkeramik culture, be it in the shape of small figurines, zoomorphic elements applied to pottery or zoomorphic vessels. However, incised images of animals on vessels seem to be completely absent[21]. In any case, cattle — alongside other domesticates — are frequent among the representational LBK artefacts. The roots of the zoomorphic pictorial universe of Bandkeramik groups definitely lie in the Carpathian and Balkano-Danubian area[22]. The cultural phenomena of the sixth and fifth millennia in these areas have produced numerous zoomorphic figurines, vessels in the shape of animals and zoomorphic vessel applications showing domesticated animals such as dogs, small ruminants and pigs. Cattle, too, are represented in significant quantities[23]. A striking depiction of a bull — with a female rider sitting on its back — found in Bulgaria has recently been published by Vassil Nikolov and dates to the local Late Neolithic (c. 5200 cal BC)[24]. The impressive, but rather short horns of the animal point diagonally forwards and suggest a domesticated animal. However, given the considerable number of cattle depictions in the Neolithic of southeast Europe, it cannot be decided in every case whether domesticated or wild cattle are shown. The identification of deer, the most frequently shown wild animal, is more straightforward. For the Early Neolithic Körös culture of the sixth millennium BC in eastern Hungary, Frank Falkenstein has been able to identify certain peculiarities, in that vessels there were also decorated with human and animal figures executed as plastic mouldings[25]. Deer and other small ruminants are frequently represented. Both animals and people are seemingly always shown

---

18   This terminology, which allows effective diachronic comparisons, is employed in accordance with Reinold Schmücker's definition of the term "Werkidentität" ("corpus/oeuvre identity"); cf. Schmücker 2003, 155–156.
19   Cf. Gleser 1995, 337–338.
20   The two Großgartach culture graves 1 and 6 in Trebur, district of Groß-Gerau, contain vessels with theriomorphic depictions which remain difficult to interpret (Spatz 1999, 245–248 with figs 120–122). They are hence not considered further here.
21   Becker 2007, 10–29; Kaufmann 1999.
22   Cf. Bánffy 2003, 16.
23   A summary is provided in Falkenstein 2007, 127–134 with figs 3–10.
24   Nikolov 2015, 24 fig. 4–5.
25   Falkenstein 2007, 131.

singly[26], with the heads of the animals pointing more often to the left[27], a fact stressed by Falkenstein and to which he accords a culturally specific significance[28].

However, searching the Neolithic and Chalcolithic corpus of east central and south-east Europe specifically for depictions of animals arranged on vessels in a frieze-like horizontal row and dating to the sixth or fifth millennium[29], we are left with a rather small number of cases. Given the large finds assemblages from settlement sites of this period, I could not claim to provide an exhaustive list here, but I would like to draw attention to two artefacts which fulfil these criteria.

In the 1960s, Sergej Karmanski uncovered a vessel base with the lower, fragmentary parts of the walls at the Early Neolithic settlement of Donja Branjevina near Odžaci in Serbia[30]. The item showed a surrounding band of most likely seven incised animals and has been attributed to the Starčevo culture of the early sixth millennium BC. While Karmanski has interpreted these animal images as a hunting scene and suggested the presence of deer and a dog, Falkenstein reaches a different conclusion: "These are unified pictures, probably of small ruminants with their heads turned backwards and arranged in alternating directions — with either their heads or tails uppermost"[31]. What can be said with certainty is that these schematically represented animals do not include cattle. Due to the bad state of preservation of the piece and the problematic interpretation of its zoomorphic depictions — a "representation" of reality or a symbolically charged scene? — any congruence with the Oberbergen piece remains superficial and is effectively limited to the depiction of animals, arranged horizontally, on the outer wall of a clay vessel.

The second artefact I would like to describe here is richly decorated and comes from the tell settlement near the thermal spa of Stara Zagora in southern Bulgaria. The vessel was unearthed during excavations led by Mincho Dimitrov, but remained unpublished at first and for decades was only known through a few photographs in exhibition catalogues[32]. It is only in 2002 that the excavator published this example together with other artefacts with zoomorphic and anthropomorphic depictions from the site[33]. Since 2010, one can also refer to a richly illustrated exhibition catalogue in which this assemblage is presented[34]. The specific item used as an analogy here[35] is an almost completely preserved beaker, 10.8 cm high, with a narrow mouth (7.2 cm in diameter) and two opposing handles. Its neck, right down to the upper attachment of the handles, is decorated all over with surrounding incisions. The whole width of the vessel's body is taken up by a frieze with six schematically represented, incised horned animals, shown in lateral view (Figure 3). The frieze is marked off at its base through one or more rows of short

---

26 As can be seen especially clearly on a vessel from Kopáncs, Kom. Szeged: Müller-Karpe 1968, plate 182 A 24; cf. Benecke 1994, 245 fig. 132.
27 Cf. Müller-Karpe 1968, plate 183 B 2-4.
28 Falkenstein 2007, 131.
29 Amongst others, I am excluding vessels with painted animal friezes, now known in some numbers from the area of the late Cucuteni culture in eastern Romania (phase Cucuteni B, early fourth millennium cal BC), as cattle do not appear to be represented (see e.g. Dumitrescu 1979, figs 153-157; Mareş 2009, 39 fig. 33).
30 Karmanski 1979, 12 with plate 41.1; 2005, 110 plate 26.
31 Falkenstein 2007, 132 (translation by the author).
32 Cf. Biegel 1986, 110 Kat.-Nr. 226 with fig. 226; Fol and Lichardus 1988, 234 Kat.-Nr. 79 with fig. 42.
33 Димитров 2002, 17 fig. 6. Unfortunately, the published drawing of the vessel and the reproduction of its complete frieze are very schematic.
34 Калчев 2010.
35 Калчев 2010, 28. Figures not numbered.

Figure 3. Stara Zagora "Thermal Spa", Upper Thrace, Bulgaria. Photo of a vessel of the late Karanovo-VI culture (after Калчев 2010, 28; courtesy of the Stara Zagora Regional Museum of History).

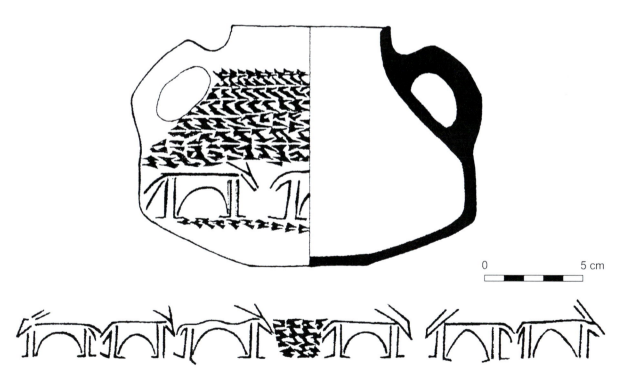

Figure 4. Stara Zagora "Thermal Spa", Upper Thrace, Bulgaria. Drawing of a vessel of the late Karanovo-VI culture (after Димитров 2002, 17 fig. 6; courtesy of the Stara Zagora Regional Museum of History).

incisions. However, the animals are not standing directly on the line thus created, but are "hovering" above it. The good state of preservation of the vessel allows us to comment on the organisation of the image and on possible relationships between the animals. First of all, the frieze does not run around the entire circumference of the vessel, but is separated into two sections of equal size by two areas of short incisions, added opposite each other underneath the handles. Each zone comprises three animals which all seem to belong to the same species. They are all shown standing up and either with their heads or tails facing each other, or arranged one behind the other and facing right (Figure 4), as is also plausible for the Oberbergen vessel. This seemingly rather "random" positioning of the animals to each other creates the impression of a scene with animals out for pasture.

Also, there are arguably clear formal parallels to the depictions on the Oberbergen vessel. On the Stara Zagora vessel, both horns are clearly visible on the heads of each single animal, so that here, too, the principle of a strictly lateral view seems to have been abandoned and the animals appear to turn towards the viewer. The animals on both vessels also share the long tails; however, on the Bulgarian piece these are shown by two lines. Both vessels could even have been made at roughly the same time, as the example from Stara Zagora was discovered in layers of the late Karanovo VI culture and hence dates soon after the middle of the fifth millennium BC. One important difference to the Oberbergen vessel concerns the orientation of the horns. In the Stara Zagora example, these always point straight back from the head. It is hence problematic to address these animals unambiguously as cattle[36]. However, these kinds of horns show affinities with the roughly contemporary sheet-gold animals in grave 36 of the Varna cemetery, where the horns are equally pointing backwards. In that case, they are also clearly curved[37], so that it is almost certainly small ruminants which are being represented.

As an interim result, the vessel from Stara Zagora can be said to offer good formal parallels to the Oberbergen example, given the principle of a row of horizontally placed animals arranged as a frieze on a container. However, in the Bulgarian case the identification of the animals as cattle is not unequivocal. Plausible, structurally congruent artefacts can only be found if Anatolia is included in the discussion[38]. As mentioned above, it can today be taken as read that the combination of Neolithic cultural traits that manifested itself in a regionally diverse form in south-east Europe from the middle of the seventh millennium onwards comprised the innovations and cultural practices of populations which first underwent the transition to a sedentary way of life in the tenth millennium, initially in eastern and soon after also in central Anatolia. Among the characteristic traits of the Anatolian-Near Eastern "Neolithic package" is the domestication of cattle[39]. Recent genetic research shows that the region along the Middle Euphrates and Upper Tigris (south-east Anatolia or Upper Mesopotamia) was probably the

---

36 As amongst others in Fol and Lichardus 1988, 234; Gleser 1995, 338. I am well aware of the fact that different races of cattle could have existed and that even the question of species identification cannot be answered with certainty given the schematic nature of the images under study. However, a cross-cultural compilation of cattle depictions from various periods (Unterberger 2011) demonstrates that cattle can be shown with their horns pointing straight backwards (see e.g. Unterberger 2001, 121 fig. 85, 129 fig. 99; but also e.g. Benecke 1994, 270 fig. 153; Eggers et al. 1964, 54–55 fig. 12f.).

37 Fol and Lichardus 1988, 70 fig. 36, 101 fig. 54.

38 Cf. Krauß 2016, 234.

39 See amongst others Masson and Rosenstock 2011, 81–83; for the applicability of the term "Neolithic package", see amongst others Çilingiroğlu 2005.

sole origin of all European domesticated cattle. It is there, in settlements of the Pre-Pottery Neolithic B (PPNB, ninth/eight millennium cal BC) that people succeeded in breeding the so-called taurine cattle (*Bos taurus*) from a local aurochs variant (*Bos primigenius*)[40]. Cattle, which are already a frequent motif in west European Ice Age art, then also came to play a central role in the worldview of sedentary early farmers in Anatolia. They appear in depictions as both wild and domesticated cattle and can be shown in a naturalistic or more schematic and abstract way[41]. The symbolic reduction of the animal to its horned head is also characteristic for this geographical region and results in a motif referred to as "bucranium", widespread in both the European and Near Eastern Neolithic[42]. Among the earliest representations are those on the relief-decorated T-pillars at the PPNA site of Göbekli Tepe near Şanlıurfa in Upper Mesopotamia (tenth millennium cal BC), which indeed already include bucrania[43]. These motifs are still being repeated millennia later on artefacts of the early Pottery Neolithic (PN) in Çatalhöyük East (seventh millennium cal BC). On the one hand, aurochs hunts are also known from this site, as on the well-known fresco in James Mellaart's "Hunting Shrine", where numerous armed human figures surround a sizeable bull[44]. On the other hand, the settlement is especially well known for certain rooms thought to have a special function and where modelled bulls' heads and horn cores or bucrania are often added to the walls[45].

Yet, vessels with a decoration referencing animals are rare in Anatolia. Particularly pertinent in this context are containers excavated by James Mellaart in Hacılar in the south-west Anatolian lakes region. These items were occasionally found in layer VI (mid-seventh millennium cal BC) and bear animal heads modelled in relief, including heavily stylised cattle heads[46]. In recent years, new fieldwork has radically changed the picture. It now appears that at the transition from the Late Neolithic to the Early Chalcolithic following Turkish terminology (*i.e.* at the turn from the seventh to the sixth millennium cal BC), settlements in central Anatolia produced a characteristic relief-decorated kind of pottery covered with a red slip and showing emblematic depictions of animals, plants and humans arranged in scenes of farming life. At Köşk Höyük in central Anatolia, Aliye Öztan's excavations have uncovered many such vessels[47], including one example with a surrounding horizontal frieze of cattle in various postures, applied in relief[48]. All the animals are depicted with their head to the right.

Similar relief-decorated vessels showing humans and animals have lately come to light during excavations at the Cappadocian settlement of Tepecik-Çiftlik, led by Erhan Bıçakçı. The animals include cattle, deer and probably also dogs[49]. Here, I would like to emphasise the fragment of a bottle with a horizontal frieze on its shoulder. Four large mammals are shown and all face to the right (Figure 5). The

---

40 Krauß 2016, 233; Masson and Rosenstock 2011, 83; Scheu 2012, 5–7.
41 For a summary, see Falkenstein 2007, 122–127 with figs 1–2.
42 Lazarovici and Lazarovici 2010, 120 fig. 14.1, 122 fig. 14.4, 125 fig. 14.10; Molist 2003.
43 Falkenstein 2007, 123 fig. 1; Schmidt 2011, 68 fig. 14, 83 fig. 36.
44 Cutting 2007, 130; Hodder 2012, 247 fig. 17.
45 Cutting 2007, 126–127; Hodder 2012, 270 fig. 9a.
46 Mellaart 1970, vol. 2, plate 112. 2, 263, plates 1 and 3.
47 Öztan 2012, 61–66 figs 29–31, fig. 33, figs 35–39.
48 Öztan 2012, 62 fig. 32.
49 Bıçakçı *et al.* 2012, 125 fig. 34, 127 fig. 37. Human figure with dog: Bıçakçı *et al.* 2012, fig. 34d; deer: Bıçakçı *et al.* 2012, fig. 34e; cattle: Bıçakçı *et al.* 2012, fig. 34b–c.

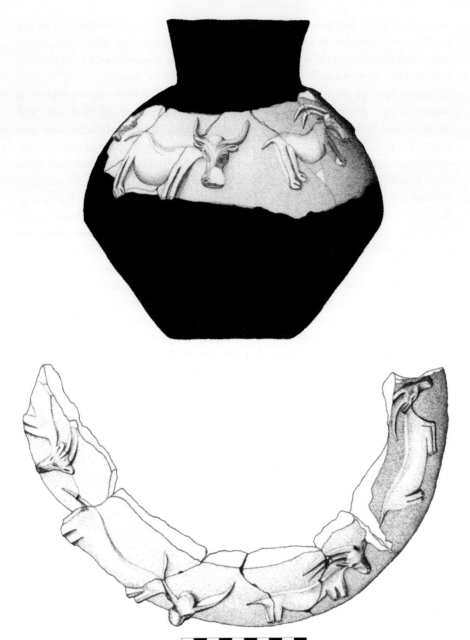

Figure 5. Tepecik-Çiftlik, Cappadocia, Turkey. Level 3. Drawing of a vessel with horned animals arranged in a frieze (after Bıçakçı et al. 2012, 125 fig. 34a. Drawing by Martin Godon; courtesy of the authors).

animals are apparently either standing up or are depicted in an attitude of repose, with characteristically bent legs. In terms of a comparison with the examples from Oberbergen and Stara Zagora, it is particularly pertinent that the bodies of the animals from Tepecik are shown in a lateral view, but the heads are depicted in a frontal view. The depiction of the horns on the Tepecik vessel is highly variable. This could suggest that different species are represented; however, bearing in mind the depiction of the legs, these must all be artiodactyls. Given the almost lyre-shaped, sweeping line of the horns, one of the animals is almost certainly a bovine, most likely an aurochs. The other animals have horns pointing straight backwards, which probably references small ruminants. In all cases, the tails seem comparatively short. In general, the animals on the vessel from Tepecik are apparently rendered in a more naturalistic manner than those from Oberbergen and Stara Zagora. But in spite of all the differences in the technical execution of the motifs and the chronological attribution of the artefacts — which are at least around 1500 years apart — there appears to be a structural and perceptual convergence in terms of the items chosen to carry images, the pictorial themes, the composition as a frieze and perhaps, at least at a general level, even in terms of image content (animals out for pasture).

The conception of the circle and hollow bodies: spherically constructed artefacts as image-bearing media

The spectacular discoveries at Göbekli Tepe and other PPN sites have made clear that animal depictions, which were long thought to be a characteristic of the Upper Palaeolithic, continue seamlessly into the Pottery Neolithic. The keeping and breeding of animals undoubtedly left profound traces in the lifeworld and worldview of sedentary post-glacial communities. It is not surprising that this should also have left pictorial traces. In spite of all the differences in the technological execution of motifs and themes, and taking into account the changes in species composition resulting from the massive warming experienced in the Holocene, which led to a different emphasis in the range of animals depicted, there is no longer a fundamental difference between Palaeolithic and Neolithic animal imagery. To the contrary: the plea, often raised in recent years with respect to Ice Age art, to jettison magico-religious interpretations in favour of a view as pictorial manifestations of idealised notions, scenes and experiences rooted in the concrete lifeworld of Upper Palaeolithic hunters[50] is just as relevant for the study of Neolithic imagery. It is in no way definite, or indeed even necessary, to see these items *a priori* as symbolically charged and connected with the religious sphere, or to postulate a related bull cult or any other animal cult[51]. Nothing prevents us from casting the animal depictions on the vessels from Tepecik, Köşk Höyük, Stara Zagora and Oberbergen in a profane light and seeing them as the outcome of defining everyday perceptions and experiences of Neolithic farmers. This is all the more relevant for the images of humans on Early Neolithic pottery, often clearly shown hunting, during harvest time or dancing[52].

It is not my aim to end on this speculative note. Given the impossibility of reconstructing the intentions behind these depictions in any meaningful way, I would like to attempt an alternative path towards appreciating the importance of such vessels in cultural processes. I would therefore like to stress the special significance of image-bearing artefacts in their own right. In terms of evolutionary biology, pottery vessels belong to a very own class of artefacts. They combine the notion of the circle, already well established in the Upper Palaeolithic[53] as the oldest surface-enclosing geometric shape peculiar to human perception, with the notion of volume. Dwight Read and Sander van der Leeuw have recently emphasised that during a period between around 10,000 and 7000 years BP, new principles

---

50 See for instance Dale Guthrie 2005, 261–281.
51 Cf. Falkenstein 2007, 135–136. An alternative interpretation which departs from a ritual reading of the site has recently been proposed by Yeşilyurt (2014).
52 For Köşk Höyük see e.g. Öztan 2012, 61 fig. 29, 64 fig. 35, 65 figs 37–38.
53 On the circle as a conceptual category of Late Palaeolithic humans, albeit in a different context, see Govedarica 2011, 38–39.

and production techniques for artefacts were developed which proved to be defining for the further development of humanity[54]. While in earlier Palaeolithic periods (during the times of *Homo heidelbergensis* and *Homo neanderthalensis*), the production of artefacts primarily involved the fragmentation and shaping of stone or wood, and the combination of several discrete elements cannot be attested very often, composite artefacts, *i.e.* those built up from several components, are already very frequent in the Upper Palaeolithic, at the time of *Homo sapiens*[55]. At least two classes of composite artefacts are particularly important: first, those created through the combination of parts made from different materials, such as wood and animal skin in the case of tents and huts, or wood and stone in the case of spears, sickles or harpoons; and second, those created from very small or fine parts made of the same material, such as strings, woven items and textiles made from fibre, bast, stalks or stems. The roots of this second kind of composite artefact, where the logic of production appears to be entirely reversed and many very small objects are used to build up a bigger one[56], do lie in the Upper Palaeolithic. But undoubtedly, it is only with the beginning of agriculture in the Near East in the tenth and ninth millennia cal BC that it gained in importance, as the number of artefacts increases markedly. This also applies to two other processes of artefact production which *Homo sapiens* only fully developed during the Neolithic: the shaping of composite substances and the concept of the hollow object. The shaping of composite substances comprises the working with materials such as plaster, clay/loam and metals. The creation of hollow objects, generally based on the geometry of the circle, was realised in the production of vessels or basketry. The making of hollow containers with both inner and outer surfaces is one of the central cognitive concepts of post-glacial *Homo sapiens*, even if the manufacture of baskets and leather tubes or bags is likely also for the Upper Palaeolithic[57]. However, the actual presence of such items during this period is currently hard to prove. The earliest portable and stable hollow shapes known today are undoubtedly stone vessels, such as have been recovered in PPN settlements. Both pottery and stone vessels have a spherical body, open at the top, and hence share the property that during their use as vessels they can only be turned around a single vertical axis if they are to maintain their primary function of wrapping, containing or presenting. The addition and subsequent viewing of a horizontal pictorial frieze takes into account the particular ordering around an artificial horizontal axis with an upper and lower boundary. What is more, the turning and passing around of such an item can also create the figurative illusion of movement, and repeated rotation that of an "endless" spatial extent. In principle, it is thus possible to capture and illustrate the dynamic character of the environment using a stationary object handled in the "world" of the Neolithic domestic context — a different kind of medium in a different sort of setting. It is therefore certainly no coincidence that images of animals are already present on PPN stone vessels in Anatolia, for instance the wild goats from Körtik Tepe[58] and the example from Hallan Çemi, where at least

---

54 Read and van der Leeuw 2008, 1965. Cf. Wilson 2012, 92–93, who reproduces this passage under the heading "The Creative Explosion", and Gamble *et al.* 2014, 185.
55 Read and van der Leeuw 2008, 1965.
56 Cf. Gleser 2016.
57 See also Gamble *et al.* 2014, 168. The concept of containers such as bags and buckets is even considered for *Homo neanderthalensis*, which has a certain plausibility as an evolutionary pre-adaptation in the course of hominin development.
58 Özkaya and Coşkun 2011, 120 fig. 20, 121 fig. 23.

one animal (probably a dog) has been preserved[59]. These containers date to the tenth millennium BC and are hence not only the earliest representatives of a new category of artefact which functioned as a medium of visual representation from the start, but in addition marked the beginning of a specific "pictorial genre" ("*Gattungsstil*"), seemingly still identifiable on the Oberbergen pot millennia later and far from its point of origin.

Concluding remarks

Based on the vessel from Oberbergen, it can be shown that in the European Neolithic, certain ideas reappear which were ultimately developed in Anatolia. To further appreciate the significance of this observation and to arrive at a satisfactory explanation, I would like to draw attention to Ulf Ickerodt's significant and fundamental study on archaeological and culture-historical comparison and interpretation. Building on the work of Dirk Krausse[60], Ickerodt adapts two categories from biological research to archaeological interpretation. In biology, similarities between organisms which have a common root are termed "homologies", while "analogies" are convergences between organisms of different origin[61]. In the sense of a natural teleonomy, similarities in this latter category are basically down to coincidences. Starting from the fact that the roots of the European Neolithic definitely lie in Anatolia, with later regional diversification without further defining external impulses from the early sixth to at least the fourth millennium, it seems opportune to use the concept of homology, which is after all based on the reconstruction of historical developmental lines, for interpreting the vessels from Stara Zagora and Oberbergen in the sense of a "tracing back of aspects of material culture"[62]. Apparently, these are the same kinds of cultural elements already found in Anatolia and rooted in a cultural relationship whereby this kind of "pictorial tradition"[63] could for instance have been transmitted over longer time scales through static worldview systems. The contrasting interpretation, that these are convergent phenomena resulting from shared practice and following some kind of functional logic, seems less likely given the context of the spread of an agricultural way of life in Europe. If the European Neolithic "lifestyle" as a whole is seen as an expression of homologous and interconnected phenomena of material and immaterial culture, and if the implications derived from this fact are not arbitrarily restricted to obvious traits such as the breeding of certain animal species or the growing of certain kinds of domesticated plants, then structural similarities in the Neolithic material of this continent must be seen as the result of a specific *tradigenetic* evolution[64] of knowledge and behaviour.

---

59 Rosenberg 2011, 75 fig. 9, 76 fig. 11.
60 Krausse 2000, 125 tab. 2.
61 Ickerodt 2010, 45.
62 Ickerodt 2010, 48 [our translation].
63 Bringéus 1990, 115.
64 On this term, see Wuketits 1997, 165.

References

Bánffy, E. 2003. Die balkanischen und lokalen (?) Wurzeln der Glaubenswelt der mitteleuropäischen Linearbandkeramik-Gruppen. *Acta Archaeologica Academiae Scientiarum Hungaricae* 54, 1–25.

Becker, V. 2007. Rinder, Schweine, Mischwesen. Zoomorphe Funde der westlichen Linearbandkeramik. In R. Gleser (ed.), *Zwischen Mosel und Morava. Neue Grabungen und Forschungen zur Vor- und Frühgeschichte Mitteleuropas. Saarbrücker Studien und Materialien zur Altertumskunde* 11, 9–95. Bonn.

Benecke, N. 1994. *Der Mensch und seine Haustiere. Die Geschichte einer jahrtausendealten Beziehung*. Stuttgart.

Bıçakçı, E., Godon, M. and Çakan, Y.G. 2012. Tepecik-Çiftlik. In M. Özdoğan, N. Başgelen and P. Kuniholm (eds), *The Neolithic in Turkey. New excavations and new research. Vol. 3 Central Turkey*, 89–134. Istanbul.

Biegel, G. (ed.) 1986. *Das erste Gold der Menschheit. Die älteste Zivilisation in Europa*. Second edition. Freiburg.

Binford, L.R. 1962. Archaeology as anthropology. *American Antiquity* 28, 217–225.

Bringéus, N.-A. 1990. *Der Mensch als Kulturwesen: Eine Einführung in die europäische Ethnologie. Veröffentlichungen zur Volkskunde und Kulturgeschichte* 44. Würzburg.

Çilingiroğlu, Ç. 2005. The concept of "Neolithic package": considering its meaning and applicability. *Documenta Praehistorica* 32, 1–13.

Cutting, M. 2007. Wandmalereien und -reliefs im anatolischen Neolithikum. Die Bilder von Çatal Höyük. In H. Siebenmorgen (ed.), *Vor 12.000 Jahren in Anatolien. Die ältesten Monumente der Menschheit*, 126–134. Stuttgart.

Dale Guthrie, R. 2005. *The nature of Paleolithic art*. Chicago.

Dehn, R. and Dieckmann, B. 1985. Sasbach, Kreis Emmendingen. *Fundberichte aus Baden-Württemberg* 10, 474–476.

Dehn, R. and Fingerlin, G. 1978. Ausgrabungen der archäologischen Denkmalpflege Freiburg im Jahr 1978. *Archäologische Nachrichten aus Baden* 22, 12–35.

Delluc, B. and Delluc, G. 2008. *Dictionnaire de Lascaux*. Bordeaux.

Denaire, A. and Lefranc, P. 2014. Les pratiques funéraires de la culture de Roessen et des groupes épiroesséniens dans le sud de la plaine du Rhin supérieure (4750–4000 av. J.-C.). In P. Lefranc, A. Denaire and C. Jeunesse (eds), *Données recentés sur les pratiques funéraires néolithiques de la Plaine du Rhin supérieure. Actes de la table ronde internationale de Strasbourg organisée par l'UMR 7044 (CNRS et Université de Strasbourg) 1 juin 2011. BAR International Series* 2633, 73–124. Oxford.

Dieckmann, B. 1978. Neue neolithische Funde bei Oberbergen im Kaiserstuhl. *Archäologische Nachrichten aus Baden* 21, 11–17.

Dieckmann, B. 1990. Die Kulturgruppen Wauwil und Straßburg im Kaiserstuhlgebiet. *Cahiers de l'Association pour la Promotion de la Recherche Archéologique en Alsace* 6, 7–60.

Димитров, М. 2002. Митологични сцени върху керамични съдове от селищната могила при Старозагорските Минерални Бани (Scènes mythologiques sur poterie du village des sources thermales de Stara Zagora). *Известия на Старозагорския Исторически Музей* 1, 9–18.

Dumitrescu, V. 1979. *Arta Culturii Cucuteni*. București.

Ebersbach, R. 2002. *Von Bauern und Rindern. Eine Ökosystemanalyse zur Bedeutung der Rinderhaltung in bäuerlichen Gesellschaften als Grundlage zur Modellbildung im Neolithikum. Basler Beiträge zur Archäologie 15*. Basel.

Eggers, H.J., Will, E., Joffroy, R. and Holmquist, W. 1964. *Kelten und Germanen in Heidnischer Zeit*. Baden-Baden.

Falkenstein, F. 2007. Tierdarstellungen und „Stierkult" im Neolithikum Südosteuropas und Anatoliens. In H. Todorova, M. Stefanovich and G. Ivanov (eds), *The Struma/Strymon river valley in prehistory. Proceedings of the International Symposium Strymon Praehistoricus Kjustendil-Blagoevgrad (Bulgaria) and Serres-Amphipolis (Greece) 27.09–01.10.2004. In the steps of James Harvey Gaul 2*, 121–138. Sofia.

Fol, A. and Lichardus, J. (eds) 1988. *Macht, Herrschaft und Gold. Das Gräberfeld von Varna (Bulgarien) und die Anfänge einer neuen europäischen Zivilisation*. Saarbrücken.

Gamble, C., Gowlett, J. and Dunbar, R. 2014. *Thinking big — how the evolution of social life shaped the human mind*. London.

Gleser, R. 1995. *Die Epi-Rössener Gruppen in Südwestdeutschland. Untersuchungen zur Chronologie, stilistischen Entwicklung und kulturellen Einordnung. Saarbrücker Beiträge zur Altertumskunde 61*. Bonn.

Gleser, R. 2016. Beginnings revisited again: about the inversion of the sequence of manufacturing, the origins of early weaving and the vertical warp-weighted loom. In K. Bacvarov and R. Gleser (eds), *Southeast Europe and Anatolia in prehistory. Studies in honor of Vassil Nikolov on his 65th anniversary. Universitätsforschungen zur Prähistorischen Archäologie 293*, 79–91. Bonn.

Govedarica, B. 2011. Die sakrale Symbolik des Kreises: Gedanken zum verborgenen Sinnbild der Hügelbestattungen. In E. Borgna and S. Müller Cylka (eds), *Ancestral landscapes. Burial mounds in the Copper and Bronze Ages (central and eastern Europe — Balkans — Adriatic — Aegean, 4th–2nd millennium B.C.). Proceedings of the international conference held in Udine, May 15th–18th 2008. Travaux de la Maison de l'Orient et de la Méditerranée 58*, 33–46. Lyon.

Hodder, I. 2012. Renewed work at Çatalhöyük. In M. Özdoğan, N. Başgelen and P. Kuniholm (eds), *The Neolithic in Turkey. New excavations and new research. Vol. 3: central Turkey*, 245–277. Istanbul.

Ickerodt, U.F. 2010. *Einführung in das Grundproblem des archäologisch-kulturhistorischen Vergleichens und Deutens. Analogien-Bildung in der archäologischen Forschung*. Frankfurt am Main.

Jeunesse, C. 1990. Le groupe de Bruebach-Oberbergen et l'horizon épi-roessénien dans le sud de la Plaine du Rhin supérieur, le nord de la Suisse et le sud de la Haute-Souabe. *Cahiers de l'Association pour la Promotion de la Recherche Archéologique en Alsace* 6, 81–114.

Калчев, П. 2010. *Неолитни жилища Стара Загора. Каталог на експозицията. Стара Загора, Регионален исторически музей*. Стара Загора.

Karmanski, S. 1979. *Donja Branjevina*. Odžaci.

Karmanski, S. 2005. *Donja Branjevina: a Neolithic settlement near Deronje in the Vojvodina (Serbia). Società per la Preistoria e Protostoria della Regione Friuli-Venezia Giulia, Quaderno 10*. Trieste.

Kaufmann, D. 1999. Einige Bemerkungen zu linienbandkeramischen Tierdarstellungen. In E. Cziesla, T. Kersting and S. Pratsch (eds), *Den Bogen spannen... Festschrift für Bernhard Gramsch zum 65. Geburtstag. Teil 2*, 333–345. Weissbach.

Krauß, R. 2016. Zur Symbolik des Rindes im europäischen Neolithikum. In K. Bacvarov and R. Gleser (eds), *Southeast Europe and Anatolia in prehistory. Essays in honor of Vassil Nikolov on his 65th anniversary. Universitätsforschungen zur Prähistorischen Archäologie 293*, 233–251. Bonn.

Krausse, D. 2000. Intra- und interkulturelle Vergleichsverfahren in der Hallstatt-Archäologie. In A. Gramsch (ed.), *Vergleichen als archäologische Methode. British Archaeological Reports International Series 825*, 119–130. Oxford.

Lazarovici, G. and Lazarovici, C.-M. 2010. Neo-Eneolithic cult constructions in southeastern Europe: building techniques and space management — a brief overview. In D. Gheorghiu (ed.), *Neolithic and Chalcolithic archaeology in Eurasia: building techniques and spatial organisation. Union Internationale des Sciences Préhistoriques et Protohistoriques. Proceedings of the XV World Congress, Lisbon, 4.–9. September 2006. BAR International Series 2097*, 119–127. Oxford.

Lüning, J. 1996. Erneute Gedanken zur Benennung der neolithischen Perioden. *Germania* 74, 233–237.

Mareş, I. (ed.) 2009. *Cucuteni culture: art and religion*. Suceava.

Masson, A. and Rosenstock, E. 2011. Das Rind in Vorgeschichte und traditioneller Landwirtschaft: archäologische und technologisch-ergologische Aspekte. *Mitteilungen der Berliner Gesellschaft für Anthropologie, Ethnologie und Urgeschichte* 32, 81–106.

Mellaart, J. 1970. *Excavations at Hacılar. Occasional Publications of the British Institute of Archaeology at Ankara*. Edinburgh.

Molist, M. 2003. Bovines in the Neolithic period in the Near East: between godhead and food. In S. Athanassopoulou (ed.), *The bull in the Mediterranean world. Myths and cults*, 102–107. Athens.

Müller-Karpe, H. 1968. *Handbuch der Vorgeschichte 2. Jungsteinzeit*. München.

Nikolov, V. 2015. Newly-unearthed types of plastic figurines from the Late Neolithic pit sanctuary at Kapitan Andreevo in southeast Bulgaria. In R. Gleser and F. Stein (eds), *Äußerer Anstoß und innerer Wandel. Festschrift für Rudolf Echt zum 65. Geburtstag. Internationale Archäologie, Studia honoraria 37*, 21–26. Rahden.

Özkaya, V. and Coşkun, A. 2011. Körtik Tepe. In M. Özdoğan, N. Başgelen and P. Kuniholm (eds), *The Neolithic in Turkey. New excavations and new research. Vol. 1: the Tigris Basin*, 89–127. Istanbul.

Öztan, A. 2012. Köşk Höyük. A Neolithic settlement in Niğde-Bor plateau. In M. Özdoğan, N. Başgelen and P. Kuniholm (eds), *The Neolithic in Turkey. New excavations and new research. Vol. 3: central Turkey*, 31–70. Istanbul.

Read, D. and van der Leeuw, S. 2008. Biology is only part of the story ... *Philosophical Transactions of the Royal Society B* 363, 1959–1968.

Rind, M.M. 2016. Das Rind in der Urgeschichte. In V. Brieske, A. Dickers and M.M. Rind (eds), *Tiere und Tierdarstellungen in der Archäologie. Beiträge zum Kolloquium in Gedenken an Torsten Capelle, 30.–31. Oktober 2015 in Herne. Veröffentlichungen der Altertumskommission für Westfalen, Landschaftsverband Westfalen Lippe 22*, 43–62. Münster.

Rosenberg, M. 2011. Hallan Çemi. In M. Özdoğan, N. Başgelen and P. Kuniholm (eds), *The Neolithic in Turkey. New excavations and new research. Vol. 1: the Tigris Basin*, 61–78. Istanbul.

Scheu, A. 2012. *Paläogenetische Studien zur Populationsgeschichte von Rind und Ziege mit einem Schwerpunkt auf dem Neolithikum in Südosteuropa. Menschen – Kulturen – Traditionen. Studien aus den Forschungsclustern des Deutschen Archäologischen Instituts 4*. Rahden.

Schlichtherle, H. 2016. Mitten im Leben. Kulthäuser und Ahnenreihen. In Archäologisches Landesmuseum Baden-Württemberg und Landesamt für Denkmalpflege im Regierungspräsidium Stuttgart (eds), *4.000 Jahre Pfahlbauten. Begleitband zur Großen Landesausstellung Baden-Württemberg 2016, 16. April bis 9. Oktober 2016*, 178–187. Ostfildern.

Schmidt, K. 2011. Göbekli Tepe. In M. Özdoğan, N. Başgelen and P. Kuniholm (eds), *The Neolithic in Turkey. New excavations and new research. Vol. 2: the Euphrates Basin*, 41–83. Istanbul.

Schmücker, R. 2003. Kunstwerke als intersubjektiv-instantiale Entitäten. In R. Schmücker (ed.), *Identität und Existenz. Studien zur Ontologie der Kunst. KunstPhilosophie 2*, 149–179. Paderborn.

Soudský, B. and Pavlů, I. 1966. Interprétation historique de l'ornement linéaire. *Památky archeologické* 57, 91–125.

Spatz, H. 1999. *Das mittelneolithische Gräberfeld von Trebur, Kreis Groß-Gerau. Materialien zur Vor- und Frühgeschichte von Hessen 19*. Wiesbaden.

Unterberger, G. 2011. *Der Stier mit der Weltsäule. Ein archaisches Mythenbild vom Bau der Welt*. Wien.

Wilson, E.O. 2012. *The social conquest of earth*. New York/London.

Wuketits, F.M. 1997. *Soziobiologie. Die Macht der Gene und die Evolution sozialen Verhaltens*. Heidelberg/Berlin/Oxford.

Yeşilyurt, M. 2014. *Die wissenschaftliche Interpretation von Göbeklitepe. Die Theorie und das Forschungsprogramm. Neolithikum und ältere Metallzeiten – Studien und Materialien 2*. Berlin/Münster/Wien/Zürich/London.

Part Three
Community, interaction and boundaries

Strategies of boundary making between northern and southern Italy in the late sixth and early fifth millennium BC

Valeska Becker

Abstract

In the sixth and early fifth millennium BC, Italy seems to be divided, as is manifest in different aspects belonging to the economic, social and religious spheres. In south and central Italy at this time, various forms of the Impresso culture appear, whereas in Upper Italy, the Fiorano culture and its regional subgroups can be found. Apart from differing pottery shapes and decorations (technique, motifs), these two large cultural phenomena can also be distinguished regarding their burial customs. Whereas burials are almost completely absent in northern Italy, the remains of several hundreds of individuals have been found in caves and settlements in central and south Italy. Finally, the division of the country also becomes apparent regarding the distribution of different raw materials. The north Italian flint from the Monti Lessini and the region around Monte Baldo does not reach across the southern border of the Po plain, whereas on the contrary obsidian from south Italy can be found only rarely in the north. The reasons for this separation may lie in the different origins of the cultural phenomena of north and south Italy.

Zusammenfassung: Abgrenzungsstrategien zwischen Nord- und Süditalien im späten 6. und frühen 5. Jahrtausend v. Chr.

Im sechsten und frühen fünften Jahrtausend v. Chr. lässt sich in Italien eine Zweiteilung beobachten, die sich an Hand verschiedener Merkmale manifestiert, die der wirtschaftlichen, gesellschaftlichen und religiösen Sphäre angehören. In Süd- und Mittelitalien sind in dieser Zeit verschiedene Ausprägungen der Impresso-Keramik verbreitet, während in Oberitalien die Fiorano-Kultur und ihre regionalen Untergruppen auftreten. Abgesehen von unterschiedlichen Keramikformen und -verzierungen (Technik, Motivik) unterscheiden sich diese beiden großen Kulturphänomene auch durch ihre Bestattungssitten. Während in Oberitalien Bestattungen fast völlig fehlen, liegen aus Mittel- und Süditalien die Reste mehrerer hundert Individuen vor, die in Höhlen und Siedlungen zutage gekommen sind. Schließlich wird die Teilung des Landes auch durch die Verteilung verschiedener Rohstoffe deutlich. Der oberitalienische Silex der Monti Lessini und der Region um den Monte Baldo dringt nicht über den südlichen Rand der Po-Ebene vor, während sich umgekehrt Obsidian aus Süditalien nur in spärlichen

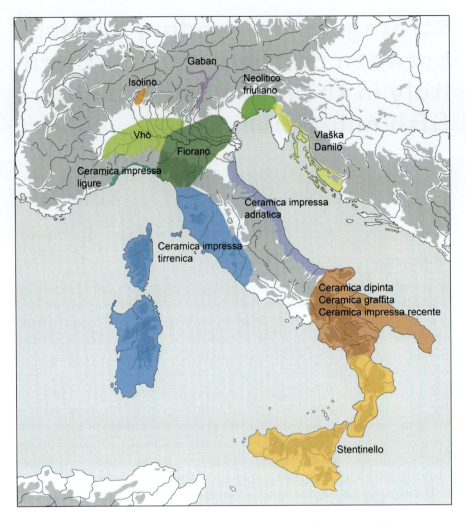

Figure 1. Ceramic groups in Early Neolithic Italy (c. 5600–4900 cal BC).

Resten im Norden findet. Die Ursachen dieser Teilung liegen möglicherweise in der unterschiedlichen Herkunft der Kulturphänomene Nord- und Süditaliens.

Introduction

The spread of a Neolithic way of life, its establishment and development in the sixth and fifth millennium BC in central Europe is well known and has formed the subject of countless studies. In contrast, the situation in regions south of the Alps is more difficult, partly due to language barriers, a complex and eclectic culture of publication and a landscape which differs drastically even over small distances. The uncertainty surrounding the prehistoric cultural situation is frequently expressed in "empty" areas or in faulty terminology on maps in introductory works[1]. More recently, however, A. Pessina and V. Tiné have succeeded in producing a lucid synthetic work on the Italian Neolithic which clearly lays out the complex relationships between

---

1   See for instance maps 9a and 10a in the Atlas of prehistoric Europe (Buchvaldek *et al.* 2007); compare the very tightly circumscribed distribution area of the Fiorano culture or the way the western Po plain is virtually empty of any cultural groups in von Schnurbein 2009, Abb. 67 (where northern Italy is shown virtually empty of finds) or Abb. 68 (in Liguria, there is actually Impresso pottery, not "Finale", and it is not really clear why the Adriatic Impresso is termed "Impressa adriatique centrale").

the different cultural phenomena, their material manifestations and their dating. Unfortunately, it is so far only available in Italian[2].

At first, the multiplicity of names for the different cultures, groups, styles and facies in late sixth and early fifth millennium BC Italy can seem confusing (Figure 1), but many of these cultural phenomena are merely local variants of two larger entities which, roughly speaking, take up the regions to the north and to the south of the Po plain respectively. This division is manifested in different material culture traits, a selection of which will be discussed in the remainder of this paper. My main aim is to suggest possible reasons for this mutual boundary marking and to attempt a clearer characterisation of the social groups responsible for this material culture patterning.

Differentiation through pottery

Decorative technique and motifs

The division of the country is most clearly visible in the pottery. This is not the place to rehearse the problems connected with the definition of archaeological "cultures" mainly on the basis of pottery, as is so often practised in Neolithic scholarship, or to repeat the lengthy discussions surrounding the archaeological culture concept[3]. It is clear, however, that the standardisations, norms and types manifested (amongst others) in pottery are ultimately based on the social practice and behaviours of individuals within a society. In contrast to certain tools and implements for which a specific shape may be determined by function, with relatively little room for deviation, the form and decoration of ceramics can be varied to a much greater extent without losing the primary function of a vessel as a container for solid or liquid substances. Therefore, the repetition of characteristics in form and decoration can express group identity and can be interpreted as standardisations within a collective[4]. I would like to stress, however, that such ceramic groups cannot be equated with ethnic groups.

As is well known, the cultural phenomena in southern Italy and along the coasts belong to the sphere of pottery decorated with impressions (Impresso-Cardial, Figure 2 top). This term covers decorative techniques characterised by the use of various implements — such as shells, spatulae, combs, flint artefacts and other bone or wooden objects — or even just the human hand (finger or finger nail impressions, pinching). Combinations with incised decoration are not excluded, but impressions do dominate the range of motifs. For this reason, the Impresso-Cardial area is often seen as a counter-model to areas using painted pottery in Anatolia, the Balkans and the Carpathian Basin, although pottery decorated with impressions is also found in settlements of the painted ware Neolithic, sometimes in high percentages[5]. Conversely, painted pottery appears in the developed Early Neolithic of southern and central Italy from about 5500 cal BC[6].

---

2   Pessina and Tiné 2008.
3   Eggert 2013; Müller 2006; Zeeb-Lanz 2003; 2006.
4   Hansen 2009.
5   This is especially the case for Early Neolithic cultural phenomena in south-east Europe, such as the Starčevo or Körös cultures: Schubert 1999.
6   The so-called *ceramica dipinta*, or painted pottery (*stile Lagnano da Piede, facies Masseria La Quercia, Passo di Corvo, Catignano*): see e.g. Bagnone and Zamagni 2003; Mallory 1989; S. Tiné 1983.

Nevertheless, the earliest Neolithic of Italy remains connected with Impresso pottery. The earliest absolute dates reach back to around 6000/5900 cal BC[7]. Quite quickly, sometimes only a few generations later, Impresso pottery is found along the western coast of Italy, especially in the caves of Liguria, while the northernmost settlements with Impresso pottery on Italy's Adriatic coast, just south of Venice, are considerably later (c. 5400 cal BC). However, this may be due to differences in the terrain: in many areas, the Tyrrhenian coast is steeper than that of the Adriatic, so that sites close to the Adriatic are more likely to have been destroyed by the sea.

The origins of impressed decoration do not lie within Italy itself, but can be traced back to the Early Neolithic cultures of the Near East. In Cilicia, in the Amuq valley and in the Levant, pottery with impressed decoration is attested from the middle of the seventh millennium BC[8]. With a slight temporal lag it is then found in western Anatolia, Thessaly, the eastern Adriatic and finally southern Italy[9].

The mechanisms of this spread, the paths it took and the persons carrying it forward are still largely unexplored. However, there are indications that the process was not purely linear. Instead, certain combinations of decorative techniques, for instance comb impressions paired with painted stripes, connect specific regions, while other areas in between do not show this kind of decoration[10]. Only larger-scale comparative studies analysing decorative techniques, motifs and styles of impressed pottery in the Mediterranean area can provide new insights into the spread of Impresso pottery.

The early Impresso pottery of southern Italy is decorated with randomly distributed dots; the rim area remains free of impressions. Only a few generations later, geometric motifs such as bands, rhomboids, trapezes, suspended triangles and zig-zag ornaments appear[11]. These strict geometric arrangements are continued into the painted pottery phases.

Wherever the impressed pottery in southern and central Italy originated — it never reached the north of the peninsula. Instead, the Fiorano culture is found here from the middle of the sixth millennium. Over time, much like the central European LBK, it can be subdivided into a series of smaller regional groups on the basis of its pottery. In spite of intensive discussion, the origin of the Fiorano culture is still unknown. Alongside individual researchers advocating a Neolithisation process driven exclusively by autochthonous Mesolithic populations[12], two scenarios are generally proposed, namely that the Fiorano culture either developed during an expansion of Impresso groups into the Po plain and northern regions[13] (and thereby completely abandoned centuries-old traditions of pottery decoration and shaping, see below), or instead that influences from outside the Po plain, namely from the Balkans and the Carpathian Basin, were the decisive element in the formation of the Fiorano culture[14].

The main difference between the Impresso area and the pottery of the Fiorano culture is that the latter is decorated with incised lines (Figure 2 lower part).

---

7 V. Tiné 2002, 137–138.
8 E.g. in Mersin-Yumuktepe, Ramad or Byblos: Balossi and Frangipane 2002.
9 See Becker 2018, 68.
10 Çilingiroğlu 2010.
11 V. Tiné 2002, 134–139.
12 Gehlen 2010.
13 Pedrotti 2001, 123–124.
14 Bagolini and Biagi 1985, 50–52; Bagolini 1990.

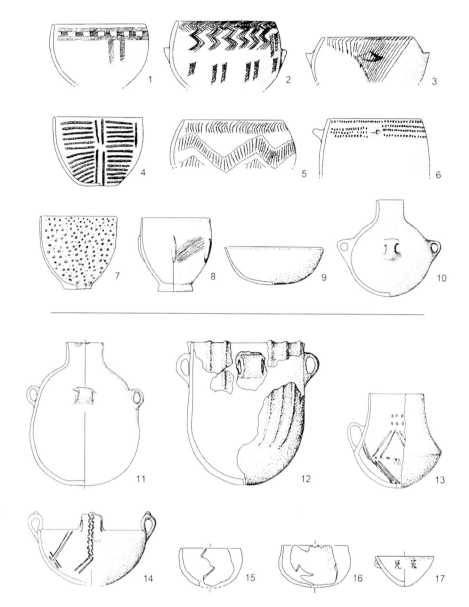

Figure 2. Ligurian (1–3), Tyrrhenian (4–6) and Adriatic Impresso (7–10), as well as pottery of the Fiorano culture (11–17). Not to scale (after Ferrari et al. 2002; Pessina and Tiné 2008).

Impressions only appear as secondary motifs and are more almond-shaped or elongated; in any case, they were definitely not produced using shells. An analysis of the pottery decoration of the Fiorano culture allows the definition of several styles characterised by arches and angles, plastic cordons, combinations of angles and plastic cordons, or angles in the rim area[15]. In general however, it is difficult to group the decorations into coherent styles, as the motifs are highly dynamic in terms of their possible combinations. Motifs can be regular and encircle the entire vessel, but there are also decorations which do not consist of repeated identical motifs. In addition, motifs can be separated by empty areas, or a vessel can be decorated in only one particular location. As the pottery of the Fiorano culture comes exclusively from settlements and is therefore highly fragmented, this apparent freedom in the

---

15   Becker 2018, 212–223.

combination and placement of motifs makes it much more difficult to define styles and hence also to provide a finer chronological subdivision.

In any case, this illustrates a further distinction between the regularly spaced and recurrent geometric motifs of the Impresso culture and the much freer and dynamic motif composition of the Fiorano culture.

Shapes

Apart from decorations, the division between northern Italy on the one hand and central and southern Italy on the other is also evident in the range of pottery shapes. Semi-spherical and globular vessels with rounded or flat bases dominate the pottery spectrum in the south; bottle-like shapes only appear with the first evidence for painted decoration.

The pottery of the Fiorano culture is completely different. The most characteristic shape is the so-called Fiorano cup (*tazza carenata*, Figure 2.13), a carinated, markedly profiled and round-based beaker with a handle. In addition, there are open bowls and bottles. Especially the predilection for attaching handles to vessels must be stressed, as handles are generally rather rare in the Early Neolithic and do not appear in the Impresso culture. Rounded bases are a further characteristic of the ceramic material, with only few exceptions. The use of very different shapes once again underlines the distinction between northern and southern Italy in the Neolithic.

Differentiation through raw materials

The division of Italy in the sixth and fifth millennium BC is not restricted to pottery, but can also be traced in the evidence for trade and the resulting material culture patterns in north and south. The study of raw materials is particularly promising for tracing economic relationships, as their sourcing, distribution and consumption can often be traced relatively clearly.

An example for a raw material which has also been recovered in areas north of the Alps is the southern Alpine flint from the Monti Lessini area or rather from the Monte Baldo on the eastern shore of Lake Garda ("Lessini flint"). This material is of high quality, easy to access and relatively close to the surface[16] and was already distributed across the Alps and as far north as the Danube in the Mesolithic[17]. The daggers made of Lessini flint and found in southern Germany have also repeatedly been discussed as indicators for trade and contact[18]. It is hence not surprising that flint from this area south of the Alps also played an important role in the Neolithic of northern Italy and is distributed across all of the Po plain. The settlement of Lugo di Grezzana at the foot of the Monti Lessini with its knapping and flint working areas provides ample evidence for the concentrated processing of this raw material from the nodule or tabular core to the finished object and its further distribution[19].

Interestingly, on the Gargano peninsula in southern Italy, the "spur" of the boot, there are varieties of flint similar to that from the Monti Lessini[20]. These

---

16 Binsteiner 1993; Goldenberg 2006.
17 Nutz 2009.
18 E.g. in Kieselbach 2010, 207–209; Tillmann 1993; 2012.
19 Cavulli 2008, 239–243.
20 Tarantini *et al.* 2011.

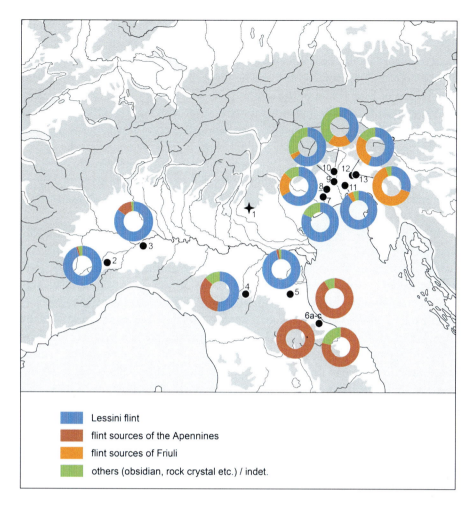

Figure 3. Distribution of Lessini flint and other flint varieties in northern Italy. 1 Lugo di Grezzana; 2 Alba; 3 Casalnoceto; 4 Savignano; 5 Lugo di Romagna; 6 Miramare; 7 Fagnigola; 8 Valer; 9. S. Vito; 10 S. Martino; 11 Piancada; 12 Sammardenchia; 13 Pavia.

are of such good quality that below-ground mines were established as early as the Neolithic. To date, not all of these shafts have been recorded, but excavations at Defensola provide a good insight into mining techniques, shaft systems and mining tools and implements[21].

If this raw material had been traded down the line, one would expect that its proportion in the various assemblages would decrease exponentially with increasing distance from the source and that core and blade sizes would also decrease, as would the proportion of cores[22]. For northern Italy, this modality of exchange seems plausible for only part of the evidence (Figure 3). On the one hand, the proportion of Monti Lessini flint diverges markedly in the settlements of northern Italy without there being a clear relation to increasing distance from the source; on the other hand, there is a clear boundary in the distribution of Lessini flint at the southern edge of the Po plain[23]. As far away as the Fiorano culture sites of Savignano and Lugo di Romagna, Lessini flint makes up 52.2 % (Savignano) or even 95.5 % (Lugo di Romagna) of the chipped stone material. In contrast, a mere 90 km further at Miramare, where several sites of the Adriatic Impresso culture were excavated, Lessini flint no longer plays any role. Instead, flint from

---

21 Galiberti 2005.
22 Scharl 2010; Zimmermann 1995.
23 For more information on flint sources, see Ferrari and Mazzieri 1998; Negrino *et al.* 2006; Pessina 2006.

the Marche region, which is also of high quality, is used almost exclusively. While flint varieties from the Apennine Mountains can occur in small percentages on settlements in the Po plain, the cultural boundary between impressed and incised pottery also seems to work as a hermetically sealed border in terms of the distribution of Lessini flint to the south.

A similar situation also applies to the distribution systems of obsidian, although it moves in the opposite direction. As the chemical composition of this material is locally very specific, its sources can be defined with great certainty. For the Italian Neolithic, the sources on Lipari, Palmarola, Sardinia and Pantelleria are the most important. While it is difficult to find, and most particularly to date, knapping areas, elemental analysis of obsidian artefacts from Neolithic sites shows that all these sources were used at the time[24].

However, while the proportions of obsidian in southern and central Italian settlements go on increasing across the sixth and fifth millennia BC, in northern Italy this raw material remains rare until the middle of the fifth millennium. This is most evident when comparing the settlements of Savignano (Fiorano culture) and Faenza-Fornace Cappuccini (Adriatic Impresso), which are a mere 80 km apart from each other. In Savignano, a single obsidian flake was found[25], while in Faenza-Fornace Cappucini 334 of the chipped stone implements were made from obsidian[26]. The cultural boundary which could already be traced using Lessini flint thus also applies to the distribution of obsidian: "this rather seems to be the result of a cultural frontier between the groups of the Po plain and the Alps, and the Impressed ware communities of the Romagna"[27].

Differentiation through mortuary ritual

Even more convincing than the two previous observations is the fact that a boundary between northern and southern Italy is also manifested in the context of mortuary rites, as this touches on the context of belief systems and religion.

Unfortunately, the data available for studying mortuary rites of the sixth and early fifth millennium BC in Italy are rather scanty; only about 320 individuals have been dated to this early horizon[28] and these are distributed unevenly across the entire peninsula. In addition, often these are not complete burials, but single skeletal elements. This suggests that burial customs in Early Neolithic Italy did not regularly involve the inhumation of complete bodies and that the human remains unearthed so far are probably more likely to be the exception rather than the rule.

In contrast to the Early Neolithic of central Europe, the Italian burials are not found in cemeteries, but are either settlement burials or have been recovered in caves[29] away from habitation sites. Often, these are crouched inhumations and the deceased have been furnished with few grave goods such as elements of clothing, vessels, tools, weapons and food offerings, and more rarely a sprinkling of red ochre.

---

24   Bigazzi and Oddone 2006.
25   Bernabo Brea and Steffè 1990, 93.
26   Tykot 1996, 57.
27   Pessina and Tiné 2008, 240 ("sembra piuttosto il risultato dell'esistenza di una frontiera culturale fra i gruppi padano-alpini e le comunità a ceramica impressa della Romagna").
28   Summarised e.g. in Bagolini and Grifoni Cremonesi 1994; Grifoni Cremonesi *et al.* 2003; Robb 1994.
29   E.g. Grotta 3 di Latronico (Mallegni 1978), Grotta dei Piccioni (Grifoni Cremonesi 2002), Grotta Continenza (Vitiello and Mallegni 1989/1990), Grotta Scaloria (Elster *et al.* 2016) and others.

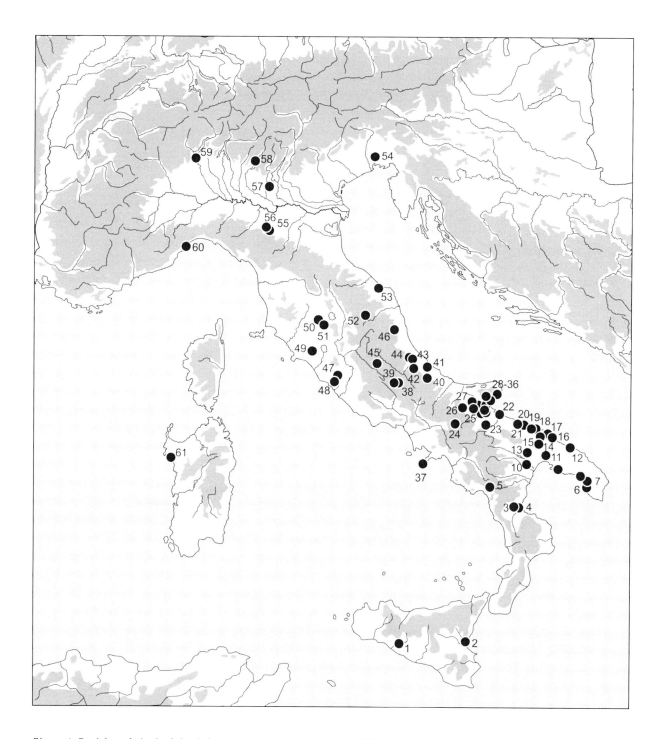

Figure 4. Burials and single skeletal elements of the Italian Early Neolithic. 1 Monte Kronio; 2 Fontanazza; 3 Grotta Pavolella; 4 Favella; 5 Grotte di Latronico; 6 Samari; 7 Torre Sabea; 8 Serra Cicora; 9 Gandoli; 10 Tirlecchia; 11 Trasano; 12 Masseria Valente; 13 Malerba; 14 Grotta Pacelli; 15 Santa Maria delle Grazie; 16 Grotta delle Mura; 17 Le Macchie; 18 Balsignano; 19 Masseria Maselli; 20 Pulo di Molfetta; 21 Carrara San Francesco; 22 Madonna di Loreto; 23 Rendina; 24 La Starza; 25 Guadone S. Rocco; 26 Diga di Occhito; 27 Ripa Tetta; 28 Masseria Fonteviva; 29 Guadone; 30 Masseria Candelaro; 31 Masseria Santa Tecchia; 32 Passo di Corvo; 33 Foggia-Villa Comunale; 34 Grotta Scaloria; 35 Murgia Timone; 36 Murgecchia; 37 Grotta delle Felci; 38 Colle Santo Stefano; 39 Grotta Continenza; 40 Lama dei Peligni; 41 Lanciano; 42 Grotta dei Piccioni; 43 Villa Badessa; 44 Catignano; 45 Grotta Belli; 46 Grotta Sant'Angelo; 47 La Marmotta; 48 Grotta Patrizi; 49 Grotta di Settecanelle; 50 Pienza; 51 Grotta dell'Orso; 52 Maddalena di Muccia; 53 Ripabianca; 54 Piancada; 55 Calerno; 56 Sant'Ilario d'Enza; 57 Casalmoro; 58 Lovere; 59 Pizzo di Bodio; 60 Arene Candide; 61 Grotta Verde.

The spatial distribution of the burials is instructive and once again illustrates the existence of a marked cultural boundary between northern and southern Italy (Figure 4). There is a clear predominance of finds in southern Italy, mostly in the agrarian settlements of the Tavoliere plain, as well as in the caves and settlements along the southern Adriatic coast. Larger numbers of settlement burials and inhumations in caves also occur in southern central Italy.

In contrast, for northern Italy there are only six known interments if one excludes the inhumation of a male from the Arene Candide cave, which was formerly associated with Ligurian Impresso pottery but was recently dated to the Chassey culture by AMS dating[30]. These six burials are briefly summarised here. The probably earliest case is the grave of a 4–5-year-old girl found in Piancada (Udine) and attributed to the Friulian Neolithic (c. 5500–4700 cal BC)[31]. The child was buried in an irregular pit, which may originally have served a different function, and was covered with hundreds of marine shells. It remained unclear whether these latter were elements of the mortuary ritual which found their way into the grave during the burial, or whether this represents detritus deposited in the pit at a later point in time. Two burials can be attributed to the Vhò group (c. 5300–4800 cal BC), which is related to the Fiorano culture. However, the two interments are rather dissimilar. At Lovere (Bergamo) a north–south oriented individual was found in a stone-lined pit covered by a mound; a bone point and an antler bead were discovered nearby[32]. In contrast, the burial at Casalmoro (Mantova) was probably oriented east–west and buried in an oval pit together with four geometric flint artefacts interpreted as arrowheads[33]. Flint flakes were also the only finds associated with the settlement burial of Calerno Cabassa (Reggio Emilia), attributed to the Fiorano culture on stratigraphic grounds. This dating also applies to the left crouched inhumation from Sant'Ilario d'Enza (Reggio Emilia), which was buried without any grave goods[34]. The human remains from Pizzo di Bodio belong to the Isolino group and are amongst the latest examples of burials from the period discussed here, dating roughly between 4800 and 4600 cal BC[35]. They form a partial burial consisting only of a left humerus and a right talus.

These six graves are distributed over a large time span and extensive geographical area and have hardly any commonalities, either in the structure of the grave or in the orientation of the body or grave goods. The skeletal remains from Pizzo di Bodio are evidence for the custom of partial burial, while the other individuals were complete inhumations.

It must be pointed out that the chances of finding burials are not as great in the Po plain as they are in southern Italy, as alluvial deposits several metres thick have accumulated on the floodplains and mask archaeological finds and features. However, settlements are known from the foothills of the Apennines and from elevated sites in the Alpine foreland, and these should have yielded settlement burials had this custom been common. In addition, dozens of caves with Neolithic material have been discovered in the karst areas around Trieste, but in none of them have burials been found. Thus, the principal reasons for the differential density of grave finds are to be sought in different cultural traditions, rather than in environmental conditions.

---

30 Biagi and Starnini 2016, 38.
31 Ferrari and Pessina 1996, 84–91.
32 Poggiani Keller 2000, 306–310.
33 Biagi and Perini 1979, 18–22.
34 Grifoni Cremonesi 2006, 92.
35 Mallegni 2000.

Figure 5. Schematic representation of decorative techniques used in northern, central and southern Italy.

Discussion

The examples described here show that Neolithic Italy can be divided into two large spheres on economic, religious and social grounds, as manifested through mortuary ritual and different aspects of material culture. In this context, pottery can be seen as standing in for a whole suite of artefacts probably produced at the household level (Figure 5). Mortuary rituals, which pertain to the religious domain, provide a superordinate interaction sphere to which many households belonged (Figure 6), and such an overarching network can also be traced using the distribution of raw materials (Figure 7), although here it is less clear which actors were involved in extraction, processing and distribution. The settlement of Lugo di Grezzana seems to occupy a special position in this network. The imagined boundary that is manifested across these different contexts runs more or less just to the south of the Po plain and was certainly permeable in some areas. For instance, single Impresso sherds are found in settlements of the Fiorano culture, while Fiorano pottery is sometimes retrieved among the ceramic material of Impresso culture sites[36].

All this begs the question as to the ultimate cause of this cultural boundary between north and south. Undoubtedly, the material expressions of the Impresso culture can be connected to the earliest agrarian communities in Italy and take their place among the circle of Mediterranean cultures producing pottery with impressed decoration. On this background, the search for the origins of the

---

36 Pessina 1998, 98.

Figure 6. Schematic representation of the distribution of mortuary customs in northern, central and southern Italy.

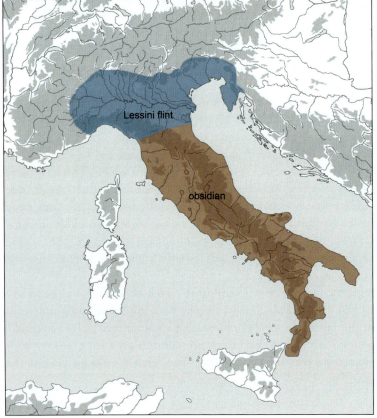

Figure 7. Schematic representation of the distribution of Lessini flint and obsidian.

Fiorano culture becomes all the more pressing, as it seems plausible that its roots are not to be found in the Mediterranean area.

This means that we will have to look again at older suggestions which traced the Fiorano culture back to influences from south-east Europe. The initiators of such a process must therefore be either the late Starčevo culture and earliest LBK, as for instance found in Hungary and Austria, or indeed the eastern Adriatic Danilo culture.

The Danilo culture can be dated to approximately between 5500 and 4800 cal BC[37] and is distributed along the shores of the eastern Adriatic. There is no doubt that it influences the Early Neolithic cultural phenomena of Friuli and the karst around Trieste[38], but neither its pottery[39] nor other items of its material culture repertoire show any similarities to Fiorano, and this quite apart from the fact that the available dates suggest these two phenomena ran in parallel, rather than one being a predecessor of the other.

This leaves the Starčevo culture and the early Bandkeramik where possible commonalities to northern Italy may be found. While such parallels have been suggested in the past[40], they are now generally rejected given the lack of any direct evidence[41]. Indeed, the most south-westerly LBK settlements in Transdanubia and the Burgenland are 350 km away from the Italian region of Friuli as the crow flies, and it is a further 150 km from there to the Po plain. Also, there are no direct parallels in terms of pottery shapes or decoration between the two areas.

Nevertheless, a connection remains possible if the post-Starčevo cultural phenomena of north-west Croatia and Slavonia are taken into account as possible mediators. These are the so-called Malo-Korenovo culture, which is sometimes described as the southernmost branch of the Bandkeramik, and the Sopot culture, which developed on a Starčevo culture substrate with influences from the early Vinča culture in Slavonia.

The main area of distribution of the Malo-Korenovo culture, first described by S. Dimitrijević[42], lies between the rivers Sava and Drava and in south-west Hungary, where its material culture is sometimes found admixed with that of the Keszthely group[43]. Its pottery is decorated with bands arranged in zig-zag, V-, meander and spiral motifs. There are as yet no absolute dates, but there are greater numbers of these for the neighbouring Sopot culture, which ranges from about 5400 to 4900 cal BC[44].

Again it is clear that the cultural phenomena based on the Starčevo culture must be discounted as possible predecessors of the Fiorano culture. However, the close connection between these phenomena is clearly illustrated by many similarities, mixed inventories and imports (Figure 8). For instance, in the karst area around Trieste and in the Danilo culture there is Malo-Korenovo culture

---

37 Forenbaher and Miracle 2006, 95 tab. 3.
38 Barfield 1972.
39 Compare the internal classification according to Batović 1979.
40 Cocchi Genick 1994, 107; Radmilli 1967; 1974.
41 Pessina 1998; Pessina and Tiné 2008, 34.
42 Dimitrijević 1961; more recently the material has e.g. been analysed by Težak-Gregl 1993.
43 See e.g. Barna 2005; Tokai 2006.
44 Krznarić Škrivanko 2011; Obelić et al. 2004. However, new AMS dates from Alsonyék in Transdanubia point to a later start around 5100 cal BC, at least at this site (Oross et al. 2016). These data and their cultural context are discussed in greater depth in Becker 2018, 238–239.

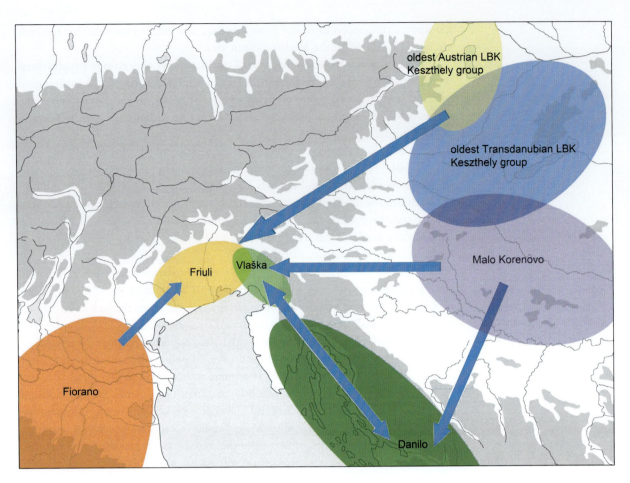

Figure 8. Communication networks of the Neolithic cultural phenomena in north-east Italy, Croatia, south-west Hungary and south-east Austria between 5500/5300 and 4900 cal BC.

pottery[45], and in Friuli, which functions as a kind of nodal point in this network, remains of the Fiorano culture, of Neolithic groups of the Friuli region and of the groups in the Trieste karst all occur[46]. The carinated Fiorano cup, which seems so foreign compared to Impresso pottery, does also not really fit with the ceramic repertoire of more north-easterly cultural phenomena, but at least carinated vessels are known from the Starčevo culture (Figure 9) and very similar types have been identified in both the Malo-Korenovo and the Sopot cultures, quite apart from the affinities which can be defined in decorative technique and motif spectrum (especially angle-arch motifs in Malo-Korenovo) (Figure 10).

Considered separately, these observations could be discounted as mere coincidence, but taken together they allow us to formulate a new hypothesis, which can now be further investigated with new absolute dates and with a much enlarged material basis (Figure 11).

The late seventh and early sixth millennium cal BC Starčevo culture is, as is well known, the substrate for the Transdanubian earliest LBK, with the two phenomena overlapping for a time and existing in parallel[47]. At the same time, the late Starčevo also formed the basis for the Malo-Korenovo culture on the one hand and the Sopot group on the other hand. It is well possible that the Fiorano culture can be added to this list as the westernmost successor of the

---

45   Dimitrijević *et al.* 1998, 89 Abb. 17; Gilli and Montagnari Kokelj 1996, 75 fig. 12,48.
46   Ferrari and Pessina 1999.
47   Bánffy and Oross 2009, 263.

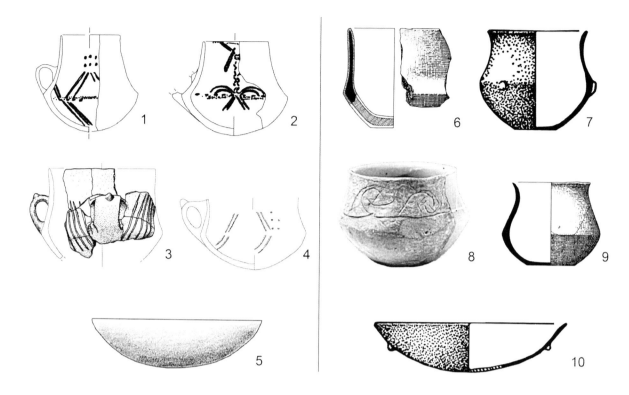

Figure 9. Comparison between vessel shapes of the Fiorano culture (1–5), the Sopot group (6, 9, 10) and the Malo-Korenovo culture (7, 8). Not to scale (after Dimitrijević 1968; 1978; 1979; Ferrari et al. 2002; Marković 2013; Težak-Gregl 1993; Tokai 2006).

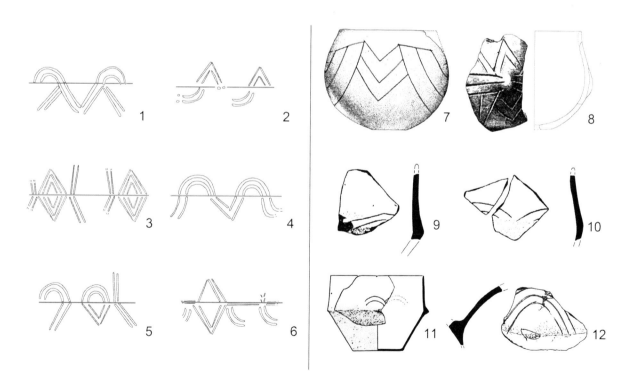

Figure 10. Comparison between decorations of the Fiorano culture (1–6) and the Sopot group (9–12) and Malo-Korenovo culture (7, 8). Not to scale (after Dimitrijević 1968; 1978; 1979; Ferrari et al. 2002; Marković 2013; Težak-Gregl 1993; Tokai 2006).

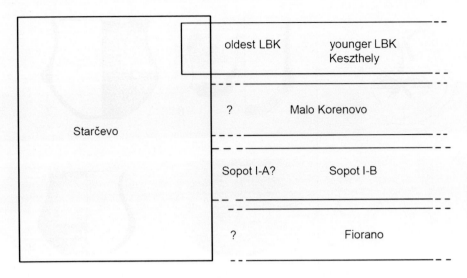

Figure 11. Schematic representation of the distribution of the Starčevo culture and its successor groupings.

Starčevo culture. This would explain the many differences between northern and southern Italy and the evident bipartition of the country in the sixth and fifth millennia cal BC. It seems that stressing one's own identity, as well as continuing traditional techniques, symbols and world views was of the highest importance for the inhabitants of Early Neolithic Italy. One reason may have been the different origin of the respective cultural complexes, rooted in divergent developments, with the two strands taking different paths for many hundreds of years before coming into contact again in the Po plain. A further reason could be the Italian landscape: the Apennines with their almost 3000 m high peaks, and the highly compartmentalised nature of the terrain more generally, could have contributed to the creation of this boundary, which was not impermeable, but nevertheless clearly visible in many aspects of life.

It is questionable whether an evaluation of genetic evidence could contribute to resolving this problem, as only few and disparate burial remains are known from the northern Italian Early Neolithic and there are also so far only restricted assemblages of human remains from the Malo-Korenovo culture and the Sopot group. The analysis of a chronologically younger individual of the Vasi a Bocca Quadrata (VBQ) culture (c. 4800–4200/4000 cal BC) from Mezzocorona (Trento) revealed a T-haplotype and hence clearly indicates Early Neolithic Anatolian origins[48]. Yet even in southern Italy, where there is enough available material for large-scale aDNA analyses, the state of research is as yet unsatisfying. It remains to be seen whether more data will in future confirm or modify the interpretation proposed here.

---

48   Di Benedetto *et al.* 2000.

References

Bagnone, D. and Zamagni, B. 2003. Lo studio della ceramica. In C. Tozzi and B. Zamagni (eds), *Gli scavi nel villaggio Neolitico di Catignano (1971–1980). Origines. Studi e materiali pubblicati a cura dell'Istituto Italiano di Preistoria e Protostoria*, 97–144. Firenze.

Bagolini, B. 1990. La neolitizzazione del versante meridionale delle Alpi centro-orientali. In M. Höneisen (ed.), *Die ersten Bauern. Pfahlbaufunde Europas. Forschungsberichte zur Ausstellung im Schweizerischen Landesmuseum und zum Erlebnispark / Ausstellung Pfahlbauland Zürich 28. April bis 30. September 1990*, 211–217. Zürich.

Bagolini, B. and Biagi, P. 1985. Balkan influences in the Neolithic of northern Italy. *Preistoria Alpina* 21, 49–57.

Bagolini, B. and Grifoni Cremonesi, R. 1994. Il Neolitico italiano: facies culturali e manifestazioni funerarie. *Bullettino di Paletnologia Italiana* 85, 139–170.

Balossi, F. and Frangipane, M. 2002. La ceramica impressa del Vicino Oriente. In M.A. Fugazzola Delpino, A. Pessina and V. Tiné (eds), *Le ceramiche impresse nel Neolitico antico. Italia e Mediterraneo. Studi di Paletnologia I*, 3–15. Rome.

Bánffy, E. and Oross, K. 2009. Entwicklung und Dynamik der Linearbandkeramik in Transdanubien. In A. Zeeb-Lanz (ed.), *Krisen — Kulturwandel — Kontinuitäten. Zum Ende der Bandkeramik in Mitteleuropa. Beiträge der internationalen Tagung in Herxheim bei Landau (Pfalz) vom 14.–17.06.2007*, 219–240. Rahden.

Barfield, L.H. 1972. The first Neolithic cultures of north eastern Italy. In H. Schwabedissen (ed.), *Die Anfänge des Neolithikums vom Orient bis Nordeuropa. Fundamenta A 3, VII*, 182–216. Köln.

Barna, J.P. 2005. Sormás-Török-földek településtörténeti áttekintése. A középső neolitikum. *Zalai Múzeum* 14, 17–36.

Batović, Š. 1979. Jadranska zona. In M. Garašanin (ed.), *Praistorija jugoslavenskih zemalja. II: Neolitsko Doba*, 473–634. Sarajevo.

Becker, V. 2018. *Studien zum Altneolithikum in Italien. Neolithikum und ältere Metallzeiten. Studien und Materialien 3*. Münster, Berlin.

Di Benedetto, G., Nasidze, I.S., Stenico, M., Nigro, L., Krings, M., Lanzinger, M., Vigilant, L., Stoneking, M., Pääbo, S. and Barbujani, G. 2000. Mitochondrial DNA sequences in prehistoric human remains from the Alps. *European Journal of Human Genetics* 8, 669–677.

Bernabò Brea, M. and Steffé, G. 1990. Il Neolitico antico a Savignano. In B. Sala (ed.), *Nel segno dell'elefante. Geologia, paleontologia e archeologia del territorio di Savignano sul Panaro*, 77–134. Savignano.

Biagi, P. and Perini, M. 1979. Scoperta di una sepoltura e di un abitato del neolitico inferiore a Casalmoro in provincia di Mantova. *Preistoria Alpina* 15, 17–24.

Biagi, P. and Starnini, E. 2016. La cultura della Ceramica Impressa nella Liguria di Ponente (Italia settentrionale): Distribuzione, cronologia e aspetti culturali. In H. Bonet Rosado (ed.), *Nel neolític a l'edat del bronze en el Mediterrani occidental. Estudis en homenatge a Bernat Martí Oliver*, 35–49. Valencia.

Bigazzi, G. and Oddone, M. 2006. Metodi per il riconoscimento della provenienza dell'ossidiana. In D. Cocchi Genick (ed.), *Materie prime e scambi nella preistoria italiana: nel cinquantenario della fondazione dell'Istituto Italiano di Preistoria e Protostoria. Atti della XXXIX Riunione scientifica, Firenze 25–27 novembre 2004*, 413–433. Florence.

Binsteiner, A. 1993. Augewählte Silexlagerstätten und deren Abbau in den Provinzen Trient und Verona. *Archäologisches Korrespondenzblatt* 24, 255–263.

Buchvaldek, M., Lippert, A. and Košnar, L. 2007. *Atlas zur prähistorischen Archäologie Europas*. Prague.

Cavulli, F. 2008. Abitare il Neolitico. Le più antiche strutture antropiche del Neolitico in Italia settentrionale. *Preistoria Alpina Supplemento* 1, 43.

Çilingiroğlu, Ç. 2010. The appearance of impressed pottery in the Neolithic Aegean and its implications for maritime networks in the eastern Mediterranean. *Türkiye Bilimler Akademisi Arkeoloji Dergisi (TÜBA-AR)* 13, 9–22.

Cocchi Genick, D. 1994. *Manuale di Preistoria. II: Neolitico*. Florence.

Dimitrijević, S. 1961. Problem neolita i eneolita u sjeverozapadnoj Jugoslaviji. *Opuscula Archaeologica* 5, 5–78.

Dimitrijević, S. 1968. *Sopotsko-Lenđelska Kultura*. Zagreb.

Dimitrijević, S. 1978. Neolit u sjeverozapadnoj Hrvatskoj (Pregled stanja istraživanja do 1975. godine). In Ž. Rapanić (ed.), *Arheološka istraživanja u sjeverozapadnoj Hrvatskoj. Znanstveni skup. Varaždin 22–25. X 1975*, 71–128. Zagreb.

Dimitrijević, S. 1979. Sjeverna zona. Neolit u centralnom i zapadnom dijelu sjeverne Jugoslavije. In M. Garašanin (ed.), *Praistorija Jugoslavenskih Zemalja. II: Neolitska doba*, 229–360. Sarajevo.

Dimitrjević, S., Težak-Gregl, T. and Majnarić-Pandžić, N. 1998. *Prapovijest*. Zagreb.

Eggert, M.K.H. 2013. „Kultur": Zum praktischen Umgang mit einem Theoriekonzept. In M.K.H. Eggert and U. Veit (eds), *Theorie in der Archäologie: Zur jüngeren Diskussion in Deutschland. Tübinger Archäologische Taschenbücher 10*, 13–61. Münster.

Elster, E.S., Isetti, E., Robb, J. and Traverso, A. (eds) 2016. *The archaeology of Grotta Scaloria. Ritual in Neolithic southeast Italy. Monumenta Archaeologica 38*. Los Angeles.

Ferrari, S. and Mazzieri, P. 1998. Fonti e processi di scambio di rocce silicee scheggiabili. In A. Pessina and G. Muscio (eds), *Settemila anni fa: il primo pane. Ambienti e culture delle società neolitiche*, 165–169. Udine.

Ferrari, A. and Pessina, A. 1996. *Sammardenchia e i primi agricoltori del Friuli*. Udine.

Ferrari, A. and Pessina, A. (eds) 1999. *Sammardenchia-Cùeis. Contributi per la conoscenza di una comunità del primo Neolitico*. Udine.

Ferrari, A., Pessina, A. and Steffè, G. 2002. Il primo Neolitico dell'Emilia centro-orientale e della Romagna. In A. Broglio (ed.), *Preistoria e protostoria del Trentino Alto Adige / Südtirol. In ricordo Bernardino Bagolini. Atti della XXXIII Riunione Scientifica dell' Istituto Italiano di Preistoria e Protostoria, Trento, 21–24 ottobre 1997, Sessione I*, 363–375. Florence.

Forenbaher, S. and Miracle, P.T. 2006. The spread of farming in the eastern Adriatic. *Documenta Praehistorica* 33, 89–100.

Galiberti, A. 2005. *Defensola. Una miniera di selce di 7000 anni fa*. Siena.

Gehlen, B. 2010. Neolithic transition processes in southern Europe: the present state of knowledge and its deficiencies in northern Italy and southwestern France. In D. Gronenborn and J. Petrasch (eds), *Die Neolithisierung Mitteleuropas. Internationale Tagung, Mainz 24. bis 26. Juni 2005. RGZM-Tagungen 4*, 607–635. Mainz.

Gilli, E. and Montagnari Kokelj, E. 1996. La Grotta degli Zingari nel Carso triestino (materiali degli scavi 1961–1965). *Atti della Società Preistorica Friuli-Venezia Giulia* 9, 63–126.

Goldenberg, G. 2006. Neolithic exploitation and manufacturing of flint in the Monti Lessini, Verona. Italy. In G. Körlin and G. Weisgerber (eds), *Stone Age — mining age. Der Anschnitt, Beiheft 19*, 83–89. Bochum.

Grifoni Cremonesi, R. 2002. Grotta dei Piccioni, Abruzzo. In M.A. Fugazzola Delpino, A. Pessina and V. Tiné (eds), *Le ceramiche impresse nel Neolitico antico. Italia e Mediterraneo. Studi di Paletnologia I*, 499–507. Rome.

Grifoni Cremonesi, R. 2006. Sepolture e rituali funerari nel Neolitico in Italia. In F. Martini (ed.), *La cultura del morire nelle società preistoriche e protostoriche italiane. Studio interdisciplinare dei dati e loro trattamento informatico dal Paleolitico all'età del Rame. Serie della Collana Origines 3*, 87–107. Florence.

Grifoni Cremonesi, R., Mallegni, F. and Tramonti, A. 2003. La sepoltura del Neolitico antico di Torre Sabea. In J. Guilaine and G. Cremonesi (eds), *Torre Sabea. Un établissement du Néolithique ancien en Salento*, 96–105. Rome.

Hansen, K.P. 2009. Kultur und Kollektiv: Eine essayistische Heuristik für Archäologen. In D. Krausse and O. Nakoinz (eds), *Kulturraum und Territorialität. Archäologische Theorien, Methoden und Fallbeispiele. Kolloquium des DFG-SSP 1171, Esslingen 17.– 18. Januar 2007*, 17–25. Rahden.

Kieselbach, P. 2010. Silex. Elementarer Rohstoff und begehrtes Importgut. In C. Lichter (ed.), *Jungsteinzeit im Umbruch. Die "Michelsberger Kultur" und Mitteleuropa vor 6.000 Jahren. Ausstellungskatalog Badisches Landesmuseum Schloss Karlsruhe*, 203–209. Darmstadt.

Krznarić Škrivanko, M. 2011. Radiokarbonski datumi uzoraka sa Sopota. In M. Dizdar (ed.), *Panonski prapovijesni osviti. Zbornik radova posvećenih Korneliji Minichreiter uz 65. obletnicu života*, 209–225. Zagreb.

Mallegni, F. 1978. I resti scheletrici umani trovati nelle Grotte n. 2 e n. 3 di Latronico. In Istituto Italiano die Preistoria e Protostoria (eds), *Atti della XX Riunione Scientifica dell'Istituto Italiano di Preistoria e Protostoria, in Basilicata, 16–20 ottobre 1976*, 215–217. Florence.

Mallegni, F. 2000. Breve relazione sui reperti scheletrici umani del primo Neolitico dal sito di Pizzo di Bodio, Bodio Lomnago (Varese). *Sibrium* 23 (1994–1999), 503–504.

Mallory, J.P. 1989. Lagnano da Piede I — an early Neolithic village in the Tavoliere. *Origini* 13 (1984–1987), 193–290.

Marković, Z. 2013. Novija razmatranja o nekim aspektima sopotske kulture u sjevernoj Hrvatskoj. *Prilozi* 29, 57–70.

Müller, J. 2006. Soziale Grenzen und die Frage räumlicher Identitätsgruppen in der Prähistorie. In S. Burmeister and N. Müller-Scheeßel (eds), *Soziale Gruppen — kulturelle Grenzen. Die Interpretation sozialer Grenzen in der Prähistorischen Archäologie. Tübinger Archäologische Taschenbücher 5*, 103–117. Münster.

Negrino, F., Salzani, P. and Venturino Gambari, M. 2006. La circolazione della selce nel Piemonte tra il Neolitico e l'Età del Rame. In D. Cocchi Genick (ed.), *Materie prime e scambi nella preistoria italiana nel cinquantenario della fondazione dell'Istituto Italiano di Preistoria e Protostoria. Atti della XXXIX Riunione Scientifica, Firenze, 25–27 novembre 2004*, 315–327. Florence.

Nutz, B. 2009. Silex in Transit. Transportwege der Steinzeit über die Alpen. In K. Oeggl and M. Prast (eds), *Die Geschichte des Bergbaus in Tirol und seinen angrenzenden Gebieten. Proceedings zum 3. Milestone-Meeting des SFB HiMAT vom 23.–26.10.2008 in Silbertal*, 283–288. Innsbruck.

Obelić, B., Krznarić Škrivanko, M., Marijan, B. and Krajcar Bronić, I. 2004. Radiocarbon dating of Sopot culture sites (Late Neolithic) in eastern Croatia. *Radiocarbon* 46, 245–258.

Oross, K., Osztás, A., Marton, T., Köhler, K., Ódor, J.G., Szécsényi-Nagy, A., Bánffy, E., Alt, K.W., Bronk Ramsey, C., Kromer, B., Bayliss, A., Hamilton, D. and Whittle, A. 2016. Midlife changes: the Sopot burial ground at Alsónyék. *Jahresbericht des Römisch-Germanischen Zentralmuseums* 94, 151–178.

Pedrotti, A. 2001. Il Neolitico. In M. Lanzinger, F. Marzatico and A. Pedrotti (eds), *Storia del Trentino. I: La preistoria e la protostoria*, 119–181. Bologna.

Pessina, A. 1998. Aspetti culturali e problematiche del Primo Neolitico dell'Italia settentrionale. In A. Pessina and G. Muscio (eds), *Settemila anni fa: il primo pane. Ambienti e culture delle società neolitiche*, 95–105. Udine.

Pessina, A. 2006. Nuovi dati sugli aspetti culturali del primo Neolitico in Friuli e suoi rapporti con l'Adriatico orientale. In A. Pessina and P. Visentini (eds), *Preistoria dell'Italia settentrionale. Studi in ricordo di Bernardino Bagolini. Atti del Convegno, Udine, 23–24 settembre 2005*, 279–301. Udine.

Pessina, A. and Tiné, V. 2008. *Archeologia del Neolitico. L'Italia tra VI e IV millennio a. C.* Rome.

Poggiani Keller, R. 2000. Lovere (Bergamo): una sequenza stratigrafica esemplare dal Neolitico Antico al Bronzo Finale in area prealpina. *Rivista di Scienze Preistoriche* 50, 297–374.

Radmilli, A.M. 1967. *I villaggi a capanne del Neolitico italiano. Archivio per l'Antropologia e l'Etnologia 97*. Florence.

Radmilli, A.M. 1974. *Popoli e civiltà dell'Italia antica*. Rome.

Robb, J. 1994. Burial and social reproduction in the peninsular Italian Neolithic. *Journal of Mediterranean Archaeology* 7, 29–75.

Scharl, S. 2010. *Versorgungsstrategien und Tauschnetzwerke im Alt- und Mittelneolithikum. Die Silexversorgung im westlichen Franken. Berliner Archäologische Forschungen 7*. Rahden.

von Schnurbein, S. (ed.) 2009. *Atlas der Vorgeschichte. Europa von den ersten Menschen bis Christi Geburt*. Stuttgart.

Schubert, H. 1999. *Die bemalte Keramik des Frühneolithikums in Südosteuropa, Italien und Westanatolien. Internationale Archäologie 47*. Rahden.

Tarantini, M., Galiberti, A. and Mazzarocchi, F. 2011. Prehistoric flint mines of the Gargano: an overview. In M. Capote, S. Consuegra, P. Díaz-del-Río and X. Terradas (eds), *Proceedings of the 2nd international conference of the UISPP commission on flint mining in pre- and protohistoric times (Madrid, 14–17 October 2009). BAR International Series 2260*, 253–263. Oxford.

Težak-Gregl, T. 1993. *Kultura linearnotrakaste keramike u središnjoj Hrvatskoj. Korenovska kultura.* Zagreb.

Tillmann, A. 1993. Gastgeschenke aus dem Süden? Zur Frage einer Süd-Nord-Verbindung zwischen Südbayern und Oberitalien im späten Jungneolithikum. *Archäologisches Korrespondenzblatt* 23, 455–460.

Tillmann, A. 2012. Grüße aus Bella Italia — ein jungneolithisches Silexdolchblatt aus Frauenberg. *Das Archäologische Jahr in Bayern* 2011, 29–30.

Tiné, S. 1983. *Passo di Corvo e la civiltà neolitica del Tavoliere.* Genova.

Tiné, V. 2002. Le facies a ceramica impressa dell'Italia meridionale e della Sicilia. In M.A. Fugazzola Delpino, A. Pessina and V. Tiné (eds), *Le ceramiche impresse nel Neolitico antico. Italia e Mediterraneo. Studi di Paletnologia I*, 131–165. Rome.

Tokai, M.Z. 2006. Adatok a Malo Korenovo kerámia délnyugat-dunántúli megjelenéséhez. *Zalai Múzeum* 15, 9–23.

Tykot, R.H. 1996. Obsidian procurement and distribution in the central and western Mediterranean. *Journal of Mediterranean Archaeology* 9, 39–82.

Vitiello, A. and Mallegni, F. 1989/1990. I reperti umani neolitici della Grotta riparo Continenza. In A. Barra, R. Grifoni Cremonesi, F. Mallegni, M. Piancastelli, A. Vitiello and B. Wilkens, La Grotta Continenza di Trasacco. I livelli a ceramiche. *Rivista di Scienze Preistoriche* 42, 87–92.

Zeeb-Lanz, A. 2003. Keramikverzierungsstil als Kommunikationsmittel: Ein Beispiel aus dem frühen Jungneolithikum Südwestddeutschlands. In U. Veit, T. Kienlin, C. Kümmel and S. Schmidt (eds), *Spuren und Botschaften: Interpretation materieller Kultur. Tübinger Archäologische Taschenbücher 4*, 245–261. Münster.

Zeeb-Lanz, A. 2006. Überlegungen zu Sozialaspekten keramischer Gruppen. Beispiele aus dem Neolithikum Südwestdeutschlands. In S. Burmeister and N. Müller-Scheeßel (eds), *Soziale Gruppen — kulturelle Grenzen. Die Interpretation sozialer Grenzen in der Prähistorischen Archäologie. Tübinger Archäologische Taschenbücher 5*, 81–102. Münster.

Zimmermann, A. 1995. *Austauschsysteme von Silexartefakten in der Bandkeramik Mitteleuropas. Universitätsforschungen zur Prähistorischen Archäologie 26.* Bonn.

The transition from the sixth to the fifth millennium BC in the southern Wetterau

Pottery as expression of contacts, boundaries and innovation

Johanna Ritter-Burkert

Abstract

Based on the archaeologically rich region of the Wetterau (Hesse), this paper reflects on the delayed uptake of Middle Neolithic stylistic elements and stresses the need for further research to accurately define the place of pottery in identity signalling practices.

Zusammenfassung: Der Übergang vom 6. zum 5. Jahrtausend v. Chr. in der südlichen Wetterau – Keramik als Ausdruck von Kontakten, Grenzen und Innovationen.

Basierend auf Komplexen aus der archäologisch reichen Wetterau (Hessen) diskutiert dieser Beitrag mögliche Mechanismen für das verspätete Auftreten mittelneolithischer Stile und weist auf bestehende Forschungslücken hin, die dem Verständnis der Rolle von Keramik als identitätsstiftendes Element materieller Kultur nach wie vor entgegen stehen.

The Middle Neolithic transition in the southern Wetterau (Hesse)

In the southern Wetterau the Early Neolithic in the form of the latest Linear Pottery culture (LBK) persisted at length — especially in comparison with the surrounding regions. It was partially contemporaneous with the early Hinkelstein culture. It can be observed that LBK settlements which showed continuity from the Flomborn phase to the end of the LBK were abandoned at the end of the Early Neolithic. There are usually no finds of the Hinkelstein culture at those sites, but rather of the Großgartach and Rössen groups. Only in the Rössen culture do overlaps with former LBK settlements occasionally exist[1]. The contrast between the many LBK finds in the southern Wetterau and the very poor archaeological material of the Middle Neolithic groups is striking. This phenomenon has also

---

1 Lindig 2002, 203.

been reported from other regions[2]. The settlements of the early Middle Neolithic lie apart from the LBK sites and only on rare occasions do pits of the Hinkelstein group occur on late LBK sites. A coexistence or overlap in time and space can therefore be hypothesised for these two cultures. For the beginning of the Middle Neolithic, the lack of built structures is characteristic, but there are large pits with masses of discarded artefacts. The pottery recovered from them is of relatively poor quality. The entire southern Wetterau is marked by major discontinuity in the settlement development during the transition phase. It is possible that some LBK sites were still in use at a time when the early Middle Neolithic was already flourishing. This would provide an explanation for the absence of direct overlap of settlement features of the two cultures. Besides, a shift of settlements in the Middle Neolithic could have been necessary because of extensive agriculture which exhausted the soils during the LBK. The LBK showed great continuity concerning house building, agriculture, burial customs and material culture, although a growing variability in pottery traditions and the development of local pottery decoration styles can be observed. The transition to Hinkelstein after almost 500 years of continuous development appears like an abrupt change, if not a complete breach. It has to be discussed whether the transition from the Early to the Middle Neolithic was caused by an economic or social crisis and if the earthworks of the latest LBK and the increased reliance on transhumance in the Middle Neolithic can be seen as signs of such a crisis[3].

The site of Friedberg B3a km 19 (Wetterau, Hesse)

The site of Friedberg B3a km 19 can serve as a kind of small-scale model of the development during the late sixth and early fifth millennium in the southern Wetterau. The site covered 21 ha and was excavated by hessenARCHÄOLOGIE in the course of road construction works in 2007[4]. An LBK settlement with an adjacent cluster of graves was uncovered. The site had been in use from the early middle LBK until the end of this culture, but no material transitional to the Middle Neolithic periods could be identified. There were some pits of the Großgartach group, but only very little pottery was found among the masses of other material (Figure 1). No other Middle Neolithic groups were present at the site, but activity resumed in the Late and Final Neolithic (Table 1).

Moreover a ^{14}C-date from a late LBK structure (Figure 2; Tables 2–3) indicates a persistence of the LBK in Friedberg B3a km 19 at a time which already saw the emergence of Middle Neolithic groups in the surrounding areas. In the vicinity, the sites of Bad Nauheim, Friedberg and Friedberg-Bruchenbrücken are settlements with continuity between Hinkelstein and Großgartach and other Middle Neolithic cultures (Figure 3)[5]. Due to the site having been built over in modern times, mechanisms of contact and the cohesiveness of settlements can no longer be reconstructed.

---

2   See also Suhrbier 2012, 141.
3   Lindig 2002, 196–202.
4   Ritter 2014.
5   Eisenhauer 2002, 287–291.

Early – latest LBK	Hinkelstein	Großgartach	Following Middle Neolithic groups	Late and Final Neolithic	Post-Neolithic
x		x		x (Michelsberg culture, Corded Ware)	x

Table 1. Early, Middle and Late Neolithic groups present in Friedberg B3a km 19.

BC	Northern Wetterau	Friedberg B3a km 19
5000 4950	Hinkelstein II	latest LBK
4900	Großgartach 1 Großgartach 2	
4800	Großgartach 3	Großgartach

Table 2. Chronological model proposed by Eisenhauer and assumed position of Friedberg B3a km 19 (modified from Eisenhauer 2002, fig. 3.3).

Sample	^{14}C age (BP)	±	δ^{13}C	cal BC (1 σ)	cal BC (2 σ)
Friedberg B3a km 19 (2007/119,34) **1**	6076	19	-22.6	5006–4949	5045–4939
Friedberg B3a km 19 (2007/119,34) **2**	6088	18	-19.9	5034–4965	5051–4946

Table 3. ^{14}C-dates from bones of pit 16 in area 4 of the site Friedberg B3a km 19 (Data: Curt-Engelhorn-Zentrum Archäometrie, Mannheim).

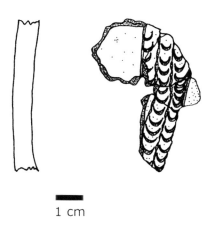

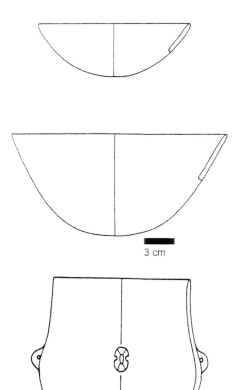

Figure 1. Middle Neolithic decorated pottery and undecorated vessel shapes from the site of Friedberg B3a km 19 (Drawing: J. Ritter).

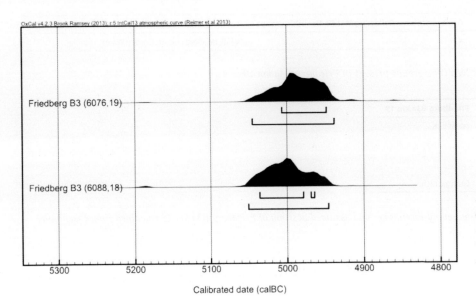

Figure 2. Probability distributions of ¹⁴C-dates from Friedberg B3a km 19 (graphic: Curt-Engelhorn-Zentrum Archäometrie Mannheim).

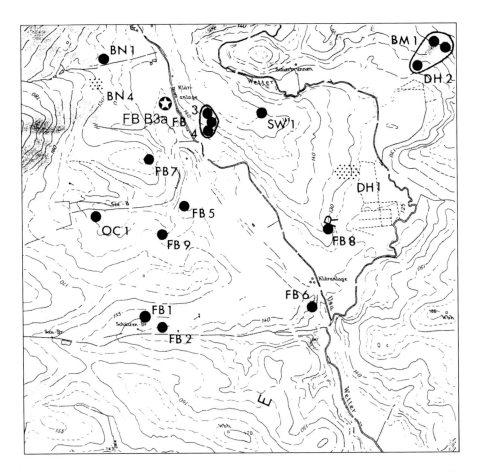

Figure 3. Map showing sites of the Middle Neolithic and Friedberg B3a km 19 (on topographic map 1:50.000). BB – Bruchenbrücken; BM – Reichelsheim-Beienheim; BN – Bad Nauheim; DH – Friedberg-Dorheim; FB – Friedberg; OC – Friedberg-Ockstadt; SW – Bad Nauheim-Schwalheim. Hinkelstein is present only in BB 2 and FB 2; the other sites have Großgartach and / or Rössen material (modified from Eisenhauer 2002, 288).

Significance of pottery for tracing cultural contacts, boundaries and innovation

The transition from the Early to the Middle Neolithic is often regarded as an innovation which manifests itself in the pottery tradition. According to the model of innovation created by Eisenhauer (2002) — adapted from Rogers and Shoemaker (1971) — an innovation spreads through communication between groups in the context of human social behaviour. This model divides communities into different categories of adoption — namely innovators, early adopters, early majority, late majority and latecomers. It implies a process of innovation comprising a stage of development, followed by diffusion after the community had decided on the innovation and its characteristics[6]. It can be assumed that a change of the social and / or economic system would have taken place in the course of innovation, but an evident transformation is only visible in the altering pottery.

The formation of the Middle Neolithic decoration style can be assumed to have been far away from the Wetterau as long as no transitional horizon emerges. In this context, one should think in terms of a process of diffusion and not of "migration"[7]. In accordance with this process, different segments of society show up as different categories of "adopters" and current research indicates that the population of the southern Wetterau has to be classified as conservative "latecomers" (Figure 4). Pottery reveals a cultural boundary in the region of the southern Wetterau, whose inhabitants persisted with LBK traditions for some time. The latest LBK is of considerable duration and finds of the early Hinkelstein culture are almost absent. The presence of a developed Großgartach then suggests a "leap" compared to the previous periods, indicating retarded adaption[8]. Diffusion of the Middle Neolithic decoration styles could be caused by contacts between groups, but the precise mechanisms remain obscure.

Cultural change — such as the transition from the Early to the Middle Neolithic — has long been attributed either to a necessity caused for instance by some form of crisis or to communication from an external centre into an established community[9]. These days, the roots of cultural change are rather traced back to the ongoing processes of identity formation within human populations, manifested in the emergence of new stylistic features in the pottery[10]. But was pottery eligible as a "medium of communication" (Eisenhauer 2002) of identity and innovation? Was a common decorative style an expression of cohesiveness and was the trans-regional Großgartach style a sign of cultural separation from LBK groups, aimed at communicating a wider range of Middle Neolithic innovations also comprising burial rites, settlement types, economy, trade contacts and resource supplies? Material culture is generally considered a manifestation of culture through material products. Especially pottery is regarded as informative concerning the ideas and behaviours of prehistoric societies[11]. Nevertheless, a potential discontinuity remains between the transfer of material

---

6 Eisenhauer 2002, 133–144.
7 Eisenhauer 2002, 131 ff.
8 For the northern Wetterau see Eisenhauer 2002, 117–118.
9 For instance the transition from Early to Middle Neolithic (namely Hinkelstein culture) in Meier-Arendt 1975, 154 ff.; 1999.
10 Link 2012, 127.
11 See the ethnographic approach and its results in Knopf 2002, 240–246.

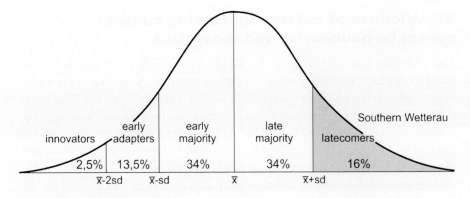

Figure 4. Categories of adaption and assumed position of the southern Wetterau (modified from Eisenhauer 2002, 140 fig. 5.4).

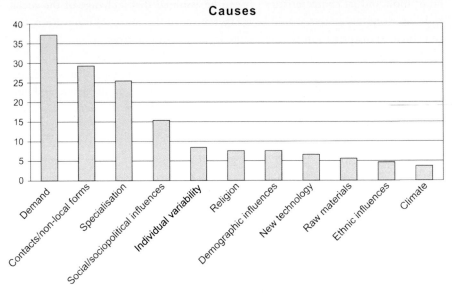

Figure 5. Causes of change in pottery traditions, based on ethnographic data (after Knopf 2002, 242).

culture and non-material aspects of past behaviours, which can partly be overcome by ethno-archaeological research[12].

An ethnographic approach can be used to draw parallels between recent and ancient cultures and investigate the causes of innovation and tradition in societies. The studies of T. Knopf (2002) concerning pottery production in recent communities mainly in Africa[13] have revealed some interesting aspects in this respect. The persistence of pottery traditions within a given community was generally accompanied by distinct behavioural norms, canons of value and a sense of identity resulting from an external dissociation, *i.e.* a boundary between neighbouring groups. Maintaining pottery traditions was moreover linked to socio-economic stability based on continuity in settlement, social and economic systems, which created stable groups with common traditions. Such groups initially remained unaffected in their pottery tradition. Pottery can be an instrument of distinction towards other groups. A change in pottery is marked by the appearance of new vessel shapes, the alteration of existing shapes and new decoration styles. Several reasons for pottery change have been documented ethnographically: demographic change, varying trade contacts, resource depletion,

---

12 Knopf 2002, 158 ff.
13 Knopf (2002, 178–246) analysed ethnographic data of pottery-producing communities in Kenya, Cameroon, Nigeria, Mali, the Maghreb, Mexico, Guatemala and the Philippines.

economic or social transitions (Figure 5). Changes in pottery production can take between several generations and up to a hundred years. Socio-economic changes are accompanied by a reorientation in economy and settlement style and an increased capacity for innovation. An abrupt shift in ceramic production could be explained by the displacement of one group by another. The means of change are often mutually dependent; for example, contact with foreign vessel shapes can cause a change in demand. Until the new pottery tradition becomes fully established, new ceramic types occur after some temporal delay or in conjunction with older types[14].

It cannot currently be decided whether the transition between the Early and Middle Neolithic corresponds to these ethnographic scenarios, but these certainly show probable options and broaden our outlook on the plurality of factors affecting innovations in pottery traditions.

References

Eisenhauer, U. 2002. *Untersuchungen zur Siedlungs- und Kulturgeschichte des Mittelneolithikums in der Wetterau. Universitätsforschungen zur prähistorischen Archäologie 89*. Bonn.

Knopf, T. 2002. *Kontinuität und Diskontinuität in der Archäologie. Quellenkritisch-vergleichende Studien. Tübinger Schriften zur Ur- und Frühgeschichtlichen Archäologie 6*. Münster.

Lindig, S. 2002. *Das Früh- und Mittelneolithikum im Neckarmündungsgebiet. Universitätsforschungen zur prähistorischen Archäologie 85*. Bonn.

Link, T. 2012. Stilwandel contra Siedlungskontinuität – zum Übergang von der Linien- zur Stichbandkeramik in Sachsen. In R. Gleser and V. Becker (eds), *Mitteleuropa im 5. Jahrtausend vor Christus. Beiträge zur Internationalen Konferenz in Münster 2010. Neolithikum und ältere Metallzeiten. Studien und Materialien 1*, 115–132. Münster.

Meier-Arendt, W. 1975. *Die Hinkelsteingruppe. Der Übergang vom Früh- zum Mittelneolithikum in Südwestdeutschland. Römisch-Germanische Forschungen 35*. Berlin.

Meier-Arendt, W. 1999. Eine Siedlungsstelle der Hinkelstein-Gruppe in Frankfurt a. M.-Sindlingen. Nochmals zur Frage des Überganges vom Früh- zum Mittelneolithikum in Südwestdeutschland. In F.-R. Herrmann (ed.), *Festschrift für G. Smolla. Materialien zur Vor- und Frühgeschichte von Hessen 8*, 497–503. Wiesbaden.

Ritter, J. 2014. Zu Chronologie und Herstellungstechniken der Bandkeramik anhand der Fundstelle Friedberg B3a km 19, Wetteraukreis. *Archäologisches Korrespondenzblatt 44*, 325–335.

Rogers, E.M. and Shoemaker, F.F. 1971. *Communication of innovations: a cross-cultural approach*. New York.

Suhrbier, S. 2012. Multikulti in Mainfranken – Der Beginn des Mittelneolithikums. In R. Gleser and V. Becker (eds), *Mitteleuropa im 5. Jahrtausend vor Christus. Beiträge zur Internationalen Konferenz in Münster 2010. Neolithikum und ältere Metallzeiten. Studien und Materialien 1*, 141–149. Münster.

---

14 Knopf 2002, 240–246.

On the relationship of the Michelsberg culture and Epirössen groups in southwest Germany in the light of absolute chronology, aspects of culture definition, and spatial data

Ute Seidel

Abstract

The relationship of Epirössen regional groups to the Michelsberg culture (MK) has so far been discussed mainly on the basis of typological arguments. Here, ^{14}C dates are presented which place the early eastern and Rhenanian Bischheim and the BBOB into the 46th/45th–44th centuries cal BC, the later Bischheim and Schwieberdingen into the 44th/43rd centuries cal BC and the Entzheim style with incised decoration as well as the Neckar-Schussenried into the 42nd/41st centuries cal BC. Riegel appears as a contemporary regional facies of Entzheim. On chronological grounds, Entzheim and flat-based Bischheim pottery in the Kraichgau can therefore not form the substrate of the MK. The mapping undertaken in this contribution follows its own methodological approach, whereby a find spot is not summarily assigned to a particular "culture". For each "culture group", a ceramic style was defined; where several styles were present on the same site, they were each given their own entry. In this way, the MK I horizon is revealed as exhibiting a relatively high degree of admixture of individual decorative styles, alongside regional preferences. In the MK II horizon, pottery styles are surprisingly homogenous at a regional scale and occur in clearly delimited areas. Finally, the function of decorated pottery is discussed.

Zusammenfassung: Das Verhältnis von Michelsberger Kultur und den epirössener Gruppen Südwestdeutschlands im Lichte absoluter Chronologie, Aspekten der Definition von Kulturen und räumlicher Verbreitungsmuster

Das Verhältnis von epirössener Regionalgruppen und Michelsberger Kultur (MK) wurde bislang vor allem mittels typologischer Argumente diskutiert. Hier werden ^{14}C-Daten vorgestellt, die ein frühes östliches und rheinisches Bischheim sowie BBOB ins 46./45.–44. Jh. cal BC stellen; jüngeres Bischheim und Schwieberdingen ins 44./43. Jh. cal BC; ritzverziertes Entzheim liegt wie Neckar-Schussenried im 42./41. Jh. cal BC; Riegel erscheint als zeitgleiche Regionalfazies von Entzheim. Entzheim und flachbodiges Bischheim im Kraichgau scheiden demnach aus chronologischen Gründen als Substrat für die MK aus. Die Kartierungen folgen einem eigenen methodischen Ansatz. Ein Fundpunkt wird nicht pauschal einer „Kultur" zugeschrieben. Für jede „Kulturgruppe" wurde ein Keramikstil definiert. Waren mehrere Stile an einem Fundort vertreten, wurde je ein eigener Datensatz angelegt. Für den Horizont MK I ergibt sich so ein Bild relativ hoher Durchmischung einzelner Zierstile, neben regionalen Schwerpunkten. Im Horizont MK II sind Keramikstile regional überraschend einheitlich und begrenzt vertreten. Die Funktion der verzierten Keramik wird diskutiert.

Introduction

This text is about the archaeological definition of "culture", following a culture definition mainly based on shapes and decoration styles of ceramics. It concerns the beginning of the central European Late Neolithic, focussing on Baden-Württemberg in south-west Germany and the adjacent area of Alsace in eastern France.

The transition from the Middle Neolithic to the Late Neolithic — "Mittelneolithikum" to "Jungneolithikum" in the south-west German terminology — is marked by the break-up of the relatively homogeneous cultural entity of the Rössen culture into regional groups, defined by ceramics. The cultural traditions in the area under investigation are represented on the one hand by small groups, whose character is mainly defined by the characteristics of their decorated ceramics, which is 6 % of all ceramics. The decoration motifs follow Rössen tradition, therefore the units were also called "Epirössen groups"[1]. The other important tradition is represented by the Michelsberg culture (MK), which — together with the Chasséen-Cortaillod-Lagozza entities — belongs to the sphere of undecorated and round-based ceramics[2], and which for about 700 years is an important factor in the central European Neolithic.

Concerning the relationship between the respective Epirössen groups and the early MK, hitherto the discussion was based mainly on typological arguments[3]; absolute dates were considered only in more recent works[4]. The Epirössen groups are estimated to have existed between 4400/4300–3900 cal BC. It is generally accepted that they were replaced by the MK successively — region by region[5]. The MK is estimated to have had a duration from 4400/4300–3600/3650 cal BC[6], but there is as yet no consensus either for the concrete chronology of its beginning or for the region of origin.

---

1 Gleser 1992; 1995.
2 Gallay 1977, 15.
3 E.g. Jeunesse *et al.* 2002/2003; Keefer 1988; Lüning 1969a; 1969b; 1971a; 1981; 1997, 58–72.
4 E.g. Gleser 2012; Nicolussi *et al.* 2013; Seidel 2004, 313–317; Strobel 2000, 434–443.
5 E.g. Gross-Klee 1998, 254; Keefer 1988, 91–99; Lüning 1997, 72; Seidel 2004, 25.
6 E.g. Höhn 2002, 178, 190–94; Lanting and van der Plicht 2000.

Concepts and questions

A look at some of the most influential and most cited works about the cultural units at the beginning of the Late Neolithic in the German south-west[7] reveals differences in the perception of "cultures". Two examples treating the beginning of the Late Neolithic ("horizon MK I") are chosen as illustration.

In 1981 Lüning mapped the cultural units "Schwieberdingen", "Aichbühl", "Rhine Bischheim", "Straßburg" and "Wauwil" together, as he assumed them to be contemporaneous (Figure 1). At the same time — in his work dedicated to the site of Schernau — he mapped a newly defined "Eastern Bischheim" or "Östliches Bischheim", which he separated from the original "Rhine Bischheim" described by Stroh[8].

In 1995 Gleser[9] (Figure 2) mapped "Schwieberdingen" and "Aichbühl" as contemporaneous; "Rhine Bischheim" was assumed to be earlier and was therefore excluded[10]; following Schmitt (1974) he re-named the "Straßburg" unit as "Entzheim", and — in dividing it into an "older" and a "younger Entzheim" — he mapped the "older Entzheim" with Schwieberdingen and Aichbühl. Additionally — following Jeunesse[11] — he dissolved the former "Wauwil group" into "Bruebach-Oberbergen" (BBOB) and "Borscht" and — in accordance with his own chronological division — Gleser mapped a "Schernau-Goldberg" as contemporaneous with MK I, and separated "Eastern Bischheim" as earlier than MK I.

Without wanting to go deeper into the history of research, the point to stress here is that the two perceptions show:

- a concept of rather closed cultural areas;
- differences in drawing borders between those cultural areas or cultural entities;
- differences in labelling the cultural entities; and
- different assumptions about the chronological position of the entities or "cultures"

To begin with the last point, until now the relationship between the Epirössen groups and the partly contemporaneous MK has been discussed mainly in the light of stylistic arguments. Within the framework of a project funded by the German Research Foundation (DFG) and the Landesamt für Denkmalpflege Baden-Württemberg (LAD) and focusing on the Late Neolithic in the Kraichgau region (DFG project "Pl 95-51/Wo 1493"), it was attempted to improve the available basis of absolute dates.

---

7   E.g. Gleser 1995; Jeunesse et al. 2002/2003; Lüning 1971a; 1981.
8   Stroh 1938.
9   Gleser 1995, 239 Karte 3.
10 Gleser 1995, 219 Karte 2 (Bischheim and Merdingen).
11 Jeunesse 1990.

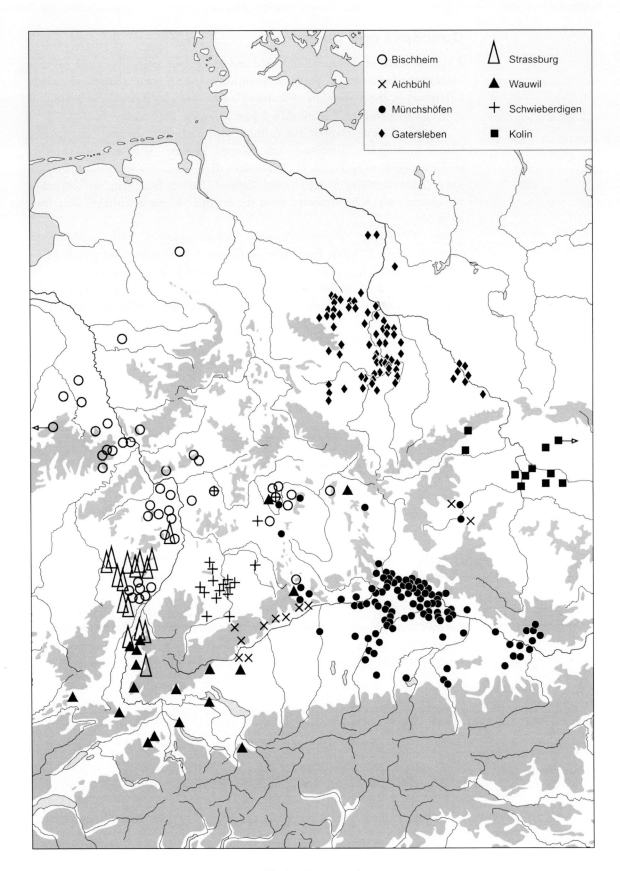

Figure 1. Earliest Late Neolithic groups, as mapped by Lüning 1981, plate 1.

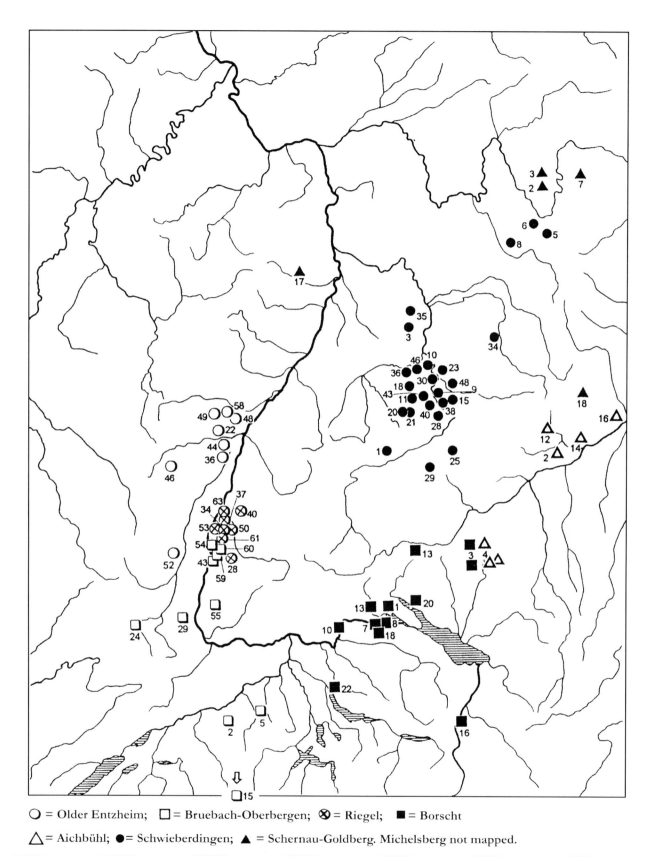

○ = Older Entzheim; □ = Bruebach-Oberbergen; ⊗ = Riegel; ■ = Borscht
△ = Aichbühl; ● = Schwieberdingen; ▲ = Schernau-Goldberg. Michelsberg not mapped.

Figure 2. Earliest Late Neolithic groups, as mapped by Gleser 1995, 239 Karte 3.

As part of the project, in a first step an inventory of all MK and Epirössen sites in Baden-Württemberg was compiled[12] and fed into an Access database (n = 748)[13]. Financed by the project, 34 dates for open, unenclosed sites could be obtained, as well as about 40 dates for the MK enclosure sites in Baden-Württemberg[14]. The multiplots presented here show 133 dates, including 23 of the new dates from the Kraichgau project, as well as already published dates for Epirössen and MK (Figures 3–9).

The validity of the dates is limited by the fact that the sample material is mostly single bones from pits[15]. There is no guarantee that a sample actually dates the context in which it was found; it is rather the totality of dates which gives a certain indication for the chronological position of a cultural unit. Moreover, many of the dates coincide with successive plateaus in the calibration curve between the 43rd and the 39th centuries cal BC; the distributions of the dates are therefore extended and sometimes bimodal, and the resulting chronology is thus less precise than it would have been had the dates fallen elsewhere on the radiocarbon calibration curve.

Nevertheless the dates contribute to a more precise idea of the beginning of the MK in Baden-Württemberg and help to clarify the origin of the MK. For the first time, absolute dates are available for the entities Merdingen, BBOB, Entzheim, "facies Riegel" and younger Rhine Bischheim on the German side. In consequence, for reasons of chronology it is not likely that the Kraichgau Bischheim and the Entzheim of the Upper Rhine were substrates for the early MK.

The multiplots

Großvillars — Kraichgau Bischheim

The first eight dates[16] (Figure 3) relate to the Bischheim of the Kraichgau, which is represented by 144 ceramic units from Oberderdingen-Großvillars near Pforzheim[17]. The ceramics represent an own local facies of Bischheim. All pots — including the decorated pots — are flat-based. This stands in contrast to the

---

12 Heumüller *et al.* 2012; Seidel *et al.* 2010; Seidel own unpublished data. This is based on the helpful catalogues of Friederich 2011; Gleser 1995; Jeunesse *et al.* 2002/2003; Keefer 1988; Lüning 1971a; Spatz 1996; as well as the archive of the Landesamt für Denkmalpflege im Regierungspräsidium Stuttgart (LAD) — Ortsakten and ADABweb — and unpublished finds kindly communicated by colleagues.

13 The structure of the Access database was kindly provided by R. Ebersbach, formerly IPNA Basel, now LAD; the database was maintained by T. Baum, IPNA Basel.

14 Unenclosed sites: 18 dates for Baden-Württemberg; one date for Oberhochstadt; one for Creglingen. Enclosures: two dates for Bruchsal-Heidelsheim "Altenberg" (pers. comm. M. Heumüller). Eleven dates from unenclosed sites had to be rejected as not being valid: nine incongruent dates from Oberderdingen-Großvillars (KIA42012–KIA42016; KIA42018–KIA42020) on bone samples kindly provided by E. Stephan, LAD; one date from Mayen Bischheim pit 3: KIA42011, 4218±30 BP, 1σ 2892–2866 cal BC, bone sample kindly provided by B.C. Oesterwind, Museum Mayen; a second date from Hochstadt-Oberhochstadt pit 24, due to insufficient collagen preservation (E. Stephan pers. comm.): MAMS17564: 5721±35 BP, 1σ 4606–4501 cal BC; $\delta^{13}C$: –47.7; collagen: 0.1 %, bone sample kindly provided by A. Zeeb-Lanz, LVR. Not shown and not discussed are the dates for deposits of human skeletal remains, as these are not the focus of discussion here and the skeletons were not associated with typologically datable material. This includes four published (Seidel 2004, 312) and three new dates (MAMS 17559; MAMS 17561; MAMS 17562) from Leonberg-Höfingen and a date for Eichstetten "Buckacker" pit 70/2 (Dieckmann 1991, Taf. 147A).

15 Where other material was dated, this will be mentioned in the text.

16 All multiplots in this chapter were created with OxCal v3.9 (Bronk-Ramsey 2003).

17 Seidel 2011b; Seidel *et al.* 2010.

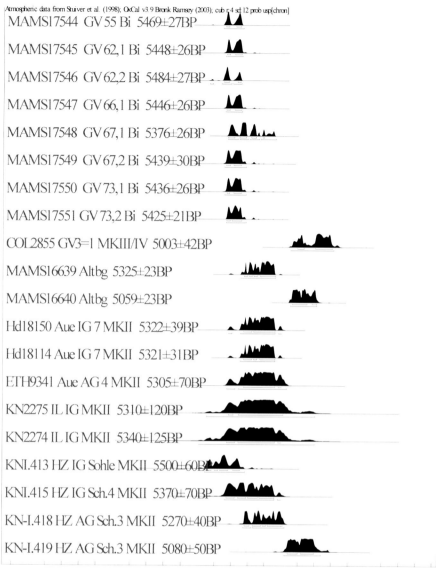

Figure 3. Multiplot for Kraichgau Bischheim and earliest MK in Baden-Württemberg.

concept of a round-based Rhine Bischheim, as defined by Stroh[18]. Among the beakers, bowls, bottles, storage bottles and pots of Großvillars only beakers are decorated. Motifs are almost exclusively single or double lines, sometimes combined with small knobs. They fit into the Rhine Bischheim "Kombinationsgruppe II" as defined by Gleser[19], whereas the decoration with triangles[20] is almost absent.

Decorated pots with flat base are defining for the "Eastern Bischheim", but here the multi-lined "Goldbergband" motif is present[21]. Decorated pots with flat base can also be found in the Schwieberdingen group, but here decoration is restricted to "metopic motifs" ("Metopen") (Figure 10.1) or placed in continuous

---

18 Stroh 1938; since used e.g. by Gleser 1995, 221; Jeunesse et al. 2002/2003.
19 Gleser 1995, 222 Taf. 19–20.
20 Gleser 1995, 222 Taf. 17–18.
21 Zeeb 1998, 107.

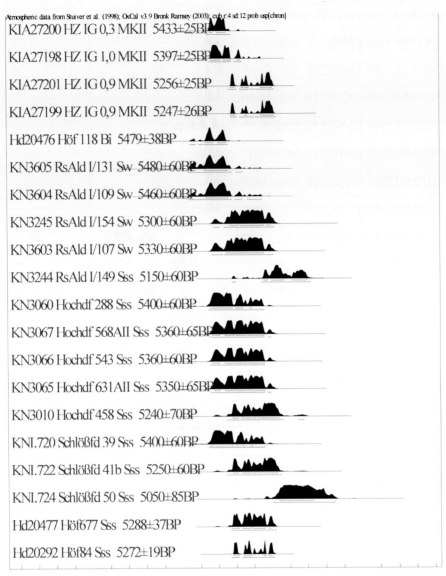

Figure 4. Multiplot for earliest MK, Bischheim, Schwieberdingen and Neckar-Schussenried in the Neckar region.

encircling decoration zones (Figure 11.1)[22]. The ceramics of Großvillars therefore represent an own local Bischheim group with flat-based beakers decorated with simple line motifs. The radiometric dates presented here were measured at the CEZ in Mannheim[23]. They lie consistently in the 54th century BP, *i.e.* 44th–43rd century cal BC (Figure 3: MAMS17544–17551).

---

22 Lüning 1969b; Seidel 2004, 158 Abb. 79.
23 These eight dates are repeated measurements. Samples were animal bones from five Bischheim pits at Großvillars. In 2010/2011 nine dates were obtained at the Leibniz Labor in Kiel (Seidel 2011b, 154–155 Tab. 2). In no case did any two dates from the same pit show comparable results, the ranges did not even overlap. Therefore, eight dates taken on the same bones were repeated at the CEZ in Mannheim. E. Stephan, LAD, kindly selected the bone samples and patiently identified the same bones for a repetition of the measurements.

Bischheim and Schwieberdingen in the Neckar region

Also the 44th–43th century cal BC is covered by absolute dates for Bischheim and Schwieberdingen now known for the Neckar region (Figure 4: Hd20476–KN3604). One date is available from Leonberg-Höfingen pit 118 for a Bischheim with simple line motif[24], four dates from Remseck-Aldingen "Halden I" for an early Schwieberdingen with simple motifs[25]. Bischheim and early Schwieberdingen in the Neckar region seem therefore to be partly contemporaneous, Bischheim being only present for a very short time. This fits with the fact of very few and heterogeneous Bischheim finds in the Neckar region, as pointed out by Gleser and Spatz[26].

Schussenried in the Neckar region

In the Neckar region the Schwieberdingen dates are followed by dates for Schussenried. The known absolute dates range between the 43rd–40th centuries cal BC (Figure 4: KN3245–Hd20292) and were obtained for Eberdingen-Hochdorf, Ludwigsburg "Schlößlesfeld" and Leonberg-Höfingen[27]. The sites represent the "Neckar-Schussenried" or "early Schussenried", which — in contrast to the "late Schussenried" of Upper Swabia — has no rectangular connection between the linear decorations of the neck and the front of the body.

Some dates cover the time after 4000 cal BC (KN3244 from Remseck-Aldingen; KNI.724 from Ludwigsburg "Schlößlesfeld"; Hd-20274 from Leonberg-Höfingen). They probably relate to a later Schussenried or even MK occupation[28]. From Remseck "Halden I" no characteristic finds are available, but adjacent to the Schwieberdingen area of "Halden I" a Schussenried area named "Halden II" was excavated[29]. A later MK occupation is attested by ceramics from "Schlößlesfeld", and by ceramics and absolute dates from Leonberg-Höfingen (Figure 5: Hd20289 and Hd20448), as well as for the Bischheim area of Großvillars (Figure 3: COL2855).

Early MK in Baden-Württemberg

For MK I in Germany no absolute dating is available as yet. The main reason is that there are no "closed assemblages" of MK I which could serve as a reliable base for a date[30]. For the MK in Baden-Württemberg radiometric dates were obtained for enclosure sites and pits on open sites. Only the earliest dates are discussed here. They come from ditch fills of enclosures.

In the Kraichgau region the earliest dates are from the enclosures Bruchsal "Aue" (Figure 3: Hd18150; Hd18114; ETH-9341)[31] and Bruchsal-Heidelsheim

---

24 Seidel 2004, 312.
25 E.g. Keefer and Joachim 1988, 27 Taf. 40.4: Remseck-Aldingen "Halden I".
26 Gleser 1992; 1995, 218–225; Spatz 1996, 405–408.
27 Keefer 1988; Keefer and Joachim 1988; Lüning and Zürn 1977; Seidel 2004.
28 Joachim 1989.
29 Keefer and Krause 1992.
30 The pit of Böhl-Iggelheim was already classified as "not a closed assemblage" by Willms (1982). It remains without material for radiometric dating. A. Zeeb-Lanz, LVR, kindly verified this in the depot of the Historisches Museum der Pfalz.
31 "Aue" inner ditch, floor level of complex 7: Hd-numbers; "Aue" outer ditch, floor level of complex 4: ETH-number (Regner-Kamlah and Seidel in press; Steppan 2003, 40).

"Altenberg" (Figure 3: MAMS166639; MAMS166640)[32]. The dates cover the 42nd/40th centuries cal BC. The samples are single bones from the ditches, in all cases from MK II contexts. A horse bone which was dated to 5465±60 BP, *i.e.* at 2σ 4451–4075 cal BC, was recovered from an MK IV context[33]. It was not included in the discussion here because of its uncertain context[34], but it currently represents the oldest absolute date for MK in the Kraichgau.

For the Neckar region dates were obtained for the enclosures of Ilsfeld "Ebene" and Neckarsulm-Obereisesheim "Hetzenberg" (Figures 3–4: KN2275–KIA 27199)[35]. They cover the 44th/43rd centuries cal BC, but the sample material is wood and one can suppose an old wood effect making the results 100–150 years older than expected[36]. This is supported by the fact that all samples were taken from contexts containing MK II ceramics[37]. In the Neckar region MK II ceramics are typo-chronologically fixed by associations with Neckar-Schussenried, the latter being dated to the 42nd/40th centuries cal BC[38].

On the basis of the currently known dates no chronological overlap of the absolute dates for the MK and the Epirössen groups can be demonstrated for Baden-Württemberg. On the other hand, the association of MK I shapes with Bischheim and Schwieberdingen ceramics is documented[39]. An absolute date not later than in the 44th–43rd centuries should therefore be expected for MK I. In this respect the first phase of digging the inner ditch of Ilsfeld gains some importance for the earliest MK in the Neckar region, as the absolute dates at Ilsfeld correspond to a later phase of the ditches during MK II. The first phase should be older than the known absolute dates. A genesis of the MK in the Neckar region[40] seems unlikely given the very limited range of segmented tulip-shaped forms in the area, compared to the wide range of variations in regions like the Paris Basin[41].

For the later MK, dates from pits seem relatively more reliable than dates from ditches. A bone from pit NN20 with MK II ceramics at Leonberg-Höfingen is dated around 4000 cal BC (Figure 5: Hd20289); pit 396 with MK III/IV ceramics falls into the 39th/38th centuries cal BC (Figure 5: Hd20448)[42]. An MK III deposition of a male adult from Großvillars contained an antler artefact which was dated to 5003±42 BP, 3945–3696 cal BC (Figure 3: COL2855)[43].

These dates for Höfingen and Großvillars fit with dendro-dates for layers with MK III and MK IV ceramics from lake-edge sites, recently compiled by Matuschik[44]. He showed that "Ösenkranzflaschen mit tief sitzenden Ösen" (bottles with low lugs), which characterise MK III, come from contexts for

---

32 Pers. comm. M. Heumüller, Kraichgau project.
33 ETH-11029: Steppan 2006.
34 Pers. comm. B. Regner-Kamlah, Kraichgau project.
35 Breunig 1987, 179; Lüning and Zürn 1977, 79; Seidel 2008, 39.
36 Stöckli 2009, 137.
37 Seidel 2008, 37–40, 104–105.
38 Keefer 1988; Lüning 1997; Lüning and Zürn 1977; Seidel 2004.
39 For compilations of structures with Bischheim and Schwieberdingen as well as earliest MK ceramics, see Gleser 1998; Lüning 1968, 135ff.; 1969b, 16ff. Taf. 5.1–3 compared to Taf. 6.5–9 (Schwieberdingen "Katharinenlinde" house structure); Willms 1982, 45–46; Zeeb 1998, 139 Taf. 19 B 13.
40 Gleser 2012, 70–71.
41 E.g. Dubouloz 1991. The genesis of the MK in the Neckar valley is discussed by Gleser 2012, 70–71.
42 Seidel 2004, 312.
43 Within the framework of a project on the Mesolithic at the University of Köln, K. Banghard, Museum Oerlinghausen, and B. Gehlen, Universität zu Köln, kindly sent the result of sample Id. Od_Gv_001. F. Healy, Cardiff University, kindly sampled the artefact in autumn 2014.
44 Matuschik 2011, 271–274.

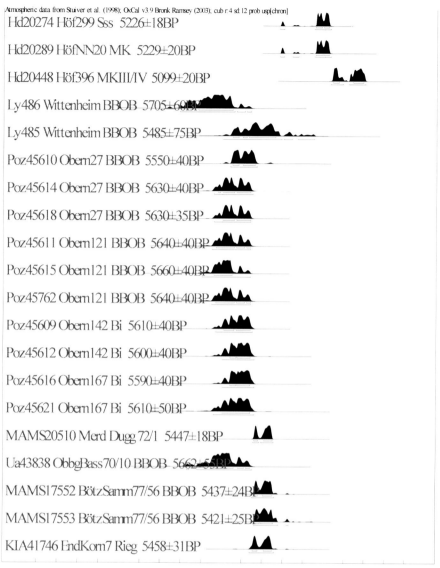

Figure 5. Multiplot for Schussenried, MK II and MK III/IV in the Neckar region, as well as BBOB, Merdingen, Rhine Bischheim and Entzheim of the Upper Rhine.

which tree-ring dates between 3919 and 3834 BC are available; for contexts with "Ösenleistenflaschen" (bottles with pan-pipe lugs), diagnostic for MK IV, tree-ring dates between 3869 and 3817 BC can be cited. In consequence, only a time span of about a century is left for MK III, instead of the three centuries previously assumed[45]. Moreover, the use of both bottle types overlapped in time, which stresses the problem of distinguishing MK III and MK IV typologically, for instance by the presence of "Ösenleistenflaschen"[46]. The ceramic assemblages of the two stages were therefore sometimes named MK III/IV[47].

---

45 E.g. Höhn 2002, 193; Seidel 2012.
46 Seidel 2012, 291.
47 E.g. Seidel 2008, 331, 388, Anhang 2; this is equivalent to Höhn's (2002) "Intervall 3c". Knoche 2013 even proposed to abolish stage MK III completely. This seems unnecessary, as there are assemblages which can be clearly identified.

Merdingen/BBOB (former Wauwil) — Upper Rhine

The group "Bruebach-Oberbergen" (BBOB) was defined for Upper Alsace and adjacent areas by Jeunesse in 1990, who separated it from the former group "Wauwil"; he assumed it to be contemporaneous with Entzheim in Lower Alsace. In 1995, Gleser separated a local "Merdingen" group from BBOB. This was identified for the southern Upper Rhine, Upper Danube and parts of the Swiss Mittelland and comprises ceramics formerly attributed to Bischheim, Wauwil and Egolzwil. In this concept, Merdingen stands chronologically between Rössen II and BBOB[48]. Jeunesse rejected this approach, claiming at the same time some Merdingen ceramics for a — regionally widespread — "initial" BBOB[49].

For BBOB, two absolute dates were published for Wittenheim, spanning the 47th–42nd centuries cal BC[50]. For Obernai, ten dates for BBOB and Bischheim were systematically obtained from charred plant remains, wood and bone[51]. They cover the 45th–43rd centuries cal BC (Figure 5). As part of the Kraichgau project, cereals from the eponymous site of Oberbergen (pit 78/10) were dated, giving a result in the 46th–44th centuries cal BC (Figure 5: Ua43838).

Animal bones from the BBOB pit 77/56 at Bötzingen "Sammelfürst" were also dated; they cover the 44th/43rd centuries cal BC (Figure 5: MAMS17552, MAMS17553). This fits with the date on a single bone from pit 72/1 at the eponymous site of Merdingen "Duggenbühl" (MAMS20510) (Figure 5: MAMS20510)[52]. The few dates suggest that Merdingen is not necessarily an earlier typological stage of BBOB, but a — probably spatially widespread — variation of BBOB.

Entzheim and the "Fazies Riegel" — Upper Rhine/ South Baden and Upper Alsace

For the Entzheim group of Lower Alsace, various propositions regarding its chronological evolution and position were made, all based on typological arguments and each achieving a different result[53]. Entzheim was recently claimed by Jeunesse and colleagues to be a substrate for the origin of the MK[54]. In 1995, Gleser separated out a "facies Riegel" based on stylistic features. He interpreted it as a local variation of Entzheim, older than the classical Entzheim[55].

---

48 Gleser 1995, 226 ff., 286 ff., Taf. 23.1 (Cravanche), Taf. 23.8 (Merdingen), Taf. 23.13–15 (Oberbergen "Baßgeige").
49 Jeunesse 1990a, 182 ff.; 1990b, 195–196; 1990c, 96 ff.; Jeunesse et al. 1998, 119–121, fig. 8.
50 Lefranc and Jeunesse 1998; Lefranc et al. 1998.
51 Croutsch et al. 2014a.
52 B. Dieckmann, U. Maier und R. Vogt, LAD, kindly provided botanic samples for Oberbergen "Bassgeige" 78/10 (Dieckmann 1991, Taf. 184–187,Taf. 51). E. Stephan, LAD, kindly provided animal bones from Bötzingen "Sammelfürst" 77/56 (Dieckmann 1991, Taf. 51, Taf. 184–187) and from Merdingen "Duggenbühl" 72/1 (Dieckmann 1991, Taf. 219, 220A).
53 Dubouloz 1991; Gleser 1995; Jeunesse 1985. Two radiometric dates measured in the 1980s for Entzheim "Desch" (F.55 Gif-2386: 3850±110 BP) and Vendenheim (Ly 866: 4870±110 BP) seemed unreliable (Jeunesse 1985, 35). As Jeunesse et al. (2002/2003, 200) state: "En absence de datations fiables, la question de la chronologie absolue est délicate" ("In the absence of absolute dates, the question of chronology remains tricky").
54 Jeunesse et al. 2002/2003, 181ff., 207ff.
55 Gleser 1995, 234.

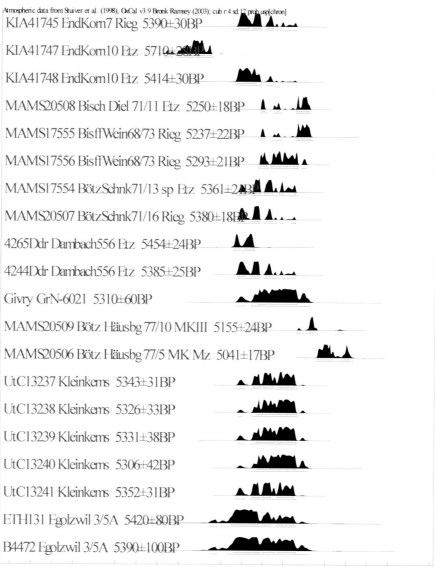

Figure 6. Multiplot for Entzheim, Riegel, MK, Munzingen, "Cortaillod" and Egolzwil of the Upper Rhine and Wauwiler Moos.

For Endingen "Kornenberg" pit 7 and pit 10, two single bones per pit were dated in the Leibniz Labor in Kiel[56]. The ceramics show features of the facies Riegel, BBOB and the Merdingen group. Both results for pit 7 and one result for pit 10 date to the 42nd/41st centuries cal BC, the other date for pit 10 falls into the 44th/43rd centuries cal BC[57] (Figures 5–6: KIA41746–KIA41748).

As the Kiel dates for "Kornenberg" were suspected to be inconsistent, more samples for Entzheim and Riegel were dated at the CEZ Mannheim as part of the Kraichgau project. Two dates for the Riegel pit 68/73 at Bischoffingen

---

56 Seidel 2011a. J. Klug-Treppe, LAD, kindly provided the material, while A. Bräuning, LAD, facilitated the dating.
57 Seidel 2011a; 2015.

"Weingarten"[58] cover the 43rd–40th centuries cal BC (Figure 6: MAMS17555, MAMS17556); dates for Bötzingen "Schneckenbühl" pits 71/16 and 71/13 fall into the 44th–41st centuries cal BC (Figure 6: MAMS20507, MAMS17554); both pits contained ceramics of the types Entzheim and Riegel[59]. Pit 73/11 at Bischoffingen "Dielen"[60] gave a result in the 42nd–40th centuries cal BC and contained typologically late Entzheim and MK sherds.

At Dambach-la-Ville in Alsace the spectacular find of two wells filled with Entzheim ceramics was made. Well 556 was dated dendrochronologically and radiometrically, using the same piece of wood (Figure 6). The sampled wood showed 150 tree rings, radiometric dates were made on rings 22 and 23[61]. The date 5454±24 BP corresponds to a dendro-date of 4265 BC, the radiometric date 5385±25 BP corresponds to a dendro-date of 4244 BC. An old wood effect for the calibrated dates in the 44th/43rd centuries cal BC is therefore proven, the building of the well is fixed to the 43rd century BC. The pottery shows almost exclusively incised decoration. As it was thrown into the wells after their abandonment, the incised pottery should date later than the construction, *i.e.* later than the 43rd century BC[62].

Radiometric dates for the Entzheim unit thus cover the 44th–40th centuries cal BC (Figures 5–6: MAMS20511–Dambach556). The Entzheim style with incised decoration probably dates to the 42nd century cal BC. This is supported by a date for Givry "Bosse de l'Tombe" in the 42nd century cal BC (Figure 6: GrN6021), as the ceramics from Givry show Entzheim influences[63]. Incised Entzheim pottery thus appears to be contemporaneous with Neckar-Schussenried. Entzheim pottery with stab-and-drag decoration ("Furchenstich") should — for stylistic reasons — be paralleled with Schwieberdingen and Bischheim, as Lüning did in 1971. Thus, Entzheim is not convincing as an older substrate for the origin of the MK. An MK substrate, being earlier than MK I, should be placed in the 46th–44th centuries cal BC, in a region which should show a local tradition of tulip shapes, which is neither the case for Baden-Württemberg nor for Alsace. Not in doubt is the fact that Entzheim assemblages contain single MK tulip beakers, for instance at the eponymous site of Entzheim pit 1 and pit 54 or at Jechtingen "Sandbrunnen"[64]. Similarly, segmented MK tulip beakers appear in assemblages of the Schwieberdingen group, together with unsegmented Schwieberdingen ceramics[65].

According to the absolute dates, the "facies Riegel" is not an older phase of Entzheim, but rather a local facies contemporaneous with Entzheim and Neckar-

---

58 See Dieckmann 1991, Taf. 63, Taf. 24–27A. E. Stephan, LAD, kindly provided the animal bones from Bischoffingen "Weingarten" pit 68/73.
59 See Dieckmann 1991, Taf. 26, 27A. E. Stephan, LAD, kindly provided the animal bones from Bötzingen "Schneckenbühl" pits 71/13 and 71/16.
60 Dieckmann 1991, Taf. 58.
61 Croutsch *et al.* 2013; 2014b. W. Tegel, Freiburg, kindly shared the then unpublished dates from Dambach and the manuscript of the lecture in 2013.
62 C. Croutsch, INRAP Sélestat, kindly facilitated an examination of the finds of Dambach and gave helpful comments in 2014.
63 Joris and Moisin 1972, 244: GrN-6021 5310±60 BP ; at 1σ: 4230–4040 cal BC.
64 Schmitt 1974, pl. I,1; XXVIII,2; Dieckmann 1991, Taf. 103.2. For pit 71/17 at Jechtingen "Sandbrunnen" no datable material is available, as verified by E. Stephan, LAD. See also Dubouloz 1998, 12.
65 Compare Lüning 1968, Beilage 5; for the beakers: Lüning 1969a, 238–239, Abb. 3A+1; 1969b, Taf. 6.5., 6.7., 6.9 (beaker), Taf. 6.6 (clay disc). The same approach can be found in Dubouloz 1998, fig. 2; Gleser 1998, Abb. 1.

Schussenried (compare Figure 4: KN3245–Hd20292). On the other hand, the overlap of dates for BBOB and Entzheim supports the reflections by Jeunesse and colleagues that BBOB could have begun over a larger area and earlier than Entzheim, then continued for a while parallel to Entzheim in Upper Alsace, while Entzheim replaced BBOB in lower Alsace[66].

The dates in the 43rd/42nd centuries cal BC for the BBOB site of Bötzingen "Sammelfürst" fit with dates for Egolzwil 3, the reference site for the former group "Wauwil" (Figure 6)[67]. The "Egolzwil" group, which includes sites like Schötz I, Egolzwil 3, Zürich "Kleiner Hafner" and Cham-Eslen, is thought to be an entity appearing without predecessor between the east and west of Switzerland[68]. A certain "spatial displacement" or moving of a cultural entity seems probable.

As the calibrated dates for Egolzwil 3 also cover the 41st/40th centuries cal BC they overlap the date ranges for the Epirössen site of Herblingen "Grüthalde" on the Swiss Rhine (Figure 7: ETH38943)[69]. The dating for "Grüthalde" and Büttenhard "Zelg"[70], both attributed to a "Kugelbecher" group (*i.e.* with globular decorated beakers), is chronologically removed from the dates for the "Kugelbecher" of the Upper Rhine in general.

Further west, four dates on charcoal from the jasper mine at Kleinkems cover the 42nd–40th centuries cal BC (Figure 6). They are associated with finds of an undecorated Cortaillod facies[71]. For the wood samples of Kleinkems an old wood effect should be taken into account. The jasper mine probably dates to the years after 4000 BC.

MK III / Munzingen Upper Rhine

For the transition MK to Munzingen along the Upper Rhine, single bones from pit 77/10 and pit 77/5 at Bötzingen "Häuslinsberg" were dated. Pit 77/10 was extraordinarily rich in ceramics, including various pots with S-profile and rounded as well as flat base[72], a low tulip beaker (type 3,1), a high bag-shaped beaker ("Beutelbecher" type 13) and a conical bowl with flat base, all defining features of MK III[73], as well as a segmented bowl with lugs[74], the segmented profile resembling NMB shapes. The dating result for pit 77/10 was 5155±24 BP or 3981–3956 cal BC, which is consistent with the estimated 40th century BC date for MK III[75].

Pit 77/5 at "Häuslinsberg"[76] contained a biconical pot with thick, rough slip and flat base, and a round-based S-shaped bowl[77]. Pit 77/5 gave a date of

---

66 Jeunesse *et al.* 1998, 132.
67 Strobel 2000, 440, 479.
68 Strobel 2000, 400; Suter *et al.* 1987. Stöckli (2009) provides references and more absolute dates which are not included here.
69 Altdorfer and Affolter 2011, 30.
70 Altdorfer and Affolter 2011, 30.
71 Engel and Siegmund 2005.
72 Dieckmann 1991, Taf. 38–45.
73 Dieckmann 1991, Taf. 38.1, 38.3–4; Lüning 1968, 23.26, 23.53.
74 Dieckmann 1991, Taf. 45.11.
75 Matuschik 2011, 271–274.
76 Dieckmann 1991, Taf. 33–35A.
77 Dieckmann 1991, Taf. 33.1., 33.5. Comparisons for the S-shaped, round-based container are difficult to find, as it is open and S-shaped like Schwieberdingen bowls, but does not have a flat base; it has no segmented profile like MK vessels and no closed mouth like Cortaillod or NMB shapes. The closest parallel comes from Gonsans (Doubs) (Gallay 1977, pl. 17,232.1).

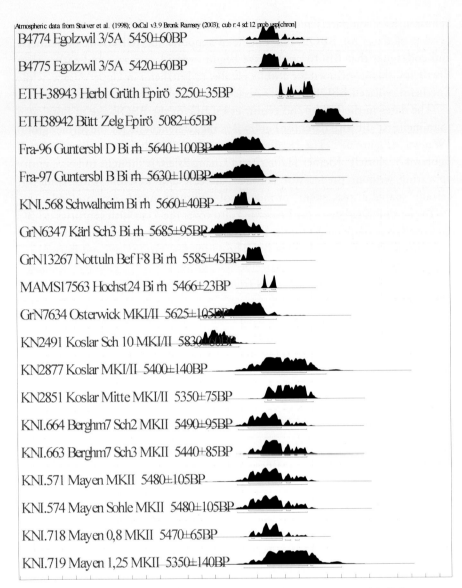

Figure 7. Multiplot for Swiss Epirössen, as well as Rhine Bischheim and earliest MK of the Middle Rhine.

5041±17 BP, 3931–3794 cal BC, which fits with the range of dendro-dates for MK III (3919–3834 BC) and MK IV shapes (3869–3817 BC) in Alpine foreland sites[78]. The two pits of "Häuslinsberg" demonstrate the close connection of the Upper Rhine valley with areas in the south-west, such as the Wauwiler Moos and Jura, and the adaption of flat-based pots as early as during MK III/IV[79].

---

78 Matuschik 2011, 271–274.
79 Seidel 2008, 322–323.

Rhine Bischheim

The dates for Kärlich and Schwalheim for Rhine Bischheim cover the 48th–45th centuries cal BC[80], for Guntersblum the 46th–44th centuries cal BC (Figure 7)[81]. Gleser discusses these high results in terms of an old wood effect as well as the use of different calibration programs[82]. In the Kraichgau project, two dates were obtained for Hochstadt-Oberhochstadt Fdst. 24[83]. The result of 4355–4263 cal BC (Figure 7: MAMS17563) confirms the existence of a late Rhine Bischheim with triangle motifs[84], already postulated by Zeeb[85]. This date corresponds to dates for Garzweiler in North Rhine-Westphalia of 4455±85 cal BC, 4295±45 cal BC and 4290±45 cal BC[86]. The date of Oberhochstadt in the 44th/43rd centuries cal BC, for a ceramic assemblage with triangle motifs, could be an argument against the chronological interpretation of triangle motifs as being older and single line motifs as being younger[87].

Early MK in the Rhine region

Currently, the earliest absolute dates for the MK in Germany are still the dates for the enclosure sites of Osterwick and Koslar 10 in North Rhine-Westphalia, Bergheim in Hessen and Mayen in the Rhineland Palatinate (Figure 7: GrN-7634–KNI.719)[88]. The dates mainly cover the second half of the fifth millennium. Osterwick and Koslar 10 have pottery classified as MK I/II and have provided the oldest dates (GrN-7634; KN-2491), beginning in the first half of the fifth millennium at the latest, *i.e.* the 48th–44th centuries cal BC[89]. Comparable early dates are neither known for south-west Germany nor for the Aisne valley, for example for Bazoches sur Vesle (MK) or Osly-Courtil (Menneville-Chasséen)[90]. From Belgium, early dates are known from Spiere "de Hel" (60th–40th centuries cal BC)[91], Ittre "Mont-à-

---

80 As Rössen ceramics are known from Schwalheim, the dating of Kärlich gains more importance.
81 Both with high standard deviations of ±100 BP: Fra-96 5640±100 BP, 1σ 4590–4350 cal BC; Fra-97 5630±100 BP, 1σ 4540–4360 cal BC (Eisenhauer 2002, 96 Abb. 3,2; Eisenhauer and Daszkiewicz 2003, 173).
82 Gleser 2012, 38–41, 70, 197.
83 Bone samples from Oberhochstadt Fdst. 24 were kindly provided by A. Zeeb, LVA Speyer. The second measurement had to be eliminated due to the lack of quality of the sample material: MAMS17564: 5721±35 BP, 1σ 4606–4501 cal BC; δ^{13}C: -47.7; collagen: 0.1 %. Kind pers. comm. E. Stephan, LAD Konstanz.
84 An AMS date for triangle and line motifs from the Bischheim pit 3 at Urmitz fell into the third millennium cal BC and therefore lies outside the possible timespan. B.C. Oesterwind, Museum Mayen, kindly provided the sample material for KIA42011, bone of an unidentifiable mammal: 4218±30, 1σ 2892–2866, 2804–2762; 2σ 2904–2851, 2813–2742, 2727–2695.
85 Zeeb 1998, 138.
86 Arora 2004, 46. Dates are published only in calibrated form with no BP date provided, therefore they are not shown in Figure 7.
87 Proposed by Gleser 2008, 136 ff. for the ceramics of Welling-Trimbs. There are no radiometric dates for Trimbs. For the ceramics, see Jürgens 2008.
88 Breunig 1987, 179; Kulick and Lüning 1972. Together with dates for Spiere "De Hel", Maastricht-Watermolen "Vogelzang" and Ittre "Mont-à-Henry" in Belgium and northern France, not displayed here, see Lanting and van der Plicht 1999/2000, 48ff.
89 Osterwick: GrN-7634: 5625±105 BP, 4598–4380 cal BC; Koslar: KN-2491: 5830±60 BP, 4877–4554 cal BC (Breunig 1987, 180; Lüning 1979; 1971b). Lanting and van der Plicht (1999/2000, 9) question the validity of this oldest date from Koslar 10, as it should date to MK II not MK I and other results from Koslar 10 are younger. This typological classification is not shared here.
90 As there are problems with bone preservation in this area, pers. comm. J. Dubouloz. The dates from Chassey-le-Camp, niv. 9, all second half of the fifth millennium cal BC, do not really contribute to this problem, as the BP dates have high standard deviations of up to 120 years: Thévenot 2005, 30.
91 Not reliable, as the BP dates have very wide standard deviations of up to 200 years.

Henry" (46th–43rd centuries cal BC) and Maastricht-Watermolen "Vogelzang" (43rd–41st centuries cal BC)[92], all classified as MK I/II.

The interpretation of the absolute dates for the beginning of the MK faces various difficulties. There is the wide standard deviation of most of the available BP dates, which makes them imprecise. An old wood effect for wood samples is to be taken into account. The samples come from ditches, which represent contexts of uncertain formation; the dates can consequently not be directly associated with ceramics. Finally, it is questionable in how far Lüning, writing in 1968, already had the possibility to distinguish between chronological, regional and chorological features.

Geschwinde and Raetzel-Fabian claim a beginning of the MK not earlier than around 4230–4040 cal BC, postulating that MK assemblages typologically older than Koslar 10, "Vogelzang" or Ittre will not be found in the future. They claim an old wood effect for the older dates, and cite only dates that reach the 43rd–41st centuries cal BC[93]. In this they follow Lanting and van der Plicht, who argue that MK I dates between 4200–4075 cal BC, and MK II between 4075–3950 cal BC[94]. As a generalisation, this is questionable, insofar as both stages, MK I and MK II, were given the same duration of 125 years even though in south-west Germany only few shapes and nearly no representative inventories for stage MK I are known; in contrast, MK II is represented by a noticeably greater number of sites and by large inventories which allow us to recognise a typo-chronological evolution within MK II[95]. Additionally, Lanting and van der Plicht are of the opinion that "import" of MK ceramics could only be found from Schussenried onwards[96]. MK tulip beakers of type 1 are already present in Schwieberdingen, and they are the basis for Lüning's typo-chronological model for the culture groups of the Late Neolithic in south-west Germany[97]. Moreover, it is widely agreed that in most regions Bischheim and MK were at least partly contemporaneous[98]. For Baden-Württemberg it was shown that the earliest absolute dates available for the MK relate to MK II contexts, and the ditch structure at Ilsfeld suggests that there should be activity predating that represented by the absolute dates. A beginning of the MK around 4400/4300 cal BC is thought possible for instance by Eisenhauer, Gleser, Höhn, Seidel and Stöckli[99].

On the other hand there is the problem of typology. That the MK typology, drawn up by Lüning mainly on the basis of south-west German sites, does not fit with the range of characteristics of ceramics in Belgium and northern France was recently outlined[100]. This is also reflected in the long-lasting discussion

---

92 E.g. Lanting and van der Plicht 1999/2000, 50–51; Vanmontfort *et al.* 1997, 123–124.
93 Geschwinde and Raetzel-Fabian 2009, 187ff., Abb. 142.
94 Lanting and van der Plicht 1999/2000, 8.
95 Seidel 2012 for Baden-Württemberg: for MK I a total of 4–5 sites; for MK II a total of 12–16 sites.
96 Lanting and van der Plicht 1999/2000, 9.
97 Lüning 1969a, 238–239, Abb. 3A+1; 1969b, Taf. 6.5., 6.7, 6.9; 1971a. The finds context of the MK beaker finds at the eponymous site of Schwieberdingen "Katharinenlinde" is one structure, most probably a pit house. For an evaluation of the circumstances see Lüning 1969b, 10 and 26 ff.; the excavation was carried out by Müller in October 1930, Inv. A 31/7-74, in contrast to the finds A 28/3.
98 E.g. Geschwinde and Raetzel-Fabian 2009, 188; Gleser 2008, 143; Höhn 2002; Lüning 1971a; 1981, 181.
99 E.g. Eisenhauer 2002, 96 Abb. 3,2; Gleser 2012, 38–41, 69; Höhn 2002, 193; Seidel 2008, 178–179; Stöckli 2002, 62ff. Abb. 100.
100 E.g. Lanting and van der Plicht 1999/2000, 10–11; Vanmontfort *et al.* 1997.

surrounding stage MK I[101]. Whereas in Willms' opinion, Lüning had too few shapes at his disposal to define a "stage MK I", Gleser presented new material from Mayen and Kollig supporting the existence of "MK I"[102]. In a PCA carried out by Dubouloz, numerous tulip beakers from Bazoches were grouped together with segmented type 1 beakers from Entzheim pit 1 and pit 54, Jechtingen "Sandbrunnen", Schwieberdingen "Katharinenlinde", Champlay, Koslar 10, Inden 9, Miel, Iggelheim and Aldenhoven 3[103]. At this time it became clear that in the Paris Basin, especially in the Aisne valley, an early MK existed. This region was in consequence accepted as the region of origin for the MK, being influenced by Bischheim and Chasséen septentrional. In the seriation for tulip beakers presented by Höhn, only the shapes from Koslar 10 were placed into the oldest "interval 1" — together with for instance beaker 1,1 from Entzheim pit 54 and the beakers from Miel. Beakers from the palisade at Mayen were placed into "interval 2a", those from Bergheim Stelle 1 and the ditch at Mayen into "interval 2b"; those from Bergheim Stelle 7 and Inden into "interval 2c" — which suggests a stylistic evolution — Koslar 10, Miel and the palisade at Mayen were attributed to MK I, Bergheim Stelle 7, Inden 9 and the ditches at Mayen to MK II[104].

In general, it must be pointed out that at all sites in the south-west, Entzheim, Jechtingen, Schwieberdingen, Ilsfeld and "Aue", typologically early MK shapes are few, and they are associated with ceramics of other cultural styles or typologically later stages. Sites with a wider range of typologically early MK ceramics, like Koslar 10, Miel or Mayen, are closer to the Paris Basin, where assemblages from Bazoches or Cuiry-lès-Chaudardes comprise a wide range of characteristics. In consequence, one must ask if the few finds "date" a "chronological stage", or in how far they are "imported" items from a neighbouring group — marking the beginning of a change in tradition.

Eastern Bischheim

The published dates for Schernau, Marktbergel, Baldingen and Creglingen[105], which cover the 46th–44th/43rd centuries cal BC, suggest a contemporaneity with the Rhine Bischheim (Figures 7–8). As the two dates for Creglingen showed a remarkable difference (Figure 8)[106], plant material from pit 273 was dated as part of the Kraichgau project (Figure 8: MAMS18689: 5338±20 BP)[107]. The result of 4238–4073 cal BC supports the more recent of the two known dates. This indicates that an Eastern Bischheim still existed at the same time as, for example, Schussenried, Entzheim and late Münchshöfen (Figure 8: Eiselsdorf, Hn-17017). Apparently the line motifs survived longer in the east than even

---

101 E.g. Doubouloz 1998 (arguments regarding MK I at Bazoches); Gleser 1995; 1998 (arguments for an existence of MK I); Höhn 2002 (MK I=1, MK I/II=2a); Schyle 2005 (MK I=2a); Seidel 2008, 110–111, 344, 413 Anhang 1; 2011b (MK I in the Neckar valley); Willms 1982, 45–46 (doubting a "full stage MK I" and attributing to MK I the sites of Miel, Aldenhoven, Koslar 10 and Cologne); Zeeb 1998, 138ff.
102 Gleser 1998; Willms 1982.
103 Dubouloz 1998, figs 2A–B. For pit 71/17 at Jechtingen "Sandbrunnen" no datable material is available, as kindly verified by E. Stephan, LAD.
104 Höhn 2002, 172 Abb. 163 and catalogue in Anhang 2.
105 Lückerath 1986, 232; Lüning 1981, 36; Spatz 1996, 407; Zeeb 1998, 139, 147.
106 Lückerath 1986, 232 (Hd-10768-10605: 5410±120 BP, 4360–4040 cal BC; Hd-10769–10606: 5750±120 BP, 4770–4450 cal BC). B. Kromer, CEZ Mannheim, kindly helped to obtain the complete information regarding the samples dated in 1986.
107 M. Rösch and T. Märkle, LAD Hemmenhofen, kindly provided cereals from pit 273.

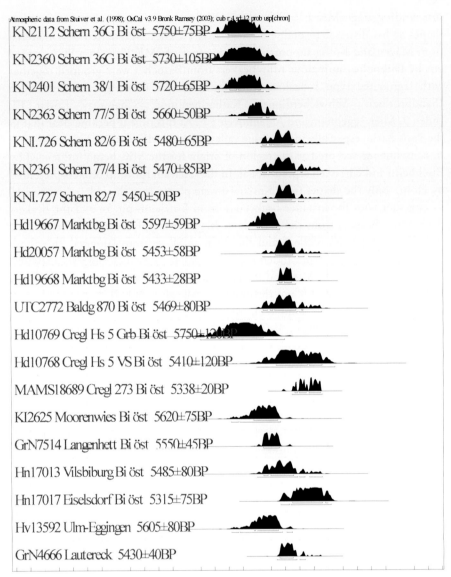

Figure 8. Multiplot for Eastern Bischheim, Schernau-Goldberg and indeterminate Late Neolithic in Franconia, Bavaria and Upper Swabia.

Zeeb-Lanz assumed[108]. At the same time, the dating of a "Schernau-Goldberg" which was claimed to be contemporaneous with MK I, and that of the preceding "Eastern Bischheim", are left open for discussion[109]. The absolute dates suggest that the older phase of Eastern Bischheim is contemporaneous with the earlier Rhine Bischheim, and the younger phase Schernau-Goldberg is contemporaneous with Aichbühl and Schwieberdingen (Figure 9)[110].

---

108 Zeeb 1998, 103 ff.
109 Gleser 1995, 189, 322.
110 As proposed by Gleser 1995, 239: Karte 3 – Figure 2 in this text.

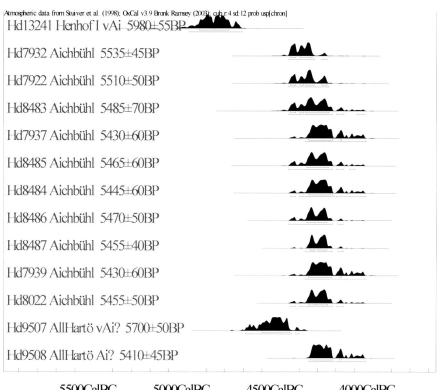

Figure 9. Multiplot for Aichbühl in Upper Swabia.

Aichbühl and Schussenried in Upper Swabia

The Aichbühl group of Upper Swabia is fixed by radiometric dates to the 44th–42nd centuries cal BC (Figure 9). Danube Schussenried is dated to the 43rd–38th centuries cal BC by more than 20 radiometric dates, mainly for the site commonly known as "Ehrenstein", but also for Riedschachen and Alleshausen "Hartöschle"[111]. Although the absolute dates for Schussenried follow without hiatus, it is generally accepted that Aichbühl appears stylistically rather isolated, not being based on a probable local Rössen, and that Schussenried does not develop from Aichbühl[112]. Rather, Schussenried emerges in a continuous process from Schwieberdingen in the Neckar region[113]. A certain relationship between Aichbühl and Münchshöfen can be recognised based on the decorative motifs. Absolute dates for Münchshöfen lie between the 44th and 40th centuries cal BC, and thus in the range of Aichbühl[114].

---

111 Strobel 2000, 434–443, 478–479. The dates are not shown here. For a graph, see Strobel 2000, 439 Abb. 374.
112 Strobel 2000, 434–443 with Abb. 374, 478–479.
113 Seidel 2004.
114 Matuschik 1992, 117; Stöckli 2009, 147–148.

A different methodological approach — mapping

For the maps in this contribution, a site was not treated as a closed unit, *i.e.* it was not ascribed completely to any one "culture group". Instead, the site was evaluated at the level of a ceramic unit. For each "cultural entity" or "culture group" under discussion, a "ceramic style" was defined. For each ceramic style present at a site, an own data set was created in the database. In this way, the concept of a closed "cultural area" or of sites of one "culture" was replaced by focusing on single pots[115]. The consequence is that for the Epirössen groups, this case study is based only on the decorated ceramics, which make up about 6 % of all ceramics; for the MK it relies exclusively on diagnostic shapes, which also include undecorated vessels.

The "informative character" of decorated ceramics has already been discussed by various authors[116]. This study follows Gleser's[117] concept for the "styles" of decorated ceramics. He defined a characteristic "disposition" of motifs, meaning the specific placement of motifs on a pot, *i.e.* something akin to an "ornamentational grammar" or "decorative logic". Here, single motifs and techniques are therefore only taken into account in a second stage and they were not mapped[118]. In this sense, a group-identifying "style" was defined by the "grammar of placement" or "disposition" of motifs, and not all motifs present in a geographical area were used for the definition of a group.

Overall, using this concept, it emerges that techniques seem not particularly specific for a "culture group", but appear "cross-culturally" as regional features. Instead, techniques have more of a chronological significance; for example, incised scratches ("Ritzverzierung") are used supra-regionally only during stage MK II, whereas during stage MK I a wide variety of stitches and stamps is used in all regions.

Single motifs are also shared "cross-culturally". For a better understanding of their use, Eisenhauer first applied Wiessner's concept of an "emblemic style" and an "assertive style" to Rössen and Epirössen ceramics[119]. An "emblemic style" is defined as a style or disposition exclusively used by a group to display its identity. An "assertive style" denotes a style which is used at the same time, but shared with neighbouring groups; it displays community and interaction[120].

In the case of the Epirössen groups, an emblemic style for Schwieberdingen would be a decoration within "windows" or "metopes" (Figure 10.1)[121]. For Rhine Bischheim, a combination of a continuous encircling band, often consisting of hanging triangles and paired with shoulder and lower decoration zones, is characteristic (Figure 10.3)[122]. For Eastern Bischheim, one could claim an encircling multilinear band ("Goldbergband") (Figure 10.2)[123]. Continuous encircling multilined bands in a diagonal position ("Aichbühler Metopen") are exclusively used in Aichbühl (Figure 10.4)[124]. Entzheim is recognisable by three decoration zones which are encircling a pot, the main zone showing stacked

---

115 A model which was in fact already followed by Gallay 1977; Lüning 1968; 1981; Schmitt 1974 and others.
116 E.g. famously by I. Hodder in 1982.
117 Gleser 1992; 1995.
118 As e.g. by Jeunesse *et al.* 2002/2003, figs 54–57; Lüning 1971a, Karte 3.
119 Eisenhauer 2002; Wiessner 1983; used since e.g. by Seidel 2004, 158–159; Zeeb-Lanz 2006.
120 Zeeb-Lanz 2006, Abb. 12.
121 Keefer and Joachim 1988, Abb. 28B, 1: Remseck-Aldingen.
122 Lüning 1971a, Taf. 14.B9: Bubenheim.
123 Zeeb 1998, Taf. 35.6: Baldingen.
124 Strobel 2000, Taf. 82.2098: Aichbühl.

"EMBLEMIC STYLE"

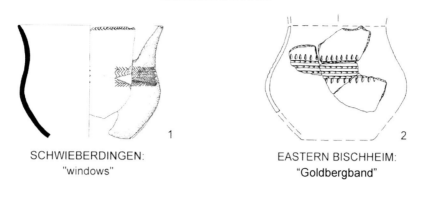

1 SCHWIEBERDINGEN: "windows"

2 EASTERN BISCHHEIM: "Goldbergband"

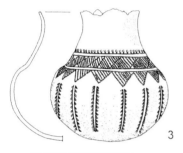
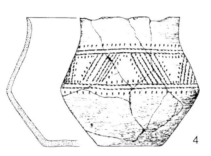
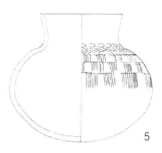

3 RHINE BISCHHEIM: hanging triangles

4 AICHBÜHL: "Aichbühl windows"

5 ENTZHEIM: repetition (chequerboard, triangles)

6 SCHUSSENRIED: main/front division Donau

7 SCHUSSENRIED: main/front division Neckar

Figure 10. "Emblemic styles", exclusively used by one group, displaying a group identity. 1: Schwieberdingen: metopic motifs ("Schwieberdinger Metopen"; Keefer and Joachim 1988, Abb. 28B). – 2: Eastern Bischheim: multi-lined "Goldbergband" (Zeeb 1998, Taf. 35,6). – 3: Rhine Bischheim: horizontal zones, hanging triangles in main zone (Lüning 1971a, Taf. 14,C9). – 4: Aichbühl: diagonal metopic motifs ("Aichbühler Metopen"; Strobel 2000, Taf. 82,2098). – 5: Entzheim: three horizontal zones, in main zone stacked motifs (chequerboard or triangles; Dieckmann 1991, Taf. 26,3). – 6: Danube Schussenried: two horizontal and four vertical zones, shoulder and front zones connected, main zone zig-zag (Lüning 1997, Taf. 33,10). – 7: Neckar Schussenried: two horizontal and four vertical zones, shoulder and front zones not connected, main zone zig-zag (Seidel 2004, Taf. 40,1).

motifs like triangles or a "chequerboard", combined with motifs above and below (Figure 10.5)[125]. Schussenried is defined by a division into two front zones with vertical motifs ("Stirnspalten") and two main zones with horizontal zig-zags ("Winkelband"); in the Neckar region, the technique of fine parallel hatches is characteristic (Figure 10.7)[126], while in the Danube region the technique of cross-hatching is used. In the Danube region the shoulder decoration is connected with the vertical motifs ("Stirnspalten") on the front of the vessel (Figure 10.6)[127].

Following this approach, these entities are at the same time connected by ceramics which show an assertive style. Schwieberdingen also uses continuous encircling motifs; they can be, but need not be, combined with an — often segmented — shoulder decoration[128]. In this respect, Schwieberdingen (Figure 11.1)[129], and to a lesser extent Aichbühl (Figure 11.4)[130], Entzheim (Figure 11.5)[131] and Chasséen[132], use horizontally continuous zig-zags ("ausgespartes Winkelband"), which later become an exclusive motif for Schussenried.

Rhine Bischheim (Figure 11.3)[133] and Eastern Bischheim (Figure 11.2)[134] share simple line motifs. Such a simple line motif can also be segmented, *i.e.* restricted to a "Schwieberdingen window" ("metope")[135]. The encircling hanging triangles of Rhine Bischheim can be found on ceramics with the motif disposition characteristic of Schwieberdingen[136], Eastern Bischheim[137], Entzheim[138] and later in the Danube Schussenried (Figure 11.6)[139].

Schwieberdingen also incorporates the continuous encircling "Goldbergband" of the Goldberg facies[140]. The continuous encircling diagonal bands or "metopes" characteristic of Aichbühl appear in the early Neckar Schussenried (Figure 11.7)[141]. An encircling band filled with diagonal hatches appears in both the Danube Schussenried[142] and in the Schernau-Goldberg group[143]. The vertical bundles of the lowest decoration zone on Entzheim pottery can be found isolated in an otherwise Bischheim disposition[144], but also combined with shoulder motifs in the Schwieberdingen disposition[145] as well as in that of early Schussenried[146].

---

125 Dieckmann 1991, Taf. 26.3: Bötzingen "Schneckenbühl" pit 71/13. Chequerboard and stacked triangles can easily be recognised as common with the Chasséen (e.g. Camp de Chassey: Thévenot 1969, pl. 27–39).
126 Seidel 2004, Taf. 40.1: Höfingen.
127 Lüning 1997, Taf. 33.10: Ehrenstein.
128 Seidel 2004, 158 Abb. 79; Lüning 1969, 13.
129 Seidel 2004, Taf. 1.3: Höfingen.
130 Strobel 2000, Taf. 80.2092: Aichbühl.
131 Jeunesse *et al.* 2002/2003, fig. 148.9: Bischoffsheim.
132 Jeunesse *et al.* 2002/2003, fig. 148, 1–7.
133 Lüning 1971a, Taf. 24.4: Holtzheim.
134 Lüning 1981, Taf. 50.7: Schernau.
135 Lüning 1971a, Taf. 15.B7: Weisenheim; Keefer and Joachim 1988, Abb. 40,4: Remseck-Aldingen I.
136 Seidel 2004, Taf. 64.6: Höfingen.
137 Lüning 1981, Taf. 64.10: Schernau.
138 Dieckmann 1991, Taf. 58.15. Bischoffingen "Dielen".
139 Strobel 2000, Taf. 35.747: Riedschachen.
140 Seidel 2004, Taf. 2.5: Höfingen.
141 Keefer 1988, Taf. 42.8: Hochdorf.
142 Strobel 2000, Taf. 32.756: Riedschachen.
143 Lüning 1981, Taf. 60.3: Schernau St. 82.
144 Lüning 1971a, Taf. 19.D7: Mundolsheim, pit 25.
145 Seidel 2004, Taf. 26.1.
146 Keefer 1988, Taf. 44.10.

"ASSERTIVE STYLE"

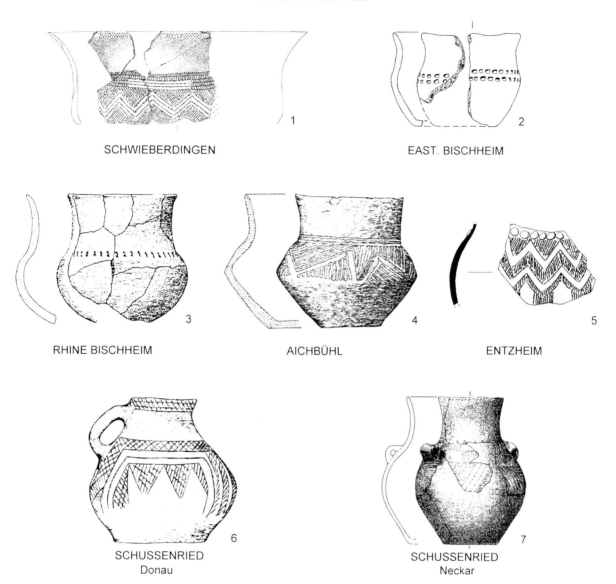

Figure 11. "Assertive styles", shared by groups, displaying interaction of neighbouring groups. 1: Schwieberdingen: zig-zag (Seidel 2004, Taf. 1,3). – 2: Eastern Bischheim: single line motifs (Zeeb 1998, Taf. 35,4). – 3: Rhine Bischheim: single line motifs (Lüning 1970, Taf. 6,18). – 4: Aichbühl: zig-zag (Strobel 2000, Taf. 83,2097). – 5: Entzheim: stacked zig-zag (Jeunesse et al. 2002/2003, fig. 148,9). – 6: Danube Schussenried: hanging triangles in four vertical zones (Strobel 2000, Taf. 35,747). – 7: Neckar Schussenried: diagonal metopic motifs ("Aichbühler Metope"; Keefer 1988, Taf 42,8).

These examples could easily be extended in number, by discussing additional motifs, and spatially, by adding further neighbouring groups. The important point to stress is that the motifs all appear within the respective disposition, *i.e.* in combination with the characteristic treatment — the presence or absence of decoration— of rim, shoulder and lowest zone of the disposition.

On the basis of this "logic of ornamentation", "grammaire ornamentale" or "disposition", "styles" were defined, and in consequence local and non-local

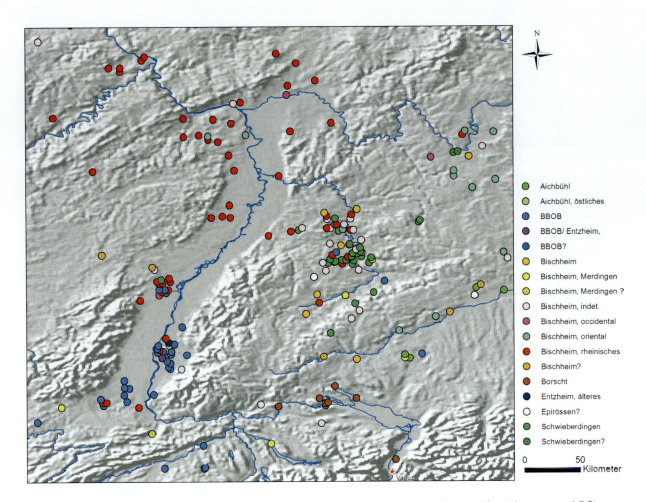

Figure 12. Map of pottery finds in the Epirössen styles dated to the MK I horizon and earlier (c. 46th–44th century cal BC).

ceramic styles were identified[147]. MK ceramics and decorated ceramics of the contemporaneous Epirössen groups were displayed here for the first time on the same maps. For stage MK I, the map shows regional concentrations of styles, but also a spatially relatively "mixed" picture. In other words, decorated ceramics — or the logic of a decoration — relatively often went beyond the area of origin (Figure 12). In clear contrast stands the map for MK II ceramics and ceramics decorated in contemporaneous Epirössen styles. Here, the areas of the respective styles are clearly limited to one region (Figure 13).

The interpretation is difficult, as only about 6 % of all ceramics were decorated during the Late Neolithic, and therefore form part of this investigation. Nevertheless, it can be noted that during horizon MK I, a greater variety of ceramic shapes was decorated by the Epirössen groups, for instance pots, bowls and bottles. Additionally, a greater variety of motifs, "motif arrangements" and techniques was applied. For example, the Bischheim unit shows a parallel use of triangle-dominated "composite" dispositions and "simple" line dispositions; Schwieberdingen a parallel use of "windows" and continuous encircling bands; following the new dates, BBOB and Merdingen show the parallel use of "composite" and "simple" dispositions, and so on. In contrast, during horizon MK II decoration was

---

147 Based on a compilation of all available drawings of decorated pots.

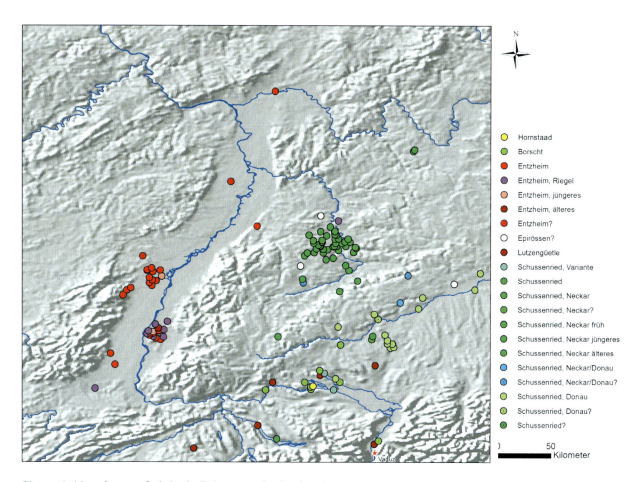

Figure 13. Map of pottery finds in the Epirössen styles dated to the MK II horizon and later (c. 44th/43rd–40th century cal BC).

restricted to few shapes, for instance mostly jars in Schussenried[148] and globular recipients in Entzheim. Often only one technique was applied, mostly the incised technique, and additionally only one specific "motif arrangement" per group was used, for instance horizontal division into four zones for Schussenried and vertically stacked zones for Entzheim. The facies Riegel combines stacked elements comparable to Entzheim with a segmentation into vertical zones comparable to Schussenried and BBOB. In terms of decoration techniques, a combination of incised ornamentation, stab-and-drag decoration (Furchenstich) and stamping is used, with hollow round stamps being characteristic.

In sum, during MK I no MK "territory" can be identified, nor is there a closed or circumscribed area for any Epirössen group. From MK II onwards, the maps allow us to recognise closed areas, opposing groups using MK ceramics and living an MK lifestyle to others with an Epirössen lifestyle and ceramics.

Discussion

For an interpretation one starting point — among many others — could be that decorated pots played a special role in social life. Preparing, sharing and consuming food and drink always has social implications. In this respect,

---

148 Only during the early Neckar-Schussenried were pots decorated, standing in the tradition of Schwieberdingen decorated "bowls".

decorated pots could have changed their social function over time. They could have served for special — ritual? — purposes only, perhaps increasingly so. One possible scenario is that during MK I decorated pots played a certain role during "ritual" events, meals or feasts, but that these events were part of a "living culture" *sensu* Eggers[149]. This means that the pots were a feature of daily life, being used — and produced? — by a wider section of the population. Therefore, the decorations were exported, locally adapted, varied and changed more easily. During MK II this living tradition could have reached the status of a "dying culture", as defined by Eggers[150]. The decorated pots would then no longer have been a part of daily life and group interaction. They could have served for the affirmation of a group identity by being linked with an identity rooted in the past, with characteristic pots used to display a certain exclusiveness. The decorated containers would then have been restricted to special occasions (persons?), which apparently involved the consumption of liquids.

Naturally the question arises if there were special pots in the MK repertoire which could have had functions comparable to that suggested here for the decorated Epirössen pots, *i.e.* pots displaying an identity. Tulip beakers are particularly suggestive in this context. As they became a type fossil of the MK for modern investigators, they could also have had significance for Neolithic people. It is well known that tulip beakers develop from a ubiquitous shape of many variations at the beginning of the MK to the rare and "exotic" shape of the tall tulip beakers at the end of the MK[151]. The latest tulip beakers — Lüning's type 4,2 — sometimes show extreme proportions and can be found as isolated finds in neighbouring groups[152]. Tall tulip beakers with round bases become the defining finds type from MK III/IV onwards. This beaker shape is restricted to an area east of the Rhine, between Lake Constance and North Rhine-Westphalia (Nottuln) and is identical with the defined distribution area of the late MK[153].

This leads to the idea that tall tulip beakers saw a change in their social function — analogous to Schussenried jars or Entzheim globular recipients. Their increasing elaboration could have coincided with an increasing exclusivity of use. Tall tulip beakers could have been reserved for a small circle of persons, and/or for only few events, recalling activities which led to the development of the originally wide tulip beaker repertoire, in other words, a former "identity" of the MK which was no longer part of the "living culture". The tulip beaker could have changed from a typo-chronological shape used in a "living culture" to a typologically resistant shape with no finer chronological implication.

In combination with typological observations, the absolute dates presented here — although far too few and therefore of preliminary character — suggest a scenario of cultural entities, perhaps even lifestyles, which were spatially moving or displaced by others. Aichbühl appears in Upper Swabia without a local stylistic predecessor and remains somewhat isolated, although stylistic links to Münchshöfen can be drawn[154]. In contrast to the continuum between Schwieberdingen and

---

149 Eggers 1986, 258–262. – In our context rather: "one element of a culture".
150 Eggers 1986, 258–262. – In our context rather: "one element of a culture".
151 Höhn 2002, 180–184; Seidel 2008, 317.
152 E.g. in the Alpine foreland, the Saale region and Prague (Höhn 2002, 190). Scollar (1961, 523) already remarked that not every region with tulip beakers must be part of the MK.
153 Höhn 2002, 187–190, Abb. 175–176.
154 Strobel 2000, 438.

Schussenried in the Neckar region[155], the Danube Schussenried does not emerge typologically on an Aichbühl substrate[156]. As the absolute dates for the Neckar Schussenried fall into the hiatus between Aichbühl and Danube Schussenried, and given that the Neckar Schussenried ends when the absolute dates for the Danube Schussenried begin[157], Paret's idea of an "exodus" of the Neckar Schussenried to Upper Swabia gains some probability[158]. The consensus view is that in the Neckar region Schussenried was replaced by MK III in the years after 4000 cal BC[159].

A comparable scenario might have played a role in the appearance of Egolzwil, which is seen as an isolated facies between Cortaillod and Pfyn[160]. Absolute dates place Egolzwil at the same time as the evolution of the round-based globular beakers ("Kugelbecher") of Merdingen and BBOB. Hypothetically, it can be proposed that the displacement of BBOB by Entzheim in Lower Alsace is connected with the appearance of Egolzwil in the Wauwiler Moos, at Lake Zurich and at Lake Zug in Switzerland, and the Fazies Riegel at the Kaiserstuhl.

The suggested scenarios for the Late Neolithic of Baden-Württemberg are a proposal for a more amplified view on ceramics, and material culture in general. At the present moment typology seems no longer to contribute to making chronology more precise. And for a definition of cultural entities it is time to develop a more differentiated perspective on material culture. Future investigation of prehistoric cultures could bring more into focus different ways of use, social significance and distribution of material culture, based on scientific foundations and for example using ethnographic case studies more systematically[161].

References

Altdorfer, K. and Affolter, J. 2011. *Schaffhauser Silex-Vorkommen und Nutzung. Wirtschaftsarchäologische Untersuchungen an den Silices der jungneolithischen Station Büttenhardt-Zelg, Schaffhausen (Herblingen-)Grüthalde und Lohn-Setzi. Beiträge zur Schaffhauser Archäologie 5.* Schaffhausen.

Arora, S.-K. 2004. Hofplätze der Bischheimer Kultur im Tagebau Garzweiler. *Archäologie im Rheinland* 2004, 45–47.

Breunig, P. 1987. *14C-Chronologie des vorderasiatischen, südost- und mitteleuropäischen Neolithikums. Fundamenta Monographien zur Urgeschichte A 13.* Köln.

Bronk-Ramsey, C. 2003. OxCal Program v3.9, Radiocarbon Accelerator Unit, University of Oxford.

Croutsch, C., Rousselet, O. and Tegel, W. 2013. Dambach-la-Ville (Bas-Rhin, Alsace). Un village de la fin du Ve millénaire. Résultats préliminaires de la fouille de la Plateforme d'Activités d'Alsace Centrale. Lecture at the 31st Colloque Internéo, 17th–19th October 2013 in Chalons-en-Champagne.

---

155 Keefer 1988, 98; Seidel 2004, 225–226, 315–316.
156 Strobel 2000, 440.
157 Seidel 2004, 27, 314ff.; Strobel 2000, 438, 478.
158 Paret 1955, 72ff.; Seidel 2004, 316; Strobel 2000, 438, 478–479 (list 14.2 "C14-Daten").
159 Keefer 1988, 91ff.; Gleser 1995, 105ff., 264ff.; Gross-Klee 1998; Seidel 2004, 233.
160 Strobel 2000, 440.
161 As an example for a different approach, see e.g. the proceedings of the workshop "Mobilities and pottery production. Archaeological and anthropological perspectives', held in Bern in June 2015 (Heitz and Stapfer 2017).

Croutsch, C., Tegel. W. and Rousselet, O. 2014a. Dambach-la-Ville – Plateforme Départementale d'Activités d'Alsace Centrale (Bas-Rhin, Alsace). Un habitat de la fin du Ve millénaire avant J.-C. Analyse dendrochronologique et premières données sur l'économie et l'environnement à travers les analyses carpologiques. *Bulletin de la Société Archéologique Champenoise* 107, 35–44.

Croutsch, C., Denaire, A., Ferrier, A., Pélissier, A., Rousselet, O. and Arbogast, R.-M. 2014b. Obernai „Schulbach/Nouvel Hopital" (Bas-Rhin, Alsace): puits et structures domestiques du Néolithique moyen. *Internéo* 10, 29–42.

Dieckmann, B. 1991. *Zum Mittel- und Jungneolithikum im Kaiserstuhlgebiet.* Unpublished dissertation, University of Freiburg im Breisgau.

Dubouloz, J. 1991. Le village fortifié de Berry-au-Bac (Aisne) et sa signification pour la fin du Néolithique dans la France du Nord. In J. Lichardus (ed.), *Die Kupferzeit als historische Epoche. Symposium Saarbrücken und Otzenhausen 06.–13.11.1988, Saarbrücker Beiträge zur Altertumskunde 55*, 421–440. Bonn.

Dubouloz, J. 1998. Réflexions sur le Michelsberg ancien en Bassin parisien. In J. Biel, H. Schlichtherle, M. Strobel and A. Zeeb (eds), 1998. *Die Michelsberger Kultur – Probleme der Entstehung, Chronologie und des Siedlungswesens. Kolloquium Hemmenhofen 1997. Materialhefte zur Archäologie in Baden-Württemberg 43*, 9–20. Stuttgart.

Eggers, H.-J. 1986. *Einführung in die Vorgeschichte* (3rd edition). München.

Eisenhauer, U. 2002. *Untersuchungen zur Siedlungs- und Kulturgeschichte des Mittelneolithikums in der Wetterau. Universitätsforschungen zur Prähistorischen Archäologie 89.* Bonn.

Eisenhauer, U. and Daszkiewicz, M. 2003. Bischheimer Keramik aus Guntersblum (Rheinland-Pfalz). *Archäologisches Korrespondenzblatt* 33, 167–186.

Engel, F. and Siegmund, F. 2005. Radiocarbon dating of the Neolithic flint mine at Kleinkems (near Efringen-Kirchen, District Lörrach, Baden-Württemberg, Germany). *Antiquity* 79, 1–5.

Friederich, S. 2011. *Bad Friedrichshall-Kochendorf und Heilbronn-Neckargartach. Studien zum mittelneolithischen Siedlungswesen im Mittleren Neckarland. Forschungen und Berichte zur Vor- und Frühgeschichte in Baden-Württemberg 123/1 & 2.* Stuttgart.

Gallay, A. 1977. *Le Néolithique moyen du Jura et des plaines de la Saone. Contribution à l'étude des relations Chassey – Cortaillod – Michelsberg. Antiqua 6.* Frauenfeld.

Geschwinde, M. and Raetzel-Fabian, D. 2009. *EWBSL. Eine Fallstudie zu den jungneolithischen Erdwerken am Nordrand der Mittelgebirge. Beiträge zur Archäologie in Niedersachsen 14.* Rahden.

Gleser, R. 1992. Bischheim und Schwieberdingen im mittleren Neckarraum – Ein Beitrag zur Chronologie und stilistischen Entwicklung der epi-rössener Keramik. *Saarbrücker Studien und Materialien zur Altertumskunde* 1, 17–60.

Gleser, R. 1995. *Die Epi-Rössener Gruppen in Südwestdeutschland. Untersuchungen zur Chronologie, stilistischen Entwicklung und kulturellen Einordnung. Saarbrücker Beiträge zur Altertumskunde 61.* Bonn.

Gleser, R. 1998. Periodisierung, Verbreitung und Entstehung der älteren Michelsberger Kultur – Rückblick und Ausblick. In J. Biel, H. Schlichtherle, M. Strobel and A. Zeeb (eds), *Die Michelsberger Kultur – Probleme der Entstehung, Chronologie und des Siedlungswesens. Kolloquium Hemmenhofen 1997. Materialhefte zur Archäologie in Baden-Württemberg 43*, 237–248. Stuttgart.

Gleser, R. 2008. Zur Keramik und den Hausgrundrissen von Trimbs. *Berichte zur Archäologie an Mittelrhein und Mosel* 13, 135–144.

Gleser, R. 2012. Zeitskalen, stilistische Tendenzen und Regionalität des 5. Jahrtausends in den Altsiedellandschaften zwischen Mosel und Morava. In R. Gleser and V. Becker (eds), *Mitteleuropa im 5. Jahrtausend vor Christus. Beiträge zur Internationalen Konferenz in Münster 2010. Neolithikum und ältere Metallzeiten. Studien und Materialien, Bd. 1*, 35–103. Berlin.

Gross-Klee, E. 1998. Michelsberg: Heterogeneität und kulturelle Einbindung in Raum und Zeit. In J. Biel, H. Schlichtherle, M. Strobel and A. Zeeb (eds), *Die Michelsberger Kultur – Probleme der Entstehung, Chronologie und des Siedlungswesens. Kolloquium Hemmenhofen 1997. Materialhefte zur Archäologie in Baden-Württemberg 43*, 249–259. Stuttgart.

Heitz, C. and Stapfer, R. (eds). 2017. *Mobility and pottery production: archaeological and anthropological perspectives*. Leiden.

Heumüller, M., Regner-Kamlah, B. and Seidel, U. 2012. Neue Aspekte zu den Siedlungsstrukturen der Michelsberger Kultur im Kraichgau. *Archäologische Ausgrabungen in Baden-Württemberg 2012*, 53–58.

Hodder, I. 1982. *Symbols in action: ethnoarchaeological studies of material culture*. Cambridge.

Höhn, B. 2002. *Die Michelsberger Kultur in der Wetterau. Universitätsforschungen zur Prähistorischen Archäologie 87*. Bonn.

Jeunesse, C. 1985. La chronologie du Néolithique alsacien. A la lumière des nouvelles découvertes et des progrès récentes des méthodes de datation absolue. *Cahiers Alsaciens d'Archéologie d'Art et d'Histoire* 28, 21–45.

Jeunesse, C. 1990a. Le Néolithique alsacien et ses relations avec les régions voisines. In R. Degen and M. Höneisen (eds), *Die ersten Bauern. Pfahlbaufunde Europas. Forschungsbericht zur Ausstellung im Schweizerischen Landesmuseum und zum Erlebnispark. Bd. 2: Einführung, Balkan und angrenzende Regionen der Schweiz*, 177–194. Zürich.

Jeunesse, C. 1990b. Eléments de type "Wauwil" dans le sud de l'Alsace. In R. Degen and M. Höneisen (eds), *Die ersten Bauern. Pfahlbaufunde Europas. Forschungsbericht zur Ausstellung im Schweizerischen Landesmuseum und zum Erlebnispark. Bd. 2: Einführung, Balkan und angrenzende Regionen der Schweiz*, 195–196. Zürich.

Jeunesse, C. 1990c. Le groupe de Bruebach-Oberbergen et l'horizon épi-roessénien dans le sud de la Plaine du Rhin supérieur, le nord de la Suisse et le sud de la Haute-Souabe. *Cahiers de l'Association pour la Promotion de la Recherche Archéologique en Alsace,* suppl. 6, 81–114.

Jeunesse, C., Lefranc, P., Kuhnle, G. and Mauvilly, M. 1998. Les sites d'habitat de Rosheim "Rosenmeer" et de Rosheim "Hexensul" (Bas-Rhin) et la relation entre les groupes de Bruebach-Oberbergen et d'Entzheim en Basse-Alsace. *Cahiers de l'Association pour la Promotion de la Recherche Archéologique en Alsace* 14, 107–133.

Jeunesse, C., Lefranc, P. and Denaire, A. 2002/2003. Groupe de Bischheim, origine de Michelsberg, genèse du groupe d'Entzheim. La transition entre le Néolithique moyen et le Néolithique recent dans les régions rhénanes. *Cahiers de l'Association pour la Promotion de la Recherche Archéologique en Alsace* 18/19, 1–280.

Joachim, W. 1989. Neue vorgeschichtliche Siedlungen in Remseck-Aldingen, Kr. Ludwigsburg. *Archäologische Ausgrabungen in Baden-Württemberg 1989*, 48–51.

Joris, J. and Moisin, P.H. 1972. Rössener Einflüsse in der Gegend von Mons (Hennegau, Belgien) und die C14-Datierung aus Givry (GrN 6021). *Archäologisches Korrespondenzblatt* 2, 243–248.

Jürgens, A. 2008. Die mittelneolithische Siedlung von Trimbs, Kreis Mayen-Koblenz. *Berichte zur Archäologie an Mittelrhein und Mosel* 13, 11–134.

Keefer, E., with contributions by E. Klein, D. Makovicz-Poliszot and R. Rottländer. 1988. *Hochdorf II. Eine jungsteinzeitliche Siedlung der Schussenrieder Kultur. Forschungen und Berichte zur Vor- u. Frühgeschichte in Baden-Württemberg 27*. Stuttgart.

Keefer, E. and Joachim, W., with contributions by J. Biel and M. Kokabi. 1988. Eine Siedlung der Schwieberdinger Gruppe in Aldingen, Gde. Remseck am Neckar, Kr. Ludwigsburg. *Fundberichte aus Baden-Württemberg* 13, 1–114.

Keefer, E. and Krause, R. 1992. *Vorgeschichtliche Siedlungen und Gräber in Remseck am Neckar. Heimatkundliche Schriftenreihe der Gemeinde Remseck am Neckar. Landschaft – Natur – Geschichte 12*. Remseck/Neckar.

Knoche, B. 2013. Zur Chronologie und Typogenese der jungneolithischen Ösenleistenflaschen. In W. Melzer (ed.), *Neue Forschungen zum Neolithikum in Soest und am Hellweg. Soester Beiträge zur Archäologie 13*, 275–298. Soest.

Kulick, J. and Lüning, J. 1972. Neue Beobachtungen am Michelsberger Erdwerk in Bergheim, Kr. Waldeck. *Fundberichte Hessen* 12, 88–96.

Lanting, J.N. and van der Plicht, J. 1999/2000. De ^{14}C-Chronologie van de Nederlandse Pre- en Protohistorie, III: Neolithicum. *Palaeohistoria* 41/42, 1–110.

Lefranc, P. and Jeunesse, C. 1998. Wittenheim (Haut-Rhin, France). Un enclos palissadé de type „Kreispalisadenanlage" dans le Rössen III du sud de la Plaine du Rhin supérieur ? *Anthropologie et Préhistoire* 109, 63–70.

Lefranc, P., Mauvilly, M., Arbogast, R.-M. and Latron, F. 1998. Un établissement du Roessen III et du groupe de Bruebach-Oberbergen à Wittenheim (Haut-Rhin). *Cahiers de l'Association pour la Promotion de la Recherche Archéologique en Alsace* 13, 85–117.

Lückerath, C. 1986. *Fünf Häuser der Bischheimer Siedlung von Creglingen-Frauental*. Unpublished Magister dissertation, University of Frankfurt/Main.

Lüning, J. 1968. Die Michelsberger Kultur. Ihre Funde in zeitlicher und räumlicher Gliederung. *Bericht der Römisch-Germanischen Kommission* 48, 1–350.

Lüning, J. 1969a. Aichbühl – Schwieberdingen – Bischheim. *Studijné Zvesti Arch. Ústavu* 17, 233–247.

Lüning, J. 1969b. *Die jungsteinzeitliche Schwieberdinger Gruppe. Veröffentlichungen des Staatlichen Amtes Denkmalpflege Stuttgart A.13*. Stuttgart.

Lüning, J. 1970. Eine Siedlung der Bischheimer Gruppe in Schwalheim, Kr. Friedberg. *Fundberichte Hessen* 9/10, 22–50.

Lüning, J. 1971a. Die Entwicklung der Keramik am Übergang vom Mittel- zum Jungneolithikum im süddeutschen Raum. *Bericht der Römisch-Germanischen Kommission* 50, 1–96.

Lüning, J. 1971b. Aldenhoven 3. *Bonner Jahrbücher* 171, 578–582.

Lüning, J. 1979. Untersuchungen zur neolithischen Besiedlung der Aldenhovener Platte VIII. *Bonner Jahrbücher* 179, 299–321.

Lüning, J. 1981. *Eine Siedlung der mittelneolithischen Gruppe Bischheim in Schernau, Ldkr. Kitzingen. Materialhefte zur Bayerischen Vorgeschichte, Reihe A, Bd. 44*. Kallmünz.

Lüning, J. 1997. Die Keramik von Ehrenstein. In J. Lüning, U. Sommer, K.A. Achilles, H. Krumm, J. Waiblinger, J. Hahn and E. Wagner (eds), *Das jungsteinzeitliche Dorf Ehrenstein III (Gemeinde Blaustein, Alb-Donau-Kreis). Ausgrabung 1960. Teil III: Die Funde. Forschungen und Berichte zur Vor- und Frühgeschichte in Baden-Württemberg 58*. Stuttgart.

Lüning, J. and Zürn, H., with contributions by K. Beckhoff, G. Nobis, M. Hopf, R. Rottländer and J. Frechen. 1977. *Die Schussenrieder Siedlung im "Schlößlesfeld", Markung Ludwigsburg. Forschungen und Berichte zur Vor- und Frühgeschichte in Baden-Württemberg 8.* Stuttgart.

Matuschik, I. 1992. Sengkofen-"Pfatterbreite", eine Fundstelle der Michelsberger Kultur im Bayerischen Donautal, und die Michelsberger Kultur im östlichen Alpenvorland. *Bayerische Vorgeschichtsblätter* 57, 1–31.

Matuschik, I. 2011. *Die Keramikfunde von Hornstaad-Hörnle I–VI. Besiedlungsgeschichte der Fundstelle und Keramikentwicklung im beginnenden 4. Jahrtausend im Bodenseeraum. Siedlungsarchäologie im Alpenvorland XII. Forschungen und Berichte zur Vor- und Frühgeschichte in Baden-Württemberg 122.* Stuttgart.

Nicolussi, K., Matuschik, I. and Tegel, W. 2013. Klimavariabilität und Siedlungsdynamik am Beispiel der Feuchtbodensiedlungen im Raum Oberschwaben, Bodensee und Nordostschweiz 4400–3400 BC. In N. Bleicher, H. Schlichtherle, P. Gassmann and N. Martinelli (eds), *Dendro – Chronologie – Typologie – Ökologie*, 69–85. Freiburg.

Regner-Kamlah, B. and Seidel, U. in press. The Michelsberg culture of northern Baden-Württemberg: a case study of a Neolithic landscape with enclosures and open sites. In *Megaliths – Societies – Landscapes. Early monumentality and social differentiation in Neolithic Europe. Proceedings of the conference in Kiel 16.–20.06.2015.*

Schmitt, G. 1974. La transition entre le Néolithique moyen et le Néolithique final en Basse-Alsace. *Revue Archéologique de l'Est et du Centre-Est* 25, 1–364.

Schyle, D. 2005. Rezension S. Reiter, Die beiden Michelsberger Anlagen von Bruchsal „Aue" und „Scheelkopf": zwei ungleiche Nachbarn. Materialhefte zur Archäologie in Baden-Württemberg 65. *Archäologische Informationen* 28, 195–199.

Scollar, I. 1961. The Late Neolithic in Belgium, Western Germany and Alsace. In B. Soudský and E. Pleslová (eds), *L'Europe à la fin du l'age de la Pierre. Actes du Symposium consacré aux problèmes du Néolithique européen 1959*, 519–548. Prague.

Seidel, U. 2004. *Die jungneolithischen Siedlungen von Leonberg-Höfingen, Kr. Böblingen. Materialhefte zur Archäologie in Baden-Württemberg 69.* Stuttgart.

Seidel, U. 2008. *Michelsberger Erdwerke im Raum Heilbronn. Neckarsulm-Obereisesheim ‚Hetzenberg' und Ilsfeld ‚Ebene', Landkreis Heilbronn, Heilbronn-Klingenberg ‚Schloßberg', Stadtkreis Heilbronn. Materialhefte zur Archäologie in Baden-Württemberg 81.* Stuttgart.

Seidel, U. 2011a. Eine jungneolithische Siedlung in Endingen am Kaiserstuhl mit ersten absoluten Daten für die „Entzheimer Gruppe". *Archäologische Nachrichten aus Baden* 83, 5–8.

Seidel, U. 2011b. Oberderdingen-Großvillars, Lkr. Karlsruhe – Eine Siedlungsstelle des Bischheimer Horizonts und der Michelsberger Kultur. In A. Denaire, C. Jeunesse and P. Lefranc (eds), *Nécropoles et enceintes danubiennes du Ve millénaire dans le Nord-Est de la France et le Sud-Ouest de l'Allemagne. Rhin Meuse Moselle Monographies d'Archéologie du Grand Est*, 143–158. Strasbourg.

Seidel, U. 2012. Wechselnde Überlieferungsdichten von Fundstellen an der Wende vom 5. zum 4. Jt. v. Chr. – Am Beispiel der Michelsberger Besiedelung im nördlichen Baden-Württemberg. In R. Gleser and V. Becker (eds), *Mitteleuropa im 5. Jahrtausend vor Christus. Internationale Konferenz in Münster 2010. Neolithikum und Ältere Metallzeiten. Studien und Materialien Bd. 1*, 291–307. Münster.

Seidel, U. 2015. Fundschau Neolithikum: Endingen „Kornenberg". *Fundberichte aus Baden-Württemberg* 35, 615–625.

Seidel, U., Regner-Kamlah, B. and Heumüller, M. 2010. Neue Ergebnisse des DFG-Projekts „Siedlungsstrukturen der Michelsberger Kultur im Kraichgau". *Archäologische Ausgrabungen in Baden-Württemberg* 2010, 22–27.

Spatz, H. 1996. *Beiträge zum Kulturenkomplex Hinkelstein – Großgartach – Rössen. Der keramische Fundstoff des Mittelneolithiums aus dem mittleren Neckarland und seine zeitliche Gliederung. Materialhefte zur Archäologie in Baden-Württemberg 37*. Stuttgart.

Steppan, K.-H. 2003. *Taphonomie – Zoologie – Chronologie – Technologie – Ökonomie. Materialhefte zur Archäologie in Baden-Württemberg 66*. Stuttgart.

Steppan, K.-H. 2006. Neolithic human impact and wild horses in Germany and Switzerland: horse size variability and the chrono-ecological context In S.L. Olsen, S. Grant, A.M. Choyke and L. Bartosiewicz (eds), *Horses and humans: the evolution of human-equine relationships*, 209–220. Oxford.

Stöckli, W.E. 2002. *Absolute und relative Chronologie des Früh- und Mittelneolithikums in Westdeutschland (Rheinland und Rhein-Main-Gebiet). Basler Hefte zur Archäologie 1*. Basel.

Stöckli, W.E. 2009. *Chronologie und Regionalität des jüngeren Neolithikums (4300–2400 v. Chr.). Schweizer Mittelland, Süddeutschland und Ostfrankreich. Antiqua 45*. Basel.

Strobel, M. 2000. *Die Schussenrieder Siedlung Taubried I (Bad Buchau, Kr. Biberach). Ein Beitrag zu den Siedlungsstrukturen und zur Chronologie des frühen und mittleren Jungneolithikums in Oberschwaben*. Stuttgart.

Stroh, A. 1938. *Eine neue keramische Gruppe der jüngeren Steinzeit in Süddeutschland. Festschrift für Gero v. Merhardt. Marburger Studien*, 234–242. Marburg.

Suter, P.J., with contributions by S. Jacomet, B. Richter, J. Schibler and P. Schubert. 1987. *Zürich "Kleiner Hafner". Tauchgrabungen 1981–1984. Züricher Denkmalpflege, Monographien 3*. Zürich.

Thévenot, J.-P. 1969. Elements chasséens de la ceramique de Chassey. *Revue Archéologique de l'Est et du Centre-Est* 20, 7–95.

Thévenot, J.-P. 2005. *Le Camp de Chassey, Chassey-le-Camp, Saone-et-Loire. Les niveaux néolitiques du rempart de « la Redoute ». Revue Archéologique de l'Est, Suppl. 22*. Dijon.

Vanmontfort, B., Casseyas, C. and Vermeersch, P.M. 1997. Neolithic ceramics from Spiere "de Hel" and their contribution to the understanding of the earliest Michelsbergculture. *Notae Praehistoricae* 17, 123–134.

Wiessner, P. 1983. Style and social information in Kalahari San projectile points. *American Antiquity* 48, 253–276.

Willms, C. 1982. *Zwei Fundplätze der Michelsberger Kultur aus dem westlichen Münsterland. Gleichzeitig ein Beitrag zum neolithischen Silexhandel in Mitteleuropa. Münstersche Beiträge zur Ur- und Frühgeschichte 12*. Hildesheim.

Zeeb, A. 1998. *Die Goldberg-Gruppe im frühen Jungneolithikum Südwestdeutschlands. Ein Beitrag zur Keramik der Schulterbandgruppen. Universitätsforschungen zur Prähistorischen Archäologie 48*. Bonn.

Zeeb-Lanz, A. 2006. Überlegungen zu Sozialaspekten keramischer Gruppen. Beispiele aus dem Neolithikum Südwestdeutschlands. In S. Burmeister and N. Müller-Scheeßel (eds), *Soziale Gruppen – kulturelle Grenzen. Die Interpretation sozialer Identitäten in der Prähistorischen Archäologie*, 81–102. Münster.

Schiepzig enclosures

Gaps in the archaeological record at the end of the fifth millennium BC in northern central Germany?

Johannes Müller, Kay Schmütz and Christoph Rinne

Abstract

What we know about the chronology of central northern Germany at the end of the fifth millennium has changed: new excavations have partially closed the gap which, 15 years ago, was still visible in the archaeological record. New results from the enclosure at Hundisburg-Olbetal, in conjunction with data from Salzmünde-Schiepzig, show that the so-called Schiepzig style began between 4300 and 4200 BC. Michelsberg and Schiepzig are closely connected. Enclosures, storage pits and similarities in material culture (vessel shape and decoration) indicate a shared social background.

Zusammenfassung: Schiepziger Erdwerke: Lücken in der archäologischen Überlieferung am Ende des 5. Jahrtausends v. Chr. in Norddeutschland?

Die chronologischen Rahmenbedingungen des nördlichen Mitteldeutschlands am Ende des 5. Jahrtausends v. Chr. haben sich verändert: Die bis vor ca. 15 Jahren festgestellte Lücke im archäologischen Fundbestand konnte partiell durch Neugrabungen geschlossen werden. Die neuen Ergebnisse aus dem Grabenwerk Hundisburg-Olbetal belegen, zusammen mit denen aus Salzmünde-Schiepzig, ein Einsetzen des Schiepziger Stils ab etwa 4300 bis 4200 v. Chr. Michelsberg und Schiepzig sind eng verknüpft. Grabenwerke, Kegelstumpfgruben und Ähnlichkeiten in der materiellen Kultur (Gefäßtypologie und -verzierung) verweisen auf den gemeinsamen sozialen Hintergrund.

Introduction

Until about 15 years ago, the overall archaeological record of central Germany, amongst others, displayed a low frequency of archaeological remains for the centuries c. 4400–3800 BC, in comparison to the preceding and following centuries. Except for 73 sites which were labelled as "Gatersleben"[1], three sites which could be associated with Jordanow and four early Michelsberg sites, no other contexts could be linked to these roughly six centuries[2]. Taking the size of

---

1 Following mainly Kroitsch 1973.
2 J. Müller 2001, 253 fig. 128; Ostritz 2000, 44–53.

the so called "Mittelelbe-Saale area" with its particularly fertile soils and other favourable settlement conditions into account, the small number of 80 sites on not less than 55,000 km² is quite remarkable. Even the few palaeoecological archives which covered the centuries in question hinted at only a low human impact on the environment[3]. In this respect a gap in the archaeological record was visible, thus it seemed probable that population density for the period and region under discussion was only low.

During the last 15 years, due to new excavations and new analytical methods the situation has changed — admittedly not dramatically, but at least new sites with archaeological features were discovered. They make new models of settlement development possible. Alongside purely pottery-focused analyses, which remained in the foreground of research for decades and resulted in the identification of varying ceramic styles, views beyond pottery development now also became possible. This paper briefly outlines the main features discovered at one such site, Hundisburg-Olbetal. As well as filling the presumed settlement gap, this enclosure site also shows a complex network of contacts, involving stylistic features of pottery, architectural elements of the enclosure, and ritual and economic practices. This is therefore one example for the dynamic cultural milieu in the second half of the fifth millennium, a time when local traditions and novel elements were admixed to create the emerging archaeological entities of the Younger Neolithic.

Research history: from ceramic styles to domestic and ritual sites

The scarcity of evidence and the resulting diversity of interpretations have left their mark in recent archaeological statements about the development of this whole region within the approximately six centuries in question, between c. 4400–3800 BC. With respect to the research history of the last three generations of archaeologists, three phases of research can be identified.

Typological identification and ceramic styles

Due to the lack of secure archaeological features (other than burials) and possibilities to apply scientific dating techniques, an immense amount of energy was expended in describing ceramic styles and typological sequences. The resulting inflation in terms of so-called local groups or typological phases (*e.g.* Epi-Rössen/Post-Rössen, Epi-Lengyel, later Gatersleben, Jordansmühl/Jordanow, Priestewitz-Kmehlen, Gröna, Schiepzig) overestimated local typological differences and underestimated general trends in ceramic development. Nevertheless, even within typochronological models that were based only on a few unsatisfactory and mostly not clearly contexted ¹⁴C dates, a lack of characteristic ceramic types within the centuries under discussion was obvious[4].

---

3   Summarised in J. Müller 2001, 268–273 fig. 143.
4   Beran 1993; Kaufmann 2007; Kroitzsch 1973; J. Müller 2001.

Absolute chronology and typochronologies of ceramic styles

Both first multivariate statistical approaches to typological sequences[5] and the few available ^{14}C dates[6] confirmed a typochronological development of ceramic styles of different cultural and spatial "origins" (late Lengyel; Bischheim/late Rössen), as well as the possibility to identify a local to regional ceramic style at least for the forty-third to the forty-first centuries BC that was also influenced by the early Michelsberg style. A co-occurrence of ceramic attributes (S-profiled funnel pots; "*Schlauchkrüge*"; amphora types) had first been isolated by Jonas Beran[7]. He linked the appearance of the few, mostly undecorated pots and sherds to a separate pre-Baalberge and post-Gatersleben ceramic style[8], which was controversially discussed[9] and recently labelled Schöningen or Schiepzig[10].

Ralf Gleser[11] summarised the small amount of existing sources for the time between the end of the Stichband-Rössen-Gatersleben styles at around 4400 BC and the earliest occurrence of Baalberge around 3800 BC. Using available ^{14}C dates and possible synchronisations with developments in other regions, he dated Rössen III-Bischheim and classic Gatersleben to c. 4580–4350 BC, thus proposing a contemporary phase of late Rössen and Gatersleben. Gatersleben is again seen in a Lengyel tradition. In consequence, Gleser labelled this phase late Rössen/late Lengyel. The probably earlier part of this phase (4350–4100 BC) includes the subtypes Gatersleben, Kmehlen and Gröna, the later part (4100–3850 BC) consists of Beran's Schiepzig group and the few Jordanow sites. In principle, this approach integrated further evidence and confirmed that the Kugelbecher/late Rössen and the late Lengyel elements typologically resulted in a combined style, as already argued in the above-mentioned correspondence analysis[12]. In consequence, the chronological sequence of ceramic styles has been clarified over the last few years (Figure 1). The renewed identification of "typical" Schiepzig pottery, as well as several new radiocarbon dates associated with Salzmünde-Schiepzig elements[13], made it possible to add further details regarding pottery development. Stratigraphies and ^{14}C dates in Hundisburg-Olbetal confirmed the division of Schiepzig into two phases (Figure 2)[14]. Also, Kaufmann's manifold local subgroups[15] were identified as resulting from different degrees of Michelsberg stylistic influences (see below)[16]. In summary, a continuous influx of Rössen and Gatersleben ceramic style traditions into the northern part of central Germany is plausible, as are influences from the late Lengyel and Epi-Lengyel areas. At this time, influences from the south-east and south-west[17], as well as from the Michelsberg area, formed a multi-cultural landscape of different but related style elements.

---

5 J. Müller 2001, 95 fig. 23.
6 Kaufmann 2007; J. Müller 2001.
7 Beran 1993.
8 Beran 1993; 1998.
9 E.g. D.W. Müller 1995; Raetzel-Fabian and Furholt 2006.
10 Kaufmann 2007.
11 Gleser 2012, 64–68.
12 J. Müller 2001, 95 fig. 23.
13 Schunke and Viol 2014.
14 Schmütz 2017, 61–65.
15 Kaufmann 2007.
16 Schmütz 2017.
17 Kaufmann 2007, 368.

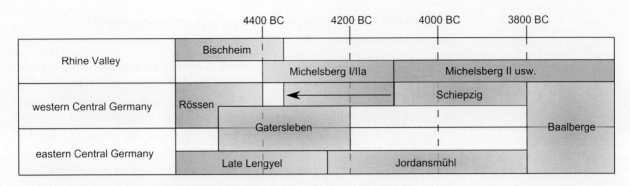

Figure 1. Sequence of pottery styles in central Germany and the Rhine valley (Schmütz 2017, 136 fig. 88).

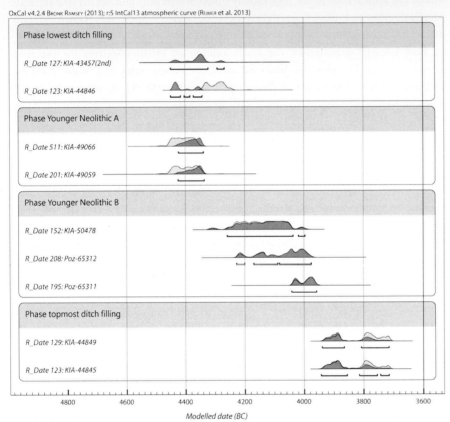

Figure 2. Absolute dating of the Younger Neolithic A (early Schiepzig) and Younger Neolithic B (late Schiepzig) in relation to the ditch stratigraphy (see Table 1 for dates; for details of modelling see Schmütz 2017, 61–69).

New archives beyond ceramics

While until the end of the twentieth century the archaeological record was mainly restricted to features with ceramic assemblages and the discourses limited to arguments about stylistic developments, new rescue excavations and research projects have furthered the study of domestic and enclosed sites of the time period under discussion. Exemplified by the settlement at Dresden, Leubnitz-Neurosta[18] and the sites of Salzmünde-Schiepzig[19] and of Hundisburg-Olbetal[20] aspects of fortification, houses, burial rites, storage facilities, subsistence economies and other aspects of daily life could be reconstructed in more detail.

---

18   Brestrich 2013; Herbig 2013.
19   Meller and Friederich 2014.
20   Müller and Rinne 2012; Schmütz 2017.

The three sites mentioned above provide new evidence that aids in closing the archaeological gap in different areas of the Mittelelbe-Saale region. Furthermore, supra-regional phenomena become visible. These are linked to the economic field of practice (new storage techniques) and the social field of practice (delimiting domestic space through early enclosures). The results of the excavation from Hundisburg-Olbetal can shed light on both these aspects.

Hundisburg-Olbetal, 4300–4100 BC

Located c. 1 km south of the boundary between the moraine landscape of the Altmark and the fertile loess soils of the Magdeburger Boerde in Saxony-Anhalt, the enclosure of Hundisburg-Olbetal is situated on a loess plateau with parabrown and chernozem soils. The causewayed enclosure (94–95 m in diameter) lies at the terrace edge about 20 m above the valley bottom, where the small river Olbe flows. The Olbe bisects the extensive loess area of the Magdeburger Boerde from north to south and 400 m further on drains into the west–east-flowing river Beber. The Beber marks the natural division between the glacial soils in the north and the loess soils in the south and flows into the river Elbe.

Research at Hundisburg-Olbetal was conducted within the framework of the DFG priority programme SPP 1400 "Early Monumentality and Social Differentiation"[21], starting with a geomagnetic prospection in 2009. The outcome of this first survey, combined with the preliminary report and the first results for the excavation of 2010, were published by Müller and Rinne[22]. The second excavation campaign followed in 2011. Final survey and excavation results were published by Schmütz[23]. Archaeobotanical, palaeopedological and archaeozoological investigations were integrated into the project[24].

Younger Neolithic features include the ditches of an enclosure and different types of pits, as well as "cultural layers". In the longitudinal trench (1770 m²), 49 m of intersecting ditches and 14 pits were excavated (Figure 3). Palaeopedological analysis confirmed that at least about 4750 tons of soil eroded due to prehistoric activities[25]. In consequence, a reduction in the depth of all features by at least 30 cm has to be taken into account.

The enclosure

The Younger Neolithic enclosure consists of five ditches which are associated with Schiepzig pottery (Figure 3). They encircle an area of 3.2 ha and their maximum length is 1.1 km. All five ditches are V-shaped. They are cut into the natural glacial sands underneath the loess layers. The inner enclosure (enclosure 1) consists of the two ditches No. 2 and No. 3. The three ditches (Nos 5, 6 and 7) of the outer enclosure (enclosure 2) increase in depth from west to east. The shallowest ditch is No. 5, which is closest to the central area.

The simultaneity of the five ditches can be deduced from the fact that they do not intersect each other and seem to reference each other. The stratigraphic

---

21 http://www.monument.ufg.uni-kiel.de
22 Müller and Rinne 2012.
23 Schmütz 2017.
24 Bönke et al. 2017; Klooß and Kirleis 2012; Rinne and Bork 2017.
25 Rinne and Bork 2017.

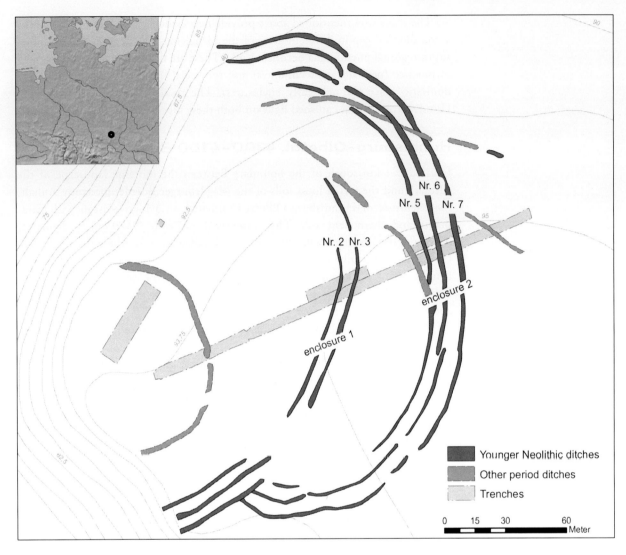

Figure 3. Hundisburg-Olbetal: the Younger Neolitihic enclosures.

analyses additionally indicate similar layers of backfill in all five ditches[26]. All of them contained four main backfill events or sets of layers (A–D), although single layers within the individual ditches may vary slightly (Figure 4). The parallel sequence of these four backfill events in all five ditches of the outer and inner enclosure suggests a simultaneous time of construction and period of use. The few artefacts retrieved from the ditches support this hypothesis. The ceramics are dated to the Younger Neolithic, more particularly the Schiepzig Group (Figure 8), with sporadic redeposited finds dated to the Early Neolithic.

The stratigraphic and typochronological analyses, combined with two radiocarbon dates from the bottom and the top layer of the backfill, indicate a date of use for the five ditches between 4350 and 4250 cal BC (see Table 1). There is pedological evidence that during this period, the ditches were used for only a short time, a couple of months or a few years, before they were deliberately infilled. At the end of the enclosure phase, the ditches were nearly completely backfilled and were only visible as small depressions on the surface[27].

26 Schmütz 2017, 59–61.
27 Schmütz 2017, 27–31.

Figure 4. Ditch section showing individual layers (1–11) and reconstructed phases of infilling (A–D) inside the Younger Neolithic ditch 6.

Context	Sample	BP	std	δ¹³C	δ¹³C std	Material	Specification
123: ditch 7 (603); fill D	KIA-44846	5435	30	25.61	0.31	charcoal	twig
127: ditch 6, fill D	KIA-43457(2nd)	5503	37	-19	0.183	animal bone	dog, collagen
129: ditch 5, fill A	KIA-44849	5010	25	22.52	0.25	fruit	cereal, indet.
142: pit, lowest layer E	KIA-44851	5060	25	25.86	0.1	fruit	cereal, indet.
152: pit, lowest layer H	KIA-50478	5315	43	-21.06	0.22	animal bone	cattle
230: pit, one layer	KIA-44856	5260	30	23.89	0.11	fruit	cereal, indet.

Table 1. ¹⁴C-dates from Schiepzig contexts from Hundisburg-Olbetal (compare Schmütz 2017, 185–186).

For the interpretation of the enclosure, the spatial layout of the ditches, their fill history and orientation are important. The inner ditches encircle an area of c. 1.8 ha, forming a semi-oval that separates the central area of the Kirschberg promontory from the rest of the plateau. A kind of entrance, 7 m wide (not excavated), is visible on the geophysical plan. The two V-shaped ditches 2 and 3 are both about 1.4 m deep and the distance between their mid-points is 6.4 m. While the water-borne sediments at the base of the ditch fills show that these features stood open for at least a few years, a second and third layer of calcareous loess are interpreted as a deliberate infilling using material from the banks that existed to the east of each ditch[28]. A similar pattern of construction and destruction was identified for the three outer ditches. This second group of ditches encircles an area of 3.2 ha. In the north and the south-west, entrance situations are visible in the geophysical plan. Furthermore, in the south this set of three ditches connects to the two-ditch system.

---

28 Rinne and Müller 2012, 355–358 fig. 8, fig. 10; Schmütz 2017, 29.

Figure 5 (above). Feature 513: one of the Younger Neolithic funnel-shaped storage pits.

Figure 6. Plan of the Younger Neolithic features showing the concentration of pits inside the enclosure.

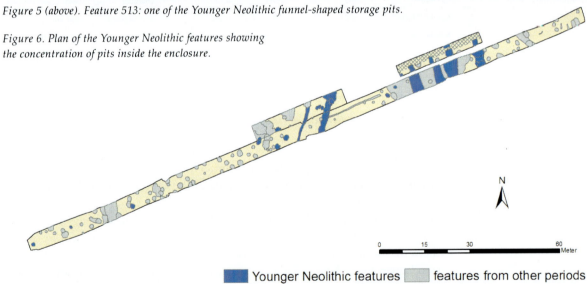

The outer three ditches are staggered in size. The innermost ditch 5 is the smallest (1.3 m wide, 1.2 m deep), followed by ditch 6 (2.3 m wide, 1.7 m deep) and the outmost ditch 7 as the largest (3 m wide, 2.15 m deep). Both for the inner and the outer part of the enclosure the smaller ditches are placed nearer the centre while the larger and deeper ditches are placed towards the outside. Archaeobotanical analysis confirmed the presence of thorny shrubs within the fills[29].

---

29 Bönke *et al.* 2017.

The decreasing depth of the ditches from outside to inside coupled with the coincidental increase of the ground elevation, the existence of banks on the inner side of the ditches, the evidence for thorny vegetation and, finally, the absence of any evidence for recutting all imply the use of the enclosure as a fortification, beside other possible functions. However, the short time during which the ditches were kept open and the deliberate destruction of the banks indicate that the site's use as a fortification was short-lived.

The storage pits

Ten truncated funnel-shaped pits, usually called beehive pits ("*Kegelstumpfgruben*" in German), were excavated at the site. Of these, some had just slightly slanting profiles, others had a marked funnel shape, such as feature 513 (Figure 5). Usually these pits are interpreted as storage pits, even if from an archaeological or archaeobotanical point of view evidence of such a hypothesis is still lacking. However, the presence of cereals and the overall design, including a funnel-like shape or even a truncated inverted bell shape, make this interpretation very plausible. Examples of truncated beehive pits are features 511, 513, 516 (Figure 5), while features 136 and 150 are more strongly funnel-shaped. The pits are 1.1–2.4 m wide at the base and 0.4–1.35 m deep[30]. In addition to the funnel-shaped pits, a few other pits yielded Schiepzig pottery. These are three through-shaped pits and one pit with a more or less flat base.

Nearly all these pits are located close to the enclosure ditches. A concentration near the inner ditches of enclosures 1 and 2 is evident (Figure 6). This area is the highest place on the plateau. Sporadic activity has also been recorded in the far western end of the longest trench. There are no features with Schiepzig finds in the whole intervening area (Figure 6). If we extrapolate the number of pits in the excavated area (1770 m²) to the whole site (32,000 m²), we can expect about 250 pits, of which about 180 would be storage pits.

Comparable, partly contemporary features are also known from Michelsberg complexes in south-west Germany, where they are also quite rare, and from a Funnel Beaker enclosure in Bohemia[31], as well as from further late Lengyel sites. In 2014, similar features were published for the site of Salzmünde-Schiepzig itself: 144 funnel-shaped pits in close vicinity to each other were documented, all of them associated with Schiepzig pottery[32]. They were dug into a loess patch at the site and are similar in shape and dimension to those from Hundisburg-Olbetal. The location of the funnel-shaped pits at Hundisburg-Olbetal and at Salzmünde-Schiepzig is also similar: in both cases, the pits were constructed close to each other in a loess area in the higher parts of the respective site[33]. Considering their potential function as storage space for grain, this location seems sensible. The risk of flooding is minimised by placing the pits in the higher areas of the site.

---

30 Schmütz 2017, 32.
31 Rinne and Müller 2012, 363.
32 Damrau *et al.* 2014, 128–129.
33 Damrau *et al.* 2014, 129.

Stichbandkeramik

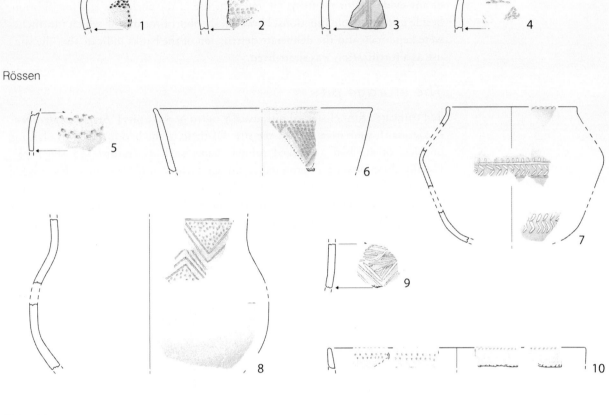

Rössen

Gatersleben

Figure 7. Examples of Stichbandkeramik, Rössen and Gatersleben pottery from Hundisburg-Olbetal. 1-11 scale 1:4, 12 scale 1:8.

Schiepzig ceramics

The site of Hundisburg-Olbetal was repeatedly used as a settlement from the LBK to the Iron Age. Artefacts from most common prehistoric ceramic styles in the research area were found on the plateau. The ceramic styles relevant to the Younger Neolithic are Rössen, Gatersleben and Schiepzig (Figures 7–8).

The Rössen finds can easily be recognised by their characteristic decoration technique consisting of double rows of incised dots that form larger ornaments. Where their profiles could be reconstructed, the vessels of the Rössen style were small beakers or bottles with round bodies. The Gatersleben style, only represented by three vessels, is reminiscent of the Rössen profile forms, only without the characteristic decorations. Just like the Gatersleben vessels, the remainder of the Younger Neolithic finds stand out because of their lack of decoration. Only

Figure 8. Examples of Schiepzig-style pottery from Hundisburg-Olbetal. 1, 3, 4, 6, 8 scale 1:8; 2, 5, 7, 9, 10 scale 1:4.

18 pieces, all of them rim sherds, were decorated. The ornaments consisted of perforated and/or everted rims with finger impressions.

The mostly undecorated Schiepzig-style vessels from Hundisburg-Olbetal have typological analogies in the assemblage from Salzmünde-Schiepzig[34]. The Schiepzig ceramic style consists essentially of the forms and decorations Beran combined into his "Schöningen group" in 1993 after he had worked with the finds from the first excavation in Salzmünde-Schiepzig[35].

Many of the characteristic forms listed by Schunke and Viol[36] were identified among the finds from Hundisburg-Olbetal, although slight variations have to be taken into account. Among the shapes represented are biconical amphorae with spherical bodies (Figure 8,4), S-profiled beakers (*e.g.* Figure 8,3), biconical

---

34   Schunke and Viol 2014.
35   Beran 1993.
36   Schunke and Viol 2014.

bowls with everted rims (Figure 8,2) and elongated, S-profiled pots with everted rims with finger impressions (Figure 8,6). Even the small cup with a distinct base (Figure 8,9) and the rounded spoon fragment (Figure 8,5) from Hundisburg-Olbetal have parallels in Salzmünde-Schiepzig.

The absolute chronology and typochronological analysis of the finds

The typochronological classification of the ceramics from Hundisburg-Olbetal was aided by a correspondence analysis combined with several radiocarbon dates. In this analysis, the Younger and Late Neolithic pit features (n=25) were examined according to the different profiles (n=12) and decorations (n=17) of the vessels they contain. In the resulting graph, a temporal sequence is visible on the x-axis, which depicts the first eigenvector (Figure 9), as is further supported by the radiometric dates.

The Younger Neolithic finds are in the positive range of the x-axis, clearly set apart from the Late Neolithic features. They are mainly influenced by the presence of amphorae, tripartite funnel beakers and bipartite bowls with funnel-shaped rims. Decorations in a strict sense are nearly non-existent. The decorations in the Younger Neolithic are normally plastic elements, ranging from short everted rims to perforated lugs, small round lugs or double lugs and distinct bases. The Late Neolithic features are defined by biconical beakers or cups with decorations typical for the Bernburg style, such as zig-zag or chequerboard decorations.

Radiocarbon dates are available for 13 out of the 25 pit features (Table 1)[37]. Transferred to the scatterplot of the correspondence analysis, they support the hypothesis of a temporal sequence on the x-axis (Figure 10). Features 136, 201, 501, 502 and 511 are at the right end of the x-axis. Pit 201 can be radiocarbon dated to the transition period from the Middle to the Younger Neolithic (KIA-49059). The date has been measured on a piece of oak charcoal, thus leaving the possibility of an old wood effect. The same can be assumed for the charcoal date from feature 511 (KIA-49066), which also dates between 4450 and 4350 cal BC. The finds from these features are mainly in the Schiepzig style. Biconical amphorae with spherical bodies and elongated, S-profiled pots with everted rims with finger impressions, two of the leading forms of the Schiepzig style, were recovered from these two early features. Additionally, rim sherds from large storage vessels with short everted rims and the small cup were found here. The vessel profiles and some other attributes are very reminiscent of the prior Rössen or Gatersleben style, but the combination of the different characteristics allows us to assign the assemblage to the Schiepzig style. Interestingly, two of the overall very rare finds that indicate possible links to the Michelsberg phenomenon were found in feature 501. The two vessels in question are a bipartite miniature beaker with a funnel-shaped rim and the only fragment of a spoon from Hundisburg-Olbetal, still showing the rudiment of a handle (Figure 8,5). The spoon also has a possible parallel among the finds from Salzmünde-Schiepzig[38]. In conclusion, an early phase of the Schiepzig ceramic style is present in Hundisburg-Olbetal, whose ceramics display typological similarities to the prior Middle Neolithic styles and a possible influence from the Michelsberg complex to the south-west. The

Figure 9 (opposite page). Pottery shapes and decoration: correspondence analysis of the Late and Younger Neolithic pit assemblages (first eigenvector 21.73 %, second eigenvector 11.06 %).

Figure 10 (opposite page). Pottery shapes and decoration: correspondence analysis of the Late and Younger Neolithic pit assemblages with associated radiocarbon dates (see Table 1).

---

37 See Schmütz 2017, 185–187.
38 Schunke and Viol 2014, fig. 3,5.

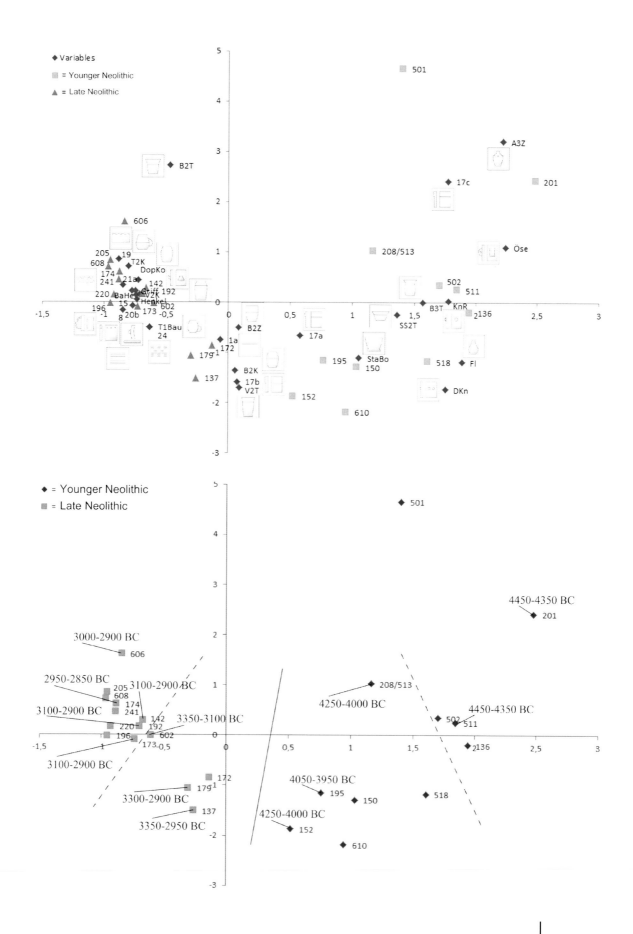

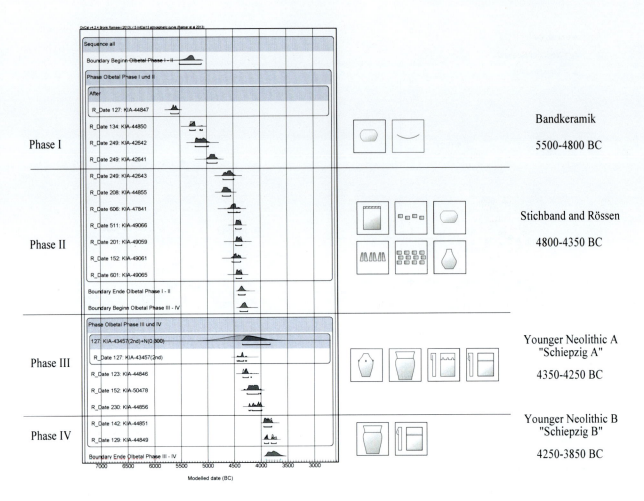

Figure 11. The phasing of Hundisburg-Olbetal, showing Middle and Younger Neolithic stylistic developments plotted against the radiocarbon chronology.

radiocarbon dates lie between 4450 and 4350 cal BC. If a possible old wood effect is taken into account, it seems justified to parallel the pit features containing early Schiepzig-style vessels with the enclosure ditches and date them both between 4350 and 4250 cal BC.

The following phase is represented by the remaining six pit features of the Younger Neolithic. Included here are three of the funnel-shaped storage pits (features 152, 195 and 208/513), which have also been radiocarbon dated. For feature 152 a goat or sheep bone (Poz-65305) and a cattle bone (KIA-50478) have been sampled. Both results date the feature to the period between 4250 and 4000 cal BC. Feature 208/513 has also been sampled multiple times and the date obtained from a cattle bone (Poz-65312) falls between 4250 and 4000 cal BC. Two samples have been taken from feature 195; a pig bone dates the feature to the period between 4050 to 3950 cal BC. It is noticeable that all features from this phase have very few finds. An explanation for this might be that these pits were used for storing cereals and not for the disposal of rubbish. The vessels from this phase are mainly large storage vessels with short everted rims and squatter S-shaped beakers with everted rims and round lugs on the shoulder. Where this feature could be observed, most of the vessels had distinct bases.

The pit features from the second phase with Schiepzig-style ceramics can be dated to the period between 4250 and 3950 cal BC. This corresponds with a radiocarbon date from an accumulation layer stratigraphically above the previously backfilled ditches, which dates between 3950 and 3850 cal BC (KIA-44849). In consequence, in Hundisburg-Olbetal Schiepzig types could clearly be associated with two chronological sub-phases.

The phasing of Hundisburg-Olbetal

The analysis of features and artefacts from the site has revealed nine phases of use, from the Early Neolithic to the Later Bronze Age. Three of these phases (Figure 11) are relevant to our time frame at the end of the fifth millennium BC[39].

Hundisburg-Olbetal Phase II

The second phase of the site dates to the period between c. 4800 and 4350 cal BC and is represented by the Stichbandkeramik, Rössen and Gatersleben ceramic styles. The finds from at least the first two styles are easily recognisable because of their characteristic decorations and decoration techniques. Defining activity areas for this phase is difficult due to the lack of features and the fact that finds were found in secondary contexts in nearly all areas of the site.

Hundisburg-Olbetal Phase III (Schiepzig 1)

This phase covers the early Younger Neolithic part of the typochronological sequence and is the time during which the enclosure was in use, between 4350 and 4250 cal BC. It is associated with the characteristic early forms of the Schiepzig style, *i.e.* S-shaped pots with everted rims with finger impressions and biconical amphorae with spherical bodies. The stratigraphy and pedological analyses have shown that the ditches of enclosures 2 and 3 were used for a short time during this phase and then purposefully infilled. Most of the activities in this time period took place in the area around the ditches.

Hundisburg-Olbetal Phase IV (Schiepzig 2)

Phase IV of Hundisburg-Olbetal covers the second part of the Younger Neolithic, following the typochronological analyses. This phase is also associated with the Schiepzig style. Three of the funnel-shaped storage pits were dated to the period between 4250 and 3850 cal BC. The dominant vessel form seems to be the large storage vessel with short everted rim. An occupation layer that lies stratigraphically above the enclosure ditches also dates to this phase.

Subsistence economy

Only a few animal bones from Hundisburg-Olbetal III and IV could be identified to species[40]. Of the 29 identified bones 18 belong to cattle, two to dogs, three to roe deer, two to red deer, three to sheep/goat and two to rodents. The assemblage of charred crop remains for the Schiepzig phase (n=300; 295 l sampled) can be considered as representative[41]. Emmer (*Triticum diccocum*; 76 %) and einkorn (*Triticum monococcum*; 20 %) dominate the crop spectrum, whereas barley (*Hordeum vulgare*; 2 %) and naked wheat (*Triticum aestivum/durum*; 2 %) are

---

39 Schmütz 2017.
40 Schmütz 2017, 74–75.
41 Klooß and Kirleis 2012.

rarely observed. In general, the crop spectrum corresponds to what is known from the central European loess areas from the Early to the Final Neolithic. At Dresden, Leubnitz-Neuostra, another Schiepzig site, a similar spectrum was observed[42]. Sickle gloss and quern fragments from Schiepzig contexts at Hundisburg further emphasise the agrarian character of the economy[43].

Interpretation

The careful and detailed analysis of archaeological features and artefacts at Hundisburg-Olbetal[44] has identified a primarily domestic site with characteristic Schiepzig pottery, which existed c. 4350–3850 BC. While the enclosure and 11 pits of different kinds belong to phase Schiepzig 1 (4350–4100 BC), three funnel-shaped pits belong to Schiepzig 2 (4100–3850 BC).

Apparently, around 4350 BC the site was fortified with fives ditches and banks, which enclosed an area of 3.4 ha. Probably due to erosion, no traces of houses or huts could be recognised. On the one hand, pits, especially possible storage pits, indicate the significance of an agrarian subsistence economy, which is visible in a cereal spectrum typical for the loess belt and in the dominance of cattle, but on the other hand human impact was still relatively small, as tell-tale colluvial processes, for instance, are lacking. The immense fortification with V-shaped ditches lasted only for a few years, but occupation continued afterwards for at least another 12 generations. In sum, we are dealing with the earliest Younger Neolithic enclosures of central Germany, which existed at the same time as early Michelsberg enclosures in other regions.

Michelsberg influence on Schiepzig

The earliest Michelsberg enclosures in Germany are situated in the west and south-west along the Rhine valley (Figure 12). They belong to phase Michelsberg I (Figure 10), the beginning dating to c. 4400 BC[45]. With an absolute date of c. 4350–4250 cal BC for the enclosure phase of Hundisburg-Olbetal, the site dates to the beginning of Michelsberg II at the latest. In the early Michelsberg, the idea of building enclosures reached the central German low mountain ranges from the south, but did not reach into the northern part of the north German lowlands. However, Geschwinde and Raetzel-Fabian[46] already showed that there is a Michelsberg influence on the area north of the Harz Mountains, even if enclosures are missing. These authors suggest an area of overlap where both Michelsberg and Baalberge styles were present. They date this incorporation of the northern Harz foreland to the period between 4200 and 4000 BC.

One possible route from the Rhine valley to the north of the Harz Mountains suggested by Geschwinde and Raetzel-Fabian follows the river valleys and passes the enclosures of Bergheim, Northeim, Einbeck and Urbach. The fragment of a tulip beaker from Haldensleben "Südhafen" proves the presence of Michelsberg

---

42 Herbig 2013.
43 Schmütz 2017, 55–58.
44 Schmütz 2017.
45 E.g. Gleser 2012, 83.
46 Geschwinde and Raetzel-Fabian 2009, 204–206, fig. 153.

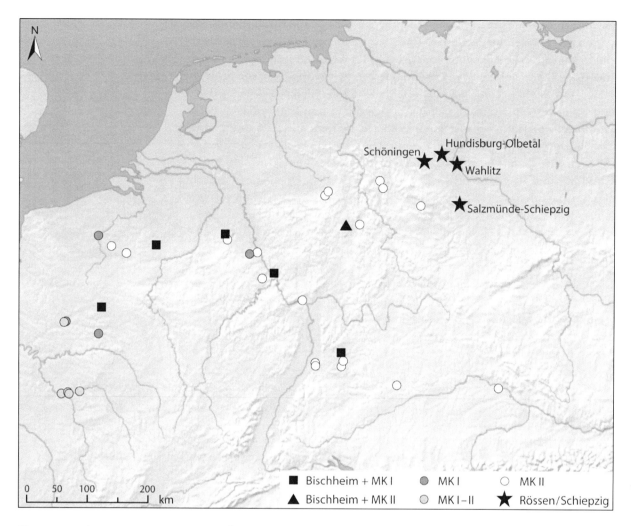

Figure 12. Early Michelsberg enclosures (after Geschwinde and Raetzel-Fabian 2012; Seidel 2008) with the addition of the secure and possible Schiepzig enclosures discussed in the text. MK = Michelsberg phase.

pottery close to Hundisburg-Olbetal, even though the beaker dates to the late Michelsberg and is therefore much younger than the enclosure[47].

In sum, chronologically and geographically it seems possible that the "idea" for the construction of this kind of enclosure derives from the Michelsberg complex in the south-west or is at least influenced by it. One feature of Hundisburg-Olbetal is unusual, however: the number and arrangement of the ditches. A total number of five ditches could otherwise only be observed at Salzkotten-Oberntudorf. All other enclosures of the early Younger Neolithic consist of one, two or rarely three ditches[48]. The construction sequence of adding two ditches to an existing enclosure with three ditches is also unusual, but a similar sequence is known from Bruchsal "Aue" in Baden-Württemberg[49].

The typological similarities between some of the characteristic shapes of the Schiepzig style and the vessels from the Michelsberg complex are evident. Beran concluded his description of the Schiepzig style with the statement that the integration of these finds into the Michelsberg complex is just a matter of

---

47 Schröter 2012, 54.
48 Schmütz 2017, 131–134.
49 Seidel 2013, 208 fig. 2.

how one understands the culture concept[50]. The close similarity in the ceramic styles of these two groups is evident. The biconical bowls with funnel-shaped rims and decorated carinations, alongside the everted rims with finger impressions, are two obvious parallels that make a connection between Michelsberg and Schiepzig styles highly likely. In consequence, the terminological difference is mainly due to research history and divergent traditions in describing local and regional variance.

Another observation that points to contacts between the Schiepzig and the Michelsberg group is the clustered construction of funnel-shaped storage pits. The eponymous site of Salzmünde-Schiepzig is a prime example, with 144 funnel-shaped pits in a 60 x 50 m area. The funnel-shaped pits were dug into the solid loess, where this sort of construction is actually stable[51]. It has already been pointed out that comparable features were also found at Hundisburg-Olbetal. Areas with many funnel-shaped pits in close vicinity to each other are rather rare on Michelsberg sites, but this may be more dependent on the duration of site use than on any other factors. About 300 storage pits were excavated at the Michelsberg site of Klingenberg near Heilbronn, where settlement activities date between Michelsberg phases II and IV[52]. These pits span 200 to 300 years. This corresponds to the results from Salzmünde-Schiepzig, where the radiocarbon dates indicate a similar time to achieve such a high number of storage pits. Thus, funnel-shaped pits with their characteristic shape and probable primary function as storage pits are present in both Schiepzig and Michelsberg contexts.

Also known from both areas is the secondary use of pits for burial purposes. There is currently a controversy concerning the depositional processes associated with human remains in Michelsberg storage pits, but several authors are arguing that these were placed there deliberately as burials[53]. Burials in funnel-shaped pits are also known from the site of Salzmünde-Schiepzig: nearly all individuals associated with the Schiepzig phase have been buried in a storage pit[54]. Jeunesse[55] has already remarked that this form of burial is common in south-west, south-east and central Europe and not a unique feature of the Michelsberg. Nevertheless, in non-Michelsberg areas this burial type exists alongside other burial practices, while in the Michelsberg area it is the only attested practice.

Combining these observations, Michelsberg influences in the early Younger Neolithic north of the Harz Mountains are obvious. The numerous similarities in the ceramic styles and the digging of clusters of funnel-shaped storage pits later used as burial places indicate contact and cultural interchange over a huge area. The new radiocarbon dates from Salzmünde-Schiepzig and Hundisburg-Olbetal suggest that the Schiepzig style emerged between c. 4350 and 4300 cal BC. This phase sees the earliest connection between the Mittelelbe-Saale region and Michelsberg.

Thus, the Schiepzig ceramic style is a combination of a continuous development from Middle Neolithic traditions (*e.g.* Rössen, Lengyel, possibly Gatersleben) and new influences from the Michelsberg complex, coming from the south-west. The more or less contemporary Jordanow style is a mixture of the same Middle Neolithic traditions with a distinct influence from the south-east

---

50   Beran 1998, 76.
51   Damrau *et al.* 2014, 128.
52   Seidel 2010, 85.
53   Jeunesse 2010; Lichardus 1998.
54   Damrau *et al.* 2014, 123.
55   Jeunesse 2010.

Figure 13. Reconstruction drawing of Schiepzig phase 1 at Hundisburg-Olbetal (S. Beyer).

associated with the Epi-Lengyel complex. Typological differences in the material culture of the Schiepzig group as documented at the sites of Schöningen, Eilsleben and Salzmünde-Schiepzig could be the effect of different levels of interaction with the Michelsberg and other groups. This would lead to several local styles that can all be combined and described as the Schiepzig style.

Many researchers have already noted that the current material basis for these highly detailed typological and chronological analyses is unfortunately rather poor[56]. A re-analysis of the undecorated pottery from older excavations would probably result in an increase in Schiepzig sites and further insights into the early Younger Neolithic in the northern part of central Germany.

Conclusion

In this paper, the absolute chronology and cultural context for the northern part of central Germany's Younger Neolithic has been outlined. The Younger Neolithic phases of the newly excavated enclosure of Hundisburg-Olbetal have been presented, including a brief description of the development of Younger Neolithic Michelsberg enclosures in general.

Hundisburg-Olbetal is associated with Schiepzig-style pottery and fits into the general development of this type of enclosures. With the site being dated to the archaeological "gap" after the transition from the Middle to the Younger Neolithic,

---

56   Gleser 2012, 63.

it belongs to the early phase of this enclosure phenomenon. Radiocarbon dates from Salzmünde-Schiepzig and Hundisburg-Olbetal indicate that the Schiepzig style is an early independent part of a new cultural and social formation at the beginning of the Younger Neolithic. Nevertheless, Michelsberg influences are also visible, on the one hand in distinct typological similarities of Schiepzig and Michelsberg pottery, on the other hand in funnel-shaped storage pits in both Schiepzig and Michelsberg contexts. Even the burials in these pits, regular or not, are a sign for shared practices in the ritual sphere. In addition, a continuation of Middle Neolithic (both Rössen and Lengyel) traditions is also observed, for instance in several typological characteristics of amphorae or in bottles that are reminiscent of the Rössen or Gatersleben style.

The existence of enclosures in central Germany during the later Middle Neolithic, before 4350 BC, is still controversial. Two Middle Neolithic sites are possible candidates[57], Schöningen and Wahlitz (Figure 12). Both presumably have a Schiepzig phase as well[58]. A re-analysis of the assemblages from these sites (and possibly several others) would probably reveal undecorated Schiepzig-style ceramics that had previously gone unnoticed. Thus there is the potential to discover more sites like Salzmünde-Schiepzig and Hundisburg-Olbetal (Figure 13) which could close the archaeological gap at the end of the fifth millennium BC. But if these sites date earlier, the general picture of an origin of the "enclosure phenomenon" in central and western France[59] has to be re-thought.

References

Beran, J. 1993. *Untersuchungen zur Stellung der Salzmünder Kultur im Jungneolithikum des Saalegebietes. Beiträge zur Ur- und Frühgeschichte Mitteleuropas*. Wilkau-Hasslau.

Beran, J. 1998. Die Michelsberger Fundgruppe in Mitteldeutschland. In J. Biel, H. Schlichterle, H. Strobel and A. Zeeb (eds), *Die Michelsberger Kultur und ihre Randgebiete — Probleme der Entstehung, Chronologie und des Siedlungswesens. Materialhefte zur Archäologie in Baden-Württemberg 43*, 73–84. Stuttgart.

Bönke, L., Nelle, O. and Rinne, C. 2017. Anthrakologische Untersuchungen der ausgeschlämmten Makroreste aus Hundisburg-Olbetal. In K. Schmütz, *Die Entwicklung zweier Konzepte? Großsteingräber und Grabenwerke bei Haldensleben-Hundisburg. Frühe Monumentalität und soziale Differenzierung 12*, 165–170. Bonn.

Brestrich, W. 2013. Die Grabung auf dem „Pfaffenberg" in Dresden, Leubnitz-Neuostra (DD-80). Ein Vorbericht und Beitrag zum Spätlengyel-Horizont im oberen Elbtal Sachsens. *Arbeits- und Forschungsberichte zur Sächsischen Bodendenkmalpflege 53/54*, 9–65.

Damrau, C., Egold, A. and Viol, P. 2014. Bestattungen der Schiepziger Gruppe. In H. Meller and S. Friederich (eds), *Salzmünde-Schiepzig — ein Ort, zwei Kulturen: Ausgrabungen an der Westumfahrung Halle (A 143). Archäologie in Sachsen-Anhalt Sonderband 21*, 122–163. Halle (Saale).

Geschwinde, M. and Raetzel-Fabian, D. 2009. *EWBSL: eine Fallstudie zu den jungneolithischen Erdwerken am Nordrand der Mittelgebirge*. Rahden.

---

57 Meyer and Raetzel-Fabian 2006.
58 Beran 1998; Schmütz 2017.
59 Klassen 2014.

Gleser, R. 2012. Zeitskalen, stilistische Tendenzen und Regionalität des 5. Jahrtausends in den Altsiedellandschaften zwischen Mosel und Morava. In R. Gleser and V. Becker (eds), *Mitteleuropa im 5. Jahrtausend vor Christus — Beiträge zur Internationalen Konferenz in Münster 2010*, 35–105. Berlin.

Herbig, C. 2013. Hasel- und Wassernüsse. Archäobotanische Untersuchungen auf dem „Pfaffenberg" in Dresden, Leubnitz-Neuostra (DD-80). *Arbeits- und Forschungsberichte zur Sächsischen Bodendenkmalpflege* 53/54, 65–77.

Jeunesse, C. 2010. Die Michelsberger Kultur — eine Kultur ohne Friedhöfe. In Badisches Landesmuseum Karlsruhe (eds), *Jungsteinzeit im Umbruch: die „Michelsberger Kultur" und Mitteleuropa vor 6000 Jahren. Katalog zur Ausstellung im Badischen Landesmuseum Karlsruhe 20.11.2010–15.5.2011*, 90–95. Darmstadt.

Kaufmann, D. 2007. „Schöninger", „Schiepziger" oder „Salzmünder Gruppe"? Neue ^{14}C-Daten zum Übergang vom älteren zum jüngeren Mittelneolithikum in Mitteldeutschland. *Archäologisches Korrespondenzblatt* 37, 365–378.

Klassen, L. 2014. *Along the road. Aspects of causewayed enclosures in south Scandinavia and beyond*. Aarhus.

Klooß, S. and Kirleis, W. 2012. Die verkohlten Pflanzenreste aus dem mehrperiodigen Grabenwerk Hundisburg-Olbetal bei Haldensleben, Bördekreis, Sachsen-Anhalt. In M. Hinz and J. Müller (eds), *Siedlung — Grabenwerk — Großsteingrab. Frühe Monumentalität und soziale Differenzierung 2*, 377–382. Bonn.

Kroitzsch, K. 1973. *Die Gaterslebener Gruppe im Elb-Saale-Raum. Neolithische Studien 2*. Halle.

Lichardus, J. 1998. Die Michelsberger Kultur strukturell gesehen. In J. Biel, H. Schlichterle, H. Strobel and A. Zeeb (eds), *Die Michelsberger Kultur und ihre Randgebiete — Probleme der Entstehung, Chronologie und des Siedlungswesens. Kolloquium, Hemmenhofen. Materialhefte zur Archäologie in Baden-Württemberg 43*, 261–275. Stuttgart.

Meller, H. and Friederich, S. (eds) 2014. *Salzmünde-Schiepzig — ein Ort, zwei Kulturen: Ausgrabungen an der Westumfahrung Halle (A 143). Archäologie in Sachsen-Anhalt Sonderband 21*. Halle/Saale.

Meyer, M. and Raetzel-Fabian, D. 2006. Neolithische Erdwerke in Mitteleuropa. Ein Überblick. www.jungsteinsite.de (article published 15h of December 2006).

Müller, D.W. 1995. Die mitteldeutschen Schlauchkrüge — eine rätselhafte Formengruppe. *Jahresschrift für Mitteldeutsche Vorgeschichte* 77, 159–175.

Müller, J. 2001. *Soziochronologische Studien zum Jung- und Spätneolithikum im Mittelelbe-Saale-Gebiet (4100–2700 v. Chr.): Eine sozialhistorische Interpretation prähistorischer Quellen. Vorgeschichtliche Forschungen 21*. Rahden.

Ostritz, S. 2000. *Untersuchungen zur Siedlungsplatzwahl im Mitteldeutschen Neolithikum. Beiträge zur Ur- und Frühgeschichte Mitteleuropas 25*. Weißbach.

Raetzel-Fabian, D. and Furholt, M. 2006. Frühbadener Elemente im Neolithikum Mitteldeutschlands: "Die Schöninger Gruppe". *Archäologisches Korrespondenzblatt* 36, 347–358.

Rinne, C. and Bork, H.-R. 2017. Bodenkundliche Untersuchungen zur Fundplatzentwicklung auf dem Kirschberg am Olbetal. In K. Schmütz, *Die Entwicklung zweier Konzepte? Großsteingräber und Grabenwerke bei Haldensleben-Hundisburg. Frühe Monumentalität und soziale Differenzierung 12*, 171–182. Bonn.

Rinne, C. and Müller, J. 2012. Grabenwerk und Großsteingräber in einer Grenzregion. Erste Ergebnisse des Projektes Haldensleben-Hundisburg. In M. Hinz and J. Müller (eds), *Siedlung — Grabenwerk — Großsteingrab. Frühe Monumentalität und soziale Differenzierung 2*, 347–375. Bonn.

Schmütz, K. 2017. *Die Entwicklung zweier Konzepte? Großsteingräber und Grabenwerke bei Haldensleben-Hundisburg. Frühe Monumentalität und soziale Differenzierung 12*. Bonn.

Schroeter, J. 2012. Ein Tulpenbecherfragment der Michelsberger Kultur. *Archäologie in Sachsen-Anhalt* Sonderband 17, 53–55.

Schunke, T. and Viol, P. 2014. Die „Schiepziger Gruppe" — eine Fundlücke wird gefüllt. In H. Meller and S. Friederich (eds), *Salzmünde-Schiepzig — ein Ort, zwei Kulturen: Ausgrabungen an der Westumfahrung Halle (A 143). Archäologie in Sachsen-Anhalt* Sonderband 21, 113–121. Halle (Saale).

Seidel, U. 2010. Satelliten der Erdwerke? Die unbefestigten Siedlungen der Michelsberger Kultur. In Badisches Landesmuseum Karlsruhe (eds), *Jungsteinzeit im Umbruch: die „Michelsberger Kultur" und Mitteleuropa vor 6000 Jahren. Katalog zur Ausstellung im Badischen Landesmuseum Karlsruhe 20.11.2010– 15.5.2011*, 82–87. Darmstadt.

Seidel, U. 2013. Das „Michelsberger Erdwerk" von Bruchsal „Aue" — ein Platz vielfältiger Aktivitäten. In H. Meller (ed.), *3300 BC. Mysteriöse Steinzeittote und ihre Welt*, 207–213. Mainz.

The jadeitite-omphacitite and nephrite axeheads in Europe

The case of the Czech Republic

Antonín Přichystal, Josef Jan Kovář,

Martin Kuča and Kateřina Fridrichová

Abstract

Polished stone tools made of jadeitite-omphacitite and nephrite represent probably the most prestigious goods of the European Neolithic before the spread of copper artefacts. This extraordinary status was derived from the high quality of both the stone raw materials and their unique appearance and rare occurrence. Today, thanks to extensive pan-European research and important finds from the last decades, we have a lot of information about jadeitite-omphacite tools in prehistoric Europe. They originate in the western Alps (in the first place from the Mont Viso Massif, Piemonte, NW Italy) and they are disseminated over an impressive distance of about 1500 km. The second group of these prestige artefacts, nephrite axeheads, played an important social and economic role in different parts of Europe, *e.g.* the Balkan Peninsula, Switzerland and the eastern part of central Europe. In this region, especially in the present-day Czech Republic, there is a significant difference in the distribution of these artefacts between Bohemia in the west and Moravia in the east of the Czech Republic.

Zusammenfassung: Beilklingen aus Jadeitit-Omphacitit und Nephrit in Europa: Das Beispiel der Tschechischen Republik

Vor der Verbreitung von Kupfer waren geschliffene Steingeräte aus Jadeitit-Omphacitit und Nephrit die wohl prestigeträchtigsten Artefakte des europäischen Neolithikums. Diesen außerordentlichen Stellenwert verdanken sie ihrer hohen Qualität als Rohmaterial, ihrem einzigartigen Aussehen und ihrer Seltenheit. Dank extensiver europaweiter Forschungen und wichtiger Neufunde der letzten Jahrzehnte verfügen wir heute über eine Vielzahl von Informationen zu prähistorischen Werkzeugen aus Jadeitit-Omphacitit in Europa. Das Rohmaterial stammt aus dem westlichen Alpengebiet (vor allem aus dem Massiv des Monte Viso, Piemont, im Nordwesten Italiens) und wurde über beeindruckende Distanzen von etwa 1500 km verbreitet. Die zweite Gruppe dieser Prestigegüter, Beilklingen aus Nephrit, spielte in verschiedenen Regionen Europas eine wichtige soziale und wirtschaftliche Rolle, z.B. auf der Balkanhalbinsel, in der Schweiz und im östlichen Mitteleuropa. In dieser Region, vor allem im Gebiet der heutigen

Tschechischen Republik, lässt sich ein klarer Unterschied in der Verbreitung dieser Artefakte zwischen Böhmen im Westen und Mähren im Osten verzeichnen.

Introduction

Nephrite and jadeitite-omphacitite artefacts have always been considered prestige goods. This fact is corroborated by their widespread occurrence all over Europe. Their unique position is due to both their composition as raw material and the attractive appearance of the finished goods. As raw materials, their fine-grained composition enables precise polishing and therefore transformation into desired shapes; the quality is unparalleled by any other contemporary material or technique. A limited supply of these materials also contributes to the prestige of these artefacts, as does their rare occurrence.

Although these two materials are almost similar in their appearance and usage, they are two different rocks. In fact, it is possible to differentiate between nephrite and jadeitite-omphacitite on several levels. They differ in their petrography, origin and occurrence. Jadeite is an alkaline pyroxene ($NaAlSi_2O_6$), and a rock predominantly composed of this silicate mineral is called jadeitite. Similarly, a rock in which a slightly different pyroxene omphacite prevails is called omphacitite[1], but in papers from the end of the nineteenth century and the first half of the twentieth century this mineral was called chloromelanite. Microprobe analyses revealed that individual pyroxene grains in such rocks have dark cores which usually have a jadeite composition, while their lighter rims are composed of omphacite. This shows the difficulties in differentiating between jadeitite and omphacitite in some cases. On the other hand, nephrite is composed mostly of a fibrous amphibole (usually actinolite or tremolite).

Methods of identification of the material

Distinguishing between these two materials is crucial for the study of the origin and distribution of the artefacts. There are several methods of identification of the material, but because the investigation focuses on unique prehistoric tools, we have to use non-destructive methods first of all. To distinguish between jadeitite and nephrite, the most readily available method is the non-destructive X-ray diffractometry. Naturally, it is necessary to adapt the device chamber for non-powdered samples, *i.e.* for whole axeheads, the dimensions of which are 10–15 cm. The surface of the artefacts needs to be well-polished. However, both jadeitite and nephrite axeheads almost always fulfil that condition.

A determination of specific gravity is another quick and effective method. According to the literature, the specific gravity[2] of nephrites ranges from 2.9 to 3.03 g/cm³, while the specific gravity of jadeite is around 3.3 g/cm³. The specific gravity of rocks transitioning into omphacitites can exceed 3.4 g/cm³. The study of six gem-quality samples of jadeitites and omphacitites from Burma and Russia[3] yielded values of 3.33–3.37 g/cm³, the most important European natural source

---

1 $(Ca,Na)(Mg,Fe^{2+},Al)Si_2O_6$.
2 Linstow 1911.
3 Coccato *et al.* 2014.

in the Mount Viso Massif, Piemonte, Italy, confirms these results[4]. The specific gravity of the samples ranged from 3.29 to 3.42 g/cm³.

A third non-destructive method is available. This is the application of magnetic susceptibility. If the axes have similar dimensions, it is possible to measure them using the Kappameter and the obtained data do not need to be recalculated. The susceptibility of both of these materials is very low. However, there are usually slight differences. Magnetic susceptibility for typical jadeitite is less than 0.15 x 10⁻³ SI, but it rises with the higher content of omphacite to 0.42 x 10⁻³ SI. Nephrite axeheads have higher values (0.22–0.57 x 10⁻³ SI) in comparison to those of pure jadeitite. Magnetic susceptibility measurements of the first author in the area of Mount Viso also showed values from 0.05–0.09 (block of albite jadeitite) to 0.20–0.27 x 10⁻³ SI (jadeitite block destroyed by collectors), but its dark green parts yielded higher results of 0.38–0.67 x 10⁻³ SI. Pebbles of light green jadeitite without pyrite from the Po river (east of Paesana) showed magnetic susceptibility around 0.16–0.17 x 10⁻³ SI, pebbles of dark green omphacitite roughly 0.58 x 10⁻³ SI. It is evident that distinguishing reliably between jadeitite, omphacitite and nephrite is not possible using only magnetic susceptibility.

To ascertain the provenance both of the jadeitite-omphacitite and the nephrite axeheads is an even more complicated task. Currently, the most efficient non-destructive method is probably diffuse reflectance spectroradiometric analysis, as used by M. Errera and P. Pétrequin[5]. They have an extensive collection of comparative spectra not only of rocks from natural sources but also hundreds of records of jadeitite-omphacitite and nephrite axeheads from the whole of Europe. Naturally, the classical petrographic (destructive) method — the preparation of a polished thin section and its investigation using electron probe micro-analysis (EPMA) — is the most precise one because it is possible to determine the chemical composition of individual pyroxene or amphibole grains, including their central or marginal parts and accessory minerals as well. In recent years, Raman spectroscopy has become accepted as one of the most efficient methods for distinguishing different "jades"[6].

List of jadeitite-omphacitite and nephrite axeheads in the Czech Republic

Compared to Bohemia, Moravia is surprisingly rich in finds of jadeitite-omphacitite and nephrite axeheads (Figure 1). This is without a doubt the consequence of the geomorphological character of the Moravian territory — its central part is the most important corridor between the Carpathians and the Bohemian Massif, connecting the Danube area with the plains of Poland and Germany. That is why the first list of eight jadeitite axeheads from Moravia was published already at the end of nineteenth century[7]. The same number of axeheads was analysed by Schmidt and Štelcl[8] using X-ray diffractometry. Přichystal[9] could already record 11 jadeitite axeheads. The last published list, compiled within the JADE 2 project, encompasses 18 jadeitite-omphacitite axeheads and one eclogite axehead. Our

---

4 Coccato 2012, 53.
5 Errera *et al.* 2012.
6 Coccato *et al.* 2014.
7 Červinka 1898.
8 Schmidt and Štelcl 1971.
9 Přichystal 2013.

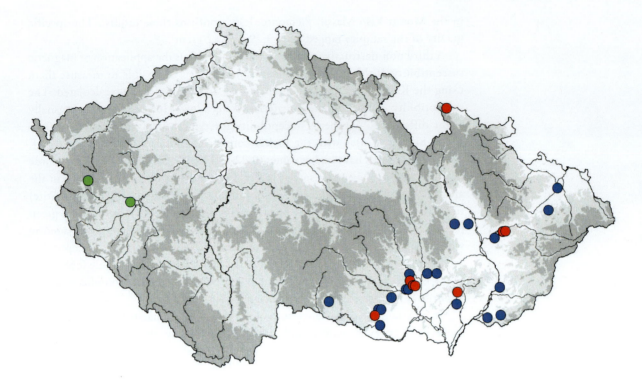

list provided here records 19 jadeitite-omphacitite axeheads studied by modern analyses and eight nephrite axeheads (five of them verified) found in Moravia. In addition, two large axeheads have also been found in Bohemia (probable imitations of jadeitite artefacts made of other rocks). We do not attempt to solve the problem of eclogite axeheads on the basis of our material, because there are more such artefacts in the Czech Republic. They are probably made partly from local eclogites, partly from eclogites of Alpine origin that occur together with jadeitite-omphacitite in the source areas of Mont Viso and the Beigua Massif. A special study is necessary to differentiate these raw materials, and we hope our contribution will show that this is well worth the effort.

Figure 1. Map of the Czech Republic with finds of jadeitite-omphacitite axeheads (blue), nephrite axeheads (red) and probable imitations of jadeitite axeheads (green).

I. Jadeitite-omphacitite axeheads

1. Brno-Líšeň, cadastral part "Na Kopaninách", found before 1889.
Basic data: flat axehead, dimensions 8.6 x 4.3 x 1.7 cm, weight 93.8 g.
Archaeological context: isolated find.
Determination: thin section[10], specific gravity 3.21 g/cm^3, non-destructive XRD, thin-section[11].
Location: Moravian Museum in Brno, No. 68 595 (up to 1973, currently not available).
References: Maška 1889; Schmidt and Štelcl 1971; Skutil 1946; Štelcl et al. 1973.

---

10 Letter by A. Arzruni, cited in Maška 1889.
11 Schmidt and Štelcl 1971.

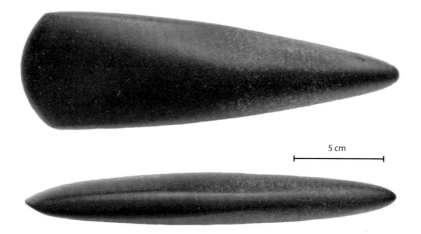

Figure 2. Large axehead from Bystročice (district Olomouc), Moravia, Czech Republic.

2. Brno-Žebětín, cadastral part "U křivé borovice", found by P. Škrdla in 2006.
Basic data: flat burnt axehead, dimensions 4.7 x 2.5 x 1.2 cm, weight 24.9 g.
Determination: magnetic susceptibility 0.01–0.03 x 10^{-3} SI, non-destructive XRD: jadeite, thin section, microprobe[12], spectroradiometric analysis[13].
Archaeological context: Lengyel (Moravian Painted Ware culture) Ib.
Location: private collection.
References: Biró et al. 2017; Přichystal et al. 2011b.

3. Bystročice, district Olomouc, cadastral part "Na dolině", found by B. Sekanina in 1929.
Basic data: large axehead (Figure 2), dimensions 22 x 6.7 x 3 cm, weight 694.2 g.
Determination: specific gravity 3.46 g/cm^3, magnetic susceptibility 0.42 x 10^{-3} SI, non-destructive microprobe[14], spectroradiometric analysis[15].
Archaeological context: isolated find.
Location: Regional Museum in Olomouc, No.7789.
References: Biró et al. 2017; Doucha 1930; Přichystal 2015; Skutil 1954.

4. Hodonice, district Znojmo, a pit in Loyd's brickyard, found by J. Palliardi in 1899.
Basic data: fragment with pointed butt, dimensions 6.3 x 4.6 x 2 cm, weight 107.4 g.
Determination: spectroradiometric analysis[16]; dimensions and weight of the studied axehead fragment from Hodonice mentioned in various papers[17] do not correspond to this artefact, described by J. Palliardi and deposited in the Moravian Museum in Brno.
Archaeological context: Lengyel I.
Location: Moravian Museum in Brno, No. 68597.
References: Biró et al. 2017; Palliardi 1889.

---

12 Přichystal et al. 2011b.
13 Carried out by M. Errera and reported in Biró et al. 2017.
14 Přichystal 2015.
15 Carried out by M. Errera and reported in Biró et al. 2017.
16 Carried out by M. Errera and reported in Biró et al. 2017.
17 Schmidt and Štelcl 1971; Štelcl et al. 1973.

5. Hovorany, district Hodonín, cadastral part "Nivky", found by D. Valentová in 1998.
Basic data: axehead, dimensions 6.6 x 4.5 x 1.9 cm, weight 127 g.
Determination: non-destructive XRD by D. Všianský (62 % jadeite, 20 % quartz, 18 % albite), magnetic susceptibility 0.08–0.11 x 10^{-3} SI.
Archaeological context: a surface find in the area of a Lengyel settlement.
Location: private collection of M. Patočka, Hovorany.
References: described for the first time in the JADE 2 project; Biró et al. 2017.

6. Jarošov, district Uherské Hradiště, cadastral part "Padělek", found before 1898.
Basic data: axehead, dimensions 5.5 x 3.7 x 0.9 cm, weight 33.4 g.
Determination: non-destructive XRD, specific gravity 3.31 g/cm^3, thin section[18].
Archaeological context: isolated find.
Location: Moravian Museum in Brno, No. 46 949 (up to 1973, currently not available).
References: Červinka 1898; Schmidt and Štelcl 1971; Štelcl et al. 1973.

7. Křepice 1, district Znojmo, field "Královka" near the Křepice hillfort, found before 1885.
Basic data: axehead, dimensions 7.1 x 3.3 x 1.6 cm, weight 69.11 g.
Determination: specific gravity[19] 3.34 g/cm^3, thin section[20].
Archaeological context: isolated find.
Location: currently unknown.
References: Maška 1888; Palliardi 1886; Skutil 1946.

8. Křepice 2, district Znojmo, in the area of the hillfort, found in 1889.
Basic data: small fragment of pointed butt, length 2 cm, weight 6.84 g.
Determination: specific gravity 3.35 g/cm^3, thin section[21].
Archaeological context: Lengyel (?).
Location: currently unknown.
References: Palliardi 1889.

9. Moravský Krumlov-Polánka, district Znojmo.
Basic data: axehead, dimensions 5.1 x 3 x 1.3 cm, weight 37.5 g.
Determination: specific gravity 3.31 g/cm^3, magnetic susceptibility 0.04 x 10^{-3} SI, non-destructive XRD by D. Všianský (96.7 % jadeite, 2.7 % omphacite, 0.6 % quartz).
Archaeological context: isolated find.
Location: Town Museum in Moravský Krumlov No.220.
References: described for the first time in the JADE 2 project; Biró et al. 2017.

10. Ostrava-Zábřeh nad Odrou, cadastral part "U korýtka" (near a ford of the Odra river), found in 1932.
Basic data: axehead (Figure 3), dimensions 10.8 x 4.5 x 1 cm, weight 114.1 g.

---

[18] Schmidt and Štelcl 1971.
[19] Maška 1888.
[20] Letter by A. Arzruni, cited in Palliardi 1886.
[21] Letter by A. Arzruni, cited in Palliardi 1889.

Figure 3. Jadeitite-omphacitite axehead from Ostrava-Zábřeh (district Ostrava), Moravia, Czech Republic.

Determination: magnetic susceptibility 0.072×10^{-3} SI, spectroradiometric analysis[22].
Archaeological context: isolated find.
Location: Ostrava Museum in Ostrava No. 61.
References: Biró et al. 2017; Moravec and Přichystal 2014.

11. Pěnčín, district Prostějov, cadastral part "Grenzsäckel", found before 1944.
Basic data: axehead, dimensions 10.6 x 5.1 x 1.7 cm, weight 146.1 g.
Determination: specific gravity 3.33 g/cm^3, non-destructive XRD, thin section[23].
Archaeological context: isolated find.
Location: Moravian Museum in Brno No. 68594 (up to 1973, currently not available).
References: Červinka 1944; Schmidt and Štelcl 1971; Skutil 1946; Štelcl et al. 1973.

12. Příbor, district Nový Jičín, found before 1877.
Basic data: axehead, dimensions 5.5 x 2.8 x 1.0 cm, weight 25.1 g.
Determination: specific gravity 3.37 g/cm^3, non-destructive XRD[24].
Archaeological context: unknown.
Location: Moravian Museum in Brno No.68593 (up to 1973, currently not available).
References: Červinka 1902; Maška 1885; Schmidt and Štelcl 1971; Skutil 1946; Štelcl et al. 1973.

13. Silůvky 1, district Brno-venkov, cadastral part "Pod kopcem", near construction of sewage plant, towards the Šatava brook, found by M. Ambrozková around 1995.
Basic data: axehead, dimensions 7.6 x 4.5 x 1.8 cm, weight 107.4 g.

---

22   Carried out by M. Errera and reported in Biró et al. 2017.
23   Schmidt and Štelcl 1971.
24   Schmidt and Štelcl 1971.

Determination: specific gravity 3.26 g/cm³, magnetic susceptibility 0.10 x 10⁻³ SI, non-destructive XRD: jadeite[25], spectroradiometric analysis[26].
Archaeological context: isolated find.
Location: private collection in Brno.
References: Biró et al. 2017; Přichystal et al. 2011b.

14. Silůvky 2, district Brno-venkov, found by M. Kuča in 2012.
Basic data: small fragment of flat pointed butt, dimensions 1.8 x 2 x 0.6 cm, weight 5.01 g.
Determination: magnetic susceptibility 0.07 x 10⁻³ SI, non-destructive XRD, spectroradiometric analysis[27].
Archaeological context: isolated find.
Location: private collection.
References: Biró et al. 2017; Přichystal 2015.

15. Tvarožná, district Brno-venkov.
Basic data: axehead, dimensions 5.7 x 3.6 x 1.3 cm, weight 54.7 g.
Determination: specific gravity 3.26 g/cm³, non-destructive XRD[28].
Archaeological context: isolated find.
Location: Moravské museum in Brno No. 68 600 (up to 1973, currently not available).
References: Červinka 1944; Schmidt and Štelcl 1971; Skutil 1946; Štelcl et al. 1973.

16. Tvarožná Lhota, district Hodonín, cadastral part "Na růsovčí", found by J. Vaculka before 1888.
Basic data: axehead without pointed butt, dimensions 8.5 x 5.0 x 1.9 cm, weight 117.8 g.
Determination: thin section[29], specific gravity 3.36 g/cm³, non-destructive XRD[30].
Archaeological context: isolated find.
Location: Moravské museum in Brno No. 68 596 (up to 1973, currently not available).
References: Maška 1888; Schmidt and Štelcl 1971; Skutil 1946; Štelcl et al. 1973.

17. Tučín, district Přerov, cadastral part "Šerý", found before 1898.
Basic data: lengthwise fragment of axehead, dimensions 8.8 x 2.2 x 1.4 cm, weight 74.6 g.
Determination: magnetic susceptibility 0.06 x 10⁻³ SI, thin section, microprobe[31]; spectroradiometric analysis[32].
Archaeological context: isolated find.
Location: Moravian museum in Brno, No. 68 599.
References: Biró et al. 2017; Červinka 1898; Přichystal 2015; Skutil 1946.

---

25 Přichystal et al. 2011b.
26 Carried out by M. Errera and reported in Biró et al. 2017.
27 Carried out by M. Errera and reported in Biró et al. 2017.
28 Schmidt and Štelcl 1971.
29 Letter by F. Berwerth, cited in Maška 1888.
30 Schmidt and Štelcl 1971.
31 Přichystal 2015.
32 Carried out by M. Errera and reported in Biró et al. 2017.

Figure 4. Nephrite axehead from Archlebov (district Hodonín), Moravia, Czech Republic.

18. Velká nad Veličkou, district Hodonín, found before 1946.
Basic data: fragment of an axehead, dimensions 5.3 x 4.4 x 1.6 cm, weight 68.6 g.
Determination: specific gravity 3.41 g/cm³, non-destructive XRD, thin section[33].
Archaeological context: isolated find.
Location: Moravské museum in Brno No. 68 598 (up to 1973, currently not available).
References: Schmidt and Štelcl 1971; Skutil 1946; Štelcl *et al.* 1973.

19. Jemnice, cadastral part "Tejnice", district Třebíč, found by L. Meduna in 1967.
Basic data: small axehead, dimensions 7.5 x 4.4 x 1.7 cm, weight 108.9 g.
Determination: non-destructive XRD by D. Všianský (98 % jadeite-omphacite, 2 % chlorite and mica), magnetic susceptibility 0.30 x 10⁻³ SI, specific gravity 3.38 g/cm³.
Archaeological context: unknown.
Location: Museum Vysočiny Třebíč.
References: Košťuřík *et al.* 1986; Mrázek 1996. The authors described it originally as nephrite based on macroscopic determination; here, it is listed for the first time as a jadeitite axehead.

II. Nephrite axeheads

1. Archlebov, district Hodonín, cadastral part "Archlebské Maliny", found by R. Muroň in 2002.
Basic data: axehead (Figure 4), dimensions 8.0 x 4.5 x 2.0 cm, weight 148.3 g.
Determination: magnetic susceptibility 0.22 x 10⁻³ SI, the same raw material as the axehead from Hlinsko determined by non-destructive XRD.
Archaeological context: a surface find in an area with artefacts of the Lengyel culture (Moravian Painted Ware culture).
Location: Museum of the Žarošice village.
References: described for the first time in this article.

---

33   Schmidt and Štelcl 1971.

Figure 5. Small nephrite axehead from Javorník (district Jeseník), Czech Silesia, Czech Republic.

2. Hlinsko u Lipníka 1, district Přerov, cadastral part "Nad Zbrušovým", Eneolithic hillfort, found in a pit during archaeological excavations by J. Pavelčík.
Basic data: small axehead, dimensions 4.5 x 3.1 x 1.0 cm, weight 26.95 g.
Determination: non-destructive XRD (82 % tremolite/actinolite, 18 % diopside), magnetic susceptibility 0.22×10^{-3} SI.
Archaeological context: Baden culture (Eneolithic).
Location: Comenius Museum in Přerov.
References: Mrázek 1996 (but his original macroscopic determination was jadeite).

3. Hlinsko u Lipníka 2, district Přerov, cadastral part "Nad Zbrušovým", Eneolithic hillfort, found during archaeological excavations by J. Pavelčík.
Basic data: fragment of an axehead.
Determination: non-destructive XRD (only tremolite/actinolite).
Archaeological context: Baden culture (Eneolithic).
Location: Comenius Museum in Přerov.
References: described for the first time in this article.

4. Javorník, district Jeseník (former district Šumperk), find circumstances unknown.
Basic data: small axehead (Figure 5), dimensions 5.8 x 2.7 x 0.6 cm, weight 18.75 g.
Determination: non-destructive XRD (only tremolite/actinolite), magnetic susceptibility 0.06×10^{-3} SI.
Archaeological context: unknown.
Location: Regional Museum in Jeseník No. 1088/63.
References: Přichystal *et al.* 2011a; 2012.

5. Plaveč, district Znojmo.
Basic data: butt fragment of not precisely identified stone tool, length about 3.5 cm.
Determination: thin section[34].
Archaeological context: Lengyel II (Moravian Painted Ware culture II).
Location: unknown.
References: Štelcl 1967.

---

34 Štelcl 1967.

6. Popůvky, district Brno-venkov, found by J. Mikulášek between 1942 and 1948.
Basic data: discoidal perforated macehead, dimensions 14.6 x 10 x 2.3 cm, weight 480 g.
Determination: according to macroscopic examination[35]; not verified.
Archaeological context: Linear Pottery culture.
Location: Moravian Museum in Brno.
References: Mrázek 1996.

7. Prštice 1, district Brno-venkov, found by J. Mikulášek in 1939–1940.
Basic data: small flat axehead, dimensions 2.8 x 2.8 x 1.1 cm, weight 16.5 g.
Determination: according to macroscopic determination[36]; not verified.
Archaeological context: Lengyel I (Moravian Painted Ware culture).
Location: Moravian Museum in Brno.
References: Mrázek 1996.

8. Prštice 2, district Brno-venkov, found in an archaeological feature during excavations by J. Mikulášek in 1939–1940.
Basic data: small hoe, length about 5 cm.
Determination: according to macroscopic determination[37]; not verified.
Archaeological context: Lengyel I (Moravian Painted Ware culture).
Location: National Museum in Prague.
References: Mrázek 1996.

III. Probable imitations of large jadeitite axeheads using other rocks in western Bohemia

1. Kříženec-Homole, village Planá near Mariánské Lázně, district Cheb; found before 1960.
Basic data: big axehead with pointed butt, dimensions 25 x 4.2 x 4.4 cm, weight 813 g.
Raw material: microdolerite[38].
Archaeological context: Michelsberg culture.
Location: West Bohemian Museum in Plzeň, inv. No. P 62959.
References: Baštová and Bašta 1989; Dobeš and Metlička 2014; Šaldová 1960; 1967.

2. Vochov, district Plzeň-sever.
Basic data: large axehead with pointed butt, dimensions 21 x 5.2 x 5.8 cm, weight 627 g.
Raw material: metabasite from Jistebsko in Jizerské hory[39].
Archaeological context: Michelsberg culture.
Location: West Bohemian Museum in Plzeň.
References: Baštová and Bašta 1989; Dobeš and Metlička 2014.

---

35   Mrázek 1996, 45.
36   Mrázek 1996, 45.
37   Mrázek 1996, 45.
38   Dobeš and Metlička 2014.
39   Dobeš and Metlička 2014.

Discussion

The territory of modern-day Moravia is comparatively rich in finds of jadeitite-omphacitite axeheads. They all share the typological feature of a triangular shape. Their butts are distinctly pointed. It is a shape typical for the Lengyel culture and is known from axeheads made of different materials found at Moravian sites, for example in Brno-Žebětín, where one jadeitite-omphacitite axehead was found, two further sites in the vicinity of Brno-Žebětín, as well as at Horákov, Kyjovice, Popůvky u Brna and two sites near Střelice u Znojma, amongst others[40]. Most of the finds mentioned were made of metabasite of the Želešice type that is found in the proximity of Brno.

There have been several handicaps in the interpretation of the distribution and the cultural role of these axeheads: the uncertain circumstances of the finds, their surface location, the polycultural nature of the sites and the fact that some of the artefacts are impossible to trace. Only the axehead from Hodonice was acquired from a reliable context — from a feature dated to Lengyel I, phase Ia[41]. The axehead from Brno-Žebětín was found during a surface survey on a site that is also dated to the Lengyel I period, phase Ib[42]. It is possible to connect some of the artefacts with some certainty with the earlier phase of the Lengyel culture (Lengyel I), specifically with phases Ia and Ib according to the relative chronology[43]. Both of these phases are chronologically concurrent according to the radiocarbon dating, falling approximately into the second quarter of the fifth millennium (6850–6450 cal BP)[44]. The connection of jadeitite-omphacitite axeheads with Lengyel I is also supported by finds from Austria, Slovakia and Hungary[45]. It corresponds very well with the maximum diffusion of the Alpine jadeitite-omphacitite axeheads in western Europe, approximately between 4600–3700 BC[46]. It is also necessary to follow the presence of jadeitite-omphacitite axeheads in different contexts because there are differently dated sites with similar finds.

The spatial distribution of the jadeite-omphacitite axeheads is linked to Moravian valleys and their edges; parts of them are concentrated in hilly areas of the Bohemian-Moravian Highland (Figure 1). Geographically, the distribution network of jadeitite-omphacitite axeheads runs south to north, from valleys in north-western Italy in the direction of Hungary, then to the Danube basin and Moravia and through the Moravian Gate to Poland. The Bohemian-Moravian Highland is the notional boundary for the spread of both the jadeitite-omphacitite and the nephrite artefacts.

Pétrequin and colleagues[47] devoted special attention to the large or oversized Alpine "jade" axeheads (meaning tools longer than 13.5 cm) and their distribution in Europe. They found almost 1800 pieces with a length between 13.5 and 46.6 cm and they believe that these long axeheads had a special value for prehistoric people as sacred things. That is why they were often deposited close to rivers, marshes, stretches of water, in front of rock shelters or isolated boulders, or at the foot of a standing stone. In the Moravian/Silesian collection there is only one such long

---

40 Cf. Kuča *et al.* 2005, fig. 16.7; Lečbychová *et al.* 2013, fig. 16.8; Salaš 1986, fig. 5.1; Trampota and Kuča 2011, fig. 17.3, 9; Vokáč 2008, 76, 207.
41 Palliardi 1889.
42 Přichystal *et al.* 2011b.
43 Čižmář *et al.* 2004.
44 Cf. Kuča *et al.* 2016.
45 Bendő *et al.* 2014; Pétrequin *et al.* 2011; Přichystal and Trnka 2001.
46 Pétrequin *et al.* 2013, 69.
47 Pétrequin *et al.* 2013.

axehead from Bystročice (length 22 cm; Figure 2) and it represents the longest "jade" tool in the eastern part of central Europe. Another one (Ostrava-Zábřeh, almost 11 cm; Figure 3) is close to the lower limit for the "oversized" category. The longest tool, that from Bystročice, was found near the Blata river and close to the Hněvotín rocky horst; similarly, the axehead from Ostrava-Zábřeh lay near an important ford crossing the Odra river (it was used for example during World War II by the Soviet and Czechoslovak armies).

The nephrite artefacts have a more restricted distribution. There are very few finds in Moravia and none in Bohemia until now. Typologically they usually do not resemble the jadeitite-omphacitite tools; however, their geographical distribution in Moravia is partly similar. Any interpretation of the distribution and chronological evaluation would be premature at this stage.

Conclusion

The polished stone tools made from nephrite and jadeite probably represent the most prestige-charged goods of the European Neolithic until the development and large-scale distribution of copper artefacts. As far as we know, all of these prestige Neolithic goods were made of European sources.

It is also possible that the importance of these prestige goods could be likened to rare resources of today, such as gold or oil. In later periods these resources were replaced by metals, which were more accessible as raw materials and easier to produce. They were also similarly exceptional in their appearance; this is possibly related to the social shift at the beginning of the fourth millennium BC.

In the past, jadeitite and nephrite artefacts have often been confused with each other due to their similar appearance. To solve this problem, the first and comparatively easy step represents the determination of specific gravity. A reliable differentiation can be achieved by investigating thin sections under a polarising microscope and using a microprobe. Unfortunately, the preparation of thin sections is a destructive method which is unacceptable for research on such precious artefacts. A very good method to reliably distinguish between jadeitite-omphacitite and nephrite tools is using a non-destructive X-ray diffractometric determination with a specially adapted X-ray diffractometer. This adaptation allows to insert and to analyse the whole artefact without causing any damage.

Our research emphasises the importance of the cooperation between archaeology and the natural sciences, in this case geology. At the moment, two distinct distribution networks of axeheads are emerging in Europe, one centred on jadeitite-omphacitite and one on nephrite. These networks and their possible social implications — for instance in terms of the high-status exchange of artefacts between elites as opposed to other models of circulation and distribution — are dependent on the exact determination of the material used for the axeheads. The relatively small sample of the artefacts in the Czech Republic already shows that the two materials tend to be mistaken for one another or indeed misidentified altogether. This, in turn, leads to the perpetuation of errors in the literature and, more crucially, to the lumping together of phenomena which, while they may be linked, must nevertheless be disentangled.

It is important to follow the development of technology and to use the least destructive methods for petrographic analysis. Only then can we gain the maximum possible amount of data and recreate as exact a picture of the past as possible.

References

Baštová, D. and Bašta, J. 1989. Osídlení západních Čech v časném a starším eneolitu. *Sborník Západočeského muzea v Plzni* 1989, 95–107.

Bendö, Z., Szakmány, G., Kasztovszky, Z., Maróti, B., Szilágyi, S., Szilágyi, V. and Biró, K.T. 2014. Results of non-destructive SEM-EDX and PGAA analyses of jade and eclogite polished stone tools in Hungary. *Archeometriai Műhely* 11, 187–206.

Biró, K., Pétrequin, P., Errera, M., Přichystal, A., Trnka, G., Zalai-Gaal, I. and Osztas, A. 2017. Des Alpes à l' Europe centrale (Autriche, République tchèque, Slovaquie et Hongrie). In P. Pétrequin, E. Gauthier and A.-M. Pétrequin (eds), *Jade. Objets-signes et interpretations sociales des jades alpins dans l'Europe néolithique*, 431–466. Besançon.

Coccato, A. 2012. *Non-destructive studies of gem quality and Neolithic jade materials*. Unpublished dissertation, Corso di Laurea Magistrale, Università degli Studi di Parma.

Coccato, A., Karampelas, S., Wörle, M., van Willigen, S. and Pétrequin, P. 2014. Gem quality and archaeological green "jadeite jade" versus "omphacite jade". In P. Ropret and J.M. Madariaga (eds), Raman in art and archaeology 2013. *Journal of Raman Spectroscopy* 45, 1260–1265.

Červinka, I.L. 1898. Otázka jadeitová a nefritová a jadeity moravské. *Věstník Klubu přírodovědného v Prostějově za rok* 1, 30–38.

Červinka, I.L. 1902. *Morava za pravěku. Vlastivěda moravská I. Země a lid, II*. Brno.

Červinka, I.L. 1944. Moravské nálezy jadeitů k otázce nefritové. *Příroda* 36, 125–128.

Čižmář, Z., Pavúk, J., Procházková, P. and Šmíd, M. 2004. K problému definování finálního stadia lengyelské kultury. In B. Hänsel and E. Studeníková (eds), *Zwischen Karpaten und Ägäis. Neolithikum und ältere Bronzezeit. Internationale Archaeologie. Studia honoraria 21. Gedenkschrift für Viera Němejcová-Pavúková*, 208–232. Rahden.

Dobeš, M. and Metlička, M. 2014. Raný eneolit v jihozápadních Čechách. *Archeologie západních Čech*, Supplement 1, 1–122.

Doucha, F. 1930. Ojedinělý nález kamenné sekyrky v Bystročicích. *Časopis Vlasteneckého spolku musejního v Olomouci* 43, 282.

Errera, M., Pétrequin, P. and Pétrequin, A.-M. 2012. Origine des jades alpins entre Provence et Adriatique. In P. Pétrequin, S. Cassen, M. Errera, L. Klassen, A. Sheridan and A.-M. Pétrequin (eds), *Jade. Grandes haches alpines du Néolithique européen. Ve et IVe millénaires av. J.-C., tome 2*, 750–821. Besançon.

Košturík, P., Kovárník, J., Měřínský, Z. and Oliva, M. 1986. *Pravěk Třebíčska*. Brno.

Kuča, M., Kazdová, E. and Přichystal, A. 2005. Sídliště staršího stupně kultury s moravskou malovanou keramikou v Brně-Žebětíně. Poznámky k fázi Ib kultury s MMK v brněnské kotlině. *Pravěk* NŘ 13, 37–89.

Kuča, M., Prokeš, L., Eskarousová, L., Kovář, J.J. and Nývltová Fišáková, M. 2016. Testing the proposed relative chronology model for the Moravian Late Neolithic using radiometric dating. In J. Kovárník (ed.), *Centenary of Jaroslav Palliardi's Neolithic and Aeneolithic relative chronology (1914–2014)*, 117–126. Hradec Králové.

Lečbychová, O., Kuča, M. and Vokáč, M. 2013. Neolitické sídliště v Popůvkách, okr. Brno-venkov – stav poznání pramenné základny k roku 2005. *Přehled výzkumů* 54, 27–45.

Linstow, O. 1911. Über Nephritegeschiebe. *Zeitschrift für Naturwissenschaften* 83, 437–444.

Maška, K.J. 1885. Sekyrka jadeitová na Moravě. *Časopis Vlasteneckého muzejního spolku v Olomouci* II, 143–145.

Maška, K.J. 1888. Příspěvky k poznání pravěku moravského Slovenska. *Časopis Vlasteneckého spolku musejního v Olomouci* X, 59–70.

Maška, K.J. 1889. Ein viertes Jadeitbeil in Mähren. *Mitteilungen der Anthropologischen Gesellschaft in Wien* 19, 42–45.

Moravec, Z. and Přichystal, A. 2014. Jadeititová sekerka ze Zábřehu nad Odrou. *Vlastivědné listy Slezska a severní Moravy* 40, 11–13.

Mrázek, I. 1996. *Drahé kameny v pravěku Moravy a Slezska*. Brno.

Palliardi, J. 1886. O jadeitové sekyrce, nalezené u Křipic na Moravě. *Časopis Vlasteneckého spolku musejního v Olomouci* III, 19–24.

Palliardi, J. 1889. Zwei neue Jadeitobjekte aus Mähren. *Mitteilungen der Anthropologischen Gesellschaft in Wien* 19, 178–180.

Pétrequin, P., Errera, M., Cassen, S., Gauthier, E., Hovorka, D., Klassen, L. and Sheridan, A. 2011. From Mont Viso to Slovakia: the two axeheads of Alpine jade from Golianovo. *Acta Archaeologica Akademiae Scientiarum Hungaricae* 62, 243–268.

Pétrequin, P., Cassen, S., Errera, M., Klassen, L., Pétrequin, A.-M. and Sheridan, A. 2013. The value of things: the production and circulation of Alpine jade axes during the 5th– 4th millennia in a European perspective. In T. Kerig and A. Zimmermann (eds), *Economic archaeology: from structure to performance in European archaeology*, 65–82. Bonn.

Přichystal, A. 2013. *Lithic raw materials in prehistoric times of eastern central Europe*. Brno.

Přichystal, A. 2015. Neolithic jadeite (jadeitite-omphacitite) axeheads in the Czech Republic and their provenance. In H. Nohálová, V. Káňa and J. Březina (eds), *21st Quaternary Conference, abstract book*, 43–44. Brno.

Přichystal, A. and Trnka, G. 2001. Raw materials of polished artefacts from two Lengyel sites in Lower Austria. *Slovak Geological Magazine* 7, 337–339.

Přichystal, A., Kovář, J.J. and Kuča, M. 2011a. Unikátní pravěká sekerka ze sbírek jesenického muzea. *Vlastivědný věstník moravský* 2011, 331–334.

Přichystal, A., Kuča, M., Kovář, J.J. and Škrdla, P. 2011b. New finds of jadeitite and nephrite axes from Moravia and Silesia. In R. Drápalová, J. Petřík, A. Přichystal and P. Valová (eds), *5th International Petroarchaeological Workshop, abstract book*, 18–19.

Přichystal, A., Kovář, J.J. and Kuča, M. 2012. A nephrite axe from the Jeseník Museum. *Časopis Slezského zemského muzea* 60, series B, 153–159.

Salaš, M. 1986. Kamenná broušená industrie z neolitického sídliště u Těšetic-Kyjovic. *Sborník prací Filozofické fakulty brněnské university* 35, series E 31, 25–48.

Schmidt, J. and Štelcl, J. 1971. Jadeites from Moravian Neolithic period. *Acta Universitatis Carolinae – Geologica* 18, No. 1–2, 141–152.

Skutil, J. 1946. Moravské nálezy jadeitových a nefritových neolitických výrobků, slezská importy. *Slezský sborník* 44, 145–156.

Skutil, J. 1954. Nález chloromelanitové sekyrky z Bystročic, okr. Olomouc. *Sborník SLUKO v Olomouci B*, 1951–1953, 177.

Šaldová, V. 1960. Dvě nová výšinná eneolitická sídliště v západních Čechách. *Archeologické rozhledy* 12, 625–627.

Šaldová, V. 1967. *Pravěk Stříbrska. Průvodce archeologickými sbírkami Vlastivědného muzea ve Stříbře*. Stříbro.

Štelcl, J. 1967. K petrografii kamenných nástrojů z některých nalezišť moravského mladšího neolitu. *Acta Musei Silesiae* 16, Series A, 143–156.

Štelcl, J., Malina, J., Schmidt, J. and Velímský, T. 1973. Petroarchaeological characteristics of jadeite artifacts of the Moravian Neolithic. *Scripta Facultatis Scientiarum Naturalium Universitatis Purkynianae Brunensis* 3, Geologia 1, 27–33.

Trampota, F. and Kuča, M. 2011. Brno-Žebětín – „Na drdi". Neolitická lokalita v kontextu Brněnska. *Sborník prací Filozofické fakulty brněnské university*, řada M 14–15, 88–112.

Vokáč, M. 2008. *Broušená a ostatní kamenná industrie z neolitu a eneolitu na jižní Moravě se zvláštním zřetelem na lokalitu Těšetice-Kyjovice*. Unpublished PhD dissertation, Masaryk University in Brno.

Disc-rings of Alpine rock in western Europe

Typology, chronology, distribution and social significance

Pierre Pétrequin, Serge Cassen, Michel Errera, Yvan Pailler, Frédéric Prodéo, Anne-Marie Pétrequin and Alison Sheridan

Abstract

In France, disc-rings made from Alpine jades and from serpentinite circulated over very long distances, as far as the Channel coast and that of Brittany. The authors offer here a typo-chronological study of these and other stone bangles, according to the types of rock used, and consider their distribution and their social significance.

Two geological source areas are identified: the Inner Alps (where disc-rings of regular shape were made, and whose rocks were the first to be exploited, from around 5300 BC at the latest) and the upper Rhine, where cobbles from the riverbed were gathered and used to make disc-rings of irregular shape from the beginning of the fifth millennium. Exactly like the circulation of the long jade adze-heads of Bégude type, that of the disc-rings of Alpine rock was underpinned by the belief systems of their users. That these objects were linked to the world of mythology is clear from the representations that were carved on monumental standing stones and on rock surfaces during the first half of the fifth millennium BC.

Zusammenfassung: Scheibenringe aus alpinen Gesteinen in Westeuropa: Typologie, Chronologie, Verbreitung und soziale Bedeutung

In Frankreich zirkulierten Armringe aus alpinen Jadegesteinen und Serpentiniten über sehr große Distanzen, teilweise bis zu den Küsten des Ärmelkanals und der Bretagne. Der vorliegende Beitrag beginnt mit einer typochronologischen Studie dieser und anderer Steinarmreifen auf Grundlage der verwendeten Rohmaterialien und geht anschließend auf ihre Verteilungsmuster und soziale Bedeutung ein. Zwei geologische Ursprungsgebiete können identifiziert werden: der inneralpine Raum (dessen lithische Materialien zuerst ausgebeutet wurden, spätestens ab etwa 5300 v. Chr., und wo regelmäßig geformte Scheibenringe hergestellt wurden) und der Oberrhein, wo aus dem Flussbett aufgelesene Gesteinsbrocken seit dem Beginn des 5. Jahrtausends v. Chr. genutzt wurden, um unregelmäßig geformte Scheibenringe herzustellen. Genau wie die Verbreitung der langen Dechselklingen aus Jadegesteinen vom Typ Bégude wurde auch die Weitergabe der Scheibenringe aus alpinen Gesteinen von den Glaubenssystemen ihrer Nutzer getragen. Dass diese Objekte mit der Welt der Mythologie verbunden sind zeigen auch die Darstellungen von Scheibenringen, die in der ersten Hälfte des 5. Jahrtausends v. Chr. auf Menhire und Felsoberflächen gemeißelt wurden.

Introduction

Schist arm-rings (bangles) of regular shape are regarded as reliable indicators of the Blicquy-Villeneuve-Saint-Germain (B-VSG) culture, dating to the first quarter of the fifth millennium BC[1]. Hundreds have been found in settlements and graves in Belgium, the Paris Basin and north-west France where they circulated in very large numbers from centres of production located on the fringes of the Armorican and Ardennes massifs. The know-how to manufacture them, however, was widespread — at least as far as the simplest versions are concerned, since these required only a small investment of time in their production. We know this because these arm-rings were not only released into circulation as finished items ready to wear, but also sometimes as raw slabs of stone or as unperforated, disc-shaped roughouts. It appears that the latter travelled as far as 200 km from their source as the crow flies[2].

In all probability, these stone bangles were mostly, if not exclusively, worn by women — but not by all women, which implies that they were a status indicator[3], not only in death (Figure 1) but also in life, to judge from the numerous fragments that have been found in settlements. It is also possible that these bangles, in common with long flint blades, had an important social value in transactions and in medium-distance exchanges within the B-VSG sphere[4].

It would appear, however, that little is known about the emergence of these schist bangles and about contemporary bangles made from other soft metamorphic rocks, as in Brittany[5]. The green-grey colour of these "pieces of jewellery" does not belong to the Linearbandkeramik tradition[6], nor does it really belong to the Cardial Impressed Ware tradition[7], where raw materials that were a white or cream colour (namely marine shells and limestone) were preferred for bangle-making. Given that the "fashion" for schist bangles was relatively short, lasting three centuries at most[8], the question remains of the origin of these green-grey bangles, and the reason for their rapid development around 5000 BC and their subsequent abandonment around the end of the first quarter of the fifth millennium. Moreover, the discovery of a hoard of five large schist bangles at Falaise (Calvados)[9] suggests that certain oversized examples had a value over and above that of a simple status marker.

In order to shed light on this question of the rise and decline in popularity of schist bangles — phenomena that have to be linked to social factors — we propose to present other models of bangle use, in this case featuring examples made from Alpine rocks[10], which have often been found associated with schist bangles in B-VSG contexts[11].

---

1 Auxiette 1989; Bonnardin 2009; Fromont 2013.
2 Fromont 2013, 627-628.
3 Bulard *et al.* 1993; Meier-Arendt 1975; Praud 2014.
4 Bostyn 1994.
5 Herbaut and Pailler 2000; Pailler 2007.
6 Bonnardin 2009.
7 Constantin and Vachard 2004; Courtin and Gutherz 1976.
8 Constantin 1999; Jeunesse 2003.
9 Fromont 2010.
10 Errera *et al.* 2012.
11 Fromont 2013; Praud 2014.

Figure 1. Tomb 1116, Longueil-Sainte-Marie/Le Barrage (Oise, France). On her right arm, the young woman wore five bangles (three of schist, two of limestone) and on her left arm, six bangles (five of schist and one of limestone). Probably Blicquy-Villeneuve-Saint-Germain culture (Bostyn et al. 2015). Excavation by Inrap, D. Maréchal. Photos: L. Petit.

The Alpine bangles were exotic in this culture, since they had been imported over long distances from the western Inner Alps or from the upper Rhine valley[12]. We hypothesise that not all bangles had the same value; their value would vary according to the relative rarity of the raw material used, the time invested in their manufacture, the distances travelled from the source and the biography of each example[13].

For the sake of clarity, in the maps that accompany this article, we have only included the bangles whose raw material has been determined analytically (through one or more of a variety of techniques: thin-section petrographic identification, X-ray diffraction analysis [XRD], spectroradiometry and macroscopic examination of diagnostic features). We have excluded other, less well documented bangles in order to avoid introducing noise and potential confusion into the distribution maps.

---

12 Pétrequin 2017.
13 Pétrequin and Pétrequin 2006; Pétrequin *et al.* 2015.

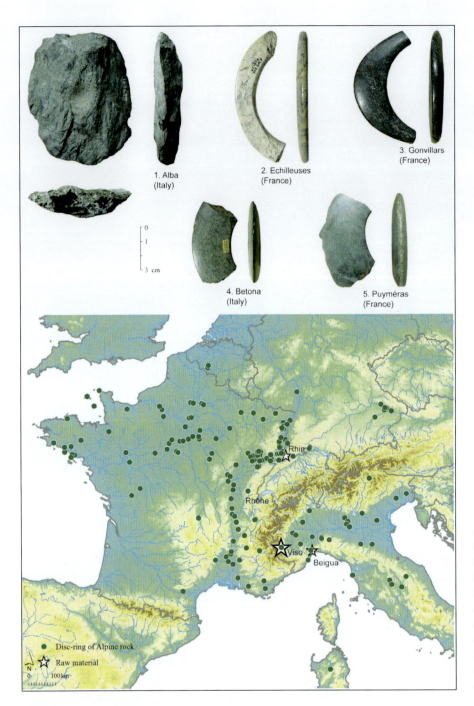

Figure 2. Distribution of communes where at least one disc-ring (of whatever type) of Alpine jade or Alpine serpentinite has been found. Photos and CAD: A.-M. and P. Pétrequin. Cartography: F. Prodéo using the base-map ESRI Data & Maps under licence MSHE Ledoux and NASA SRTM.

Regular-shaped disc-rings with a triangular-section hoop, made from jade or serpentinite

Even though some colleagues remain to be convinced[14], there can be no doubt concerning the Alpine origin of what we call "disc-rings" — thus named because they are always flat, with a hoop that is more or less broad, and because it has not been demonstrated that all had always been worn as arm-rings/bangles. Effectively, the only outcrops of jades that were exploited during the Neolithic

---

14   Fromont 2013.

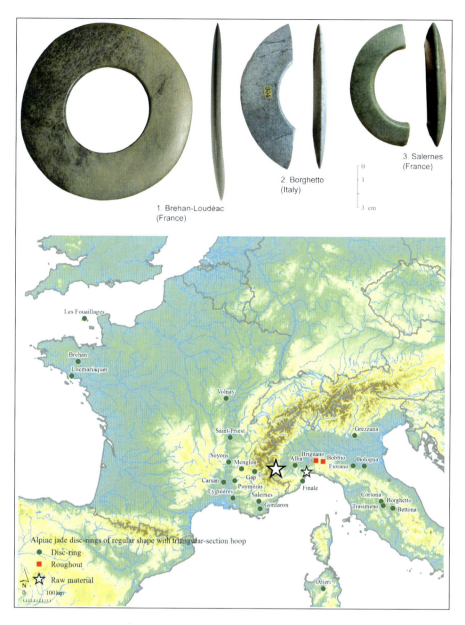

Figure 3. Distribution of communes where at least one disc-ring of regular shape with triangular-section hoop, of Alpine jade, has been found. Photos and CAD: A.-M. and P. Pétrequin. Cartography: F. Prodéo.

(namely jadeitites, omphacitites and very fine-grained eclogites) are located in the Inner Alps, in the massifs of Mont Viso and Mont Beigua[15]. Furthermore, if one considers the distribution of all the disc-rings made from jades and serpentinites (combining all the typological groups; Figure 2), it is evident that the main concentrations are those on the French side of the Alps and the Rhône valley on the one hand, and Alsace and the Belfort Gap on the other. In both cases these are close to the regions where the only known roughouts have been found (see Figures 3, 4 and 7 for the roughouts).

---

15   Pétrequin *et al.* 2012c.

We accord pride of place to the disc-rings of Alpine jades, all of which have hoops of triangular section. There is a fundamental reason for doing so: we are dealing with the rarest kind of disc-ring, not only in terms of the precious raw material used (mostly jadeitites, but also omphacitites and very fine-grained eclogites) but also in terms of the amount of time that was needed to make them. No experimental replication of a disc-ring of jadeitite — one of the toughest rocks known — has yet been attempted, but to judge from the experimental replication of long polished axeheads of this material, we can suggest that it would have taken several hundred hours of careful pecking and of lengthy polishing to produce one.

The only known roughouts have all been discovered in northern Italy (Figure 3), with the finished versions being exported to central Italy and Sardinia in one direction, and to the valleys of the Rhône and Saône in another direction. The only exceptions — being remarkable examples of very long distance circulation, at 850 km from Mont Viso as the crow flies — are to be found in Brittany and the Channel Islands, and in particular in the hoard of three large jadeitite disc-rings found at Bréhan-Loudéac (Morbihan; Figure 3.1). It is no coincidence that Brittany, and in particular the Gulf of Morbihan, should have constituted a major area of attraction for Alpine disc-rings (and, as we shall see, for other types of disc-ring as well). This area had also been a magnet for long polished axe- and adze-heads made of jades[16].

Since so few of these Alpine jade disc-rings have been found in reliable and dateable contexts, there remains a serious problem concerning their chronology. In north Italy, these precious objects are attributed to the end of the Early Neolithic, around 5300–4900 BC[17], with a currency that may continue into the period of the Finale Ligure/Arene Candide cave use within phase 1 of the Square-Mouthed Pottery culture (VBQ). The same is true for the example from Salernes/grotte de Fontbrégoua (Var, France), which was associated with late Cardial pottery[18]. In Brittany, by contrast, the sole reasonably well-dated example is that found at Locmariaquer/Mané er Hroëck (Morbihan: Figure 12.2). This was found in the central chamber of a giant Carnac-type tumulus that may date from around the middle of the fifth millennium BC or slightly earlier[19].

It is scarcely credible that this chronological disjunction could just be due to the slowness of the transfers or to a prolonged re-use over generations — even though these may be the first reasons that spring to mind. The disc-rings found in Brittany are oversized in comparison to most of the Italian examples. An alternative explanation — which we prefer — is that disc-rings were being made in the French Alps, and that this production continued long after the Italian production ceased at the beginning of the fifth millennium. The two hypotheses are not mutually exclusive.

The jade rings, which are very rare even in their zone of production in Piedmont, always follow the same design, with a pointed triangular-section hoop. Here we are certainly not dealing with "jewellery" that was available for all to wear. On the contrary, their circulation as far as Brittany, with the hoard from Bréhan-Loudéac and the find from the monumental tomb of Mané er Hroëck at Locmariaquer, indicates that these objects were manipulated and that their transfer only occurred

---

16 Cassen *et al.* 2012; Pétrequin *et al.* 2012b.
17 Bagolini and Pedrotti 1998; Moser 2000; Pessina and D'Amico 1999; Ribero 2015; Tanda 1977.
18 Courtin and Gutherz 1976.
19 Cassen *et al.* 2012; Lefebvre and Galles 1863.

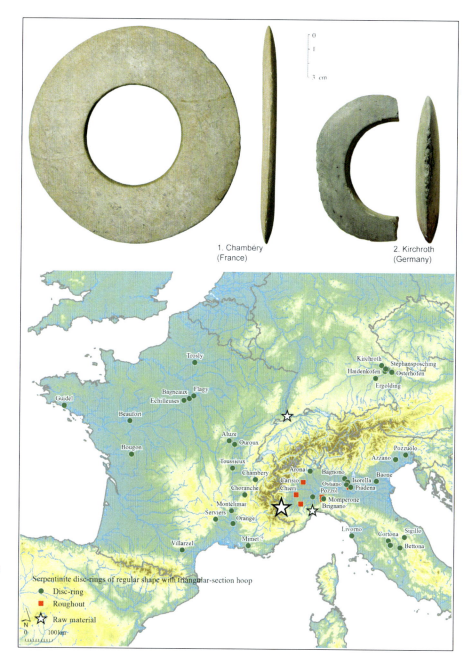

Figure 4. Distribution of communes where at least one disc-ring of regular shape with triangular-section hoop, of serpentinite, has been found. Photos and CAD: A.-M. and P. Pétrequin. Cartography: F. Prodéo.

between members of the elite, since we are evidently dealing with "object-signs" of high social value[20].

Let us continue to isolate the components of the general map of the distribution of Alpine rings (Figure 2), in order to understand the organisation of their flow from northern Italy (which is considered to be the origin of the idea, if not of the rings themselves) towards north-west Europe. Other regular-shaped disc-rings with a triangular-section hoop were made from serpentinite. These are significantly more numerous than the examples made from Alpine jades, and this is understandable given that serpentinites are very abundant in the Alps

---

20   Pétrequin *et al.* 2012a.

(even though not all are usable) and that the amount of time required to make a serpentinite disc-ring carefully will not have exceeded twenty hours.

All the roughouts have been found upstream of the Po plain. But we should not forget the famous hoard found at Chambéry/La Ferme des Combes (Savoie)[21] that comprised five large rings that were unfinished and never worn (Figure 4.1). These may have been imports from across the Alps in Italy, even though such rings with very wide hoops are rare in northern Italy; as we have suggested above, they could actually have been made on the French side of the Alps.

The circulation of serpentinite disc-rings with a triangular-section hoop (Figure 4.2) — or else the idea of using them, along with copies of them — reached Lower Bavaria, probably during the period 5000–4700 BC, when the Stichbandkeramik culture was developing[22]. Other, more numerous serpentinite disc-rings of this shape circulated towards the valleys of the Rhône and the Saône, the Paris Basin (where they are associated with the B-VSG culture) and finally Brittany, as attested by the example from Guidel (Morbihan)[23], which once more demonstrates the power of attraction of the Carnac area.

Chronologically, the situation is exactly the same as for the rings of Alpine jades, with which they are certainly contemporary, at least in part: one finds examples with hoops of modest width in northern Italy down to the end of the sixth millennium, while from the beginning of the fifth, production on the French side of the Alps took over, with oversized examples with very wide hoops being frequent. Nevertheless, there is no definitive proof that the triangular-section disc-rings of serpentinite were used after the end of the B-VSG. This is, however, an observation that needs to be treated with prudence, given the small number of examples that have come from datable contexts.

Regular-shaped disc-rings with quadrangular section made from serpentinite

Despite being of indubitable Alpine origin, the regular-shaped serpentinite disc-rings with a quadrangular section and wide hoop (Figure 5) are rare in northern Italy, with just one example being known from a secure context at Pozzuolo del Friuli/Sammardenchia (Friuli-Venezia Giulia), and dating to the end of the sixth or the very beginning of the fifth millennium[24]. By contrast, most of the examples have been found in the Paris Basin, associated with B-VSG material or in an aceramic grave attributed to the B-VSG at Jablines/Les Longues Raies (Seine-et-Marne) (Figure 5.1)[25]. The currency of this type of disc-ring is demonstrated in Brittany, where the example found at Pleuven/Pen Houat Salaün (Finistère) seems to have been associated with pottery stylistically close to that from the eponymous Cerny site[26]. Likewise, in Morbihan — the region that kept on being a pole of attraction for exotica — several disc-rings with wide hoops have been found in graves that were the precursors for the earliest giant mounds of the Carnac area. Here they were associated with repolished adze-heads of Bégude type, made of Alpine jades. With its four serpentinite disc-rings and two Bégude-type adze-heads,

---

21 Thirault 2004.
22 Eibl 2016.
23 Herbaut and Pailler 2000.
24 Pessina and D'Amico 1999.
25 Bulard *et al.* 1993.
26 Nicolas *et al.* 2013.

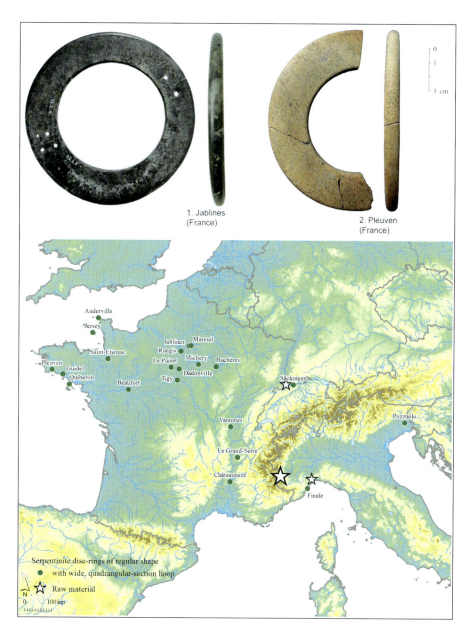

Figure 5. Distribution of communes where at least one disc-ring of regular shape with wide, quadrangular-section hoop, of serpentinite, has been found. Photos and CAD: A.-M. and P. Pétrequin. Cartography: F. Prodéo.

the hoard from Quiberon/Fort Saint-Julien is the best-known of these probably funerary deposits[27]. We propose to date this hoard to just before the middle of the fifth millennium — or at least anterior to the classic Carnac mounds such as that of Carnac/Saint-Michel, which is well dated, by three radiocarbon dates[28], to the mid-fifth millennium. The chronological overlap (at least partial) between disc-rings with a triangular-section hoop and those with a quadrangular-section hoop is thus established, even though the latter could, theoretically, have appeared somewhat later than the former — a point which remains to be demonstrated. However, the significance of the difference between these two variants — with the triangular-section examples essentially being Italian and Alpine (Figure 4) while

---

27   Cassen and Pétrequin 1999; Cassen *et al.* 2012; Herbaut and Pailler 2000.
28   Cassen *et al.* 2011; 2012.

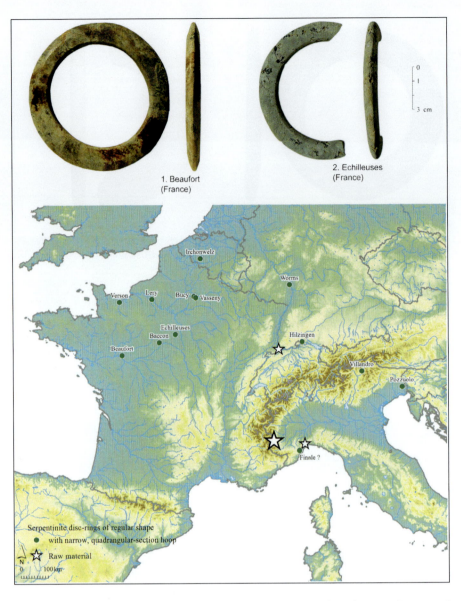

Figure 6. Distribution of communes where at least one disc-ring of regular shape with narrow, quadrangular-section hoop, of serpentinite, has been found. Photos and CAD: A.-M. and P. Pétrequin. Cartography: F. Prodéo.

the quadrangular-section examples are mainly concentrated in the Paris Basin and Brittany (Figure 5) — is not yet fully understood.

Regarding this question, the serpentinite disc-rings with a narrow hoop (Figure 6.1 and 6.2) are particularly interesting. They are most numerous in B-VSG contexts between the Loire and Belgium (Figure 6)[29], and the six examples from the female grave XLV from the cemetery of Worms-Rheingewann (Rhenish Palatinate, Germany)[30] demonstrate stronger links with the Paris Basin than with the producers in the Alps.

Two observations allow us to propose that these disc-rings with narrow, quadrangular hoops were not just manufactured in the Alps. Firstly, their distribution (Figure 6) is noticeably different from that of wide-hooped disc-rings (Figure 5); several of these narrow-hooped examples are located further away from their potential Alpine sources than those with medium-width or wide hoops.

---

29   Fromont 2013.
30   Meier-Arendt 1975.

Secondly, some of these disc-rings show signs of having been repolished on the edge of the hoop, as though someone had sought to modify the diameter of the hoop and its section shape (Figure 6.2).

Our hypothesis, already set out elsewhere[31], is that disc-rings with a wide, triangular-section hoop could have been repolished, once they had arrived in the Paris Basin, in order to modify their diameter and section, thereby conforming to the regional norms that pertained for the B-VSG schist disc-rings. This hypothetical process of repolishing is even more evident in the case of the irregular-shaped disc-rings of Alsatian type.

Alsatian-type disc-rings of irregular shape

The characteristic feature of Alsatian disc-rings of irregular shape[32] — called "Alsatian" because most have been found in Alsace — is the use of flat cobbles of more or less oval shape. Their outline was either left unchanged or only minimally modified, while their central perforation is circular (Figure 7.3). Thus, these disc-rings are easy to recognise, even when found as fragments. Most have been made of serpentinite taken from the recent alluvial deposits of the upper Rhine valley, upstream and downstream from Basel (Figure 7, the white star on the map). Just one small centre of production is known, at Bad Säckingen (Baden-Württemberg, Germany), and here all the stages of manufacture are represented, from roughing-out by grinding both faces within a hollow to longitudinal, "buttonhole"-style perforation by means of bifacial grooving, followed by enlargement and regularisation of the circular perforation, through rubbing with a sandstone file[33]. Other production villages no doubt remain to be discovered, given the suspected importance of the production of these bangles; and the use of other types of stone to manufacture this type of bangle is known, such as pelite-quartz cobbles at Plancher-les-Mines (Haute-Saône, France) in the southern Vosges[34].

Found in the form of fragments in settlements, or else complete and deposited in pairs in certain graves, probably female (Figure 10.1), the irregular-shaped Alsatian bangles have most often been found in Großgartach and Rössen contexts. It is suspected that they first appeared from the end of the Linearbandkeramik culture in Alsace and that they were in use throughout the first half of the fifth millennium[35]. It is justifiable to ask whether this use of natural, ovoid forms to make stone bangles had been inspired by the bangles made from *Spondylus* shell, whose flow to this region had been interrupted at the end of the sixth millennium[36], even though it continued in west-central Europe. However, against this idea is the fact that in the region of Lyon (and thus outside a Danubian-tradition context), at the same time, there was small-scale production of irregular-shaped bangles, made from cobbles that differ from the Alsatian examples in having a pointed triangular hoop section — a feature that derives directly from the Italian and Alpine tradition[37].

---

31 Pétrequin 2017; Pétrequin *et al.* 2015b.
32 Glory 1948.
33 Gersbach 1969.
34 Pétrequin 2017; Pétrequin *et al.* 2015b.
35 Denaire and Mauvilly 2012; Jeunesse 1995.
36 Bonnardin 2009.
37 Pétrequin 2017.

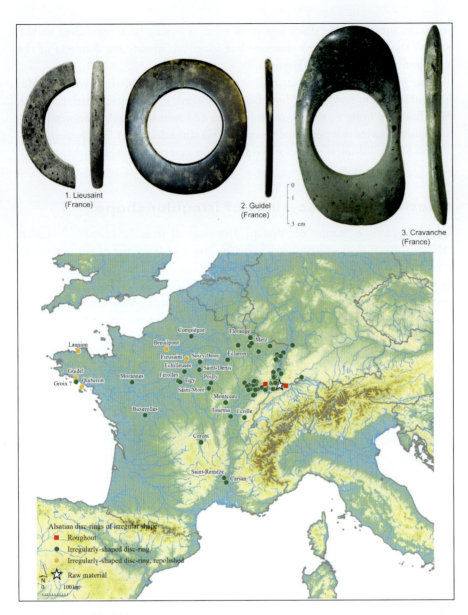

Figure 7. Distribution of communes where at least one Alsatian-type disc-ring, of irregular shape, has been found. Most are of serpentinite. Photos and CAD: A.-M. and P. Pétrequin. Cartography: F. Prodéo.

For as long as only a few examples had been known, the distribution of irregular-shaped disc-rings had appeared to be limited strictly to Alsace, Lorraine and the Belfort Gap, with just a single example having travelled as far as Corent (Puy-de-Dôme, France), in the north of the Massif Central[38]. However, after the systematic study of disc-rings undertaken as part of *Projet Jade 2*, the situation changed significantly. The number of known examples has doubled, in particular in the north of the Jura, while around 20 others allow us to demonstrate that they had circulated as far as the Paris Basin and the Loire valley (Figure 7), travelling over a distance of 600 km from the neck of the Rhine at Basel towards the west (and thereby towards Brittany).

Moreover, we have demonstrated that at least five serpentinite disc-rings of regular shape, with a quadrangular-section hoop, had resulted from the reshaping — probably in the Paris Basin — of Alsatian irregular-shaped bangles, no doubt

---

38 Jeunesse 1995.

in order to make them resemble more closely the more classic shape of the schist bangles of the B-VSG culture. The example from Guidel (Morbihan, France) (Figure 7.2), among others, leaves no room for doubt in this respect. As had been the case with the Alpine disc-rings found in the Paris Basin (Figure 6), the examples of repolished Alsatian disc-rings that had been rendered more regular in outline are all located in the Paris Basin and to its west. The most distant example is that from Lannion/Kervouric (Côtes-d'Armor), discovered in a B-VSG context and radiocarbon dated to 5002–4840 cal BC[39]; this lies some 840 km from the neck of the Rhine as the crow flies.

An east–west circulation of sex-specific signs

The typological approach described above, which also takes into account the raw materials used to manufacture disc-rings, now allows us to follow the circulation of Alsatian products (from the Rhine) on the one hand, and of Alpine products (from the Inner Alps) on the other (Figure 8).

In examining the disc-rings of Alsatian origin, one needs to take account of the selection of flat cobbles of serpentinite (Figure 8, top left). These cobbles are rare in the alluvial deposits of the Rhine, becoming available only after serious flooding, with its concomitant shifting of the alluvial banks and of the course of the meanders. Experimentally, the time required to make a medium-sized irregular-shaped Alsatian disc-ring is of the order of 20 hours. Thus, it was the rarity of the serpentinite cobbles, and not the time invested in the manufacture of the disc-rings, that gave them their high "price". As for the exchanges of these objects, these were above all orientated towards the west and the Paris Basin, while there seems to have been a firm frontier to the east, limiting their easterly movement (Figure 8). We shall return to the significance of this boundary, which ran southwards along the Rhine and the Black Forest.

The raw materials used to make the Alpine disc-rings were also serpentinites, but rarely in the form of fluvial cobbles. Primary outcrops at high altitude had certainly been exploited (Figure 8, top right), as well as secondary deposits in the form of large blocks with rounded edges. The latter were exploited using a hard hammer, in order to extract plaques (Figure 2.1). Despite the abundance of serpentinite outcrops and blocks in the Alps, and contrary to what one may imagine, examples of serpentinites that were good for flaking and hammering are rare. Similarly, flat slabs of jadeitite are very rare and some must have been gathered at high altitude in the Mont Viso massif, between 1700 and 2400 metres above sea level[40]. In the case of the disc-rings of Alpine jades, their value will have been linked to the expeditions to the mountain that were necessary to obtain the raw material, to the spectacular Alpine location of the raw materials, and to the time that had to be invested in manufacturing a single disc-ring in jadeitite or omphacitite.

The number of Alpine disc-rings that were released into circulation was far higher than the number of Alsatian disc-rings (Figure 8). Their distribution is also more extensive, stretching from northern Italy to Brittany. It was in and around the Paris Basin that the distributional overlap between the Alsatian and Alpine disc-rings occurred.

The contrast between the Alpine and the Alsatian disc-rings is even stronger if one takes into account all the disc-rings with a wide, triangular-section hoop made

---

39   Juhel 2015.
40   Pétrequin *et al.* 2012c.

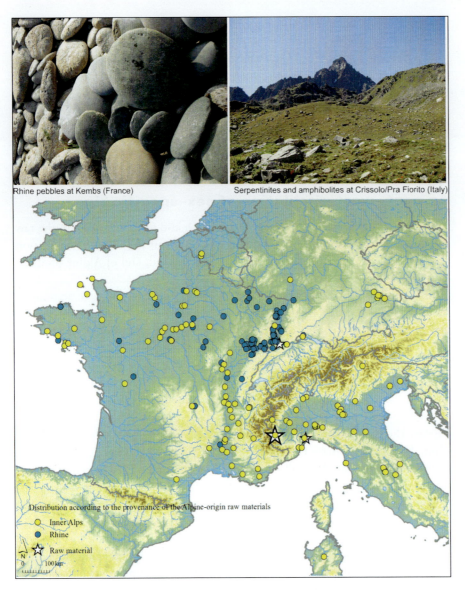

Figure 8. Origins of the Alpine raw materials: comparative distribution of disc-rings made from rocks from the Inner Alps and of those made from rocks taken from the river-bed along the upper Rhine near Basel. Photos: P. Pétrequin. Cartography: F. Prodéo.

from Alpine rock — that is, including chlorite schists and amphibolite-family rocks, among the rock types whose origin is harder to pinpoint. In this regard, two large disc-rings of nephrite need to be mentioned: one found at Languidic/Park Petit Trecoët (Morbihan, France) (Figure 5)[41] and the other found at Pozzuolo del Friuli/Sammardenchia (Friuli-Venezia Giulia, Italy)[42]. These examples — which are exceptional as much for the quality of the precious raw material as for the high level of skill required in their manufacture — have been found at the two extremes of the distribution of Alpine disc-rings (Figure 9), in Brittany to the west and at Friuli to the east. Nevertheless, they share the same origin: one of the nephrite outcrops in Swiss Valais, situated between 1900 and 2600 metres above sea level. Some of these outcrops are on the fringes of glaciers (Figure 9.2).[43]

41   Herbaut and Pailler 2000; Pailler 2007.
42   Pessina and D'Amico 1999.
43   Pétrequin 2017.

Figure 9. Distribution of disc-rings made from Alpine nephrite. The example from Languidic (Morbihan, France) is of nephrite from the Swiss Valais, extracted at an altitude between 1800 and 2600 metres above sea level. Photos and CAD: A.-M. and P. Pétrequin. Cartography: F. Prodéo.

In the Alps, it is likely that the same people were responsible for gathering and roughing-out disc-rings and for creating large axe- and adze-heads, working where access to the rare raw materials was sometimes difficult. This no doubt enhanced the social value of these objects and led to their widespread distribution.

In showing, on the same map (Figure 10), the distribution of Alpine disc-rings and that of large Bégude-type adze-heads made from Alpine jades — all generally dating to the end of the sixth millennium and the first half of the fifth — it is clear that their diffusion was virtually identical, as we had previously claimed on the basis of a much smaller number of examples[44]. The limits of this distribution (*i.e.* the areas where these sixth/early fifth millennium imports are not found) are as follows:

- To the north, Great Britain, which was not yet affected by Neolithic colonisation;
- To the north-east, Germany, which was scarcely concerned with Alpine artefacts before the expansion of the Michelsberg culture from 4300 BC;

---

44 Pétrequin *et al.* 1998.

Figure 10. Comparative distribution of disc-rings of rocks from the Inner Alps and of large adze-heads of Bégude type in Alpine jades. Photos and CAD: A.-M. and P. Pétrequin. Cartography: F. Prodéo.

- To the east, central and Balkan Europe, regions that had developed their own system of social values, in which copper featured prominently[45];
- To the south-west, the Iberian peninsula, into which only a small number of large Alpine axe- or adze-heads penetrated (and no disc-rings); those that did arrive here are mostly found along the Atlantic coast, towards the outcrops of variscite[46];
- And to the south-east, southern Italy and Sardinia, where small jadeitite axe/adze-blades predominate.

---

45   Pétrequin *et al.* 2012a.
46   Cassen 2011; 2012.

320 | Contacts, boundaries and innovation in the fifth millennium

It is noteworthy that none of these limits of diffusion corresponds to the limits of a cultural entity (insofar as researchers identify Neolithic communities on the basis of pottery styles). It seems more likely that the limits related to different societies' world-views[47]. We have already discussed this point elsewhere, in considering Alpine axe- and adze-heads[48].

While all the evidence points to the artefacts in question having been attributed a sex[49] — with the ring-discs being female and the axe- and adze-heads being male, as attested in female and male graves[50] — not a single example has been found, in the whole of the distribution area, where an Alpine disc-ring has been closely associated with a Bégude-type adze-head. The earliest instances where these female and male signs have been found together date to the end of the first half of the fifth millennium; the context for these is the oldest monumental graves of Carnac type around the Gulf of Morbihan, at Quiberon and Locmariaquer, as noted above. Thus, it seems to be that it was in Morbihan — a great pole of attraction for Alpine jades in general — where the physical synthesis of male and female object-signs from the Alps operated.

Disc-rings and status markers

There is a pressing need to understand the value, the meaning and the social significance of disc-rings made from Alpine rocks. Are we simply dealing with individual pieces of jewellery? Were the arm rings worn every day or was their use reserved for ceremonies and for funeral gifts? And how might one explain the dynamic of the long-distance circulation of Alpine and Alsatian disc-rings, in contrast to the more restricted circulation of schist rings, which was limited to regional exchange systems and within which the rings only travelled up to 200–250 km as the crow flies? Such are the points (among others) that need to be considered here.

It is first necessary to determine whether all the Alpine bangles were designed to be worn on the upper arm, above the elbow, as is suggested by the skeleton from the grave at Jablines/Les Longues Raies (Yvelines, France)[51]. Roberto Micheli believes this to be the case with the Italian bangles[52]: he presents a diagram showing a correspondence between the interior diameter of 67 Italian examples and the width of the distal epiphysis of the humerus of 21 individuals belonging to the Square-Mouthed Pottery culture[53]. What he does not say, however, is that no stone bangle has ever been found in a grave in northern Italy. Notwithstanding this, the data are consistent with his view.

However, Micheli's study omitted the extremes of the range of ring diameters, and this introduces a possible bias. Among the Italian stone bangles, at least eight are of extremely small size, with an internal diameter of between 33 and 40 mm; these include examples from Alba, Brignano Frascata and Finale Ligure/Grotta Pollera[54]. We are therefore led to suspect that in addition to those disc-rings that

---

47 Godelier 2015.
48 Pétrequin *et al.* 2012a.
49 Pétrequin and Pétrequin 2006.
50 Pétrequin 2017.
51 Bulard *et al.* 1993.
52 Micheli 2012.
53 Micheli 2012, 244, fig. 3.
54 Ribero 2015.

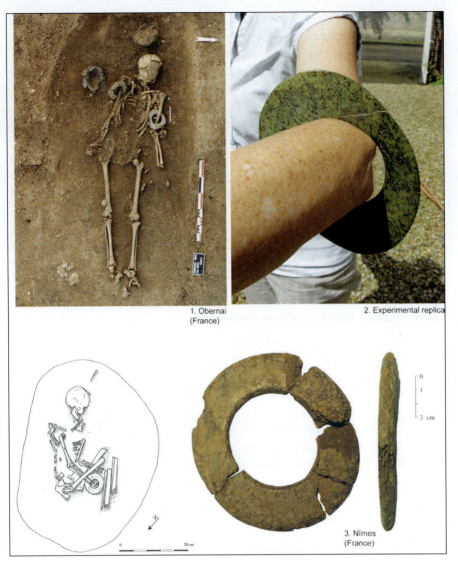

Figure 11. Disc-rings from funerary contexts, plus experimentally-made disc-ring. 1. Grave at Obernai (Bas-Rhin, France), Großgartach culture, excavation by Inrap, C. Feliu; 2. Experimental disc-ring made by D. Buthod-Ruffier; 3. Grave SP 1194, Nîmes/Esplanade Sud (Gard, France), excavation by Inrap, M.L. Hervé, A. Garnotel and C. Noret. Photos and CAD: P. Lefranc (no. 1), P. Pétrequin (no. 2), A. Garnotel and P. Séjalon (no. 3).

were made to suit human morphology, there were other, very small examples that were designed simply to be suspended or to be attached to a garment. Our hypothesis is supported by the seven representations of rings that figure on the torso of the anthropomorphic figure with "feathers" or "projecting rays", engraved on the decorated boulder at Buthiers/La Vallée aux Noirs (Seine-et-Marne, France)[55]. Moreover, on this same panel, a ring of larger diameter was represented on top of (or engaging with) the proximal end of the haft of an axe with a large polished blade. Likewise, we can ask ourselves whether the rings engraved on the standing stone at Lutry/La Possession (Vaud, Switzerland) — a stele that has wrongly, in our opinion, been attributed to the Final Neolithic[56] — might also be a representation of disc-rings attached to a garment[57].

The very small rings have not just been found in northern Italy. At least one has been found in southern France: at Lussas/dolmen de Rieu (Ardèche),

---

55 Cassen 2017; Cassen *et al.* 2014.
56 Burri-Wyser 2016.
57 Cassen 2017.

where it was reused, with a double perforation; and at Olargues/grotte de Lauriol and Saint-Étienne-d'Albagnan/grotte de Bonnefons 2 (Hérault), all in "rock or greenschist" and attributed to the Final Neolithic — even though they were found uncontexted, in assemblages spanning a long time[58].

It would therefore appear that not all the disc-rings were "functional" bangles, inasmuch as their engraved representations are associated with mythological images. One might justifiably object that it is impossible to identify the type of stone used for the disc-rings shown in these engravings, even though we are clearly dealing with large versions of this artefact type. Nevertheless, their clear association with images of axeheads which, typologically, can only be of Alpine jades strongly suggests that the disc-rings thus portrayed also had an Alpine origin.

Let us return to the disc-rings of average size. The sheen on the interior of the hoop shows that these had been worn for a considerable period, despite the evident discomfort that will have ensued from wearing the outsized and/or irregular-shaped examples (Figure 11.2). Such non-ergonomic disc-rings will have restricted the movement of the arm and would probably have interfered with, or rendered impossible, certain (female) activities.

Given the low frequency of stone rings in funerary offerings (Figure 1; Figures 11.1 and 11.3), it is widely held that these "bangles" were socially distinctive forms of personal adornment, used to mark a particular status among women[59]. A question that nevertheless remains to be answered is this: were these bangles — in some cases very cumbersome pieces of jewellery — only worn on special occasions, or were they worn every day? The presence of broken examples in villages or in temporary cave sites might suggest the latter, when the risk of breakage was particularly high. This applies as much to the regular-shaped Alpine bangles as to the irregular-shaped Alsatian examples.

It seems acceptable to suggest that these objects were markers of status (of certain women) and were specific object-signs, assigned to the world of women by being transposed there. It is now necessary to consider the weight of this social convention, which rested on imaginary beliefs that were shared by all and were probably regulated by men[60].

The imaginary world of the Alpine disc-rings

It will no doubt have been men — the producers in Piedmont, on the French side of the Alps and in Alsace — who manufactured the disc-rings, just as it will have been men who made the polished axe- and adze-heads of Alpine jades[61]. Following the model of the sexual division of labour proposed by Alain Testart[62], men will have defined and materialised the signs that were allocated to women, and rather than wearing them themselves — which would have constituted an unacceptable inversion of the genders — the men attributed them to certain women as a sign of distinction. However, as noted above, there was one association between male and female "object-signs": this was in the "funerary" hoard from Quiberon/Fort

---

58   Barge 1982.
59   Bostyn *et al.* 2015; Bulard *et al.* 1993; Denaire and Mauvilly 2012; Micheli 2012; Praud 2014.
60   Godelier 2015; Pétrequin and Pétrequin 2006; Pétrequin *et al.* 2017.
61   Pétrequin *et al.* 2017.
62   Testart 1986.

Figure 12. 1: Oversized disc-ring from Ouroux-sur-Saône (Saône-et-Loire, France, of serpentinite); 2: large axehead found with its butt end placed within the hoop of a disc-ring (both of Alpine jades) at Locmariaquer/Mané er Hroëck (Morbihan, France); 3: engravings on the standing stone of Saint-Micaud (Saône-et-Loire, France), showing the association between a disc-ring and an axe with a polished stone axehead. Photos and CAD: S. Cassen, V. Grimaud, L. Lescop (no. 3) and A.-M. and P. Pétrequin.

Saint-Julien (Morbihan), in which four highly-polished adze-heads of Bégude type (male signs) were associated with four large disc-rings (female signs).

The finds from the grave of Locmariaquer/Mané er Hroëck (Morbihan) allow us to clarify the meaning of this funerary association between sexually-opposed

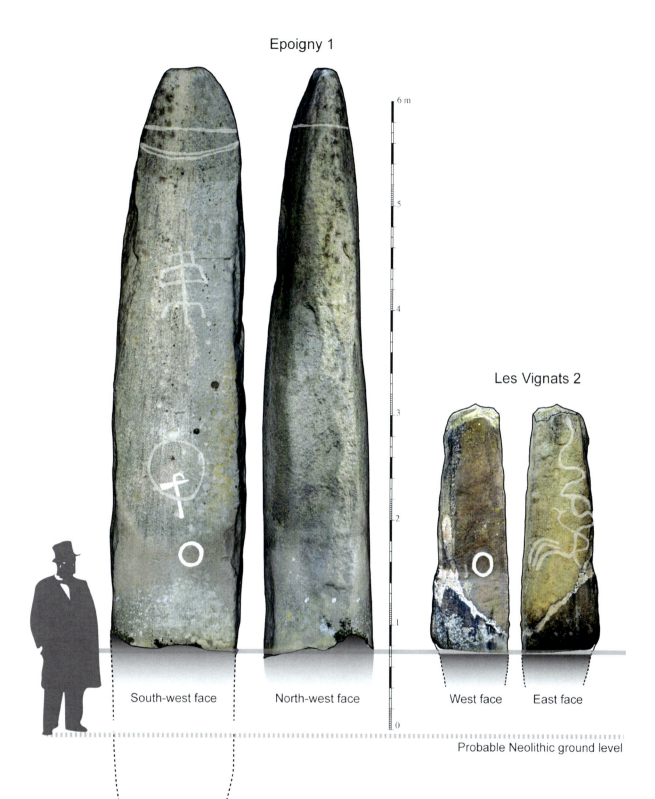

Figure 13. The standing stones at Epoigny 1 (Couches, Saône-et-Loire, France) and Les Vignats 2 (Saint-Clément-sur-Guye, Saône-et-Loire, France). The engravings were recorded using photos taken under oblique rotating light and integrated within a photogrammetric model. Imaging and modelling: S. Cassen and V. Grimaud.

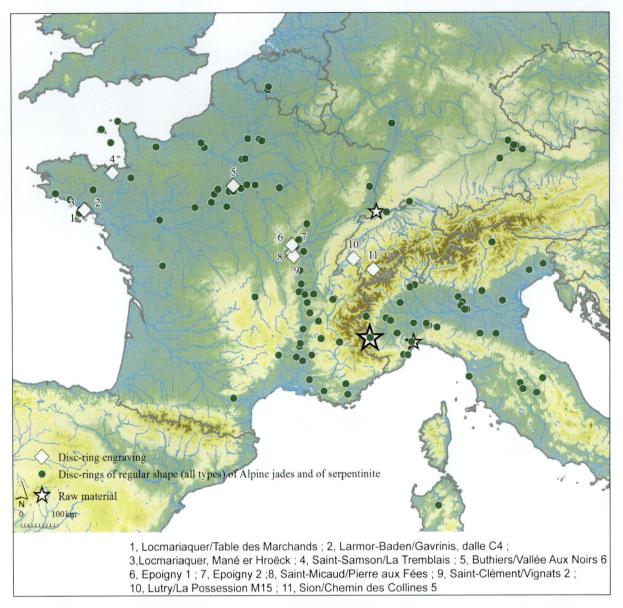

1, Locmariaquer/Table des Marchands ; 2, Larmor-Baden/Gavrinis, dalle C4 ;
3, Locmariaquer, Mané er Hroëck ; 4, Saint-Samson/La Tremblais ; 5, Buthiers/Vallée Aux Noirs 6
6, Epoigny 1 ; 7, Epoigny 2 ; 8, Saint-Micaud/Pierre aux Fées ; 9, Saint-Clément/Vignats 2 ;
10, Lutry/La Possession M15 ; 11, Sion/Chemin des Collines 5

Figure 14. Distribution of engravings of disc-rings, in relation to the distribution of disc-rings made from rocks originating in the Inner Alps. Cartography: F. Prodéo.

signs: among an extraordinary collection of other exotic "object-signs" there was found a very long Carnac-type Alpine axehead, with its butt end placed through the hoop of a jade disc-ring (Figure 12.2). This arrangement was completed by two variscite pendants, placed at the blade end of the axehead[63]. This arrangement conveys an unequivocal message, which we have interpreted in terms of the ideal reproduction of society, whereby an exceptional man, buried under a gigantic mound, controlled the copulation of a male sign penetrating a female sign[64].

It could be argued that, since these finds came from an excavation that took place during the second half of the nineteenth century, the observations of the diggers lack scientific value. However, this would be to decry the high quality of the research undertaken at that time in these giant mounds — work that has not been bettered in the 150 years since. Moreover, other literally stupefying observations

---

63 Cassen *et al.* 2012; Lefebvre and Galles 1863.
64 Pétrequin *et al.* 2012a.

made at the time — namely of axeheads planted vertically in the ground, axeheads deposited as pairs, axeheads that had been deliberately reworked or broken in the chambers of Carnac mounds — have been lent credence since the 2000s, when certain old research paradigms were (finally) taken seriously and brought into play[65].

In addition, the recent study of standing stones and engraved boulders in Brittany, the Gâtinais, Burgundy and south-west Switzerland has shown *inter alia* that several representations of disc-rings (Figures 12.3 and 13) were integrated within the various mythologies of these regions, just as axeheads of Alpine jade were[66]. Moreover, the figurative associations between axeheads or complete axes and disc-rings are not rare, with examples including Saint-Micaud/La Pierre aux Fées (Saône-et-Loire, France) (Figure 13) and Épogny (Saône-et-Loire) (Figure 13, Épogny 1), not forgetting Buthiers/La Vallée aux Noirs (Seine-et-Marne), as described above.

Among the mythological designs, the disc-ring could feature as the sole and central image on the face of a standing stone, as at Épogny/Les Vignats 2 (Figure 13). The motif was thus no less important than the images of axeheads or axes; these two "object-signs" were indissociable, just as the actual disc-rings and axeheads had been in the chamber of Mané er Hroëck. It is to this belief system that we can arguably attribute certain large disc-rings of serpentinite, such as the magnificent example dredged from the river Saône at Ouroux-sur-Saône (Saône-et-Loire, France; Figure 12.1).

The representations of disc-rings engraved on monumental standing stones and the actual Alpine disc-rings, some of which are oversized, are material expressions of the links between the western Alps and the Gulf of Morbihan, by way of Burgundy and the centre of the Paris Basin (Figure 14). Along the principal routes travelled by Alpine jade objects towards the Atlantic[67], this distribution reflects the social values that were shared in part, but certainly also adapted and interpreted in novel ways in the different regions[68].

Thus the integration of these disc-rings within a belief system rich in mythology, if not actual religion, could account for the dynamic of their trans-cultural circulation over almost a thousand kilometres as the crow flies.

Where do the schist bangles of the Blicquy-Villeneuve-Saint-Germain culture fit into this picture?

In the scenario that we have proposed, there are still many lacunae and uncertainties because disc-rings of Alpine rock have only rarely been found in contexts that can be dated with any precision.

However, some conclusions can be drawn regarding the disc-rings originating in the Inner Alps, namely:

- The earliest examples appeared in the Tyrrhenian Impressed Ware culture over the course of the sixth millennium, in the form of regular-shaped disc-rings with a triangular-section hoop, made from limestone. These are more

---

65 Pétrequin *et al.* 2012a.
66 Cassen 2017; Cassen *et al.* 2017.
67 Pétrequin *et al.* 2017.
68 Cassen 2017.

numerous within this geographical zone than in Cardial Impressed Ware contexts in the south of France;
- From 5300 BC at the latest, regular-shaped disc-rings with a triangular-section hoop — but made in Alpine rock types, jades and serpentinites — were being made in north Italy, using raw materials that had been taken from the Inner Alps to the west of the Po plain. This production was particularly intense during the last three centuries of the sixth millennium, and there was possibly a localised continuation in Liguria into the currency of the first phase of the Square-Mouthed pottery culture;
- The earliest exports of disc-rings across the Alps towards Burgundy must have coincided with this peak of Italian production, pre-dating the time when secondary-production centres on the French side of the Alps took over the production of wide-hooped serpentinite disc-rings, many of them being very large;
- Production of disc-rings of Alpine rock declined rapidly a little before 4500 BC.

As regards the Alsatian disc-rings, made using serpentinite cobbles selected from the alluvial deposits of the Rhine:

- The earliest well-dated ring-discs belong to the beginning of the Großgartach culture, around 4900–4800 BC, although there are indications that they were being used as early as c. 5000 BC;
- Production and export regularly occurred throughout the first half of the fifth millennium, subsiding only when the large Rössen cultural entity split up.

Like the large polished Bégude-type adze-heads of Alpine jades, whose distribution they share, disc-rings of Alpine rock (of all types) were, for the most part, drawn towards the west and north-west, in the direction of the English Channel and the Breton coast, with a remarkable concentration in the Paris Basin (Figure 15). Such a westerly-orientated circulation — one that runs inverse to that of the central European and Balkan influences — suggests that over western Europe the disc-rings became integrated into the systems of religious belief and mythology that pertained to Alpine jades[69], while contemporary and concurrent mythologies elsewhere in Europe blocked their expansion in other directions[70].

Thus, the disc-rings were integrated into the representations engraved on monumental standing stones and on rock surfaces on the one hand, and into the funerary rituals of exceptional people, buried in the earliest Carnac mounds around the Gulf of Morbihan, on the other hand. Shortly after the middle of the fifth millennium the disc-ring — a female "object-sign" — was to disappear from the iconographic systems and from the funerary practices around Carnac, while the long polished axe- or adze-head of jade was to become the male "object-sign" par excellence. This occurred just before the expansion of the Michelsberg culture in north-west Europe.

From a chronological point of view, the schist disc-rings of the Blicquy-Villeneuve-Saint-Germain culture thus appear to be subordinate to the system pertaining to Alpine disc-rings. They appeared later than the Early Neolithic

---

69 Pétrequin *et al.* 2012a; 2017.
70 Bernabò Brea and Cultraro 2012; Pétrequin *et al.* 2017; Schlichtherle 2016.

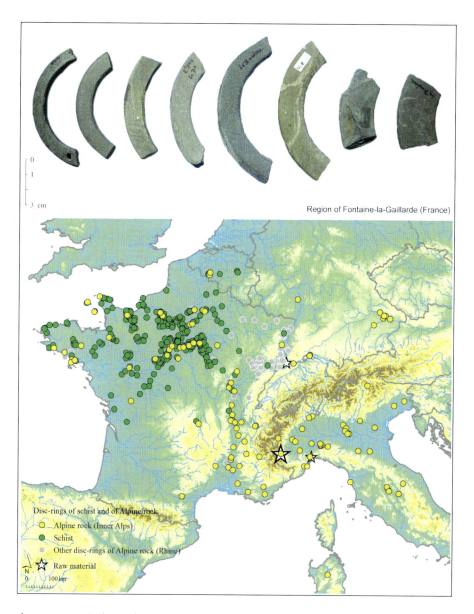

Figure 15. Comparative distributions of the disc-rings made from rocks originating in the Inner Alps and of those of schist, belonging to the Blicquy-Villeneuve-Saint-Germain culture. Photo: P. Pétrequin. Cartography: F. Prodéo.

disc-rings in Italy, and certainly disappeared well before the export of Alpine and Alsatian examples began to decline. Nevertheless, thousands of schist disc-rings were produced during a relatively brief period, from around 5000 BC to around 4700 BC, and circulated in large numbers in the B-VSG and affiliated cultures[71]. The vigour of the B-VSG system and the demand for bangles was so important that the Alpine and Alsatian examples continued to be drawn to the Paris Basin and Brittany. The latter were appropriated through being repolished — as we have already noted in the case of some polished axe- and adze-heads of Alpine jades, which were repolished in the Paris Basin and then around the Gulf of Morbihan — in order to make the cross-section shape of the serpentinite disc-rings conform to the B-VSG norms. In contrast to the dynamic of the disc-rings made from Alpine rocks that circulated over long distances, the cycle of production of schist examples was short and intense: the hundreds of examples whose schist source has

---

71 Fromont 2013.

been determined show that they were produced in many small centres[72] and that their circulation paths criss-crossed. To these we should add the schist disc-rings that were made in Brittany; their impact was not negligible[73].

With such large numbers of bangles being put into circulation in the B-VSG culture, a contradiction arises: on the one hand, these rings are too numerous in settlements to be considered just as "object-signs" of status, but on the other hand, their rarity in funerary assemblages, in the graves of women, seems to offer proof of their function as a status marker.

In order to resolve this conundrum, the most coherent hypothesis (whether correct or otherwise) is to consider most of the schist bangles of the B-VSG culture as a kind of currency, whose value will have been based on the integration of certain specific bangles into the system of myths — as demonstrated elsewhere in the case of the Alpine disc-rings. To produce, to give, to exchange and to store up these schist bangles (considered to be female signs) will therefore have been the ways to regulate social relations and the circulation of women and of goods — a social function that is well known from ethnology[74]. Thus, the system of compensation payments could have collapsed due to the large number of bangles released into circulation, which will have led inexorably to the devaluation of their social value[75].

What is being presented here is a testable hypothesis, offered as a way of escaping from the current widespread desire to explain everything in terms of economic relationships in Neolithic societies, despite all the ethnographic evidence from tribal (and modern) societies.

Acknowledgements

This work was undertaken as part of *JADE2 "Interprétations sociales des objets-signes en jades alpins dans l'Europe néolithique"*, a project funded by the Agence Nationale de la Recherche (ANR-12-BSH3-0005-01) and carried out under the auspices of the MSHE C.N. Ledoux, CNRS and the University of Bourgogne Franche-Comté, Besançon.

References

Auxiette, G. 1989. Les bracelets néolithiques dans le nord de la France, la Belgique et l'Allemagne rhénane. *Revue Archéologique de Picardie* 1–2, 13–65.

Bagolini, B. and Pedrotti, A.L. 1998. L'Italie septentrionale. In J. Guilaine (ed.), *Atlas du Néolithique européen, volume 2 A, l'Europe occidentale. ERAUL 46*, 233–341. Liège.

Barge, H. 1982. *Les parures du Néolithique ancien au début de l'Age des métaux en Languedoc*. Paris.

Bernabò Brea, M. and Cultraro, M. 2012. La statuetta femminile di Vicofertile (PR) nel contesto neolitico italiano e transadriatico: confronti tipologici e significati simbolici. *Atti della XLII Riunione Scientifica dell' Istituto Italiano Preistoria e Protostoria, Preistoria Alpina* 46 (I), 185–193.

---

72 Fromont 2013.
73 Pailler 2007.
74 Godelier 1984.
75 Pétrequin *et al.* 2015.

Bonnardin, S. 2009. *La parure funéraire au Néolithique ancien dans les Bassins parisien et rhénan. Rubané, Hinkelstein et Villeneuve-Saint-Germain. Mémoire de la Société Préhistorique Française* XLIX. Paris.

Bostyn, F. 1994. *Caractérisation des productions et de la diffusion des industries lithiques du groupe néolithique du Villeneuve-Saint-Germain.* Unpublished PhD thesis, University of Paris X.

Bostyn, F., Arbogast, R.-M., Clavel, B., Hamon, C., Kuhar, C., Maréchal, D., Pinard, E. and Praud, Y. 2015. Habitat et sépultures du Blicquy/Villeneuve-Saint-Germain à Longueil-Sainte-Marie "Le Barrage" (Oise). In F. Bostyn and L. Hachem (eds), *Hommages à Mariannick Le Bolloch. Revue archéologique de Picardie* 3–4, 155–206.

Bulard, A., Degros, J., Drouhot, C., Duhamel, P. and Tarrête, J. 1993. L'habitat des Longues Raies à Jablines (Seine-et-Marne). In J.C. Blanchet, A. Bulard, C. Constantin, D. Mordant and J. Tarrête (eds), *Le Néolithique au quotidien. Actes du XVIe colloque interrégional sur le Néolithique. Documents d'Archéologie Française*, 41–62. Paris.

Burri-Wyser, E., Chevalier, A., Falquet, C., Favre, S., Steudler, S. and Weidmann, D. 2016. *Destins des mégalithes vaudois. Lutry, La Possession / Corcelles, Les Quatre menhirs et La Vernette / Concise, En Chenaux et Fin de Lance / Onnens, Praz Berthoud. Fouilles 1984–2012. Cahier d'Archéologie romande 159.* Lausanne.

Cassen, S. 2012. L'objet possédé, sa représentation: mise en contexte général avec stèles et gravures. In P. Pétrequin, S. Cassen, M. Errera, L. Klassen, J.A. Sheridan and A.-M. Pétrequin (eds), *Jade. Grandes haches alpines du Néolithique européen. Ve et IVe millénaires av. J.-C. Cahiers de la MSHE C.N. Ledoux, tome 2*, 1310–1353. Besançon.

Cassen, S. 2017. D'un signe à l'autre, des Alpes à l'Atlantique: représentant et représenté. In P. Pétrequin, E. Gauthier and A.-M. Pétrequin (eds), *Jade. Objets-signes et interprétations sociales dans l'Europe néolithique. Cahiers de la MSHE C.N. Ledoux, tome 4*, 883–909. Besançon.

Cassen, S. and Pétrequin, P. 1999. La chronologie des haches polies dites de prestige dans la moitié ouest de la France. *European Journal of Archaeology* 2, 7–33.

Cassen, S., Pétrequin, P., Boujot, C., Dominguez-Bella, S., Guiavarc'h, M. and Querré, G. 2011. Measuring distinction in the megalithic architecture of the Carnac region: from site to material. In P. Pétrequin, S. Cassen, M. Errera, L. Klassen, J.A. Sheridan and A.-M. Pétrequin (eds), *Megaliths and identities. Third European Megalithic Studies Group Meeting, Kiel, 13–15 May 2010*, 225–228. Bonn.

Cassen, S., Boujot, C., Dominguez-Bella, S., Guiavarc'h, M., Le Pennec, C., Prieto Martinez, M.P., Querré, G., Santrot, M.E. and Vigier, E. 2012. Dépôts bretons, tumulus carnacéens et circulations à longue distance. In P. Pétrequin, S. Cassen, M. Errera, L. Klassen, J.A. Sheridan and A.-M. Pétrequin (eds), *Jade. Grandes haches alpines du Néolithique européen. Ve et IVe millénaires av. J.-C. Cahiers de la MSHE C.N. Ledoux, tome 2*, 918–995. Besançon.

Cassen, S., Grimaud, V., Lescop, L. and Caldwell, D. 2014. Le rocher gravé de la Vallée aux Noirs, Buthiers (Seine-et-Marne). Campagne 2013. *Bulletin du Groupe d'études, de recherches et de sauvegarde de l'art rupestre* 65, 25–37.

Cassen, S., Grimaud, V. and Lescop, L. 2017. Les compositions gravées en Bourgogne. In P. Pétrequin, E. Gauthier and A.-M. Pétrequin (eds), *Jade. Objets-signes et interprétations sociales dans l'Europe néolithique. Cahiers de la MSHE C.N. Ledoux, tome 4*, 847–882. Besançon.

Constantin, C. 1999. Problèmes de chronométrie de la succession Rubané–culture de Blicquy/Villeneuve-Saint-Germain. In J. Evin, C. Oberlin, J.P. Daugas and J.F. Salles (eds), *^{14}C et archéologie, 3e Congrès international, Mémoires de la Société Préhistorique Française 26*, 161–164. Paris.

Constantin, C. and Vachard, D. 2004. Anneaux d'origine méridionale dans le Rubané récent du Bassin parisien. *Bulletin de la Société Préhistorique Française* 101, 75–84.

Courtin, J. and Gutherz, X. 1976. Les bracelets en pierre du Néolithique méridional. *Bulletin de la Société Préhistorique Française* 73, 352–369.

Denaire, A. and Mauvilly, M. 2012. Guémar "Rotenberger Weg", première grande nécropole Grossgartach et Roessen (Néolithique moyen) en Alsace. *Internéo* 9, 73–85.

Eibl, F. 2016. *Bayerische Gruppe der Stichbandkeramik und die Gruppe Oberlauterbach. Definition, Verbreitung und Untersuchungen zu Entwicklung sowie kultureller Stellung.* Saarbrücken.

Errera, M., Pétrequin, P. and Pétrequin, A.-M. 2012. Spectroradiométrie, référentiel naturel et étude de la diffusion des haches alpines. In P. Pétrequin, S. Cassen, M. Errera, L. Klassen, J.A. Sheridan and A.-M. Pétrequin (eds), *Jade. Grandes haches alpines du Néolithique européen. Ve et IVe millénaires av. J.-C. Cahiers de la MSHE C.N. Ledoux, tome 1*, 440–533. Besançon.

Fromont, N., with contributions by A. Hérard and B. Hérard. 2010. Un dépôt d'anneaux en pierre du Néolithique ancien à Falaise, « zone d'activités Expansia II ». *L'Anthropologie* 114, 199–237.

Fromont, N. 2013. *Anneaux et cultures du Néolithique ancien. Production, circulation et utilisation entre massifs ardennais et armoricain. BAR International series 2499.* Oxford.

Gersbach, E. 1969. *Urgeschichte des Hochrheins (Funde und Fundstellen in den Landkreisen Säckingen und Waldshut). Badische Fundberichte 11.* Freiburg im Breisgau.

Glory, A. 1948. Les disques-bracelets d'Alsace. *Bulletin de la Société Préhistorique de France* 45, 174–179.

Godelier, M. 1984. *L'idéel et le matériel.* Paris.

Godelier, M. 2015. *L'imaginé, l'imaginaire et le symbolique.* Paris.

Herbaut, F. and Pailler, Y. 2000. Les anneaux en pierre dans le massif armoricain. In S. Cassen (ed.), *Eléments d'architecture. Exploration d'un tertre funéraire à Lannec (Erdeven, Morbihan). Constructions et reconstructions dans le Néolithique morbihannais. Propositions pour une lecture symbolique. Mémoire XIX*, 353–385. Chauvigny.

Jeunesse, C. 1995. Les anneaux irréguliers du Sud de la plaine du Rhin supérieur et la question des bracelets en pierre du Néolithique danubien. *Cahiers Alsaciens d'Archéologie, d'Art et d'Histoire* XXXVIII, 5–34.

Jeunesse, C. 2003. Ensembles mixtes et faciès de transition. Contribution à la chronologie du Néolithique ancien du Bassin parisien. In C. Desplat (ed.), *Actes du 125e Congrès national des Sociétés historiques et scientifiques, Lille, 2000*, 429–447. Paris.

Juhel, L. 2015. *Bretagne, Côtes-d'Armor, Lannion, Kervouric. Un habitat du Néolithique ancien.* Unpublished report, Inrap Grand Ouest.

Lefebvre, M. and Galles, R. 1863. Mané-er-Hroëck. Dolmen découvert sous un tumulus à Locmariaquer, *Bulletin de la Société Polymathique du Morbihan*, deuxième semestre 1863, 18–33.

Meier-Arendt, W. 1975. *Die Hinkelstein-Gruppe. Der Übergang vom Früh- zum Mittelneolithikum in Südwestdeutschland. Römisch-Germanische Forschungen 35.* Berlin.

Micheli, R. 2012. Raw materials, personal ornaments and Neolithic groups: some observations on stone bracelets of the Early Neolithic of northern Italy. In M. Borrell, F. Borell, J. Bosch and M. Molist (eds), *Xarxes al neolític. Circulació i intercanvi de matèries productes i idees a la Mediterrània occidental (VII–III mil·lenni aC). Congrès international, Gava et Bellatera, 2–4 février 2011, Rubricatum 5*, 241–248. Gavà.

Moser, L. 2000. Il sito neolitico di Lugo di Grezzana (Verona). I materiali archeologici della campagna di scavo 1993. In A. Pessina and G. Muscio (eds), *La neolitizzazione tra oriente e occidente. Convegno di studi, Udine, 1999*, 125–150. Udine.

Nicolas, E., Marchand, G., Henaff, X., Juhel, L., Pailler, Y., Darboux, J.R. and Errera, M. 2013. Le Néolithique ancien à l'ouest de la Bretagne: nouvelles découvertes à Pen Hoat Salaün (Pleuven, Finistère). *L'Anthropologie* 117, 195–237.

Pailler, Y. 2007. *Des dernières industries à trapèzes à l'affirmation du Néolithique en Bretagne occidentale (5500–3500 av. J.-C.). BAR International Series 1648.* Oxford.

Pessina, A. and D'Amico, C. 1999. L'industria in pietra levigata del sito neolitico di Sammardenchia (Pozzuolo del Friuli, Udine). Aspetti archeologici e petroarcheometrici. In A. Ferrari and A. Pessina (eds), *Sammardenchia-Cüeis. Contributi per la conoscenza di una comunità del primo neolitico*, 23–92. Udine.

Pétrequin, P. 2017. Quatrième partie: bracelets et anneaux-disques. In P. Pétrequin, E. Gauthier and A.-M. Pétrequin (eds), *Jade. Objets-signes et interprétations sociales dans l'Europe néolithique. Cahiers de la MSHE C.N. Ledoux, tome 3*, 600–757. Besançon.

Pétrequin, A.-M. and Pétrequin, P. 2006. *Objets de pouvoir en Nouvelle-Guinée. Catalogue de la donation Anne-Marie et Pierre Pétrequin. Musée d'Archéologie Nationale, Saint-Germain-en-Laye.* Paris.

Pétrequin, P., Croutsch, C. and Cassen, S. 1998. A propos du dépôt de La Bégude: haches alpines et haches carnacéennes pendant le Ve millénaire. *Bulletin de la Société Préhistorique Française* 95, 239–254.

Pétrequin, P., Cassen, S., Errera, M., Klassen, L. and Sheridan, J.A. 2012a. Des choses sacrées… fonctions idéelles des jades alpins en Europe occidentale. In P. Pétrequin, S. Cassen, M. Errera, L. Klassen, J.A. Sheridan and A.-M. Pétrequin (eds), *Jade. Grandes haches alpines du Néolithique européen. Ve et IVe millénaires av. J.-C. Cahiers de la MSHE C.N. Ledoux, tome 2*, 1354–1423. Besançon.

Pétrequin, P., Cassen, S., Gauthier, E., Klassen, L., Pailler, Y. and Sheridan, J.A. 2012b. Typologie, chronologie et répartition des grandes haches alpines en Europe occidentale In P. Pétrequin, S. Cassen, M. Errera, L. Klassen, J.A. Sheridan and A.-M. Pétrequin (eds), *Jade. Grandes haches alpines du Néolithique européen. Ve et IVe millénaires av. J.-C. Cahiers de la MSHE C.N. Ledoux, tome 1*, 574–727. Besançon.

Pétrequin, P., Pétrequin, A.-M., Errera, M. and Prodéo, F. 2012c. Prospections alpines et sources de matières premières. Historique et résultats. In P. Pétrequin, S. Cassen, M. Errera, L. Klassen, J.A. Sheridan and A.-M. Pétrequin (eds), *Jade. Grandes haches alpines du Néolithique européen. Ve et IVe millénaires av. J.-C. Cahiers de la MSHE C.N. Ledoux, tome 1*, 46–183. Besançon.

Pétrequin, P., Cassen, S., Chevillot, C., Cornen, G., Denaire, A., Duteil, Y., Pailler, Y., Prodéo, F. and Villes, A. 2015. Bracelets en schiste et anneaux-disques en jadéitite, en serpentinite ou en amphibole. In P. Ambert and A. Chancerel (eds), *Signes de richesse. Inégalités au Néolithique. Catalogue d'exposition, Les Eyzies, Musée National de Préhistoire*, 35–42. Paris.

Pétrequin, P., Pétrequin, A.-M., Gauthier, E. and Sheridan, J.A. 2017. Mécanismes sociaux: les interprétations idéelles des jades alpins. In P. Pétrequin, E. Gauthier and A.-M. Pétrequin (eds), *Jade. Objets-signes et interprétations sociales dans l'Europe néolithique. Cahiers de la MSHE C.N. Ledoux, tome 3*, 521–599. Besançon.

Praud, I. 2014. Parure et haches en roches alpines dans le Bassin parisien. In R.-M. Arbogast and A. Greffier-Richard (eds), *Entre archéologie et écologie, une Préhistoire de tous les milieux. Mélanges offerts à Pierre Pétrequin. Annales Littéraires de l'Université de Franche-Comté 928*, 187–198. Besançon.

Ribero, M. 2015. *I bracciali litici italiani. Aggiornamenti e nuove proposte interpretative a quaranta anni dalle prime ricerche*. Unpublished dissertation, Università degli Studi di Torino.

Schlichtherle, H. 2016. Wandbilder in neolithischen Pfahlbausiedlungen des Bodensees. Überlegungen zur Deutung von Bildern und Zeichen des südwestdeutschen Neolithikums. In G. Bosinski and H. Strohm (eds), *Höhlen, Kultplätze, sakrale Kunst. Kunst der Urgeschichte im Spiegel sprachdokumentierter Religionen*, 207–243. Paderborn.

Tanda, G. 1977. Gli anelloni litici italiani. *Preistoria Alpina* 13, 111–155.

Testart, A. 1986. *Essai sur les fondements de la division sexuelle du travail chez les chasseurs-cueilleurs. Cahiers de l'Homme, nouvelle série XXV*. Paris.

Thirault, E. 2004. *Echanges néolithiques: les haches alpines. Préhistoires 10*. Montagnac.